Phonology

Introducing Linguistics

Praise for Andrew Spencer's *Phonology*

'Andrew Spencer's textbook provides an excellent introduction to the field. Not only does it present the essentials of phonological analysis in a clear and accessible manner, it incorporates sufficient theory to acquaint students with a range of current research issues.' *Elizabeth Hume, Ohio State University*

'A clear, up-to-date introductory text. The chapters on syllables, and on rules and domains, are particularly well done.' *Moira Yip, University of California, Irvine*

'This is a lively and accessible introduction to phonology for under-graduates. Its focus on English makes it useful for potential linguists as well as for potential teachers of English as a second language.' *Ellen Broselow, State University of New York at Stonybrook*

Phonology

Theory and Description

Andrew Spencer

Department of Language and
Linguistics
University of Essex

First published 1996
Reprinted 1996

Blackwell Publishers Ltd
108 Cowley Road
Oxford OX4 1JF, UK

Blackwell Publishers Inc.
238 Main Street
Cambridge, Massachusetts 02142, USA

British Library Cataloguing in Publication Data
A CIP catalogue record for this book is available from the British Library

Library of Congress Cataloging in Publication Data
Spencer, Andrew.
Phonology: theory and description / Andrew Spencer.
p.   cm. — (Introducing linguistics; 1)
Includes bibliographical references and index.
ISBN   0–631–19232–8 (hb: alk. paper) — ISBN   0–631–19233–6 (pb: alk. paper)
1. Grammar, Comparative and general—Phonology. 2. English language—
phonology. I. Title. II. Series.
P217.S64   1996   95–12748
414—dc20

Commissioning Editor: Steve Smith
Editorial Coordinator: Alison Dunnett
Desk Editor: Jack Messenger
Production Controller: Lisa Eaton
Text Designer: Lisa Eaton

Typeset in 10.5 on 12pt Plantin
by Graphicraft Typesetters Limited, Hong Kong
Printed and bound in Great Britain by T. J. Press Ltd, Padstow, Cornwall

This book is printed on acid-free paper

Для одной хитрой рыжей морды

Contents

Figures

Tables

Preface
(Mainly for
the Teacher)

This book arose out of a need to teach introductory phonology to students who did not need to know a great deal about the theoretical aspects of the subject, but did need to get some experience of what phonologists do and why they do it. The course therefore stresses analytical techniques rather than theory construction or the evaluation of competing theoretical models. In practice this means taking a somewhat eclectic view of theory, and subordinating doctrinal issues to the more practical goal of learning how to see patterns in phonologies and understanding how phonological systems work.

However, it is all but impossible to teach a subject like phonology without reference to a host of other languages. Nor is it desirable that any student, with whatever practical objectives, should be given the impression that phonology can be conducted in a typological vacuum. There are topics that can (in principle and with many intellectual convolutions) be taught on the basis of English, but which only require a short paragraph and a couple of examples from a different language. Some phenomena, like vowel harmony, simply can't be sensibly illustrated on the basis of English alone. It should be part of any anglicist's training to appreciate to some extent at least, where English stands with respect to the rest of the linguistic world.

For these reasons, I have organized this book in two strands, the first a concise and selective survey of general phonological theory, the second a more detailed description of certain aspects of phonology. The descriptive function, however, is subservient to the broader aim of showing the student how phonology is done (by phonologists, not anglicists). This means that I have left out a number of 'interesting' phenomena, of the kind that an anglicist might wish to know, on the grounds that they are not needed to make a particular point. However, one of the aims is that the text should provide the wherewithal for a properly informed exploration of the more exhaustive descriptive literature. At the same time, it is intended as an introduction to the basics of phonology and can therefore be used as a precursor to the subject before tackling more detailed and exhaustive expositions such as Kenstowicz (1994).

The resulting compromise isn't perfect. There are important aspects of theory left untouched. One set of omissions is tone and intonation. I have bypassed these topics because I don't know enough about them, and because it seems to me that they are best dealt with in a separate, more specialist course. My limited experience teaching such things suggests that students find even the intonation of their own language very difficult without careful practical eartraining, and the study of tone systems of wholly unfamiliar languages is simply unrealistic in undergraduate programmes other than those specializing entirely in linguistics or in tone languages (especially where the teacher lacks expertise in the area).

A theoretical domain which I have left largely untouched is lexical phonology (and especially, Lexical Phonology). There are plenty of lexical processes discussed in the text (e.g. English lexical stress for one) but I have not presented an introduction to current theoretical models. This is a serious breach with prior pedagogic tradition and demands commentary. I strongly feel that contemporary theories of morphophonemics are *too difficult* for the novice. First, it is difficult to understand the machinery of most varieties of lexical phonology without a reasonably sophisticated understanding of at least the basics of morphology, and this goes beyond the remit of an introductory course. Second, to appreciate fully the argumentation of any variety of Lexical Phonology, it is necessary to motivate a sizeable fragment of grammar which invariably leads to fairly 'abstract' underlying forms (e.g. the English vowel inventory of SPE or Halle and Mohanan 1985) and a complex battery of rules (e.g. those surrounding the alleged Great Vowel Shift of synchronic English). Weaker students are apt to be put off by all this, since they can't see the purpose of it. The better students may well be confronted with a culture clash – in their syntax classes they are quite likely to be taught that the goal of linguistic theory is to solve the logical problem of language acquisition by eliminating the rule component of the grammar. The next day, they have to navigate their way through a maze of ordered, morphologically conditioned, none too phonetically natural rules in order to generate a finite set of items (plus, if they're lucky, a set of suggestions on how to avoid generating the exceptions).

For these reasons, I have bitten the bullet and left out the lexicon. To be sure, there are plenty of lexical rules and alternations left to illustrate what is an indispensable part of the cultural baggage of the phonologist. However, I have limited myself to drawing what I take to be the mainstream distinction between lexical and postlexical processes and making limited reference to it (notably in the section on underspecification and structure preservation).

This decision explains why an entire chapter is devoted to (of all things) *postlexical* processes in English. These are the processes which are relatively natural, phonetically, and which illustrate the interaction between segmental processes and prosodic categories fairly readily. One price to be paid for this is that the non-native speaker is put at a slight advantage with respect to native speakers (note the position of the negative morpheme!). Non-native anglicists are likely to be much more aware of postlexical distinctions than the naive native speaker, partly because they have been taught them, partly because they can hear them more easily, and partly because it is usually of great interest to the non-native student of English to know the facts of the matter. On the other hand, anglophone students of modern languages need to know what underlies their pronunciation of English if they are to acquire a decent pronunciation of the target language. (I know that conscious knowledge of sound patterns is neither necessary nor sufficient for acquiring the phonology of L2, but it usually helps.) This is particularly true of accent and rhythm: it is no more possible to get the segmental phonology of a language right with the wrong rhythmic organization than it is possible to play a violin sonata in tune without first getting the rhythm right. The importance of this far from self-evident link between rhythmic organization and the rest of phonology in part underlies my insistence on introducing ideas such as rhythmic alternations in English, and the conditioning of segmental processes by prosodic domains.

I have not actually assumed prior knowledge of basic articulatory phonetics and the IPA, but I presume that the typical student will have already been exposed to such things in a first year introduction to general linguistics. The first chapter is therefore partly review of previously studied material and partly consolidation, but also scene setting. In particular, I mesh the phonologist's labial-coronal-dorsal typology onto the IPA account of places of articulation, so don't skip the chapter completely!

Chapter 2 puts the reader in touch with elementary notions of phonology. I have added a very sketchy typological survey, on the grounds that students are too often launched in medias res without really knowing what phonological processes look like in the broader scheme of things. Many of the themes introduced in that section are taken up later, and it is a prerequisite for chapters 5 and 6. I feel it is important for students to have a view of processes and of the skeletonic structure of phonological representations before getting to grips with the minutiae of distinctive features and rule writing. The third chapter presents a fairly traditional view of syllable structure. The next chapter, essentially on features, presents the classical arguments from classification and sets the scene for feature geometry in the chapter that follows. I have introduced a limited conception of underspecification, first, because I am not convinced by Radical Underspecification (and especially Coronal Transparency), second, because the expositional payoff given by Radical Underspecification in a modest introduction of this sort is minimal, and third, all bets will be off anyway with the advent of Optimality Theory. Chapter 5 is where processes are introduced, yoked to feature geometry. Never mind the fact that we 'know' now that this early species of geometry is 'wrong' – I believe that it is much more important to anchor feature geometry, with its imposing tree structures and not necessarily perspicuous notational conventions, in something relatively familiar, i.e. the IPA description. The scant virtues of being thoroughly up-to-date are outweighed by the greater vice of being off-putting. The prosodic domains grounding of processes is admittedly rather skimpy (you can't expect a beginner to do syntax in phonology classes), but I feel the area is sufficiently important to be worth teaching (one of the virtues of ditching generative morphophonemics is that it frees up time for such luxuries).

Chapter 6 can be seen as the culmination of the segmental part of the book. I have taken the liberty of completely reinterpreting that old warhorse, Aspiration (which is now Deaspiration), but don't lose heart – I've salvaged what I can of a mainstream account as a prelude to my own analysis and this will do service for the more faint hearted, for whom my rule inversion will prove too radical. But try my version – it's far simpler and illustrates how to write phonological rules much better than any of the standard analyses. Otherwise, this chapter is a fairly mainstream contemporary interpretation of standard analyses. I've been surprised at just how vague and incomplete the literature on English is in places. There's ample scope for more advanced students/classes to take up some of these phenomena and conduct project work on prosodic domain conditioning, dialect differences, effects of speech rate and so on.

The final two chapters are on stress, accent and rhythm. A shorter course could content itself with just, say, chapter 7 and brief discussion of some of the issues in chapter 8. There is probably sufficient material in chapter 8 (and sufficiently many unanswered questions!) to support fairly lengthy discussion of these issues in a more leisurely course. In keeping with the emphasis on analytical techniques rather than theory construction, I have (somewhat reluctantly) resisted the temptation to present the Halle/Vergnaud approach to parametrization. It's sufficient at this level that students be capable of understanding how to analyse stress systems and become familiar with the mechanics. At the very end, in the section of chapter 8 dealing with eurhythmy, I have permitted myself the luxury of presenting several competing analyses of one set of phenomena, though without drawing firm conclusions. This final section can be treated as a prelude to a more advanced course where evaluation of theoretical models is the principal objective.

At every stage the theoretical model has been chosen with pedagogy in mind rather than theoretical purism. This means that I have, on occasions, presented analyses which I do not necessarily believe in. For example, I am personally inclined towards a moraic view of the world, but it seems to me that the syllable building approach taken here is easier for the beginner to understand. And conversion from rhymes to moras is conceptually simpler than vice versa. A brief foray into moras is there for reference, but a detailed exposition should be left for specialist advanced courses.

The exercises in any linguistics textbook should be regarded as integral to the text. Just occasionally, a new theoretical point is smuggled into an exercise. They are there for several purposes – for the solitary reader to monitor progress, for the hard pressed instructor who doesn't have the opportunity to construct a suite of exercises of their own, and as a fallback for the instructor with their own exercises but who might welcome one or two new ones. However, this is not a programmed instruction package – you don't have to get the answers to all the questions to chapter 4 right before being allowed to proceed to chapter 5 (though this would undoubtedly help). Some of the exercises presuppose that the student speak either (1) English or (2) some other language. If the reader doesn't fall into both categories simultaneously this simply means that not all the exercises are suitable for all readers. However, non-native speakers can very profitably attempt questions about the nitty-gritty of English by quizzing native speakers. This in itself is very instructive and (compared to a lot of the hoops we compel our students to jump through) is usually *fun*. So please encourage non-native speakers to do exercises on English.

Preface
(Mainly for
the Student)

This is an introduction to how to do phonology. Phonology is the study of the sounds used in languages: the way they pattern with respect to each other, the way they are used to make up words and phrases, and the changes they undergo. By working through this course you should acquire enough knowledge of phonological theory to enable you to understand much of what phonologists do. At the same time you should be able to use that knowledge to gain a better understanding of your native language, of other languages you might be studying and especially of English.

A decent appreciation of the sound structures of English is important whether you are studying English as your native language or as a foreign language, but it is also important if you are a speaker of English studying other languages. This is because many of the problems which face a language learner in acquiring a good accent are caused by interference from the native language. If you know how English works you've obviously got a better chance of avoiding such pitfalls. This is especially true of those aspects of sound structure that are not reflected in the writing system, and which are usually rather hard for native speakers to hear.

The book contains a good deal of discussion of English phonology and some chapters are devoted entirely to English. This is essentially for practical reasons: many students of linguistics need to know about English.

However, English is a convenient language to use if only because I can guarantee that all readers of the book know the language. Nonetheless, in order to understand the way even simple phonological theory works it is useful and sometimes necessary to look at other languages. Moreover, even if your primary concern is with the structure of English, it's important to have some sort of feel for the way other languages work. In addition, looking at data or exercises from other languages allows you to test out your practical analytic abilities without the benefit of knowing the 'answer' beforehand. The examples from languages other than English, however, are always relevant to English in the sense that they illustrate a phenomenon which is of importance to the structure of English. So, if you're a student or speaker of English and you feel that you're being asked to delve into intricacies of an exotic language which has nothing to do with English, it's possible that you're missing at least part of the point.

Although I discuss a variety of theoretical issues in this book, my principal concern is not with the construction of phonological theories themselves. The theory is there to give us tools with which to analyse phonological structures and patterns. For this reason, I have usually chosen just one theoretical approach out of many and shown how that approach solves certain problems and allows us to understand particular phenomena. This doesn't mean that you should regard that approach as the last word (there's no such thing in science!). If you go on to study phonology at a more advanced level you'll encounter other ways of doing things. However, from this course you'll get a feel for how phonology works and how to organize phonological data in such a way as to get an explanation of why things are the way they are.

The exercises are an important part of any textbook. Some of the ones in this book are to help you monitor your progress and essentially ask you to apply what you've just learnt to a new body of data. Some of them go further and ask you to think about the issues in greater depth. Other exercises introduce you to interesting aspects of the phonology of English. Some of the exercises can have more than one function. As with any textbook, you should also invent your own simple feedback exercises. At the end of a section take the crucial examples discussed in the text and try to analyse them without referring to the book. (Don't be surprised at how difficult this seems at first!)

The essence of doing linguistics is seeing patterns in something we take for granted, language. This is a very unnatural thing to – language didn't evolve for the benefit of linguists – and the techniques can be a bit unnerving at first. But once you've got over the initial sense of strangeness you'll find yourself able to see (and hear) fascinating things which were completely hidden before. I'd like to think that this book will help open up some of that hidden world, and that you'll enjoy exploring it.

Acknowledgements

Several cohorts of students cheerfully submitted themselves to earlier drafts of this text. They helped introduce innumerable improvements and I thank them collectively. Iggy Roca commented on some very embryonic incarnations. I am particularly indebted to reviewers, one anonymous, the other Elizabeth Hume, who provided detailed comments and criticisms. In addition to spotting various typos and other aberrations, they encouraged me to alter the content and organization in a number of important ways. I am grateful to the University of Essex for its enlightened policy on study leave, without which this book would still be a collection of stapled photocopies.

Figures 1.2, 1.3(a) and 1.3(b) are taken from *A Course in Phonetics*, 3rd edn, by Peter Ladefoged and are reproduced by permission of the publisher, Harcourt Brace & Company.

Abbreviations and Symbols

(For abbreviations of distinctive features see chapter 4, appendix 4.3.)

AdjP	adjective phrase
ATR	Advanced Tongue Root (see chapter 4, appendix 4.3)
Aux	auxiliary (verb)
C	consonant
CG	Clitic Group
Co	coda
ESR	English Stress Rule
G	glide
Gen	Genitive (case)
I	Intonational Phrase
IPA	International Phonetic Alphabet
L	liquid
N	nasal; noun
N/A	not applicable
Nom.	Nominative (case)
NP	noun phrase
NSP	Nominal Strident Palatalization (Polish)
NSR	Nuclear Stress Rule

Nu	nucleus
Num	number
NumP	number phrase
O	onset
OCP	Obligatory Contour Principle
P	preposition; plosive
pl	plural
PP	prepositional phrase
Pwd	Phonological (Prosodic) Word
R	rhyme
RP	Received Pronunciation
RS	Raddoppiamento Sintattico (Italian)
sg	singular
SPE	*The Sound Pattern of English* (Chomsky and Halle 1968)
SR	surface representation; Strong Retraction
SSA	Stray Syllable Adjunction
SSG	Sonority Sequencing Generalization
U	Utterance Phrase
UR	underlying representation
V	vowel; verb
Vel Pal	Velar Palatalization (Slavic)
VP	verb phrase
σ	syllable
φ	Phonological Phrase

chapter 1

Preliminaries
to Phonology

1.0 Introduction

In this chapter I will present a review of the central themes of phonology
in section 1.1 and devote the bulk of the chapter to the real task of describing speech sounds and the way speech sounds can be written down. This
is the essential foundation for any serious study of phonology, but it also
illustrates a number of important features of the kind of linguistic analysis
that we will be concerned with in the rest of the book. Most of the discussion is devoted to individual speech sounds, but in section 1.3 we will also
touch briefly on the structure of the syllable, and such questions as stress
and intonation. Finally, section 1.4 will raise some broader questions concerning the reasons why phonologists study what they study.

1.1 The Nature of Phonology

1.1.1 Phonetics and phonology

The study of speech sounds is partitioned between two distinct but related
disciplines, **phonetics** and **phonology**. Both terms come from the Greek

word meaning 'sound', and there is a fair degree of overlap in what concerns the two subjects. Thus, the boundaries between phonetics and phonology are very difficult to draw, and there is a good deal of controversy amongst linguists as to exactly where they should lie. Despite the differences, it is clear that each of these subdisciplines relies on the other to a large extent, in the sense that phonological analyses have to be grounded in phonetic facts, and phonetic research has to be geared towards those capacities of the human vocal tract which subserve language specifically (as opposed to, say, eating or breathing). In this subsection I will sketch in outline the relationship between phonetics and phonology, presenting what I take to be the mainstream view amongst phonologists.

Phonetics is essentially the study of the physical aspects of speech. This means the acoustic bases of speech (linked most closely with speech perception) and the physiological bases of speech (linked most closely with speech production). Thus, phonetic research might investigate the collection of frequencies of sound observed in the production of particular types of vowel, or it might examine the precise movements of the tongue in producing the sound 's'.

Phonology is concerned with the linguistic patterning of sounds in human languages. This means phonologists will be interested in all those aspects of sound production and perception which can be controlled (albeit unconsciously) by a mature native speaker in order to achieve a particular linguistic effect. It also means that phonologists are concerned with those abstract patterns in the sound systems of languages that have to be learned by a child (or indeed adult) acquiring the language. In this respect phonology is concerned with something psychological, mental, or in contemporary terms, cognitive.

Phonology is not specifically concerned with aspects of speech production or perception which are purely the result of the physical properties of the system. For instance, it is often said that the articulation of the 'k' sounds in the words car and key differ from each other slightly. In the 'k' of key the tongue is brought slightly towards the front of the mouth in comparison with the 'k' of car. Anticipating the next section, we could say that it effectively becomes slightly palatalized. The reason for this , of course, is that the 'ey' vowel of key drags the tongue forward slightly, because that vowel is produced with the tongue slightly further forward in the mouth than the 'a' vowel of car. In fact, it is more or less impossible to pronounce a clear and pure 'ey' type vowel immediately after the kind of 'k' sound found in car. In other words, it would appear that some degree of fronting in these circumstances is physiologically inevitable.

This kind of phenomenon is of great interest to those speech scientists who study the precise way in which human speech sounds are produced and their influence on each other during speaking. When discussing cases such as this in which the articulation of one sound has an uncontrollable articulatory effect on a neighbouring sound we often use the term **coarticulation**.

The study of coarticulation is of great importance for a full understanding of exactly how the speech production system works. However, since the speaker isn't really in control of coarticulation phenomena it is effectively impossible to make use of them within the linguistic system. A linguistic system is built on the idea of **contrasts**. By selecting one type of sound instead of another we can, for instance, distinguish one word from another. Thus, we can distinguish the words *cane* and *gain* by choosing as the first consonant either 'k' or 'g'. However, not all languages do this, and in some the speaker may even have a free choice as to which sound to use. The fact that the distinction between 'k' and 'g' is significant in English is something which anyone acquiring the language (e.g. an English speaking child) has to learn. However, no language, it seems, can make use of the very slight (and to the ears of phonetically untrained English speakers inaudible) difference between the 'k' sounds of *key* and *car*. To this extent we can say that this difference is a purely phonetic fact of no immediate phonological interest, in the sense that phonological theory doesn't need to have any special account of it. We can also say that, as far as the phonological system is concerned, the two varieties of 'k' are really just minor variants of <u>one</u> sound.

On the other hand, in some languages the fronting or palatalization effect would be emphasized, so that a word form such as *key* would be pronounced with a noticeable accompanying 'y' (called a palatalized 'k'), or might even be pronounced in the same place as the 'y' sound (when it would be called a palatal sound). This sort of thing happens in a number of Slavonic languages, for instance, such as Russian or Polish. Such a pronunciation would be different then from the English pronunciation (and perhaps from other dialects of the language). It would be part of what distinguishes that language or dialect from other languages and dialects and would be part of what the child would have to learn in order to speak the language accurately, with a correct accent. It would thus be the proper concern of a phonologist.[1]

It is very important that we try to account for all the phonetic variation that is potentially under the speaker's control, even if we can easily find phonetic 'justification' for a given process. For instance, in a great many languages the 'n' sound is pronounced rather like any consonant which immediately follows it. For example, in a phrase such as *in Greece* spoken at normal rate without undue care, the 'n' of *in* is pronounced rather like the 'ng' sound of *sing*, and not like the true 'n' sound of *sin*. This is due to the influence of the 'g' of *Greece*. This is because it is very natural for the speech apparatus to anticipate the place of articulation of a following sound, in that it reduces the amount of oral gymnastics required by cutting out the need to move the tongue from near the teeth for 'n' to the back of the mouth for the 'g' sound. This will become somewhat clearer when we discuss assimilation of place of articulation in the next sections. Given that exactly the same thing happens in language after language one might be tempted to assume that this was just another example of coarticulation, i.e. that such accommodation to the following sound was an inevitable physiological consequence of the vocal tract mechanism and couldn't be controlled by speakers. However, that would be a mistake. Although in a language like English or the Slav language Polish, we do observe this, in Russian, which is very closely related to Polish, no such phenomenon is observed. Thus the 'n' of the word *anglija* 'England' is pronounced as an 'n' not as the 'ng' sound (in transcriptional terms it is [anglijə], not [*aŋglijə]). Indeed, the latter pronunciation is a common error amongst foreign learners of Russian.

1.1.2 Phonemes

I have said that phonology deals with the linguistic patterning of sounds. There are several ways in which this manifests itself. The first, most obvious, question that a phonologist would ask when confronted with an undescribed language is 'what sounds does the language make use of?' In other words, the first aspect to the phonology of a language is the sound inventory. Even here we might note that what is phonetically possible is not necessarily realized in phonology. For example, no language seems to use a sound made by closing off the glottis (i.e. the voice box), building up air pressure inside the mouth by raising the larynx, and then expelling this suddenly from between almost closed lips. This sound is not difficult to make (indeed, it is actually quite a common occurrence, being used as a gesture of disparagement, and usually referred to as a 'raspberry'). So just because a sound is physically possible and can be produced in a controlled fashion doesn't mean that it will occur in a phonological system. On the other hand, the kind of click noise that we can make to register disapproval ('Tut-tut!' or 'Tsk-tsk!') is used in some languages of Southern Africa as a normal speech sound (and such clicks occur in great variety in some of those languages).

Once we have established the inventory of sounds used in a language, we will wish to know what relationships those sounds have to each other. An important distinction traditionally drawn is between those sounds which are used **contrastively** and those which are **variant** pronunciations of contrastively used sounds. Put simply, the contrastive sounds of a language are those which, like 'k' and 'g' in English, can be used in that language to distinguish one word from another. The sounds used contrastively are called **phonemes**.[2] However, a given phoneme may in fact be realized as a number of different sounds depending on the phonological context in which it is found. Such variant pronunciations are called **conditioned variants** or **allophones** of a phoneme. The phenomenon itself is called **allophony**.

A familiar case of allophony is provided by the 'p t k' sounds of words such as in *pan, tan* and *can*. These differ in quality from the corresponding sounds in *span, Stan* and *scan*. As we will see, sounds such as 'p t k' are called *plosives*. The initial plosives of *pan, tan, can* are accompanied with a slight puff of air, **aspiration.** This aspiration, however, is lacking in *span, Stan, scan*, which have **plain** plosives. However, the lack of aspiration in the *s-* initial words is due to the presence of the 's' and is wholly predictable. There are no words in English distinguished solely by the aspiration of a plosive. For our purposes the distribution of plain and aspirated voiceless plosives can be summarized (oversimplifying considerably) by principle 1.1:[3]

1.1   An initial voiceless plosive on its own is aspirated, but after [s] it is plain (unaspirated).

I have place the letter 's' inside square brackets, [s]. This is to indicate that the letter is being used as the name of a speech sound. Whether a plosive is preceded by [s] or not constitutes the phonological context for the allophonic variation.

This situation can be contrasted with that found in a language such as Hindi, illustrated in 1.2 (from Ladefoged 1993: 145):

1.2   a. pal   'take care of'
            pʰal   'edge of knife'
        b. tan   'mode of singing'
            tʰan   'roll of cloth'
        c. tal   'postpone'
            tʰal   'place for buying wood'
        d. kan   'ear'
            kʰan   'mime'

The raised 'h' in the Hindi words represents aspiration. Examples of this sort, which differ in just one respect, are called in linguistics **minimal pairs.** The examples of 1.2 demonstrate the phonological importance of aspiration in Hindi. The word /kʰan/ 'mine' in Hindi is very similar to the English word *can*, but phonologically the two tokens of [kʰ] in the English and Hindi words are different. This is because in English there is no possible contrast between [k] and [kʰ], as there is in Hindi. In other words, there is no way that just this pair of sounds could serve, on their own, to distinguish different words.

The idea that allophones of a phoneme are conditioned variants of that phoneme brings with it a further important notion, that of **distribution.** This is one of the most important concepts in linguistics. To return to our aspirated plosives, we have seen that the plain plosives are found in certain positions (or contexts, or environments) while the aspirated plosives are found in different positions. In other words, the two types of sound are distributed differently. Now there are several ways in which the distribution of two sounds, A and B, can be related, among them being the following:

Figure 1.1   Types of distributional relationships

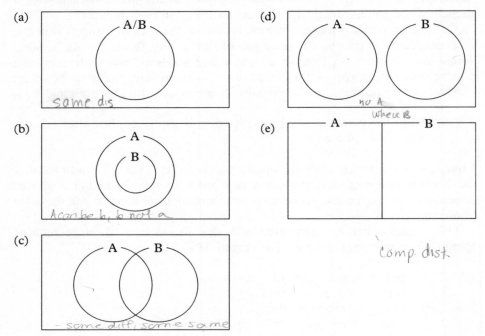

(a)   A/B   *same dis*

(b)   A B   *A can be b, b not a*

(c)   A B   *— some diff, some same*

(d)   A B   *no A where B*

(e)   A B   *comp. dist*

(a)   The sounds may have exactly the same distribution.

(b)   The distribution of A may include all the positions where B is found, with some A positions not occupied by B. (We would then say that the set of B positions is properly included in the set of A positions.)

(c)   There may be overlapping distribution, with some of the A and B positions being the same, while some of the A positions are not shared by B and vice versa.

(d)   The sets of positions may be entirely disjoint, that is, no A occurs where a B occurs, and vice versa.

These possibilities are sketched in the form of Venn diagrams in figure 1.1.

The important type of distribution for our understanding of phonemes is that of figure 1.1 (e). This is like (d) except that the two sets of positions are exhaustive. The A positions therefore complement the B positions and vice versa.[4] This kind of distribution is known therefore as **complementary distribution**. This is the situation we have with our aspirated and plain plosives. Ignoring the oversimplification in the description here, we can say that there are two basic positions, immediately after [s] and not after [s]. If we think of the A sound as the aspirated plosive and the B sound as the unaspirated, then we can say that there is just one B position, namely, after

[s], and one A position, namely, not after [s]. The two positions complement each other (since a sound cannot be simultaneously after [s] and not after [s].

The point of complementary distribution is that two sounds with such a distribution could never form a minimal pair. ||

For example, the [tʰ] and [t⁼] of *tan* and *Stan* cannot form part of minimal pairs because unaspirated [t⁼] must be preceded by [s] while aspirated [tʰ] can never be preceded by[s]. Thus, [tʰ] and [t⁼] will, by definition, never have the opportunity to be used contrastively. The basic intuition here is that only phonemes can be used to distinguish one word from another and [tʰ] and [t⁼] are merely variants of one single phoneme, /t/. Complementary distribution is important in trying to figure out which sounds correspond to independent phonemes and which are just allophones of phonemes. If two sounds are in complementary distribution and therefore cannot form minimal pairs they are unlikely to be independent phonemes. || It is more likely they are conditioned variants of one and the same phoneme. This is the conclusion we would draw from our example with aspirated and plain plosives.

To see this more clearly, suppose that in a street the neighbours believe that there are two different men living in the same house, a bus driver and a night security guard. In the morning the neighbours see the bus driver leave for work in his bus driver's uniform and come home in the evening. Then a little later they see the night security guard leave for work in his security guard's uniform and return at dawn the following day. Now suppose the neighbours think about the situation for a little while and realize that they never see the bus driver and the security guard at the same time (say, in the local shops). In other words, suppose the bus driver and security guard are in complementary distribution. Then, it might dawn on some of the neighbours (those who have studied phonology, perhaps), that the two men are actually one and the same man doing two jobs. Thus, the man himself corresponds to a phoneme, and the two incarnations or 'realizations' as bus driver and security guard correspond to two allophones.

So far I have spoken as though some sounds are phonemes and others sounds are conditioned variants, or allophones. So far this has been a harmless oversimplification. However, it is a very misleading way of thinking of the notion of the phoneme (though it is unfortunately the way that many beginners picture this notion). The problem is that it is not the case that some sounds are used contrastively and others are not. Instead we must distinguish two different notions of 'speech sound', one a concrete, phonetically based notion (the actual sounds of a language as they might be heard and transcribed in a careful phonetic record), and another more abstract notion.

This means that we should distinguish two different levels of analysis. At the first, more concrete, level (which we could call, though with caution, the 'phonetic' or better, the 'allophonic' level) we have the inventory of speech

\allophonic

sounds used in a language. We can call these sounds the **phones** of the language. We will continue to write phones between square brackets. These will include in English and in Hindi the sounds [p pʰ k kʰ] etc. The phones are all those sounds which a language makes use of. At the next, more abstract, level we distinguish a set of sound types. These are the phonemes, and they do not necessarily correspond in a direct way to any particular physical (phonetic) sound. Rather, they are the units which serve to build up individual words and hence which distinguish one word from another. Unfortunately, we are obliged to use the same letter symbols to write down phones as we use for phonemes (though in chapter 4 we will see a more sophisticated way of representing speech sounds). The usual way to distinguish a symbol for a phone from one for a phoneme is to put the phonemes in slashes, / . . . /. Hence, we can say that in Hindi we can identify the phonemes /p pʰ t tʰ t tʰ k kʰ/. In English the corresponding phonemes would be limited to the set /p t k/, though English also has the phones [p pʰ t tʰ t tʰ k kʰ]. Then we need to ask what phones correspond to these phonemes. In Hindi (given the meagre data at our disposal here), there is a rather simple situation, illustrated in 1.3:

1.3

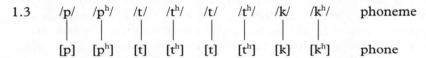

In other words there is a simple one:one relationship between phonemic and phonetic levels (for this set of sounds). In English we get 1.4:

1.4

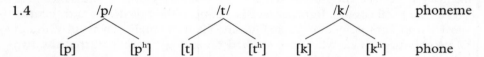

Here we see that there are two phones corresponding to each of the three phonemes: [p pʰ] correspond to two separate allophones of the phoneme /p/.

It might be asked at this point why we choose to represent the phonemes in 1.4 with the symbols /p t k/ rather than, say, /pʰ tʰ kʰ/, or, indeed, entirely different symbols with no relation to phonetic transcription, such as /P T K/. First, phonologists tend to assume that the basic form of a phoneme is identical to its most widespread allophone. In addition, it is generally assumed that the basic form of a phoneme will be phonetically somehow 'simpler' than other forms. However, neither of these assumptions is necessary. Although an aspirated plosive is generally felt to be in some way more 'complex' than a plain plosive, I shall, in fact, argue in chapter 6 against tradition and claim that it is the aspirated variant that is basic. Moreover, it is sometimes necessary to assume that the basic phoneme is phonetically distinct from all of its allophones (though this is rather rare). The decision can only be the result of a careful analysis of the phonological system. We chose that solution which gives us the simplest, most elegant overall description of the system. This point will be expanded on in chapters 4 and 6.

Our discussion of phonemes and their allophones shows us why we need to distinguish two different senses of the expression 'speech sound'. In the English and Hindi examples we can distinguish six sounds in the sense of phones, [p pʰ t tʰ k kʰ]. However, in Hindi we also distinguish six sounds in the sense of phonemes, while in English we only have three sounds in the sense of phonemes. The important point is to realize that the word 'sound' can be ambiguous between a relatively concrete meaning (phone) and a relatively abstract meaning (phoneme).

Given our notational conventions governing square brackets and slashes, [. . .] vs. / . . . /, we can write or **transcribe** words such as those of 1.5 in two ways, using a phonemic or 'broad' transcription (1.6) or a phonetic or 'narrow transcription'[5] (1.7):

1.5   a. pan   b. tan   c. can
      d. span   e. Stan   f. scan

1.6   a. /pan/   b. /tan/   c. /kan/
      d. /span/   e. /stan/   f. /skan/

1.7   a. [pʰan]   b. [tʰan]   c. [kʰan]
      d. [span]   e. [stan]   f. [skan]

In 1.6 we no longer seem to represent which plosives are aspirated and which are not. But we can appeal to 1.1 above to recover this information and derive the representations in 1.7.

What governs the choice of the phoneme symbol? For instance, what would stop us assigning allophones to phonemes in the following way?

1.8   /p/   /t/   /k/   phoneme

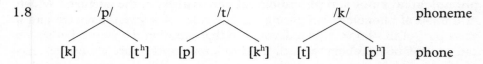

      [k]   [tʰ]   [p]   [kʰ]   [t]   [pʰ]   phone

If we did this we would get the following phonemic transcriptions:

1.9   a. /kan/ = *pan*   b. /pan/ = *tan*   c. /tan/ = *can*
      d. /stan/ = *span*   e. /skan/ = *Stan*   f. /span/ = *scan*

This may seem absurd, but the point is that the representations of 1.9 give us exactly the same information as those of 1.6. In other words, we might say that the representational system illustrated in 1.8, 1.9 is a **notational variant** of the usual one. To see this, think of the schemas in 1.6, 1.8 as just a set of instructions how to pronounce a word. You should verify that if you follow the crazy schema in 1.8 and apply principle 1.1 you will still get the correct pronunciation of the words. Another way to see the same point is to replace all the phoneme symbols with, say, Roman numerals, the corresponding plain allophones with arbitrarily chosen even Arabic numerals, and the aspirated allophones with arbitrary odd Arabic numerals. In this way, we would replace the triple {/p/, [p], [pʰ]} in 1.4 with, say, {IV, 4, 7}. Then it becomes obvious that it simply doesn't matter which symbols we chose for our phonemes and their allophones as long as they are differentiated from each other.

The reason that 1.8 seems crazy is because it brings with it the claim that the members of the pairs {[k] [tʰ]}, {[p] [kʰ]}, {[t] [pʰ]} are variants of each other. However, this goes against common sense. This is because [p] is rather similar phonetically to [pʰ], [t] to [tʰ] and so on, and it seems more natural therefore to associate those pairs than the ones in 1.8. It is interesting to realize, however, that the notational convention is just that, a convention which makes the system look a little more sensible. Strictly speaking there is nothing wrong with the system in 1.8. This, in fact, is a flaw in a notional system such as this which restricts itself to naming phonemes and their allophones with a single symbol (possibly enriched with a few diacritics). We will see that the problem disappears once we adopt a more sophisticated solution to the problem of describing sounds in chapter 4.

One practical problem with the notation is that it encourages us to imagine that the phoneme /p/ is 'essentially' the sound (phone) [p]. This is very misleading, however, as our notational experiment in 1.8 should have taught us. Rather, what we must say is that we have a phoneme /p/ which has two physical (phonetic, allophonic) **realizations**, [p], [pʰ].

Finally, we have discussed at some length the relationships between phonemes and their realizations. However, it should be borne in mind that the other side of the coin in performing this kind of analysis is the set of principles such as 1.1. We will see later that these principles are embodied in the **phonological rules** and **phonological constraints** of the language. Much of the job of phonology is figuring out the rules of a given language and a great part of this book will be devoted to that question. However, before we can address that problem we will need to know much more about the sorts of sounds found in the world's languages and we will also need to develop an unambiguous and efficient way of writing down those sounds (i.e. a transcription system). This is the topic of the next section.

1.2 The Phonetic Basis: Articulatory Segmental Phonetics

Many readers will have at least some familiarity with much of the subject matter of this section: articulatory phonetics and the transcriptional system of the International Phonetics Association (IPA). This will not, therefore, be an introduction aimed for the complete beginner in this area. Those who know literally nothing about the area should first consult the appropriate books or chapters mentioned in the further reading at the end of the chapter. The section will thus be a brief review of these basic concepts, together with certain additional notions and information which will be of use when we look at phonology proper. The section is headed 'articulatory phonetics' because the predominant mode of description is in terms of how the speech sounds are produced. This is not to say that the acoustic properties of sounds are unimportant, merely that they have had less influence on the development of phonological theory than articulatory properties. The section heading also refers to 'segmental' phonetics. By 'segment' we simply mean an individual speech sound. Now, it is an intriguing problem to determine how it is we know where one segment ends and the next begins, a problem that tends to be masked by the false sense of comfort offered by our alphabetic writing and transcription systems. However, we will ignore such niceties and assume that we know how to segment the speech stream into individual sounds. In a later section we will look at sound phenomena which stretch beyond (or over and above) the segment, that is **supra-** **segmental** phenomena such as stress, rhythm and intonation.

In order to talk about the sound system of a language we need to be able to write about that system. In particular, we need to be able to write down the sounds of the language in a reasonably unambiguous fashion. This is problematical for languages which lack a writing system of any sort, or which use a picture-based system which bears little relationship to the sound system (e.g. Egyptian hieroglyphics or modern Chinese ideograms). Alphabetically written languages like English often have bizarre spelling conventions, so that a single sound such as 'f' can be written as 'f' (*fun*) 'ff' (*affair*), 'ph' (*phone*), or even 'gh' (*enough*). On the other hand, some letters remain unpronounced such as the 'k' of *knight*, or have a complex relation to the pronunciation of other sounds (such as the 'gh' of *knight*, compared with *knit*, where the 'gh' represents a change in the sound conveyed by the letter 'i'). However, even languages which are 'phonetically' spelt pose serious problems when we come to provide a really accurate record of pronunciation. We will see in what way in due course.

The first tool needed to solve this problem is a commonly accepted transcription system. In this book we will use the alphabet of the International Phonetics Association (IPA), given in appendix 1.1. This is essentially a chart of symbols, together with a set of additional, diacritic symbols, which will allow us to register any sound used by any language. To follow the description of articulations, refer to the diagram of the vocal tract in appendix 1.2.

1.2.1 Consonants

We will begin with the consonant system. It is traditional in IPA descriptions to distinguish three aspects or **parameters** of a sound: its voicing, its

voicing
place
manner

place of articulation, and its manner of articulation. This way of looking at things is, of course, reflected in the usual way that sounds are described when the IPA classification is used, e.g. describing a sound [b] as a voiced bilabial plosive. We can see this, too, from the traditional construction of the chart, which lists places of articulation from left-to-right, manners of articulation from top-to-bottom, and pairs voiced and voiceless sounds in each cell. This organization is something of an oversimplification, but it makes a good starting point.

It will be convenient to begin by discussing manners of articulation first, and then place of articulation. Finally, we will discuss voicing under the more general heading of laryngeal articulations and airstream mechanisms.

The first thing we need to understand in considering speech sounds is the source of the sound itself. This is the larynx or voice box. For our purposes, we can think of this as a box of cartilage in the throat across which lie two strips of tissue, the vocal cords or vocal folds. These are attached to an immovable part of the larynx, the thyroid cartilage, at one end and movable parts, the arytenoid cartilages, at the other. By moving the arytenoids it is possible to change the tightness or tension of the vocal cords. If we push air forcefully out from the lungs through the larynx when the cords are slack nothing much happens (we get a 'breathy' sound characteristic of heavy breathing). However, if we tighten up the vocal cords then we experience the phenomenon of **phonation**. This occurs when the sides of the vocal folds are brought together in such a way that outgoing air causes the sides to vibrate against each other. This gives rise to a very rapid sequence of impulses, a little like a baby's rattle only much faster. These impulses are sufficiently fast to give us the illusion of a continuous sound.

Given this source of sound we can then modify it by changing the shapes of the cavities inside the vocal tract as the air moves out from the sound source, the larynx. As the cavity shapes change, as a result of movements of the tongue, lips and other articulators, so the way that the air in them vibrates will also change. This takes us onto our next important concept, that of **resonance**. Some sounds involve a relatively large degree of resonance or **sonorance** in the buccal cavity (the throat, mouth and nasal passages) and these are generally referred to as **sonorants**. Other sounds involve much less sonorance and these are termed **obstruents**. The precise meaning of 'sonorance' (or 'sonority') in this context is still not very clear, and we will discuss this concept in more detail in chapter 3. However, the basic idea is that certain types of cavity will resonate, producing a relatively pure type of sound. An example would be an empty milk bottle, which produces a musical note when you blow across the opening. Another type of sonorant chamber would be the inside of a cathedral with a strong echo. However, if you produce a noise by friction (e.g. sawing a piece of wood) or percussion (e.g. by knocking two pieces of wood together) you will produce a non-resonating sound. Roughly speaking, the obstruents are those sounds made by friction or a sudden burst of sound within the vocal tract,

while sonorants are those in which some part of the tract is made to resonate. The most obvious case of a sonorant would, then, be a vowel. ⟶ highest
sonority

1.2.1.1 Manners of Articulation The obstruents are divided into three broad
classes: **plosives**, **fricatives** and **affricates**. There are two crucial aspects
to such sounds. The first is that they are all made by closing of the nasal
passages so that air cannot escape through the nose. This is achieved by
raising the **velum** or (**soft palate**), the soft part of the roof of the mouth,
beyond the dome of the **hard palate**. Raising the velum closes off the
opening from the back of the throat to the nose (the nasal port). The result
is that the air can only pass through the mouth, and we have an **oral** sound.
The second characteristic of the obstruents is that they involve a significant
narrowing or closure of the oral tract, thereby reducing the resonance. This
narrowing is known as **stricture**. Plosives are made with a complete stricture in the vocal tract, stopping the air which is being pushed out from the
lungs from escaping through the mouth. At the same time, we prevent the
air from escaping through the nasal passages. We can think of this as occurring in two phases. For instance, in making the sound [b] we close off the
vocal tract at the level of the lips (the 'closure phase'). Since the air cannot
escape, pressure builds up. Then, the blockage is released (the 'release phase')
and the result is a sudden burst of sound corresponding to the plosive.

A fricative is made by means of an incomplete stricture, that is we almost
shut off the vocal tract at some point, but not quite. For instance, in making
the sound [f] we bring the top teeth and bottom lip very close together, but
without making a complete, airtight closure. The result is that air is forced
out of the mouth through a very narrow passageway. This means that the
air is at a relatively high pressure and as it flows rapidly along the articulators
it generates turbulence or friction, which we hear as noise. The precise
nature of that noise depends on exactly which articulators are used and
exactly how they are positioned. Since it is possible for air to pass through
the vocal tract we often refer to fricatives as a type of **continuant** sound.
When the air is prevented from passing through the mouth, as in the case
of plosives, we have a **stop** sound.

An affricate is a sound which starts out rather like a plosive and finishes
rather like a fricative. We can think of it as a plosive whose release phase has
been prolonged. There has been much discussion of how to distinguish an
affricate such as English [ʧ] in *the chop* from a genuine sequence of plosive
followed by fricative, e.g. the [t ʃ] in *that shop*. The essential difference is one
of length and timing: an affricate tends to last about as long as, say, a single
fricative, while a sequence tends to last as long as two consonants. Occasionally, the two types of situation contrast with each other. In Polish, for
instance, we find the affricate [ʧ] in the word *czy* [ʧ ɨ] '(question particle)'
but a consonant sequence (in careful pronunciation, at least) in *trzy* [t ʃ ɨ]
'three'.

Among the sonorant consonants a very important class is the nasals.

These are formed by allowing the air to pass through the nasal passage. This is achieved by lowering the velum, thus allowing air to escape through the nose. If the rest of the vocal tract is stopped up, as in the case of [b], then we get a **nasal stop**, [m]. This is an example of a stop which is not a plosive (in fact, it is not even an obstruent). The production of nasal stops is the commonest use of nasal resonance. However, there are other types of nasal sounds, especially nasalized vowels, which we will briefly discuss later.

I mentioned that fricatives are a subtype of continuant sound. We can also produce continuants which do not involve friction or turbulence. In the IPA tradition these are called **frictionless continuants** or **approximants**. These are sounds which do not involve an obstruction in the buccal cavity sufficient to cause either complete blockage of the oral tract (as for a noncontinuant stop), or a high degree of turbulent noise (as with a fricative). It is common in phonological discussion to divide these sounds into two subgroups, the **glides** and the **liquids**.

Glides are exemplified by such sounds as [w] and [j]. They are closely related to the vowels [u] and [i]. Indeed, you can gradually turn these vowels into glides in a sequence such as [aua] or [aia] by just making the articulation of the [u, i] increasingly lax and rapid. The result will be [awa] and [aja]. In French, we can take the front rounded vowel [y] and get the corresponding glide [ɥ]. In chapter 3 I expand on this way of looking at glides.

Liquids are essentially 'l'- and 'r'- sounds, or more technically **laterals** and **rhotics**. However, this is a pretty mixed bag, especially when we consider the rhotics. There are several ways of pronouncing an 'r' sound. In the standard (British and American) English sound (IPA [ɹ]) we have a frictionless continuant or approximant, very reminiscent of a glide in its production and behaviour. In American English (and many other varieties) the -tt- of a word like *better* is pronounced almost like a 'd' sound (IPA [ɾ]). This is produced by rapidly flicking the tip of the tongue at the gum ridge. Such a sound is called a **tap** or **flap** and in many languages it represents a type of rhotic (for example, it is one of the two rhotics of Spanish). We can place the tongue tip against the gum ridge and force air through the gap forcefully enough to start the tip itself vibrating. This gives us a **rolled** or **trilled** 'r' (IPA [r]). In varieties of English which lack this, it is the sort of 'r' sound produced when uttering the exclamation *brrrr!* on a cold day. In some sense these articulations, whilst very different in their acoustic effects, are all related. This is clear from the fact that it is often the case that different dialects of one and the same language may differ precisely in the manner in which the rhotic sounds are produced. English, French and German all show such dialectal variation in the pronunciation of rhotic sounds. When we consider places of articulation we will see that there is even more variation in these sounds, and I shall return to them briefly later in this section.

Lateral sounds are produced by allowing the air to pass by one or both sides of the tongue. For the English [l] the tongue is in roughly the position

Table 1.1 Places of articulation

Name	Passive articulator	Active articulator(s)
Bilabial	Both lips	(Both lips)
Labiodential	Lower lip/upper teeth	
(Inter)dental	Teeth	Tongue tip/blade
Alveolar	Gum ridge	Tongue tip/blade
Alveo-palatal/palato-alveolar/Postalveolar	Gum ridge/hard palate	Tongue blade
Retroflex	Hard palate	Tongue tip
Palatal	Hard palate	Tongue blade
Velar	Soft palate (velum)	Tongue body (dorsum)
Uvular	Uvula	Tongue body
Pharyngeal	Pharynx wall	Tongue root
Glottal(laryngeal)	Larynx	—

it would be for a [d] sound. Other types of 'l' sound will be discussed after we have introduced places of articulation and voicing.

1.2.1.2 Places of articulation As I have pointed out, by changing the shape of the cavities within the oral tract we can change the type of sound eventually produced. This is because certain components of the sound generated in the larynx are filtered out by certain configurations of the tract, while other components are amplified. It should be appreciated that the source of sound remains the larynx and the vibrations of the vocal folds. The rest of the vocal tract modulates this sound in various ways.

The next point to bear in mind is the distinction between **active** and **passive articulators**. This is seen most clearly when we consider a sound such as [s]. Here the tongue tip is brought towards the gum ridge leaving just enough of a chink to cause friction. The fact that it is the gum ridge (or alveolar ridge) where this takes place is important since at any other place the sound would be different. However, the gum ridge is not itself moved, and is thus the passive articulator. On the other hand, the tongue tip is actively brought against the gum ridge so this is the active articulator. Again, it is important that it be the tip of the tongue; if, for instance, the blade of the tongue were used we would get a sound more reminiscent of [θ] than [s].

Traditionally, we distinguish places or points of articulation in terms of the passive articulator. These are shown in table 1.1, together with an indication of the commonest active articulator used in the languages of the world.

A word of explanation is due here. There is no obvious sense in which one or other articulator is active or passive in the case of bilabials (though for labiodentals it makes more sense to say that the movable articulator, the lower lip, is active). For glottals there is no active articulator – this type of sound refers to the way in which the vocal folds are manipulated to produce a particular type of sound. This is discussed in more detail in section 1.2.1.3 on airstream mechanisms.

In most cases interpretation of these descriptions should be fairly straight-forward, given the diagram in appendix 1.2. The problematic sound types for most readers will be those which are uncommon in European languages, such as the uvulars and pharyngeals. The uvula is the tip of the soft palate. By bringing the body of the tongue against it we produce a sound similar to a velar. It is also possible to produce a uvular tap or trill. Pharyngeal sounds are made by bringing the root of the tongue back towards the back of the throat. Such sounds are not especially common in the world's languages, but neither are they particularly rare. It is next to impossible to bring the tongue root so far back as to make a complete closure, so we don't find cases of pharyngeal plosives. However, Arabic, for instance, has voiced and unvoiced pharyngeal fricatives, [ʕ] and [ħ].

When we examine the way that the sounds of a given language pattern together we generally find that the places of articulation behave as though they belonged to larger groupings. The bilabial and labiodental sounds often group together, and since both sets crucially involve one of the lips, we will call them **labials**. This is an important group of sounds, present in virtually every language of the world. Another important group is that whose active articulator is the body or dorsum of the tongue, the velars and the uvulars. These are referred to as **dorsals**, though if a language has no uvular sounds the class is often just called **velars**. Again, most languages have some sort of dorsal sound, with velars being much more frequent than uvulars.

Velar sounds are those like English [k g ŋ], produced by making a con-striction with the tongue body against the soft palate (velum). Many lan-guages also have velar fricatives [x ɣ]. A rather rare sound is the velar affricate [kˣ]. Similar to the velars are the uvular sounds. The uvula, recall, is the soft piece of flesh at the end of the velum and a uvular stop can be made by bringing the dorsum of the tongue against the uvula to give [q G N]. The uvulars are much rarer sounds than the velars, and it is especially rare for a language to have a uvular sound but no velar. Uvular fricatives are perhaps more familiar to European and American speakers (the voiced uvular fricative [ʁ] occurs in Standard French and German). The Eskimo languages (e.g. West Greenlandic, Inuit, Inuktitut, Yup'ik) have a rich series of uvular sounds.

The pharyngeal and glottal sounds often behave as a group (in the rela-tive small number of language which have two or more of these types) and it is customary nowadays to refer to them as **gutturals** (though other terms are sometimes used).[6] In many languages gutturals are lacking, or are only marginal sounds in the system.

Glottal sounds are common in the world's languages. Many languages

Table 1.2 Place of articulation groupings

LABIAL	CORONAL	DORSAL (VELAR)	GUTTURAL
Bilabial Labiodential	Dental Alveolar Palato-alveolar Retroflex Palatal	Velar Uvular	Pharyngeal Glottal

have a glottal fricative [h] (including the standard varieties of English), made by spreading apart the vocal folds. This gives the effect of 'heavy breathing' and produces a fricative type of sound, though at the level of the larynx. We can therefore regard [h] as a voiceless laryngeal fricative. The glottal stop [ʔ] is also found in all dialects of English, though not generally as a phoneme in its own right. However, in a great many languages throughout the world the glottal stop is a fully fledged consonant phoneme.

Finally, we come to the most important group, comprising those articulations stretching from the dentals to the palatals. Their articulatory common property is that they are all made by raising the front part of the tongue. This means the tongue tip or the blade of the tongue, but not the body of the tongue. The general term given to this group is **coronal**. It is a very important group of sounds. Coronals of one sort or another are found in every language so far described. This particular classification is not part of the original IPA descriptive scheme (though something like it has been used informally for a long time). We will see in chapter 4 that it imposes a very useful level of organization on the description of place of articulation. These broad groupings are summarized in table 1.2.

There are further remarks we can make about the way the consonant system is described. A number of languages distinguish a separate set of retroflex sounds. These are produced by curling the tongue tip backwards and articulating the sound against the hard palate or the boundary between the hard palate and the gum ridge. These sounds are particularly well represented in the languages of the Indian subcontinent and Australia, where they often fulfil the role of a particular place of articulation. For example, in Malayalam, a Dravidian language of Southern India, we find the following sounds (Ladefoged 1993: 159):

1.10	kʌmmi	'shortage'	bilabial
	pʌn̪n̪i	'pig'	dental
	kʌnni	'Virgo'	alveolar
	kʌɳɳi	'link in chain'	retroflex
	kʌɲɲi	'boiled rice and water'	palatal
	kʌŋŋi	'crushed'	velar

In many languages we also find retroflex plosives, fricatives, and liquids. This (as Ladefoged points out) is a rather strange situation because retroflexion in some ways is more a manner of articulation (witness our description in terms of the curling up of the active articulator). We will follow Ladefoged in treating retroflexion as, potentially at least, a type of place of articulation, but bearing in mind that this may in some cases be a little misleading.

The case of retroflex sounds shows that the distinction between place and manner is not always clear cut, and in some respects somewhat artificial. A different type of problem arises with respect to affricates. I have described these sounds as a plosive followed by a fricative, forming a single segment. However, in a number of cases the plosive element is more important (so that the affricate behaves like a kind of plosive) while in others it is the fricative component that is predominant, so that the affricate is a special manner of articulation for a given place. For example, some languages have four plosives, labial, alveolar/dental, palatal and velar; /p t c k/ (Icelandic, Czech and Hungarian are like this). However, in many languages the place of the palatal plosive /c/ (a rather rare sound) is taken by some sort of postalveolar, palato-alveolar or palatal affricate (e.g. Polish, some dialects of Czech).

The next aspect of the pronunciation of consonants which must be discussed is **secondary articulation**. This occurs when an additional vowel-like articulation is overlaid on the basic sound. In effect, this means articulating the consonant with a simultaneous glide. This is not the same as a consonant + glide cluster (though in practice it can often be very difficult to hear the difference).

One of the commonest secondary articulations is **palatalization**, the addition of a [j] glide to the consonant. Notice that a palatalized sound is not the same as a palatal sound. For example, in Russian the palatalized [nʲ] is an alveolar/dental sound made with the tongue tip against the teeth or the gum ridge. It is not made with the dorsum of the tongue against the hard palate, as is the case with a true palatal sound. Instead, the tongue blade is simultaneously bunched up against the hard palate while the dental or alveolar sound is being articulated. In effect, then, we superimpose a [j] sound on the [n] sound. The same is true of other palatalized consonants in Russian, such as [tʲ], [sʲ], [pʲ] etc. Again, these are not sequences of, say, [p + j], indeed, such sequences do exist, and are audibly different from the simple palatalized sounds. Thus, the name [pʲotr], 'Pyotr (= Peter)' begins with a single, palatalized p-sound, while the verb form [pʲjot] 'drinks', begins with the same palatalized p-sound followed by the glide [j].

If the added glide element is [w] we get **labialization**. Thus, a sound which is transcribed as [kʷ] consists of a [k] and simultaneously a [w] sound. The duration of the entire segment is more or less that of a plain [k] (or [w]). **Velarization** involves superposition of a vowel quality corresponding to a [w] or [u] sound but without the lip rounding (in transcription this is represented as [ɯ]). This is achieved by raising the dorsum of the tongue towards the velum while articulating the basic consonant sound. In many dialects of English the 'l' sound is pronounced like this, at least in some positions in the word. Velarization is represented by a tilde ~ through the sound [ɫ]. Finally, a number of languages, most famously Arabic, have a process of **pharyngealization**. This can be thought of as the superposition of a retracted [ɑ] sound on the consonant. To do this the tongue root must be brought back simultaneously with the production of the consonant. In a number of languages (including Arabic) it can be difficult to distinguish velarization from pharyngealization (the acoustic effects are similar).

There are other aspects of pronunciation of consonants which are beyond the scope of this introduction. Particularly interesting from the articulatory point of view are consonants with **double articulation** (e.g. a labial velar sound such as the [gb] of Igbo, which is a [b] simultaneous with a [g]) and the very numerous click sounds of a number of languages of Southern Africa such as Zulu. (See Ladefoged 1993 for a detailed description.)

1.2.1.3   Other aspects of consonant systems   The approximants or frictionless continuants deserve further discussion. We will start with the liquids, laterals and rhotics. In introducing these sounds I pointed out that the rhotics can appear in a great variety of guises, with widely differing places and manners of articulation. In 1.11 I have listed some of these together with an indication of which languages exemplify them.

1.11	ʋ	labiodental approximant	(English dial)
	ɹ	dental/alveolar approximant	(English)
	r	dental/alveolar trill	(Spanish)
	ɾ	dental/alveolar flap	(Italian)
	ɻ	retroflex approximant	(English)
	ɽ	retroflex flap	(Malayalam)
	ʐ	retroflex fricative/glide	(Mandarin)
	ɼ	palato-alveolar trilled fricative	(Czech)
	R	uvular trill	(French, German)
	ʁ	uvular fricative	(French, German)

It is notoriously difficult to determine what unifies all these sounds, particularly when we consider that a good many fricatives are included in the list, which, of course, excludes a definition in terms of frictionless sounds. In addition, in many languages a number of these sounds seem to pattern as other than rhotics. For instance, the voiced uvular fricative of the Eskimo group of languages seems to be just that, i.e. an obstruent, just like the voiced velar fricative. At the same time the labiodental approximant [ʋ] generally behaves like a labial glide (similar to [w]), as in Dutch or Ewe. On the other hand, in Mandarin Chinese it is difficult to know what criteria would determine whether the [ʐ] sound should be treated more as a liquid (akin to [l]) or as a kind of fricative (like [ʒ]).

Laterals, which we met at the end of section 1.2.1.1, provide another example of a frictionless continuant. They differ amongst themselves chiefly in voicing and place of articulation. The better known examples of laterals are all coronals, though velar laterals have been reported, particularly in the languages of the Pacific. In addition to alveolar laterals ([l]), we have palatal and retroflex laterals in languages such as Malayalam ([ʎ], [ɭ]). In a number of Australian languages (Dixon 1980) we have a distinction between an apical lateral, produced with the tongue tip against the teeth or gum ridge, and a laminal lateral, in which the tongue blade is placed in much the same place as for English [θ].

The other type of sound described as a frictionless continuant is the glide. This is essentially a high vowel sound which has lost its ability to form a syllable and which therefore behaves somewhat like a consonant. Thus, if we take [i] and pronounce it as a consonant we get [j], and likewise, [u] corresponds to [w].

The structure of the syllable will be briefly introduced in section 1.3.2. There I point out that every syllable has a peak or nucleus, which is typically a vowel. However, in some languages consonants can form the peak of a syllable, and behave just like vowels. In this case we speak of syllabic consonants. In the names of the Czech towns Plzeň and Brno we have two syllables, the first of which bears the stress. But the peak of each syllable is a liquid: [pl̩zeɲ], [br̩no] ([r] is an alveolar trill in Czech). Syllabicity is indicated in our transcription by a subscripted diacritic mark. In other languages other types of consonant can be syllabic. Most commonly we find nasals, that is [n], sometimes [m], and less frequently [ŋ]. In certain languages obstruents can be syllabic. A number of native languages on the northwestern seaboard of America have such consonants.

1.2.1.4 Airstream mechanisms The third parameter of the traditional IPA classification is **voicing**. Sounds may be voiced or unvoiced. However, this simple distinction is actually rather complex both in phonetic and in phonological terms. The problem is in deciding what constitutes voicing. In acoustic terms a voiced segment has one of two characteristics. If the sound is a continuant (e.g. a fricative or a sonorant) then we can say that voicing means simply ensuring that the vocal folds continue to vibrate during the production of the sound. This characterizes the difference between [s] and [z]. Any fricative or affricate can be voiced or unvoiced, including, for instance, the glottal fricative [h], which appears in a voiced form [ɦ] in Czech and Ukrainian. Depending on the language, voicing can affect any sonorant. Thus, Welsh has voiced and voiceless *l*- and *r*- sounds ([l l̥] [r r̥]), Burmese has voiced and voiceless nasals ([n̥ m̥]).

Liquids are generally voiced sounds but they can also be voiceless. This is rather uncommon with rhotics, but it is found reasonably often with laterals. If we devoice /l/ we get a sound represented by the 'devoicing' diacritic, a small circle placed under the sound: [l̥]. However, a voiceless sonorant of this kind can be hard to distinguish from a voiceless fricative. Many languages make use of voiceless lateral fricatives as part of the consonant system. The IPA symbol for such as sound is [ɬ]. A fricative is an obstruent, of course, and not a sonorant, and as such the voiceless lateral fricative has a voiced counterpart, [ɮ]. By introducing a stop phase just before the release of the fricative we obtain an affricate. A lateral affricate is transcribed in IPA as a digraph, a joined [t] and [l]: [tl]. (In some transcriptions especially for Native American languages you will see other symbols, such as [ƛ].) In languages which have a large number of laterals we often find fricatives and affricates patterning with the other obstruents (as in Archi, discussed below).

For plosives, which are really just a shortlived explosive burst, a definition in terms of simultaneous voicing is not meaningful. Instead, a voiced plosive is one which is immediately <u>followed</u> by vibration of the vocal folds. If the onset of vocal fold vibration is delayed by a short period (say, about 50 msecs) then we hear the sound as lacking voice. If we delay even further then we may hear the sound as aspirated. This is acoustically very much like pronouncing the consonant with a following [h] (though some languages distinguish between genuine sequences of consonant + *h* and aspirated consonants). The period between the offset of the plosive and the beginning of vocal fold vibration is known as **Voice Onset Time**, or **VOT**.

Some VOT values are shown schematically in figure 1.2. This shows five different values of VOT for a bilabial stop, ranging from fully voiced, partially voiced, voiceless, slightly aspirated and strongly aspirated. In figure 1.2.1 the vocal folds are kept close together for the whole articulation, so that they are able to vibrate and cause voicing. Hence, voicing, indicated by the wavy line at (c), precedes the closure phase of the [b] and runs through it without a break. In 1.2.2 the vocal folds are allowed to open slightly at the beginning of the articulation and this induces a partial devoicing of the sound at its onset. In the voiceless, unaspirated stop, [p], in 1.2.3, the devoicing lasts for exactly the duration of the closure phase. However, in 1.2.4 and 1.2.5 the opening of the lips and the consequent release of the plosive occurs slightly (1.2.4) or significantly (1.2.5) before the voicing starts up again. There is therefore a period of voicelessness after the plosive, which can, for example, run into the following vowel. This gives the effect of weak or strong aspiration.

Much research has been conducted on VOT values for various types of sound in different languages. It turns out that the precise timing of the VOT depends on a number of factors including the place of articulation of the sound. However, a large number of languages (including English) make use of this phonetic difference to convey a general category of voiced/voiceless plosive. In other languages, there is a distinction between voiced/plain voiceless/aspirated voiceless (e.g. Korean). In a number of languages of India (Hindi, Bengali and so on) we even find a type of aspiration for a voiced

Figure 1.2   A diagrammatic representation of stops (between vowels) differentiated by voice onset time

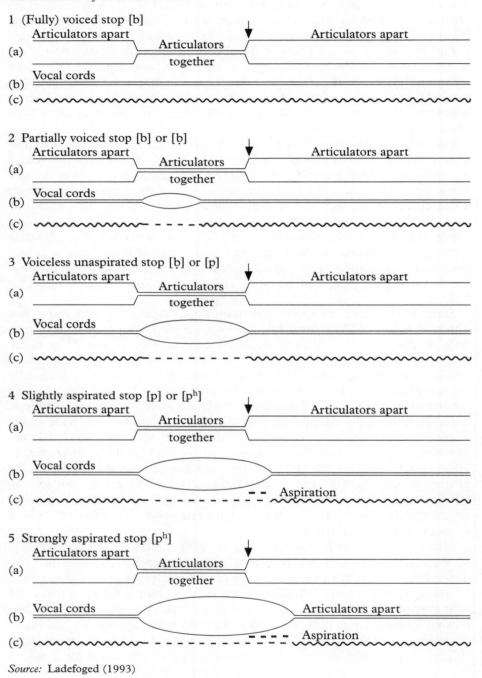

1 (Fully) voiced stop [b]

Articulators apart

(a)

Articulators together

Articulators apart

(b)   Vocal cords

(c)

2 Partially voiced stop [b] or [ḅ]

Articulators apart

(a)

Articulators together

Articulators apart

(b)   Vocal cords

(c)

3 Voiceless unaspirated stop [ḅ] or [p]

Articulators apart

(a)

Articulators together

Articulators apart

(b)   Vocal cords

(c)

4 Slightly aspirated stop [p] or [pʰ]

Articulators apart

(a)

Articulators together

Articulators apart

(b)   Vocal cords

(c)   Aspiration

5 Strongly aspirated stop [pʰ]

Articulators apart

(a)

Articulators together

(b)   Vocal cords   Articulators apart

(c)   Aspiration

Source: Ladefoged (1993)

stop. In simplified terms we may think of this as the superposition of a voiced [ɦ] sound on the consonant.

The final aspect of consonant production which must be mentioned is the airstream mechanism. I noted at the beginning that it is necessary to provide a source of noise in order for spoken language to work and that this is usually provided by expelling air from the lungs through the voice box or larynx. This is referred to as an **egressive** airstream, and since the air comes originally from the lungs it is further called a **pulmonic egressive** airstream. However, this is not the only way to make a noise using the vocal tract. Another way is to breathe *in*, as when uttering a gasp of astonishment. This so-called **ingressive pulmonic** airstream is not a very practical way of making speech sounds, however, and languages don't seem to make systematic use of it (though it is found in certain types of speech disorder).

There is a way of using a ingressive airstream mechanism, however, which is found in a variety of languages across the world. Consider a [b] sound. With an egressive pulmonic airstream mechanism the hold phase is followed by release as the lips are brought suddenly apart and the air escapes from the lungs. Suppose, however, that we suddenly lower the larynx at exactly the same time that we open the lips. What will happen then is that for a very short time, air will rush into the vocal tract, before being pushed out by the air coming from the lungs. This is known as an **ingressive glottalic** airstream mechanism, and it produces a set of sounds known as **implosives**. These are always voiced sounds, since it would be impossible to perform the manoeuvre without voicing the consonant. Implosives are particularly associated with the languages of Africa, though they occur as well in certain Mayan languages of Central America, and some of the languages of the Far East. They are also a characteristic pronunciation of voiced sounds in the speech of the profoundly deaf (perhaps because it is easier for a deaf person to feel the downward movement of the larynx and thus be certain that they have pronounced a sound with some sort of voicing). The implosive correlates of the pulmonic egressive sounds [b d g] are transcribed as [ɓ ɗ ɠ].

The movability of the larynx permits another type of airstream mechanism. Suppose we wish to pronounce a [p] sound, but instead of releasing the sound in the normal way we suddenly raise the larynx, just before opening the lips. This will mean that air will be forced out of the mouth, not from the lungs, but from the larynx itself, which will act as a kind of piston head. The acoustic effect is a kind of 'popping' sound accompanying the plosive. This effect will be shortlived, of course, because the larynx can only move a small distance and in any case the effect will quickly be overtaken by air coming from the lungs. Sounds of this sort are called **glottalized** sounds or **ejectives**. Since the larynx has to be closed for the effect to work, this can only be achieved with voiceless plosives, not voiced ones. Ejectives are found in a great many languages of the world, though in familiar European languages it is only found as a marginal dialectal phenomenon (it is encountered occasionally in certain Northern British English varieties). In

IPA an ejective is transcribed by adding an apostrophe to a consonant symbol [p' t' k'].

In some ways an egressive glottalic airstream mechanism is similar to a type of secondary articulation. This is particularly obvious when we realize that it is not just plosives which can be glottalized. A number of languages have series of glottalized fricatives, affricates, liquids, nasals or even glides. Since there is no hold phase for these sounds, these will not, strictly speaking, be ejectives; rather, they will be fricatives, which have a glottal constriction superimposed upon them. In that respect, we can think of them as truly glottalized sounds (in the same sense that [pʲ] is a palatalized sound). However, it is still convenient to reserve the term 'secondary articulation' for those instances in which a vowel-like colouring is given to a sound. These often develop historically from the effects of neighbouring vowel qualities, while glottalization usually arises in other ways.

To provide illustration of some of these types of secondary articulation and additional airstream mechanism we can turn to Archi, a Daghestan language of the Caucasus, spoken by a few hundred people in Southern Russia. The languages of the Caucasus are famous (or notorious) for their complex consonant systems, and Archi has one of the richest (though not the most complex by any means). The consonant inventory is summarized in table 1.3:

Table 1.3 Archi consonants

Lab	Dent	Lat	Alv	Pal-Alv	Vel	Uvul	Phar	Glott
p̄ b	t̄ d	tl	ts	tʃ	k̄	q		ʔ
pʰ p'	tʰ t'	tl'	ts' t̄s'	tʃ' t̄ʃ'	kʰ k'	q' q̄'		
	tʷ tʷʰ	tlʷ tlʷ'	tsʷ t̄sʷ'	tʃʷ tʃʷ'	kʷ gʷ	qʷ		
					kʷʰ kʷ'	qʷ'		
		ɬ	z	ʒ		ʁ	ħ	h
		ɫ ɫ̄	s s̄	ʃ ʃ̄		χ χ̄		
			zʷ	ʒʷ		ʁʷ		
		ɫʷ ɫ̄ʷ	sʷ s̄ʷ			χʷ χ̄ʷ		
m	n	l	j					
		r						

Source: Based on Kibrik et al. (1977: 224)

The Archi system has a particularly well developed set of obstruents. It includes sounds described as **fortis** by Kibrik et al. (1977). Fortis sounds are produced with greater tension and intensity than plain sounds. A sound pronounced with less intensity and more laxly than a plain sound is described as **lenis**. In Archi, the fortis sounds are generally pronounced longer than corresponding plain sounds. For instance, the verb forms /lap̄us/ 'to throw' or /ʔas̄as/ 'to shake' are pronounced [lap̄p̄us], [ʔas̄s̄as] with doubled [p̄] [s̄] sounds. This doubling is known as **gemination**. We will discuss this phenomenon in a little more detail in chapter 3. Kibrik et al. stress that the geminated fortis consonants are different from sequences of identical lenis consonants that just happen to come together as the result of word formation processes. Thus, the geminated /s/ of [k'os-sas] 'touch a knife' is still lenis and not fortis, and thus should be distinguished from the geminated /s̄/ of [ʔas̄s̄as]. In [k'os-sas] the geminated [s] arises because we have combined two morphemes ('knife' and 'touch') to form a compound. However, in [ʔas̄s̄as] the geminated [s̄] is part of the morpheme 'to shake' itself. This latter type of geminate, which is an inherent part of a morpheme, is often called a **true geminate**. We often distinguish it from the type found by combining two morphemes, as in [k'os-sas], which we call a **fake geminate**. It is not uncommon for languages to bar true geminates but permit fake ones. Indeed, this is the case with English. neutral vs nonneutral

In addition to the fortis/lenis distinction Archi has labialized sounds (e.g. [tʷ]), aspirated sounds ([pʰ]) and glottalized sounds [k']. A labialized sound may additionally be aspirated [tʷʰ] or glottalized [kʷ']. Notice that the affricates, affricate laterals, [tl], alveolars [ts] and palato-alveolars [tʃ] can be glottalized, too, and behave like plosives in this respect. The fricatives, on the other hand, only admit the fortis/lenis contrast and labialization. The Archi system is comparatively unusual in having a large number of lateral sounds. Thus, it has lateral affricates (labialized and/or glottalized), [tl, tl', tlʷ, tlʷ'], voiceless (fortis and/or labialized), [ɬ ɬ̄ ɬʷ ɬ̄ʷ] and voiced plain [ɮ]. Indeed, there are so many laterals that they almost give the impression on a chart of constituting a separate place of articulation. However, we should remember that laterals have different places of articulation themselves, in that they can be retroflex and palatal as well as alveolar or dental. There are even cases reported of velar laterals, though in the great majority of languages laterals are restricted to the coronal range of place of articulation.

1.2.2 Vowels

We now turn to a very brief consideration of the vowel sounds. As with consonants, we can distinguish vowels in terms of the **quality** (the precise combination of sound frequencies which make it up, determined by the position of tongue, lips and other articulators) and **quantity** (how long the sound lasts).

1.2.2.1 Vowel quality The most important aspects of vowel quality are **tongue height**, **frontness/backness** and **lip rounding**. Thus, we will typically distinguish high vowels [i u] from low [a] or mid [e o], front vowels [i e æ] from back [u o a] and rounded [y u ʉ o ø œ ɔ ɒ] from unrounded [i ɯ ɨ ɤ e ɛ ʌ ɑ].

The precise relationship between the way in which vowels get articulated

Figure 1.3(a)   A formant chart showing the frequency of the first formant on the ordinate (the vertical axis) plotted against the distance between the frequencies of the first and second formants on the abscissa (the horizontal axis) for eight American English vowels

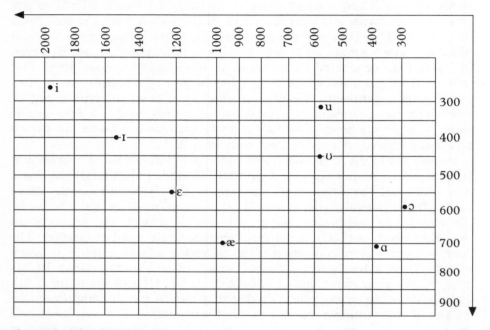

Source: Ladefoged (1993)

and their acoustic properties is rather complex. However, a simple version of the story goes as follows: high vowels are produced by raising the body of the tongue beyond some notional 'mid point' (roughly where the tongue would be for a schwa); low vowels are produced by lowering the tongue body; front vowels involve forward motion of the tongue body, while back vowels involve retraction of the tongue body. Round vowels are produced by rounding the lips, while unrounded vowels lack this gesture.

To understand the acoustic effects of these gestures we need to understand the concept of **formant**. When a voiced sound makes the vocal tract resonate the resulting sound consists of several components. This is because the vibrations from the vocal folds produce sounds at a great variety of frequencies and the vocal tract will amplify some of these depending on its configuration. Therefore, a vowel can be thought of as a mixture of sounds at these different frequencies. The main frequency, of course, is that of the vocal folds, the **fundamental frequency**, F_0. However, the next two frequencies up are very important for the description of vowels. These additional frequencies are called formants, the **first formant**, F_1 and the **second**

Figure 1.3(b)   The frequencies of the first three formants in eight American English vowels

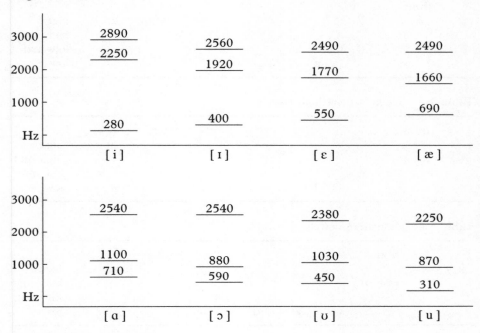

Source: Ladefoged (1993)

formant, F_2. The first formant corresponds very roughly to the resonances created in the upper front part of the mouth, and the second formant corresponds to those created in the lower back part. In figure 1.3 I give the values of the two formants for eight vowels in American English (modified from Ladefoged 1993: 212). The frequencies are measured in Hertz (Hz). The higher the vowel the lower is F_1. For front vowels, the higher the vowel the higher is F_2, though this correlation doesn't work very well with back vowels (partly because of the asymmetric shape of the vocal tract and partly because of the effects of lip rounding on F_2).

To return to the articulatory characterization, the oversimplification in my description is evident in the story for the tongue body. It is misleading to think of there being three heights and two poles of frontness/backness, for it is easy to produce a continuum of front-back or high-low gestures. For instance, we can start with a high front [i] sound and gradually lower the tongue body to a low front [a] sound. In point of fact, the traditional IPA description includes four degrees of vowel height, and three degrees of frontness/backness (front – central – back). This generates the **cardinal vowel** chart, shown in table 1.4. This type of chart is an idealization in the sense that it attempts to describe the most 'extreme' vowel qualities. For instance,

Table 1.4 Cardinal vowels

	front			back			
i						u	high
	e				o		high-mid
		ɛ			ɔ		low-mid
			a	ɑ			low

Table 1.5 Secondary cardinal vowels

	front			back			
y						ɯ	high
	ø				ɤ		high-mid
		œ			ʌ		low-mid
			Œ	ɒ			low

Table 1.6 Hungarian vowels

	front			back			
i iː y yː						u uː	high
	eː ø øː						high-mid
		ɛ			ɔ ɔː		low-mid
			aː	ɑ			low

the symbol [i] represents the highest and frontest vowel sound possible. The vowels which are transcribed using the [i] symbol in various languages may not be quite as high and quite as front as the 'ideal' cardinal. However, this is relatively unimportant. The point is to have some sort of descriptive reference system, and the chart in table 1.4 is adequate to these purposes.

The first thing to notice in this table is that there are two sorts of mid vowel, the **close-mid** or **high mid** [e, o] and the **open-mid** or **low mid** [ɛ ɔ]. The next point is that some of these cardinal vowels are rounded (essentially the nonlow back vowels, [u o ɔ]) while the others are unrounded. We can construct a chart in which these values are reversed, giving us table 1.5, the set of **secondary cardinal vowels**.

The two cardinal charts don't include all the vowels found in the world's languages. A number of English vowels are missing for a start. However, a good many languages make use of some subset of the sixteen cardinals. The vowel system of Hungarian, shown in table 1.6, is a fairly rich system of this sort.

Notice that Hungarian distinguishes long and short vowels; some of the long vowels don't have short equivalents and vice versa. However, in general, vowels come in short/long pairs in Hungarian and in this system /eː/

Table 1.7 ATR and non-ATR vowels

i y					u m	high, ATR
ɪ ʏ				ʊ		high, non-ATR
	e ø		ɣ o			mid, ATR
	ɛ œ	ʌ ɔ		ɜ		mid, non-ATR
		a ɑ				low

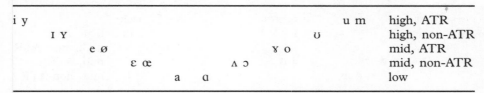

behaves like the long equivalent of /ɛ/ and /aː/ behaves like the long equivalent of /ɒ/. This type of covariation is not uncommon in real vowel systems.

A further articulatory dimension for vowels is added when the root of the tongue is included. In a number of languages vowels differ as to whether they are made with the tongue root in its normal resting position or in a position pushed forward from this, **advanced tongue root** (ATR). This ᴬᵀᴿ distinction is very important in a whole host of languages of Africa as well as elsewhere. Advancing the tongue root in this way tends to have an effect on vowel quality. For one thing the ATR vowels tend to have a more tense articulation. In addition, if we take the vowels [ɛ ɔ] and pronounce them with an advanced tongue root we obtain vowels which acoustically are more or less what we would transcribe as [e o]. For many phonologists this is the correct way of characterizing the so-called half-closed mid vowels. Since this correlates in many languages with differences for other vowels such as the [i ~ ɪ] or [u ~ ʊ] distinction, this permits us to link related sets of vowels in a way that is not possible using the traditional cardinal vowel system. In table 1.7 I have presented a representative sample of ATR and non-ATR vowels, for comparison with the standard cardinal vowel charts.

We next need to mention the problem of **central vowels**. Again, it is possible to produce infinitely many gradations of frontness or backness. However, for most purposes the simple front/back dimension is sufficient in the description of a given language. This is because a vowel pronounced with a central articulation will generally behave either as though it were really a back vowel or really a front vowel. If we wish to compare different languages or dialects it often turns out to be useful to distinguish central vowels from front or back. This, however, is a rather controversial area, and phonologists are not yet decided on how best to approach the question of central vowels. The two central vowels most commonly encountered are the high central unrounded [ɨ] and the mid central unrounded schwa [ə]. In addition, there is the high central rounded [ʉ] and the rounded schwa [θ], together with a low central unrounded vowel, found, for instance, in Portuguese, [ɐ].

This characterization of the vowels permits us to describe the vowel system of English, with one exception. We have not yet introduced the sound represented by the IPA 'ash' symbol [æ], found in 'strong' (conservative) British RP and most American dialects. This sound is a little higher and

Table 1.8 Commonly identified vowel sounds (from IPA)

front		central		back		
i y		ɨ ʉ			u ɯ	high, ATR
	ɪ ʏ			ʊ		high, non-ATR
	e ø	ɘ ɵ		ɤ o		mid, ATR
	ɛ œ		ʌ ɔ			mid, non-ATR
	æ ɐ					
	a	ɑ ɒ				low

fronter than [a] but a little lower than [ɛ]. With these sounds we have the main set of vowel sounds distinguished in the most recent version of the IPA chart, shown in table 1.8.

Any of the vowel types so far mentioned can be given various types of 'secondary' articulation. A number of languages have **nasalized vowels**, in which the nasal passage is open during the production of the vowel leading to resonance of the nasal cavities, just as when a nasal consonant is produced. French, Portuguese and Polish make much use of such vowels, though they can be heard in a great many languages, including English. In IPA transcription nasalization is shown by placing a tilde ~ above the vowel, as in the four nasalized vowels of standard (Parisian) French: [ɑ̃ ɛ̃ ɔ̃ œ̃]. Likewise, we find **pharyngealized** and **glottalized** vowels, in which the pronunciation is accompanied by a retraction of the tongue root (roughly as with pharyngealization of consonants) or a creaky type of phonation. Some languages have voiceless vowels, which, in effect, are whispered.

1.2.2.2 Vowel quantity We next turn to vowel quantity. Many languages distinguish short vowels and long vowels. This is the vocalic equivalent of consonant gemination which we have just seen with Archi. In general, a long vowel lasts roughly twice as long as a short vowel, though the precise difference depends on the language, the quality of the vowel, and a number of other factors.

A related quantity distinction is that between **monophthongs** and **diphthongs**. The definition of 'diphthong' is not entirely straightforward. It is basically two vowels pronounced in the same time as a single vowel. Thus, it effectively consists of two half vowels, the first of which undergoes a rapid transition into the other. One of the members of the vowel sequence making up a diphthong will always dominate over the other. If the dominant member is the first of the sequence, as in English [aɪ], then we speak of a **falling** diphthong. English only has falling diphthongs. However, in many languages we find diphthongs of the form [ɪa] where the dominant member is the second. Such diphthongs are called **rising**. A simple vowel is called a monophthong, whether long or short.

A very small number of languages (e.g. Icelandic) distinguish long and

Table 1.9   English vowels: monophthongs

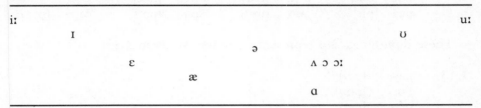

Figure 1.4   English vowels: diphthongs

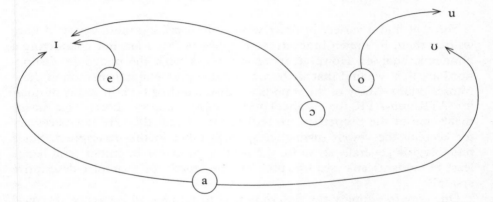

short diphthongs. Usually, however, a diphthong behaves very much like a long monophthong. One of the difficulties in describing diphthongs is in deciding when we have a diphthong (such as English RP [aɪ], [aʊ] on standard British descriptions) and when we have a vowel + glide sequence (for falling diphthongs), as with the usual American description of these vowels as [aj], [aw], or a glide + vowel sequence for rising diphthongs, [ja], [wa]. A very short high vowel can be more or less indistinguishable from a glide in many languages, so it is difficult to make a principled choice. I shall discuss this problem in more detail in chapter 3.

1.2.2.3   The English vowel system(s)   To round off this discussion of vowels we must consider the ways of transcribing the English vowels. The system I shall describe may or may not be the same as that of your own speech. As mentioned in the preface I have opted to give a system which is something of a compromise between General American and British RP. A detailed comparison of British and American vowels is given in Kreidler (1989) together with a very useful comparison of transcriptional system used by various anglicists.

In table 1.9 and figure 1.4 I give the English monophthongs and diphthongs other than those which are only found before a written 'r'. These vowels are represented by the following words:

1.12   pit [pɪt]   pet   [pɛt]   pat [pæt]
        pot [pɒt]   putt [pʌt]   put [pʊt]
        pea [piː]   poo   [puː]   paw [pɔː]   Papa [pəpɑː]

These diphthongs are represented by the words in 1.13:

1.13   pay   [peɪ]
        Po   [pou]
        pie   [paɪ]
        point [pɔɪnt]
        pow   [paʊ]

You will find a variety of other ways of transcribing these vowels. I have written them in square brackets, to emphasize that I am not conducting a phonemic analysis. However, if we are to ask what the phonemic distinctions are then we find that we have too much phonetic information in these transcriptions. Many of the sounds are distinguished both in terms of quality (ATR/non-ATR, for instance) and quantity (long vs. short). This means that some of the properties are redundant, in that they are not necessary for keeping the vowels distinct from each other in the description. Since phonologists generally strive for the neatest, most parsimonious (and hence least redundant) analysis, this prompts the search for a simpler descriptive system.

One way to simplify the description is to remove all reference to vowel length. Thus, we can consider length to be an 'accidental' concomitant property of vowels of a certain quality. Essentially, such analyses take the 'tenseness' or ATR quality of [iː uː] and consider these as having primacy over length. In addition, they regard the diphthongs in *pay, Po*, to be modified types of long vowel (which is how they are pronounced in some accents, e.g. in certain parts of the North of England). The remaining diphthongs are then represented as a sequence of short vowels followed by a glide. Thus, the fairly representative US system of transcription adopted in Fromkin and Rodman's (1993) introductory textbook is as shown in table 1.10.

Table 1.10 A typical US transcription system

i							u
	ɪ					ʊ	
		e		ə		o	
			ɛ		ʌ ɔ		
			æ				
				a			

Monophthongs
aj   aw (or æw)   ɔj
True diphthongs

Table 1.11 English vowels analysed in terms of quantity (length)

iː i						u uː
	e			ə		
					ʌ ɔ ɔː	
			a aː			

This gives us the following transcriptions for the words of 1.12, and 1.13:

1.14   pit   /pɪt/   pet   /pɛt/   pat   /pæt/
        pot   /pat/   putt   /pʌt/   put   /pʊt/
        pea   /pi/   poo   /pu/   paw   /pɔ/   Papa   /pəpa/

1.15   pay   /pe/
        Po   /po/

1.16   pie   /paj/
        point   /pɔjnt/
        pow   /paw/

Since we have removed the redundancy in the representations in order to arrive at a phonemic analysis, we can transcribe these words using slashes.

Although it is common to consider length as secondary and quality as primary, it is also possible to regard the length distinction as primary and the quality distinction as secondary (which in general reflects historical development somewhat better). In that case, we can ignore the ATR and other quality differences, provided the vowels pair off into longs and shorts. This may pose a bit of a problem, since in many accents we do not find such a neat pairing off. However, the trick works for enough cases for this analysis to have been adopted at various times. For example, we might adopt the transcription system of table 1.11.

1.17   pit   /pit/   pet   /pe/   pat   /pat/
        pot   /pɔt/   putt   /pʌt/   put   /put/
        pea   /piː/   poo   /puː/   paw   /pɔː/   Papa   /pəpaː/

The diphthongs can then be represented as in 1.18:

1.18   pay   /pei/
        Po   /pou/
        pie   /pai/
        point   /pɔint/
        pow   /pau/

The question of whether to analyse English vowels principally in terms of length or quality is a vexed one and there is no agreed approach. Indeed,

Table 1.12 British English r-coloured vowels

ɪə			ʊə
	əː		
ɛː		ɔː	
		ɑː	

the phonologist may sometimes adopt one analysis and another time the other depending on the precise question under investigation. For example, Morris Halle, the most distinguished figure in generative phonology, adopted an analysis in terms of tenseness in the most important generative phonological study (Chomsky and Halle 1968), but in an extremely influential paper some fifteen years later he adopted a length analysis (Halle and Mohanan 1985).

When we have a vowel followed by 'r' in the spelling, we tend to get two different types of vowel depending on the dialect. In one set of dialects, the 'r' is preserved in speech. Such dialects or accents are called **rhotic** (from the Greek word *rho*, which is the name of the letter corresponding to 'r' in the Greek alphabet). Such accents are found throughout the US and in many parts of Britain, especially Ireland and Scotland. However, RP, as well as most dialects of Australasia, drops any 'r' which is not at the beginning of a syllable (i.e. which is in the coda – see section 1.3.2 below). Such accents are called **non-rhotic**. These are dialects in which the historically present 'r' sound has been lost. However, before disappearing, it had time to affect the pronunciation of the preceding vowel. Such vowels are often called **r-coloured**. In table 1.12 I give my own pronunciation (modified British RP) for the r-coloured vowels.

1.19	pier	[pɪə]
	pear	[pɛː]
	purr	[pəː]
	poor	[pʊə]

In my speech the vowel of *pore* is exactly the same as the vowel of *paw*, [pɔː] and the vowel of *Parr* is identical to that of *pa*: [pɑː].

In many US dialects, these r-coloured vowels would be pronounced with the tongue in the position of a retroflex consonant, and would often be transcribed as a vowel followed by /r/. Adopting the system of table 1.10 we obtain 1.20:

1.20	pier	/pir/
	pear	/pɛr/
	purr	/pər/
	poor	/pur/

In 'strong' RP there are also such things as triphthongs, a development of
r-coloured diphthongs. Thus, in that dialect the words *pyre*, *power* would be
pronounced [paɪə], [paʊə], but as one syllable. This pronunciation is on the
wane. My own pronunciation of such words is disyllabic (i.e. with two
syllables), sometimes with a glide between the two syllables, to give: [paɪjə],
[paʊwə].

For much of this book we will not be concerned with the correct
phonemicization for the surface vowel inventory of English. For this reason, I shall give the redundant transcription, indicating both length and
quality differences. When we come to look at syllable structure we will find
it convenient to bear the length differences in mind rather than the quality
differences.

To summarize, I give the transcriptions of the suite of words used so far,
which I shall be adopting in the book:

1.21   a. pit   [pɪt]   pet   [pɛt]   pat   [pæt]
            pot   [pɔt]   putt   [pʌt]   put   [pʊt]
        b. pea   [piː]   poo   [puː]
            paw   [pɔː]   Papa   [pəpɑː]
        c. pay   [peɪ]
            Po   [poʊ]
            pie   [paɪ]
            point [pɔɪnt]
            pow   [paʊ]
            pier   [pɪə]
            pear   [pɛː]
            purr   [pəː]
            poor   [pʊə]

The vowels of 1.21a are short. In English, the only short vowels that can
occur at the end of a word are [ə ɪ]. Otherwise, word-finally the short vowels
must be closed by a consonant. The vowels of 1.21b are long vowels. The
examples of 1.21c are the diphthongs. They are all falling diphthongs. Since
[ɪə], [ʊə] fall to a central vowel, the schwa, they are often called **centring
diphthongs**.

1.3   Suprasegmentals

1.3.1   Prosody

So far we have spoken about individual speech sounds, or segments. However,
there are a number of important aspects to the phonological organization of

a language which go beyond simply the list of phonemes and their allophonic variants. Earlier in this chapter I followed a well-established tradition in referring to these as 'suprasegmentals'. They include stress, length, and tone and intonation. Stress and rhythm together with intonation are often called **prosody** (though this term and its derivatives tends to be used in a variety of other technical senses as well).

Many languages have a stress system in which one or more syllables in a word are pronounced more forcefully than others. The phonetic realizations of 'stress' vary from language to language (see chapter 7). In some languages the position of stress is entirely predictable, in that it always falls on a particular syllable in the word (e.g. the first, or the penultimate or whatever). In such cases, stress cannot be used contrastively, to distinguish one word from another, though it does have a useful function with regard to speech perception, since it can help the listener determine where word boundaries come. In other languages (including, to some extent, English) stress is contrastive. In a good many languages stress interacts in complex ways with the segmental phonology, whether it is contrastive or not, and thus it can be a very important factor in the phonological system as a whole.

The patterns of alternation between stressed and unstressed syllables is called **rhythm**. This is an important factor in many languages for organizaing the pronunciation of stretches longer than a single word, i.e. phrases. Rhythmic factors often have an important influence on the way individual segments are pronounced, and in many instances the acquisition of a good native-like accent in a foreign language depends more on achieving the right rhythmic structures than anything else.

A distinction which needs to be clarified at the outset is that between stress and rhythm, on the one hand, and intonation on the other. To be sure, the two types of phenomena are closely connected. However, intonation is the change in the pitch of the voice throughout an utterance. Every utterance is spoken with what is effectively a kind of tune. We can illustrate some of the tunes (or **intonation contours**) of English by considering a single, monosyllabic utterance, spoken in different ways depending on the context. This is shown in 1.22:

1.22   a.   Me   b.   Me?   c.   Me?   d.   Me!

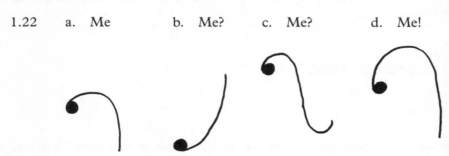

Utterance 1.22a would be used, for instance, as a neutral answer to a question such as 'Who did Tom give the letter to?' The voice starts at a mid pitch and falls to a low pitch, but not too abruptly. Utterance 1.22b starts low and rises. Utterance 1.22c, however, starts high, then falls abruptly to a low pitch and (only) then rises (slightly) at the end. Both 1.22b and c would convey a questioning tone (hence the '?'), as in response to a statement like 'We thought Tom might have given the letter to you.' Utterance 1.22d is the converse of 1.22c intonationally, in that it starts low, rises abruptly to a high pitch and then tails off, falling to a mid pitch. This tends to convey emphasis and excitement, as, say, in response to a question such as 'Who won the 100 meter sprint?'

In a good many languages different tunes are used to differentiate individual words. Such languages are called **tone languages**. Probably a good deal more than half the world's languages use tone in this way, though in European languages it is limited to a very peripheral phenomenon in Norwegian and Swedish, and remnants of the old Indo-European tone system which remain in Serbo-Croat, Slovene, Latvian and Lithuanian. It is somewhat difficult to get to grips with the phonological systems represented by tone without a good deal of practical experience of a tone language. It is also rather difficult to gain a proper appreciation of intonation contours without a good deal of practical training in listening to and transcribing intonation contours. For this reason, a consideration of intonation and of tones is beyond the scope of this text. However, both topics are very important to the development of recent phonological theory and are an important part of any advanced study of phonology. Suggested reading in intonation and tone is given at the end of this chapter.

An aspect of the phonologies of many languages which sometimes turns out to be closely related to stress concerns the length of segments, especially vowels. In many languages with stress a stressed vowel is phonetically longer than a corresponding unstressed vowel. This is true, for instance, of Russian. However, this is not always the case. Greek has a stress system similar in many respects to that of Russian, yet the length of a vowel under stress is more or less the same as when it is unstressed. In Russian (and Greek) vowel length is never contrastive. Thus, we could say that a lengthened vowel under stress in Russian is simply an allophonic variant of the (lengthless) vowel phoneme. However, as we know from section 1.2.2, in other languages vowel length is one of the factors which distinguishes one word from another. Czech, another Slav language, has contrastive vowel length, though its stress system is noncontrastive (the stress always falls on the first syllable of the word). Indeed, historically, Russian stress and Czech vowel length are different developments of one and the same tonal system, that of Proto-Slavic, their common ancestor. Thus, there are words in Czech distinguished solely by vowel length, such as *kruːtje* 'turkey', *krutje* 'cruelly'. In like fashion, we have seen that some languages distinguish long (doubled, geminated) consonants from short ones. Estonian even has a three-way length contrast, distinguishing short, long and overlong consonants.

1.3.2 Representing the syllable

Last, but by no means least, it is important to mention the role that syllables play in a phonological description. Although there is no agreed phonetic characterization of the notion 'syllable', it is clear that the structure of syllables is often of considerable importance for the phonological organization of the language. Moreover, syllablic organization seems to play an important role in speech perception and production. Children appear to be aware of syllable structure from a very early age (though they show much less articulated or direct awareness of the existence of segment-sized units, at least until they learn to read an alphabetic writing system). The whole of chapter 3 is devoted to syllable structure, so I will just give a foretaste here of the basic phenomena.

English, like a good many languages, has a system of poetry based on the final part of the syllable. Even very young children recognize that words like *bat, cat, rat, sat*, rhyme with each other. If we ask ourselves what it is that makes a pair of words rhyme, we quickly realize that it is typically the final part of the final syllable. More specifically, it is the vowel plus its following consonants. Thus, we can split up a word like *cat* into two parts or constituents, /k/ + /æt/. The second we will call the **rhyme** and the first the **onset**. The onset is a string of one or more consonants.

All syllables have to have some sound which functions as the **peak** or **nucleus**. This is usually a vowel, but it can be a syllabic consonant as in *bottle* [bɔtl̩] or *button* [bʌtn̩]. The nucleus is thus the only obligatory part of the rhyme. For this reason, it is often regarded as the **head** of the rhyme (borrowing a notion from syntax), and by extension, we often refer to the nucleus as the head of the whole syllable. Where a syllable ends in one or more consonants, we can split up the rhyme into two constituents, the nucleus and a **coda**, which is a sequence of one or more consonants. In English, it is possible to have syllables which lack an onset, e.g. *eye, I, aye* [aɪ], *in, own, acts*. Moreover, it is possible to have syllables which have no final consonants, as in the words *pay, spy, do*, and in non-rhotic accents, *car, four, sure* and so on. Syllables which lack a coda are called **open syllables**. Those that have a coda are called **closed syllables**.

Using a fairly complex syllable such as the word *strengths*, we can represent this picture of syllable structure by means of a tree diagram (the convential way in which linguists represent constituent structure), as in 1.23:

1.23

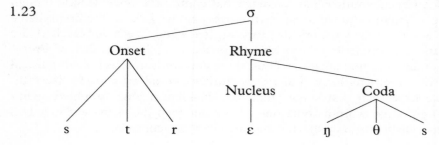

Notice that we use the Greek letter σ (sigma) to represent 'syllable'. We'll see later that 1.23 may be an oversimplified representation of the syllable structure, but for the moment we'll assume that this is a typical type of syllable.

The fact that consonants and vowels are grouped into a higher order structure, the syllable, is very important for the development of phonological theory, and we will devote the whole of chapter 3 to an investigation of the nature of syllables and the role in the phonological system. In chapter 5 we will see ways in which phonological processes make reference to syllable structure.

1.4 Phonology and Universal Grammar

Having seen some of the factual questions that are raised in the study of phonological systems, we will close by asking why phonologists study these things at all. There are essentially two reasons why a linguist might be interested in phonological systems. The first is relatively practical: the linguist may wish to be able to provide as complete and detailed a description as possible of one particular language or dialect of a language such as English. This is of interest in itself, of course, but will often have considerable importance for other practical concerns. For instance, such knowledge is essential to the speech and language pathologist, who has to treat children who are not acquiring the sound system of their language properly, or people who, through illness or injury, have lost some of their capacity to speak. Teachers need to know much about the sound structure of English to teach it to foreign learners. Likewise, speech technologists building communication systems or talking computer systems need to understand a great deal about the structure of the language they are working on. Even singers nowadays need to have a practical command of the way that English and other languages were spoken in the Middle Ages and Renaissance in order to sing songs from those periods with an accurate pronunciation.

Anyone wishing to develop such a description of a single language needs to have some sort of descriptive framework, simply in order to be able to lay out the relevant facts. Such a framework is provided by theoretical linguists, who consider 'language' as a whole and try to develop a theory of how languages are structured and why they are structured the way they are and not some completely different way. The key concept in theoretical linguistics is that of explanation. The theoretician wants to know not just what happens, but also how it happens, and, as far as possible, why it happens. In some cases explanation can be rather trivial. For instance, no language will make use of sounds that are impossible for a normal human vocal tract to produce, or which are beyond the range of human hearing. In most cases, however, the explanation is much more elusive and hence

Figure A1.1 The International Phonetic Alphabet

THE INTERNATIONAL PHONETIC ALPHABET (revised to 1993)

CONSONANTS (PULMONIC)

	Bilabial	Labiodental	Dental	Alveolar	Postalveolar	Retroflex	Palatal	Velar	Uvular	Pharyngeal	Glottal
Plosive	p b			t d		ʈ ɖ	c ɟ	k g	q ɢ		ʔ
Nasal	m	ɱ		n		ɳ	ɲ	ŋ	ɴ		
Trill	ʙ			r					ʀ		
Tap or Flap				ɾ		ɽ					
Fricative	ɸ β	f v	θ ð	s z	ʃ ʒ	ʂ ʐ	ç ʝ	x ɣ	χ ʁ	ħ ʕ	h ɦ
Lateral fricative				ɬ ɮ							
Approximant		ʋ		ɹ		ɻ	j	ɰ			
Lateral approximant				l		ɭ	ʎ	ʟ			

Where symbols appear in pairs, the one to the right represents a voiced consonant. Shaded areas denote articulations judged impossible.

CONSONANTS (NON-PULMONIC)

Clicks		Voiced implosives		Ejectives	
ʘ	Bilabial	ɓ	Bilabial	ʼ	as in:
ǀ	Dental	ɗ	Dental/alveolar	pʼ	Bilabial
ǃ	(Post)alveolar	ʄ	Palatal	tʼ	Dental/alveolar
ǂ	Palatoalveolar	ɠ	Velar	kʼ	Velar
ǁ	Alveolar lateral	ʛ	Uvular	sʼ	Alveolar fricative

SUPRASEGMENTALS

ˈ	Primary stress	ˌfoʊnəˈtɪʃən
ˌ	Secondary stress	
ː	Long	eː
ˑ	Half-long	eˑ
˘	Extra-short	ĕ
.	Syllable break	ɹi.ækt
|	Minor (foot) group	
‖	Major (intonation) group	
‿	Linking (absence of a break)	

TONES & WORD ACCENTS

LEVEL		CONTOUR	
e̋ or ˥	Extra high	ě or ˩˥	Rising
é ˦	High	ê ˥˩	Falling
ē ˧	Mid	e᷄ ˦˥	High rising
è ˨	Low	e᷅ ˩˨	Low rising
ȅ ˩	Extra low	e᷈ ˧˦˧	Rising-falling etc.
↓	Downstep	↗	Global rise
↑	Upstep	↘	Global fall

VOWELS

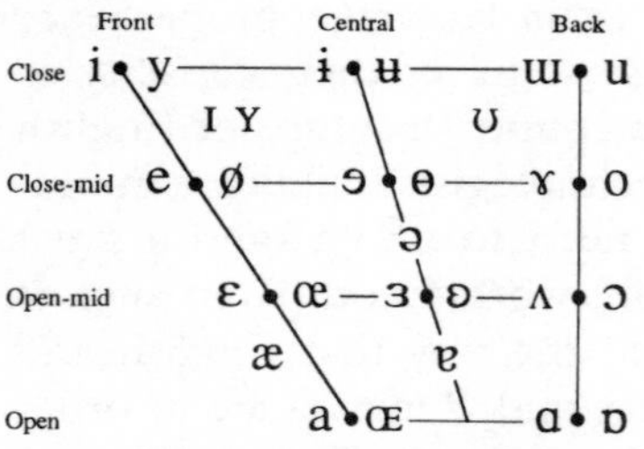

Front
Central
Back
Close
Close-mid
Open-mid
Open
i y
ɨ ʉ
ɯ u
ɪ ʏ
ʊ
e ø
ɘ ɵ
ɤ o
ə
ɛ œ
ɜ ɞ
ʌ ɔ
æ
ɐ
a ɶ
ɑ ɒ

Where symbols appear in pairs, the one to the right represents a rounded vowel.

DIACRITICS Diacritics may be placed above a symbol with a descender, e.g. ŋ̊

̥ Voiceless	n̥ d̥	̤ Breathy voiced	b̤ a̤	̪ Dental	t̪ d̪
̬ Voiced	s̬ t̬	̰ Creaky voiced	b̰ a̰	̺ Apical	t̺ d̺
ʰ Aspirated	tʰ dʰ	̼ Linguolabial	t̼ d̼	̻ Laminal	t̻ d̻
̹ More rounded	ɔ̹	ʷ Labialized	tʷ dʷ	̃ Nasalized	ẽ
̜ Less rounded	ɔ̜	ʲ Palatalized	tʲ dʲ	ⁿ Nasal release	dⁿ
̟ Advanced	u̟	ˠ Velarized	tˠ dˠ	ˡ Lateral release	dˡ
̠ Retracted	i̠	ˤ Pharyngealized	tˤ dˤ	̚ No audible release	d̚
̈ Centralized	ë	~ Velarized or pharyngealized	ɫ		
̽ Mid-centralized	e̽	̝ Raised	e̝ (ɹ̝ = voiced alveolar fricative)		
̩ Syllabic	ɹ̩	̞ Lowered	e̞ (β̞ = voiced bilabial approximant)		
̯ Non-syllabic	e̯	̘ Advanced Tongue Root	e̘		
˞ Rhoticity	ə˞	̙ Retracted Tongue Root	e̙		

OTHER SYMBOLS

ʍ	Voiceless labial-velar fricative	ɕ ʑ	Alveolo-palatal fricatives
w	Voiced labial-velar approximant	ɺ	Alveolar lateral flap
ɥ	Voiced labial-palatal approximant	ɧ	Simultaneous ʃ and x
ʜ	Voiceless epiglottal fricative		
ʢ	Voiced epiglottal fricative		
ʡ	Epiglottal plosive		

Affricates and double articulations can be represented by two symbols joined by a tie bar if necessary. k͡p t͡s

Source: International Phonetic Association

Figure A1.2   Schematic diagram of the vocal tract

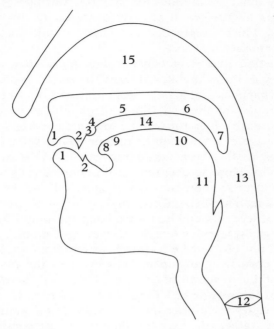

1	Lips	9	Tongue blade
2	Teeth	10	Tongue body (dorsum)
3	Gum ridge (alveolar ridge)	11	Tongue root
4	Palato-alveolar region (alveopalatal region)	12	Larynx (voice box)
5	Hard palate	13	Pharynx
6	Soft palate (velum)	14	Oral cavity
7	Uvula	15	Nasal cavity
8	Tongue tip		

interesting. For example, why are syllable onsets in English of the form *bn-*, or *lp-* impossible, despite the existence of such clusters in other languages? As we will see in chapter 3 this is a consequence of a general principle governing sequences of sounds which seems to hold for all languages, in one form or another.

One of the consequences of the principle explaining the absence of *bn-* or *lp-* onsets in English is that languages which do permit such onsets will also permit onsets of the more familiar type, say, *br-* or *pl-*. Statements of this sort, of the form 'If a language has X it will also have Y (though not necessarily vice versa)' are intended to be statements true of all human languages. Hence, they are called **universals**. The type of universal just cited, of the form 'if A, then B', is known as an **implicational universal**. An important goal of linguistics is to establish the universals of human language, that is, to characterize what constitutes a human language (as opposed to any other communication system), abstracting away from individual languages themselves. It is easy to dream up theoretically possible sound systems, which in practice are never found, because they would violate one or another universal.

Another question that is of considerable importance to contemporary linguistic theory is: how do children learn the sound system of their native language? As it happens, not a great deal of research effort has been devoted to the actual course of the acquisition of phonology by children, though there is quite a sizeable literature on the way that children learn to articulate words from the age of a few months to four or five years of age. However, in phonology, as in other branches of linguistics, there is an intriguing problem of learnability. How do children learn phonological systems so rapidly? It is very difficult to see how they could figure out for themselves the general principles which are being discovered by linguists. Generative linguists, on the whole, believe that children learn language so quickly and with such apparent ease (whilst learning lots of other things simultaneously, of course) that they could not possibly be learning entirely from scratch. Rather, children must be born with an innate knowledge of the more general principles, that is, of the universals of language. This innate knowledge is referred to as **Universal Grammar** or **UG** for short. The term is a little misleading in that the principles themselves do not constitute the grammar of any particular language; rather, they set the limits on what constitutes a possible human language. As we proceed through the book we will encounter a good many phonological principles of UG.

FURTHER READING

Introductions to the phonetic bases of phonology can be found in Abercrombie (1967), Catford (1988), Clark and Yallop (1990), Ladefoged (1993). Lieberman and Blumstein (1987) and Borden and Harris (1984) are good introductions to the acoustic and physiological aspects of the subject.

Kreidler (1989) is a useful source on different transcription systems. A standard source for US pronunciation is Kenyon and Knott (1953). Jones (1967) and Gimson (1993) provide standard accounts of (rather conservative) British RP. However, in many ways a definitive source is Wells (1990), who provides both British and US pronunciations for about 75 000 words.

For information about intonation and tone (which I do not address in this book) you can consult the following:

Intonation

Bolinger (ed.) (1972), Bolinger (1986), Cruttenden (1986), Couper-Kuhlen (1986), Crystal (1969), Gibbon (1976), Halliday (1980), Kreidler (1989), Ladd (1980, 1992), Pierrehumbert (1988).

Tone

Hyman (1975), Goldsmith (1990), Katamba (1989), Odden (1994), Pike (1948), Roca (1994), Yip (1994).

EXERCISES

1.1 Give the IPA symbol for each of the following:

- voiced uvular nasal stop;
- alveolar implosive stop;
- voiced retroflex lateral approximant;
- voiceless palatal affricate;
- voiced labiodental nasal stop.

1.2 Using the IPA chart give a description of the following sounds:

ɣ ʬ ɸ ʐ χ ɳ ç tɕ ɦ

1.3 *Some* (though not all) of the following words of English (British RP accent) have been incorrectly transcribed. Make appropriate corrections.

acknowledges	[æɡknɔlɛʤəz]
appearance	[əpɡaɹəns]
athletics	[æthlɛtɪx]
competition	[kɔmpətition]
condescending	[kɔndɪsɛndɪŋ]
irreparable	[ɪɹɛpɹəbl]
lioness	[laɪənɛss]
potato	[pəteɪtoe]
recruitment	[ɹɪkɹuːtmənt]
Romans	[Rouməns]

1.4 Even phonemes

The sounds [ç h s] are in complementary distribution in native words in the Olsk dialect of Even, a Tungusic language spoken in Yakutia, Siberia (Novikova 1960: 71). What governs this distribution? [[i̯e] [i̯æ] are rising diphthongs consisting of [i] + [e]/[æ]]

nısa	'bead'	çi̯ævʊs	'rotted'
huːn	'blows'	bʊlʊs	'sad'

hɛr	'bottom'	hɔːn	'his skill'
hor	'cave'	hɛssə	'sole'
hɑt	'foundation'	çilʲ	'soup'
hoːksi	'hot'	hɔvʲɛːt	'Soviet'
çɪrqɑn	'knife'	busqʲɪ	'spectacles'
hɑːn	'knows'	ɔsɪqɑm	'star'
çiep	'pocket'	hulɑ	'vein'
hʊl	'poplar'	us	'weapon'

h → # __ V

ç → # __ high front vowels

S - elsewhere.

chapter 2

Phonological Processes

2.0 Introduction

In this chapter we will extend the notion of phonological alternation introduced in chapter 1, and see how phonologists have couched alternations in
terms of a process applying to one type of representation to derive another
representation. This notion of derivation is very important in contemporary
linguistics, and in phonology in particular, and we will dwell in some detail
on a specific instance to see how the idea can be used to account for the
patterning of data. In the following section we will take up these ideas and
generalize from them by constructing the outlines of a theory of the way
that phonological alternations come about. This type of theory, while very
simple in overall structure, has been extremely influential in the development of phonology since the 1960s.

The third section briefly introduces an important distinction between
relatively natural, 'automatic' phonological processes and those which have
become 'fossilized' over time, which in many cases have become phonetically unnatural, and which frequently have exceptions. The final section will
then provide an overview of some of the types of phonological alternation
or process commonly found in the world's languages. Most of the examples

in that section will be from languages other than English, though for most of these processes similar types of phenomena can be found (sometimes in a rather hidden guise) in one or more dialects of English too.

2.1 An Example: Fricative Devoicing

We will start with a simple example from the phonology of English. In the following sets of transcriptions (borrowed from Gimson 1980: 293, Hawkins 1992: 188, or specially constructed) the first represents a reasonably careful, particularly distinct pronunciation, while the second represents a more natural, less stilted articulation:

2.1				
	a.	five past	[faɪvpɑːst]	[faɪfpɑːst]
	b.	love to go	[lʌvtəgou]	[lʌftəgou]
	c.	as well as can be (expected)	[əzweləzkənbɪ]	[əzweləskənbɪ]
	d.	has to go	[hæztəgou]	[hæstəgou]
	e.	loathe to go	[louðtəgou]	[louθtəgou]
	f.	breathe slowly	[briːðsloulɪ]	[briːθsloulɪ]

What these examples show is that certain sounds change into other sounds under certain conditions. We are witnessing the operation of a phonological rule or process, which transforms one representation (that of 'slow' or 'careful' speech) into another.[1]

   If we restrict our attention to the behaviour of segments, we can say that any phonological process has three aspects to it:

1   a set of sounds which undergo the process;
2   a set of sounds produced by the process;
3   a set of situations in which the process applies.

We can represent the idea of a phonological process taking place (in other words, the application of a phonological rule) by means of an arrow. Thus, the change represented in 2.1a can be represented by 2.2:

2.2   /v/   →   [f]

This rule tells us that a **target** or **affected segment** undergoes a process or **structural change**. In this case it is a process of devoicing. Without this process the /v/ phoneme would have been realized as its principal allophone, namely, [v]. However, as a result of the devoicing process it is realized as the sound [f], which is, of course, the principal exponent of the phoneme /f/. This means that we can no longer distinguish between a /v/ phoneme and a genuine /f/ phoneme in this position. When this happens we say that the contrast between the two phonemes has been **neutralized**, and the process is a **neutralization** process.

However, 2.2 doesn't tell us that the change only takes place in certain **environments**, or **contexts**. In the case of 2.1a the /v/ has been devoiced under the influence of the voiceless obstruent /p/. In fact, the /v/ has acquired the same value for voicing as this subsequent sound, so that in this respect the [f] sound is more similar to the [p] of 'past' than a [v] sound would have been. We therefore say that a process of **assimilation** has taken place. Since it is a following sound which is influencing a preceding sound we can be more specific and call this **regressive assimilation**. The converse process, in which sound A influences sound B in the sequence AB, is called **progressive assimilation**.

In point of fact, analyzing this as assimilation is something of a leap, since we haven't examined enough evidence to be sure that this is the cause of the change. In principle, it could be due to anything. The reason we would assume an assimilation rule is that there are many other similar examples occurring in similar circumstances. These are represented in the other examples of 2.1. The data that we've been presented with suggest, in other words, a *hypothesis* about the relationships we've observed. Doing phonology is the process of setting up such hypotheses and then testing them against the data. Very often we need to revise or completely abandon our first hypotheses as a result of the testing process. We can never in fact prove that we have the best analysis – we may have overlooked some important fact, or there may be a simpler way of accounting for the data. This is true of all hypothesis testing.

The first thing we need to do is to isolate the set of sounds which are the targets for this process. From the data in 2.1 they are /v ð z/. These are transformed into /f θ s/, i.e. into corresponding voiceless sounds. Our hypothesis is that this change is triggered by a following voiceless consonant. The following consonants in each case are respectively *p t k t t s*, all of which are voiceless. We can say that the process is **conditioned** or **triggered** by these sounds. We can notate this as in 2.3:

2.3   voiced fricative   →   voiceless /____ voiceless

This is to be interpreted as follows: a voiced fricative is transformed into the corresponding voiceless sound when it appears in the environment specified by the slash. The bar after the slash (often called the **focus bar**) marks the position of the segment undergoing the process. In this case, the rule says that it happens immediately before a voiceless sound. Rule 2.3 is thus equivalent to 2.4, exemplified by 2.5:

2.4	voiced	+	voiceless	→	voiceless	+	voiceless
	fricative		sound		fricative		sound

2.5	v	+	p	→	f	+	p

The notation in 2.4 factors out the environment in which the change occurs.

A complete characterization of the process demands that we know precisely which sounds undergo the process, precisely what sounds they are transformed into, and precisely what sounds condition the process. This means we need to know whether these three sets are exhaustive. To investigate this we first need to try out as many other sounds as we can in the positions of /v ð z/ in the examples of 2.1 to see if they undergo a similar voicing assimilation process. It is fairly clear that vowels fail to devoice. Thus *three past* would not be pronounced [θri̥ːpɑːst] (where the circle under the vowel indicates voicelessness). Nor do the sonorants such as /l/ or the nasals devoice, as we can see from 2.6 (The asterisk * is used in its usual sense in contemporary linguistics to indicate an unacceptable or ungrammatical form):

2.6	a.	will to live	[wɪltəlɪv]	*[wɪl̥təlɪv]
	b.	in case	[ɪnkeɪs]	*[ɪŋ̊keɪs]
	c.	come to think	[kʌmtəθiŋk]	*[kʌm̥təθiŋk]

Finally, voiced plosives don't undergo the rule (at least not in RP according to Gimson 1980: 294):

2.7	a.	bad to worse	[bædtəwəːs]	*[bættəwəːs]
	b.	job to do it	[dʒɔbtəduːɪt]	*[dʒɔptəduːɪt]
	c.	leg to stand on	[lɛgtəstændɔn]	*[lɛktəstændɔn]

However, it does seem that the voiced affricate /dʒ/ undergoes the process:

| 2.7 | d. | bridge to cross | [brɪdʒtəkrɔs] | [brɪtʃtəkrɔs] |

It's logical to ask whether /ʒ/ participates in this process. Unfortunately, /ʒ/ is a rare sound in English, and very few words end in it. Those that do are loan words, which are usually assimilated to English by changing the /ʒ/ to /dʒ/, e.g. *garage* /gərɑːdʒ/. However, it seems to me that the phrase *garage to let* would generally be pronounced [gərɑːʃtəlet] in all but careful speech.

We can therefore characterize the targets of the rule as the voiced fricatives and affricates. However, we can, in fact, retain our rather simpler formulation and restrict the rule to fricatives, by recalling that an affricate is, in a certain sense, composed of a plosive followed by a fricative (see section 1.2.1.1).[2] Intuitively speaking, this set of sounds seems to constitute a natural grouping. If the process had applied to, say, /v m g/ but no other voiced sounds we would probably wonder why it didn't also apply, for instance, to /z/ or /n/ or /d/. Such a natural grouping is very important in phonology and receives the name **natural class**. We'll see a further example later in this chapter, and in chapter 4 we will discuss this individual case in rather more detail, as well as the whole notion of natural classes. For the moment, we should think of a natural class of sounds as being a class of all those sounds in the language concerned which share some property or properties. Thus, the sounds {v ð z ʒ} are exactly those sounds which are at once voiced and also fricatives. The class {v z ʒ} wouldn't be a natural class because it would exclude /ð/. Similarly, the classes {v ð z ʒ b} or {v ð z ʒ s} wouldn't be natural classes because they would include extraneous sounds, /b/ and /s/ respectively, which don't have both the properties of being voiced and of being a fricative.

We've seen that in each case a devoicing process occurs, without any other obvious change. What of the environments? We can investigate this aspect by replacing voiceless sounds with voiced ones to see if this has any effect. In 2.8 I've done this for the examples of 2.1 (though I've had to change the words used):

2.8	a.	five before	[faɪvbɪfɔː]	*[faɪfbɪfɔː]
	b.	love declared	[lʌvdɪklɛːd]	*[lʌfdɪklɛːd]
	c.	as well as going	[əzwɛləzgouɪŋ]	*[əzwɛləsgouɪŋ]
	d.	has the answer	[hæzðɪænsə]	*[hæsðɪænsə]
	e.	loathe disruptions	[louðdɪsrʌpʃn̩z]	*[louθdɪsrʌpʃn̩z]
	f.	breathe deeply	[briːðdiːplɪ]	*[briːθdiːplɪ]

Clearly, the devoicing doesn't take place before a voiced sound.

To summarize, English has a process by which the voiced fricatives /v ð z/ are devoiced when they are immediately followed by a voiceless consonant. This process of Fricative Devoicing takes place when the two words concerned 'form part of a close knit group' in Gimson's words (1980: 293). We'll come back to this point later in chapter 5. Fricative Devoicing illustrates just one of a great many different types of phonological process. Other types involve the wholesale deletion or insertion of sounds or even syllables, as well as other rather more complex cases. In the final section I'll give a survey of the main types of process.

2.2 Underlying Representations (URs)

As a result of the process of Fricative Devoicing a word like *five* seems to end up with two distinct pronunciations, [faɪv] and [faɪf], though we may be accustomed to thinking that a word usually has just one pronunciation. This illustrates a very important aspect of phonology. Because of the phonological context in which the word finds itself, its pronunciation has altered. This situation is called **alternation**, and the two pronunciations are called **alternants**. Much of the task of phonology is to account for this phenomenon of alternation in a principled fashion.

When we come to describe an alternation such as this, it is usual to assume that one of the alternants is the basic pronunciation, and the other is derivative of it. In our example of Fricative Devoicing it would appear that the pronunciation [faɪv] is the basic one. We couldn't say, for instance, that the careful pronunciation [faɪvpɑːst] could be derived from the casual pronunciation [faɪfpɑːst] by a converse rule of Fricative Voicing. This is because, as it turns out, such a thing doesn't happen in English. For instance, in the phrase *laugh together* there is no careful pronunciation in which the /f/ voices: *[lɑːvtəgɛðə]. This means that the form [faɪvpɑːst] must be more basic than [faifpɑːst].

The form *faiv*, which represents the basic, unaltered pronunciation before any phonological processes have had chance to operate, is called the **underlying form** or **underlying representation**, often abbreviated to UR. The form *faif*, the actual pronunciation after the operation of the rule, is called the **surface form** or **surface representation** (SR). The process of applying a set of rules to URs to give SRs in this way is often referred to as a **derivation**. We say that we **derive** the SR from the UR by means of the rules. For this reason a surface representation is sometimes referred to as a **derived form/representation**. However, when a series of rules applies this term can refer to any of the intermediate stages in the derivation too.

It is usual to write the UR in slant brackets, /faɪv/, and the SR in square brackets, [faɪf]. This corresponds to the distinction in traditional phonetic transcription practice between a broad / . . . / and narrow [. . .] transcription. However, the analogy is rather misleading. This is because an underlying representation is more than just a phonemic representation, i.e. a string of phonemes in the traditional sense. This will become more obvious as we see more examples. Admittedly, for many of the examples we discuss the representation we take to be 'underlying' will correspond more or less to a phonemic transcription, but the concept of 'underlying representation' is more abstract than this, and we will see, in later chapters especially, that it goes rather beyond the notion of phoneme. In order to draw this distinction more clearly, I will often adopt the notational convention of writing URs between double slashes: //faɪv//. I will, however, use single slashes to represent intermediate steps in a more complex derivation.

I will illustrate the importance of URs in more detail using some very well-known facts concerning the pronunciation of the regular plural ending (and similar suffixes) in English. The pattern of change in the phonological shape of a morpheme is referred to in general terms as **allomorphy**. In English plurals, for instance, we find that the plural suffix, *-(e)s* in the orthographic (written) form, is pronounced in three different ways:

2.9   a.   cat   cats   [kæt]   [kæt-s]
      b.   dog   dogs   [dɔg]   [dɔg-z]
      c.   walrus   walruses   [wɔːlrəs]   [wɔːlrəs-əz]

The plural suffix surfaces as [s], [z] or [əz].[3] Our job in this section is to determine what governs this allomorphy.

As we saw in discussing the process of Fricative Devoicing in section 2.1, we need to set up a hypothesis about what might be happening, and then bring our empirical observations to bear on that hypothesis. If the data don't include counterexamples then we can accept our hypothesis as correct, until some other researcher digs up a counterexample. In fact, even if we find counterexamples, we might not necessarily want to abandon our thesis. This is because counterexamples sometimes turn out to be simply exceptions. Language tends to be ridden with exceptions, and just because, say, we can find irregular plural forms (such as *children, oxen, sheep*) doesn't mean to say that there isn't an important set of words which behave regularly. But even if we do come up against a frank counterexample, the hypothesis might be useful in guiding the search for new data, and shouldn't be abandoned until it can be replaced by a superior hypothesis.

There is, of course, no procedure which will guarantee that we can dream up a suitable hypothesis to get us going. This is where linguistic and scholarly creativity come in, together with experience of what is typical in phonological systems. However, a good way to attack a problem of this kind is to collect as many different types of data as possible and see what patterns emerge.

In fact, I've already given you much more information than a linguist would get attacking this problem cold, because I've said that there are just three different allomorphs. This is the sort of conclusion that is readily reached from scanning a large and varied selection of carefully transcribed examples. What phonological factors might condition the allomorphy? It can hardly be attributed to the sounds on the right because there aren't any. Presumably, then, it is the material to the left which governs the change.

Now, in general, a context which affects a target segment will be adjacent to that target. This may not necessarily mean exactly adjacent. Many languages have rules, for instance, changing a vowel depending on the quality of the following vowel, disregarding intervening consonants. However, adjacent segments are a good place to start when looking for a conditioning environment. In the present case, that means systematically investigating the effect of the final segment or segments on plural allomorphy. In 2.10 we see some more examples in which I've manipulated the final segments (though in a fairly unsystematic fashion).

2.10	a.	cows	-z	b.	apes	-s
	c.	crocodiles	-z	d.	doves	-z
	e.	eagles	-z	f.	flamingoes	-z
	g.	giraffes	-s	h.	kangaroos	-z
	i.	lions	-z	j.	monkeys	-z
	k.	ostriches	-əz	l.	partridge	-əz
	m.	snakes	-s	n.	starlings	-z
	o.	thrushes	-əz	p.	toads	-z
	q.	tortoise	-əz	r.	warthogs	-z
	s.	wombats	-s			

We now sort these according to the plural allomorph. In 2.11 I've indicated the singular form in transcription:

2.11   a.   -z   cows   /kaʊ/   crocodiles   /krɔkədaɪl/
                    doves   /dʌv/   eagles   /iːgl̩/
                    flamingoes /fləmɪŋou/   kangaroos   /kæŋəruː/
                    lions   /laɪən/   monkeys   /mʌŋkɪ/
                    starlings   /stɑːlɪŋ/   toads   /toud/
                    warthogs   /wɔːthɔg/
        b.   -s   apes   /eɪp/   giraffes   /dʒɪræf/
                    snakes   /sneɪk/   wombats   /wɔmbæt/
        c.   -əz   ostriches   /ɔstrɪtʃ/   partridge   /paːtrɪdʒ/
                    thrushes   /θrʌʃ/   tortoises   /tɔːtəs/

The /z/ allomorph appears after the following sounds: /aʊ, l, v, l̩, ou, uː n, ı, ŋ, d, g/, the /s/ allomorph occurs after /p f k t/ and the /əz/ allomorph is found after /tʃ, dʒ, ʃ, s/.

I've illustrated the plural allomorphy with a selection of extant English words. However, it's interesting to note that this type of allomorphy is the consequence of a process which is totally **productive**. What this means is that the process is a living part of the language, which cannot, in fact, be overridden by speakers. In an important sense, it is part of what a speaker of English knows by virtue of knowing how to speak English. We can tell that the process is productive because it applies to completely new words which a speaker may well never have heard before. For instance, if I were to market a children's puppet and called it a wug, everyone would know that the plural would be wugs and that it would be pronounced [wʌgz] (and not, say, [wʌgəz]). Moreover, even children as young as four know this (as shown by the classic experiments of Berko 1958). The alternation in the form of the plural morpheme is phonetically quite natural (we will see this in more detail later in the book), though there are quite a few other, equally natural, possibilities that the language might have opted for. Thus, English could easily have had a rule which said that the plural ending was deleted, i.e. simply not pronounced, after [tʃ, ʃ] etc, or which had the allomorph [əz] everywhere except after a vowel, when it surfaced as [z], or any number of other possibilities. Thus, the allomorphy is not determined in a completely mechanical fashion, and children learning English have to acquire this knowledge as part of their grammar of the language.

We now turn to figuring out how to characterize the process. What hypotheses do these data generate? The sounds preceding /z/ are very heterogeneous, including vowels, sonorant consonants and obstruents. The sounds preceding /s/ are all voiceless obstruents and those preceding /əz/ are affricates and fricatives. If we are dealing with a genuine phonological process (and not just some random assemblage of idiosyncratically determined choices) then we would expect these three sets of sounds to form a natural grouping. In other words, we would expect each member of the three groups to have something in common with the other members which distinguished it from the other two groups. This, in fact, is just another way of saying that the sounds should form themselves into natural classes.

The most natural-looking class is that preceding /s/, the voiceless obstruents. Suppose we assume then that /s/ appears after a voiceless obstruent. Now we observe that all the sounds preceding the /z/ allomorph are themselves voiced. This suggests a preliminary hypothesis: *the /s/ allomorph appears after voiceless sounds and the /z/ allomorph appears after voiced sounds.*

Unfortunately, this doesn't account for the /əz/ allomorph at all, so our initial hypothesis can't be the whole truth. However, we can test it against further data, to see how far it will take us. The data shown in 2.11c, governing the distribution of the /əz/ allomorphy are problematical for several reasons. First, given our initial hypothesis we would expect words ending in /s, ʃ, tʃ/ to be followed by /s/ and those ending in /dʒ/ to be followed by /z/. Second, we need to know what unites the sounds in this group.

To approach the second problem first, it turns out that the sounds which condition the /əz/ variant are the following: /s z ʃ ʒ tʃ dʒ/ (you should check that this is so – see ex. 2.6). In the next chapter we will found out exactly what unites these sounds. For the present we'll note that they are all fricatives or affricates (which, of course, are sounds which include a fricative component), and they are all coronal sounds (as opposed to say, /f/, which, though a fricative, is labial). The traditional term for this grouping of sounds is **sibilant**. We'll accept that this is a natural grouping without further comment for the moment. This means that we can propose a secondary hypothesis: *sounds ending in a sibilant are followed by /əz/.*

We now have the ingredients of an explanation of the plural allomorphy. However, our two hypotheses only tell us about the distribution of the allomorphs. The other side of the problem is the actual set of phonological forms assumed by these allomorphs. It is apparent that they are similar: the variant which appears after voiceless sounds is itself a voiceless sound, /s/, while the allomorph which appears after a voiced sound is the voiced correlate of /s/, namely /z/. Finally, the post-sibilant form is this same voiced sound preceded by schwa.

What this suggests is that the allomorphy should be accounted for by assuming that the three allomorphs are really just different ways of pronouncing the same form, just as [faɪvpɑːst] and [faɪfpɑːst] are different ways of pronouncing the same form. This means that we must discover a basic or underlying form for the suffix and then construct a set of phonological rules which turn that underlying form into the three derived forms. There are four possibilities for the underlying form: //s//, //z//, //əz//, 'something else'. Again, we need to investigate this question by beginning with guesswork and testing out our hypothesis. The simplest solution to the quest for an underlying form is to choose one of the surface alternants or variants as the basic one. The allomorph which appears most frequently and in the greatest variety of contexts is /z/, so let's select this as basic. We'll assume that there are no important processes affecting the singular noun stems themselves. This means that our starting point in the *cats, dogs, walruses* examples will be the representations of 2.12:

2.12   a. kæt + z   b. dɔg + z   c. wɔːlrəs + z

Nothing further need be said about //dɔgz// since this is the surface form. However, we need to devoice the /z/ in 2.12a. Let's therefore assume a rule of Devoicing such as that stated in 2.13:

2.13   z   →   s   /voiceless consonant ____

In order to obtain /wɔːlrəsəz/ from //wɔːlrəs+ z// we need to insert a schwa. This is a rule of *Epenthesis*, which we can state as in 2.14:

2.14   ∅   →   ə   /sibilant ____ z

Armed with these two rules, let's see if we can derive the right surface representations (SRs) from the underlying representations (URs) of 2.12. The derivations are shown in 2.15:

2.15   a. //kæt + z//   b. //dɔg + z//   c. //wɔːlrəs + z//
              s   N/A   s Devoicing
             N/A   N/A   N/A Epenthesis
             kæts   dɔgz   *wɔːlrəss Output

Something has gone wrong. The problem is that Devoicing will always apply to /z/ following a voiceless sibilant, destroying the environment for Epenthesis. This means that Epenthesis will never have a chance to apply.

   The obvious way around this problem is to stipulate that the rules apply in the opposite order, as in 2.16:

2.16   a. //kæt + z//   b. //dɔg + z//   c. //wɔːlrəs + z//
              N/A   N/A   ə Epenthesis
               s   N/A   N/A Devoicing
             kæts   dɔgz   wɔːlrəsəz Output

This gives the desired result.

   Thus, by postulating a common underlying form for the plural morpheme, we can derive the three surface allomorphs by means of a set of phonological rules. In the present case, we also need to appeal to a specially stipulated **rule ordering**. Rule ordering is a controversial device which not all phonologists accept. There is a wide variety of ways in which rules can

Figure 2.1 Schematic model of generative phonology

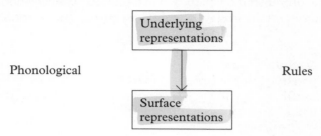

be ordered with respect to each other, and some of these will be discussed in more detail in chapter 5. For the present it is sufficient to know that such a thing is a possibility.

The result of our derivations is a set of surface representations which reflects the allomorphy of the suffix. This allomorphy is determined entirely by the phonological composition of the noun stem on this analysis. We can therefore call it **phonologically conditioned allomorphy**. The resulting model of phonology is represented diagrammatically in figure 2.1: This is the form of the 'classical' model of generative phonology. It remains the basis for nearly all contemporary theories of phonology.

2.3 Lexical and Postlexical Phonological Processes

In chapter 1 we discovered that English voiceless stops are aspirated in certain positions. This phenomenon is part of the phonology of the language. We can say that it is part of the native speaker's unconscious knowledge of his/her language. Interestingly, it is something which is not under the conscious control of the speaker. It is perfectly possible for a human being to pronounce a form like [p⁼ɪn] where [p⁼] indicates lack of aspiration, and indeed this is the only correct pronunciation in languages such as French, Spanish or Russian. But it is very difficult for a native speaker of English to withhold aspiration without special phonetic training. Indeed, this is one of the hallmarks of the foreign accent which marks out English-speaking learners of those languages.

One consequence of this is that the process of aspirating voiceless stops is exceptionless. Thus, when English borrows loan words with voiceless initial consonants from, say, Russian, (for instance, *perestroika*), such words will be pronounced with aspiration which they lack in the source language. For this reason we often refer to such processes as **automatic processes**. In the case of aspiration the process specifies the distribution of particular allophones of a set of phonemes, so such processes are often referred to as allophonic processes.

A slightly different type of process is illustrated in 2.17, where I compare a careful pronunciation with a more relaxed, conversational pronunciation (I ignore certain irrelevant subtleties in the transcriptions, such as aspiration):

2.17   careful   casual
      a.   pəteɪtou   pteɪtou   'potato'
      b.   tərɪfɪk   trɪfɪk   'terrific'
      c.   pəliːs   pliːs   'police'

optional

The casual variants are the result of deleting the first, unstressed, vowel of the word. Now, this type of process is characteristic of ordinary English conversation (even in the speech of purists who claim to frown on this as 'sloppy'). However, it is not an obligatory process. It is governed by how quickly and carefully the speaker wishes to articulate. We can therefore refer to such a process as **optional**. On the other hand there is no alternative to aspirating an initial voiceless stop, so such a process would be called obligatory. An **obligatory** automatic process is one which applies in all speech styles, while an optional process is one which is governed by factors such as register, style, rate of speaking and so on.

Now consider the examples in 2.18:

2.18   a.   extend   extensive
            deride   derisive
       b.   progress   progressive
            dismiss   dismissive

Here we have a suffix -*ive* which takes a verb and creates a related adjective. In my pronunciation, whenever this suffix is added to a verb stem ending in /d/ it replaces that phoneme with /s/. This means that there are two forms of each of the stems in the 2.18a examples: [ɛkstɛnd] ~ [ɛkstɛns], [dɪraɪd] ~ [dɪraɪs]. In other words, we again see two alternants and the alternation is induced by the suffixation of -*ive*.

This always happens when an adjective is created from a verb by this particular affix. This means that there are no such -*ive* adjectives of the form . . . *d-ive*. In other words it would be impossible have two such -*ive* adjectives which were identical except that one had the form . . . *d-ive* and the other the form . . . *s-ive*. This is interesting, because normally, of course, /d/ and /s/ are independent phonemes whose function is precisely to distinguish one word from another. When we have this kind of situation we sometimes say that the phonemic contrast has been suspended in the particular context. Another, more frequent, term used is neutralization. The /d ~ s/ contrast is neutralized in the context of a following -*ive* deverabal adjectival suffix.

In this example the precise morphological function of the affix is important.

If we look at an apparently identical suffix it turns out to show different behaviour. Thus, we can also add *-ive* to nouns to get an adjective, as in *mass ~ massive*. However, when this is added to a stem in *-d* no neutralization of /d/ and /s/ takes place, as we can see from *gerund ~ gerundive*.

An alternation such as /d/ ~ /s/ only applies to certain sorts of words, stems or morphemes. Since the alternation is governed by the nature of individual morphemes, words or word structure, we often refer to it as a **lexical process**. The set of processes of this kind, dependent of specific properties of individual words or morphemes is often called the **lexical phonology** of the language. Other, earlier, terms for the same idea are **morphophonology** (stressing the crucial interaction between phonology and morphological structure) and **morphophonemics**.

This last term is taken from the terminology of structural linguistics of the 1930s. However, it brings with it the implication that phonemes are involved. In fact, in the vast majority of such processes examined in the world's languages, the process replaces one phoneme or set of phonemes with another. Thus, there is no sense in which we could claim that /s/ is an allophone of /d/ in a word like *extensive*. What has happened is that the phoneme /d/ in *extend* has been <u>replaced</u> by the phoneme /s/. One consequence of this is that there can no longer be a phonemic contrast between /d/ and /s/ immediately before this particular suffix, in other words the contrast is neutralized in this context. This is the typical case with such alternations. This is not to say that automatic processes cannot also relate one set of phonemes to another. In fact, the Fricative Devoicing process we saw earlier is an example of an automatic process which neutralizes the voicing contrast in fricatives. The point is that it is typical for a lexical process to replace one set of phonemes with another. In other words, the standard cases of lexical alternations are always neutralizations.

Over and above lexical alternations, we may find further automatic (e.g. allophonic) processes can apply, treating the new phoneme just as if it had been there all the time. However, it never seems to be the case that an automatic process can 'feed into' a lexical process. For this reason, these automatic processes are often called **postlexical processes** and the whole set of these is often referred to as the **postlexical phonology**. Moreover, some of these processes are triggered only when two separate words come together to form a phrase, hence, such rules are also often known as the **phrasal phonology**.

One important difference between the rules of phrasal phonology and the lexical phonology is that the phrase phonology processes are expected to be phonetically 'natural' in a certain sense. It is not easy to explain what precisely is meant by this term, so suffice it to say that there are some processes (like aspirating voiceless stops) which seem to have their basis in the physiology of the speech organs (without being determined exhaustively by purely phonetic considerations, as I stressed at the beginning of this subsection). Now, many lexical alternations could easily be viewed as phonetically natural processes. However, many of the processes which have been described in the lexical phonologies of languages would never be expected to occur as natural phonological processes in the phrase phonology of a language. This even applies to lexical processes which are actually quite common in the world's languages. We'll see examples of this later in the book, and especially in chapter 4.

2.4   Summary of Common Segmental Processes

We have seen how in English a voiced fricative becomes a voiceless sound under the influence of a following voiceless segment. This type of assimilation is generally regarded as a natural phonological process, because it is generally supposed that it is in some sense 'easier' to articulate a two voiceless segments together than to quickly change the voicing from one consonant to the next. Although this concept of 'ease of articulation' is a somewhat murky one, it is influential in determining which sorts of phonological process are considered natural, and hence to be expected, and which are 'unnatural' and hence in need of some additional explanation. In this section I shall review a few of the more important types of process that are regarded as natural.

2.4.1   Assimilations and dissimilations

We continue with assimilations. These can take place in two directions: right-to-left (regressive, anticipatory assimilation) or left-to-right (progressive, perseverative assimilation). Fricative devoicing is an example of regressive assimilation, the devoicing process observed in the plural allomorphy of the previous section is a case of progressive assimilation.

A type of assimilation which plays an important role in many languages is called **harmony**. Most commonly this affects vowels (hence, **vowel harmony**). This is found in a wide variety of languages and operates in a number of different ways. In 2.19 we see some Hungarian nouns inflected in a case form meaning (amongst other things) 'about, concerning':

2.19   a.   teːrkeːprøːl   'map'
              føldrøːl   'land'
              yɟrøːl   'business'
              siːnrøːl   'colour'
        b.   laːɲroːl   'girl'
              uːrroːl   'gentleman'
              fogroːl   'tooth'

(These examples are in broad IPA transcription, not the official Hungarian orthography.)

Clearly, there is a case suffix which has two allomorphs, *-roːl/røːl*. The first of these has a back vowel /oː/, and the second has the corresponding front vowel /øː/. Moreover, the front vowel allomorph occurs after stems which have front vowels (2.19a), while the back vowel allomorph occurs after stems which have back vowels (2.19b). We can therefore say that the vowel of the suffix has assimilated along the front-back dimension to the value of the stem vowel. As it happens, the /roːl/ allomorph occurs independently elsewhere in the language, and one traditional way to describe the situation is therefore to say that the UR for the suffix is //roːl// and that in the examples of 2.19a the suffix vowel is changed from back to front under the influence of the stem.

An interesting feature of this process is that it systematically ignores intervening consonants. This is typical of vowel harmony. Such a phenomenon is sometimes referred to as a case of 'action-at-a-distance'. However, it is interesting that in genuine harmony systems the basic process takes place between vowels in adjacent syllables.

Much less commonly we find consonant harmony. One type of language where this crops up with great regularity however is child language. For instance, many children go through a stage of 'Velar Harmony' when a coronal consonant at the beginning of a word harmonizes with a velar consonant at the end. Typical examples of this would be those of 2.20:

2.20   gɔg   'dog'
         keɪk   'take'
         ŋɪk   'Nick'

Although assimilations are considered natural, there are circumstances when we find the opposite process occurring, that is, two neighbouring sounds which are similar become dissimilar as one or both undergo some phonological change. This is a process of **dissimilation**. An example of this in historical development is provided by Greek. Ancient Greek permitted two obstruents to appear in onsets. In the modern language when this happens they may be either fricatives or plosives. However, there is a strong tendency for a pair of plosives or a pair of fricatives to turn into a fricative + plosive pair. Some examples are given in 2.21 (a description of Greek can be found in Mackridge 1985 and Joseph and Philippaki-Warburton 1987):

2.21   fθinos   >   ftinos   'cheap'
         sxolio   >   skolio   'school'
         epta   >   efta   'seven'
         okto   >   oxto   'eight'

This can also be seen in alternations with certain types of verb stem. The passive aorist (a kind of past tense) form normally has a suffix *-θik*, as seen in 2.22:

2.22   a.   agap-a-   'love'
             agap-i-θik-e   'he was loved'
        b.   fer-   'carry'
             fer-θik-e   'he was carried'
        c.   stel-   'send'
             stal-θik-e   'he was sent'

However, when the passive aorist stem ends in a fricative we get dissimilation of the suffix:

2.23   a.   akus-   'hear'
             akus-tik-e   'he was heard'
        b.   ðex-   'receive'
             ðex-tik-e   'it was received'
        c.   γraf-   'write'
             γraf-tik-e   'it was written'

2.4.2 Fortitions and lenitions (strengthenings and weakenings)

Now we briefly consider processes associated loosely with the idea of 'strength'
(or 'weakness') of articulation. I shall illustrate this with an example from
the historical development of Greek (though this presumably corresponded
to a genuine, i.e. synchronic, process at some stage in the history of the
language). In Ancient Greek there were voiced plosives /b d g/:

2.24   biblos   'book'
        hodos   'road'
        dyo   'two'
        grapʰoː   'I write'
        pragmata   'things, deeds'

However, there were no voiced fricatives corresponding to these sounds. In
Modern Greek, the old voiced plosives have been largely replaced by voiced
fricatives:

2.25   vivlos   'Bible'
        oðos   'road'
        ðio   'two'
        γrafo   'I write'
        praγmata   'things, deeds'

Similarly, in Japanese we find a process under which a voiceless stop between two vowels becomes voiced under certain circumstances, as when a
compound is formed from two other words, a phenomenon known as
Rendaku (these data are taken from Itô and Mester 1986: 50):

2.26   a.   ori   'fold'
             kami   'paper'
             tana   'shelf'
             tsukuri   'make'
        b.   origami   'origami (paper folding)'
             origamidana   'origami shelf'
             origamidanadzukuri   'origami shelf making'

It is generally felt that there is a sense in which a fricative is a 'weaker'
articulation than a stop, and a voiced segment 'weaker' than a voiceless one.
Phonetically, the justification for this is that a more tense and energetic
articulation is needed for voiceless sounds or for plosives than for voiceless
sounds or fricatives. Consequently, processes such as this are often referred
to as weakenings or (more commonly) **lenitions**.

In a number of languages there is a distinction between aspirated consonants (usually plosives) and non-aspirated ones. Again, the aspirated series
is usually associated with greater energy and is frequently weakened. In
most forms of Quechua there is a distinction between voiceless aspirated
plosives and voiceless plain plosives. However, in some dialects this distinction is no longer observed and the aspirated plosives have become plain.
One the other hand, slightly more complex phenomena are sometimes
observed. Greek, too, had a distinction between aspirated and plain voiceless plosives. However, in Greek the aspirated sounds underwent lenition,
though the voiceless plain stops were untouched. The aspirates became
fricatives, as we can see from 2.27:

2.27   Ancient Greek   Modern Greek
        a.   grap^{h}oː   ɣrafo   'I write'
        b.   t^{h}alassa   θalasa   'sea'
        c.   k^{h}roːma   xroma   'colour'

Finally, geminated consonants are regarded as 'stronger' than single consonants. In keeping with the general tendency towards weaker articulations
in Greek, the frequent geminated consonants of Ancient Greek have been
entirely replaced by single consonants:

2.28   Ancient Greek   Modern Greek
        a.   hellas   elas   'Greece'
        b.   thalassa   θalasa   'sea'
        c.   ennea   enea   'nine'
        d.   kappa   kapa   'kappa (letter of
                                                 Greek alphabet)'

Likewise, approximants (glides and liquids) are regarded as weaker than
corresponding obstruents. The ultimate form of lenition is total disappear-
ance. This has happened in the history of a good many languages, especially
to velar stops.

A general, though not exhaustive, scheme for lenitions would be roughly as in 2.29:

2.29   plosives > fricatives > approximants > zero   *P > F > A*
       aspirated > plain voiceless > voiced   *A > Voiceless > Voiced*

As can be seen from many of the examples presented above, consonants tend to be lenited between two vowels. Another common site for lenition is the end of a syllable (this is one of the reasons why codas in a given language often admit a narrower set of consonants than onsets). On the other hand, as a language changes historically whole classes of sounds may lenite completely, and get replaced by another set of consonants, as we saw with Greek in examples 2.27/28.

Corresponding to the lenitions, though rather less common, are converse processes, where a sound is produced more forcefully. These are known as **fortitions**. It is misleading, however, to think of them as just lenitions run in reverse. We don't find zero suddenly becoming a velar fricative, for instance. However, there are certain contexts in which a set of sounds is replaced by the corresponding set somewhere to its <u>left</u> in the hierarchy in 2.29. The case of the devoicing of obstruents in word final position in a good many languages (e.g. Russian, German) is an example of this. The development of Schwyzertüütsch (Swiss German) provides an interesting case. The original stop series of earlier Germanic, which gave rise to English and Standard German /p b t d g k/ has changed in Swiss German, so that the voiced stops /b d g/ have become unvoiced stops, but pronounced in a relatively 'lax' fashion. The technical term for this is lenis. On the other hand, the unvoiced /p t/ have become unvoiced (unaspirated) stops pronounced more energetically and with greater muscular tension. Such stops are called fortis. The fate of original /k/ is rather intriguing. In some words it has suffered lenition to the (lenis variant of the) corresponding fricative, /x/, in others it corresponds to the fortis plosive, while in yet others, especially loan words, it has undergone further fortition to a velar affricate [kˣ] (a characteristic sound of the language). This is illustrated in the sets of words in 2.30 (adapted from Baur 1969) comparing Standard German with Schwyzertüütsch (I represent a fortis articulation in the Swiss examples by doubling the consonant):

2.30 | | Standard German | Swiss German | |
       |----|-----------------|--------------|----------|
       | a. | kalb | xalp | 'calf' |
       | | bakɴ | paxə | 'bake' |
       | | folk | volx | 'people' |
       | b. | ekə | ekkə | 'corner' |
       | | lak | lakk | 'varnish'|
       | c. | kameːl | kˣameːl | 'camel' |
       | | rykɴ | rukˣə | 'move' |
       | | ʃtok | ʃtokˣ | 'storey' |

2.4.3   Insertions, deletions and coalescence

The processes we've seen so far involve just the pronunciation of individual segments. However, a good many processes affect the way that groups of segments are pronounced. We can group these into three broad types: insertions (epenthesis), deletions (truncation), and coalescence. In the first two we are usually looking at processes which are governed by the structure of syllables or larger groupings of sounds.

It is extremely common to find that a language inserts a segment (usually a vowel, less commonly a consonant) into a string of segments which would otherwise violate the syllable structure principles of the language. A striking example of this is provided by Koryak, a paleosiberian language spoken in Kamchatka. In Koryak it is not unusual to find words which lack underlying vowels altogether. Such a thing is unpronounceable, however, because Koryak imposes strict conditions on syllable structure. Basically, the most complex type of syllable allowed in Koryak has the form CVC. Therefore, if a word has a UR of the form, say, CCVC or CVCCCVC a vowel has to be introduced among the certain of the consonants to break up the illegal cluster. Here are some examples (taken from Zhukova 1972; /l'/ represents a palatalized /l/):

2.31	təmək	'kill' *tə*
	pəŋlok	'ask'
	wəwwən	'stone'
	jəlləjəl	'branch'
	ʔənnəŋəjtəgəjŋən	'catch (of fish)'
	pəl'həl'həgəjŋən	'river flow'

It might be wondered how we know that these schwas are all inserted epenthetically. There are basically two reasons. First, there seem to be very few occasions when we need to regard schwa as an independent phoneme in words of Koryak. There do not seem to be any minimal pairs in which a schwa contrasts with some other form, and the position of the schwa in the great majority of words is entirely predictable from the phonological shape of the word. The second reason is that the schwa regularly disappears if it is not needed, in other words, we have evidence from *alternations* between schwa and zero. Thus, in the verb *təmək* we need two schwas, to avoid an illegal cluster (i.e. to avoid *CCVC, *CVCC). However, in inflected forms of the verb we alter the implied syllable structure by the addition of affixes. Some prefixes such as *t-* '1sg subject' or *mt-* '1pl subject' end in a consonant while others such as *na-* '3pl subject' end in a vowel. If we add these to a verb such as *pənlok* 'ask' then we obtain different results, as shown in 2.32:

2.32	a.	təpŋəlon	'I asked him'
	b.	mətpəŋlon	'we asked him'
	c.	napŋəlo-n	'they asked him'

This is easy to understand if we assume that none of the schwas is present in the URs of these words, as shown in 2.33:

2.33   a. //t-pŋlo-n//
        b. //mt-pŋlo-n//
        c. //na-pŋlo-n//

We now move from left-to-right and try to group all the consonants and vowels into syllables respecting the CVC template. If we encounter a cluster that couldn't in principle be syllabified then we insert a schwa. This gives us the required results.

Languages sometimes impose restrictions on the distribution of vowels, such as the places in a word where they may appear, or what kinds of vowel sequence are permitted. One common restriction rules out word initial vowels. In Czech, for instance, a word may not begin phonetically with a vowel, and there are also severe restrictions on sequences of vowels. However, phonologically it is perfectly possible to begin a word with a vowel. Where this happens a glottal stop is inserted. However, the glottal stop in Czech is not a phoneme. If a vowel-initial stem receives a consonant-final prefix then the glottal is no longer required and hence is not inserted. This can be seen in 2.34:

2.34   a. ʔoperovat   'to operate'
            voperovat   'to transplant (tissue, organ)'
        b. ʔutʃitel   'teacher'
            podutʃitel   'junior teacher'

In Koryak we see epenthesis functioning to make clusters of consonants pronounceable. Another common strategy for dealing with such clusters is to delete certain of the consonants. To a limited extent this happens in the lexical phonology of Koryak. A number of verb roots begin with consonant clusters, of which the first member is lost when there is no prefix. Some examples are shown in 2.35:

2.35   a. təlqutək   'I stood up'
            qutti   'he stood up'
            root: (l)qt   'stand up'
        b. tətwak   'I was'
            waj   'he was'
            root: (t)wa   'be'

This seems to be restricted to certain types of verbs, however, and isn't observed with other word classes.

In Russian we see a general process simplifying certain types of 'difficult' consonant cluster. This is often seen when we attach a suffix to a root form.

In the examples in 2.36 (taken from Avanesov 1972: 148) we see various simplifications following suffixation:

2.36   a. mest-o   'place'
            mest + nɨj   'local'   *t - deletion*
            [mesnɨj]

        b. zvjozd-ɨ   'stars'
            zvjozd + nɨj   'stellar'   *d - deletion*
            [zvjoznɨj]

        c. sovesʲtʲ   'conscience'
            sovesʲtʲ + lʲivɨj   'conscientious' *t - deletion*
            [sovesʲlʲivɨj]

        d. marksist   'Marxist'
            marksist + skij   'marxist'   *t - deletion*
            [marksisskij]

        e. istets   'plaintiff'
            istts + ɨ   'plaintiffs'
            i[sts]ɨ (NB vowel deletion)

        f. irland-ija   'Ireland'
            irland + skij   'Irish'
            [irlanskij]

        g. gigant   'giant'
            gigant + skij   'gigantic'   *t - deletion*
            [giganskij]

        h. serdets   'heart (genitive pl)'
            serdts + e   'heart (nominative sg)'
            [sertse] (NB vowel deletion)

Here what is happening is that a /t d/ in the middle of a cluster is dropped. In some words this is obligatory, though in others there is a tendency to try to restore the /t d/ in very careful speech.

It is not uncommon to find languages which avoid vowels at the end of a word. This type of vowel truncation is illustrated by the Chukchee examples in 2.37 (taken from Skorik 1961: 41. Chukchee is a close relative of Koryak):

2.37   a. ajkol   'bed'   ajkolat   'beds'
        b. tʃawtʃəw   'nomad'   tʃawtʃəwat 'nomads'
        c. milut   'hare'   milutet   'hares'
        d. əwik   'body'   əwikit   'bodies'

Clearly, the plural suffix is -t. However, when this (or indeed any other suffix is added), a vowel appears on the end of the stem. The nature of this vowel can't be predicted phonologically, so it makes sense to assume that it is present in the underlying representation of the stem and deleted in word final position. Thus, the URs for the examples of 2.37 would be //ajkola//, //t͡ʃawt͡ʃəwa//, //milute//, //əwiki//. With a small number of exceptions, vowels are not found at the end of a stem where this coincides with the end of a word (though it is common for word-final suffixes themselves to end in a vowel).

Chukchee also illustrates another common phenomenon: the simplification of vowel sequences. This can be seen from the following examples, again provided by Skorik 1961:

2.38	a.	ʔaat͡ʃek	'youth'	ʔaat͡ʃek-en	'belonging to a youth'
		qora-ŋə	'reindeer'	qoren	'belonging to a reindeer'
	b.	migt͡ʃiret-ək	'to work'	ge-migt͡ʃiret-linet	'they worked
		umeket-ək	'to gather'	g-umeket-linet	'they gathered'
	c.	milger	'rifle'	ge-milger-e	'with a rifle'
		ilir	'island'	g-ilir-e	'with an island'

Here, the first vowel in the sequences /a e/, /e u/, /e i/ in the URs //qora-en//, //ge-umeket-linet//, //ge-ilir-e// is being simplified by deletion of the first of the vowels.

One particularly frequent process which can be related to deletions is the simplification of 'doubled' or geminated consonants to singleton consonants. We often find that a language fails to permit geminated consonants but that morphological processes place identical consonants side by side. Languages differ as to how they respond to this situation. In Serbo-Croat, for instance, there are no geminates word internally. Therefore, if a word has, say, a prefix ending in the same consonant as that at the beginning of the following stem, the resulting geminate is simplified, as can be seen in the examples of 2.39:

2.39	a.	lomiti	'break'
		odlomiti	'break off'
	b.	umirati	'die'
		odumirati	'die out'
	c.	derati	'tear'
		oderati	'tear off'
	d.	trcati	'run'
		otrcati	'run away'

Here we see that there is a prefix *od-* with roughly the meaning of 'away, from'. This has the allomorph *ot-* before a voiceless consonant. When added to a stem beginning in /d t/ (2.39c, d) the resulting cluster /dd/, /td/ is simplified to /d/ and /t/.

Coalescence of segments is a widespread phenomenon, when two distinct sounds blend together to produce a single sound which is an amalgam of the two original sounds. Coalescence is particularly frequent with vowels, a very common example being the coalescence of a diphthong such as /ai/ or /au/ to a single vowel /e/ or /o/. This has happened in the history of a great many languages and remains as part of the lexical phonology of Sanskrit, many Bantu languages and certain Romance languages. Its effects can be seen in the orthography of French: the sequences -ai-, -au-, as in *mais* 'but' or *cause* 'cause' are pronounced as in /mɛ/ and /koz/. The contemporary spelling reflects an earlier pronunciation when the vowels were still diphthongs.

Consonants can coalesce with each other, too. Czech has an affricate /tʃ/, as well as a fricative /ʃ/. However, when a sequence /t + ʃ/ is formed, the cluster is pronounced like the affricate:

2.40   a.   star-iː   'old'
              star-ʃiː   'older'
        b.   tlust-iː   'fat'
              tlustʃ-iː   'fatter'
        c.   mlad-iː   'young'
              mlatʃ-iː   'younger'

In 2.40a we see the comparative suffix -*ʃiː*. However, in combination with /t/ (2.40b) or /d/ (2.40c) the cluster /t + ʃ/ or /d + ʃ/ is simplified to the affricate [tʃ]. Thus, the root *mlad-* gives *mlat-ʃiː* (with devoicing) and then *mlatʃiː*. We can regard this as a simplification because an affricate in Czech (as in many languages) is a single segment (albeit a complex one). For example, it only lasts as long as a single consonant such as /t/ or /ʃ/. Therefore, at the very least we have to say that we have lost one of our 'segment slots' in the examples of 2.40.

2.4.4   Lengthenings and shortenings

In many languages short vowels become long under certain circumstances. The most common situation is for a stressed vowel to be longer than unstressed vowels. Thus, in Russian there is no contrast in vowel length. However, in a word such as *rúki* 'hands' the stressed [u] vowel is longer than the unstressed [u] vowel of *ruki* 'of a hand'. Conversely, the stressed [i] of *ruki* is longer than the unstressed [i] of *rúki*.

In English a vowel is slightly longer before a voiced obstruent than in other positions. Thus, the vowel of *bid* is slightly longer than that of *bit*, and the vowel of *bead* is longer than that of *beat*. Since the vowel of *bee* is roughly the same length as that of *bead*, it would appear that this is a case of vowel shortening before a voiceless consonant.

It is not uncommon to find languages in which a consonant is deleted and

at the same time the preceding vowel lengthens, to make up for the lost
consonant, so to speak. This process is known as **compensatory lengthening**. It can be illustrated by the examples in 2.41 from Latin (the data
are taken from Hayes 1989: 260):

2.41   kasnus   →   kaːnus   'grey'
        kosmis   →   koːmis   'courteous'
        fideslia →   fideːlia 'pot'

2.4.5 Metathesis and reduplication

This completes our description of the most important phonological processes. Two other types might also be distinguished, though they are not so
important for the description of specifically phonological systems. The first
of these is metathesis. This refers to the reordering of segments. A typological survey can be found in Ultan (1978). Metathesis is sometimes found in
the lexical phonology of languages, though it is not obvious that it is ever
observed as an automatic, connected speech process. It frequently occurs in
all languages as a type of speech error and is a common feature of child
phonology. Examples of this sort would be pronunciations such as /aks/ for
ask, or /aminal/ for animal. Not infrequently such speech errors are passed
onto the next generation of speakers and this results in a diachronic change.
Thus, a great many of the examples of metathesis cited in the phonology
literature come from historical linguistics. An example from the history of
English involves a particularly common phenomenon, the metathesis of a
vowel and liquid. Thus, the words *bird, frost,* and *horse* in Old English were
pronounced (roughly) /brid, forst, hros/ (Wright and Wright 1928: 111).
   Another type of process which is quite frequent in the lexical phonological systems of languages is reduplication. Phonologically, this is a rather
complex phenomenon, and in many respects it is better regarded as a morphological process rather than a phonological one. It is not found, for instance, as an automatic phonological process in any language. However, it
is a process which involves a phonological modification of the morphemes
it affects and as such can be seen as lying on the boundary between phonology and morphology.
   A typical type of reduplicative processes involves repeating the first CV or
CVC of a word. Examples from Tagalog are shown in 2.42:

2.42   a.   sulat   'writing'
             susulat   'write (future)'
        b.   basa   'reading'
             mambasa   'to read'
             mambabasa   '(act of) reading'
        c.   magsulatsulat   'write intermittently'

In 2.42a the first CV sequence of the root is reduplicated (su+sulat), while in 2.42b the same happens to a root which already has a prefix, *mam-*. In 2.42c the whole morpheme is reduplicated.

In the Tagalog examples the reduplicated material is prefixed. In the Chukchee examples from 2.43 we see the first CVC sequence of a root reduplicated to the right of a noun root in the absolutive (basic) case form, thus functioning as a suffix (the schwas in 2.43a are epenthetic):

2.43   a.   tirk-ək   'sun (locative)'
             tirkətir   'sun (absolutive)'
       b.   nute-k   'earth (locative)'
             nutenut   'earth (absolutive)'

In some languages we find partial reduplication, in which part of the reduplicative affix is specified already and the rest is copied from the stem to which the affix attaches. Ancient Greek provides an example:

2.44   a.   ly-oː   'I release'
             le-ly-ka   'I have released'
       b.   tiːm-oː   'I honour'
             te-tiːm-eːka   'I have honoured'
       c.   t^{h}yː-oː   'I sacrifice'
             te-t^{h}y-ka   'I have sacrificed'
       d.   grap^h-oː   'I write'
             ge-grap^h-a   'I have written'

Notice that the first consonant is reduplicated but the vowel is always /e/ regardless of the first vowel in the root. Notice, too, how only the first consonant of the cluster *gr-* is reduplicated in 2.44d, and how the aspiration of the /t^h/ in the root *t^{h}yː* in 2.44c is not copied in the reduplicated prefix.

This completes our outline of the types of phonological processes found in the world's languages. As we proceed we will see a variety of each type exemplified by English and other languages.

FURTHER READING

Introductions to the formalism of generative phonology can be found in a variety of sources. Particularly recommended are Hyman (1975) and Kenstowicz and Kisseberth (1979).

Schane (1973) gives a simple overview of some of the commoner processes, from the point of view of classical (SPE) generative phonology. Katamba (1989) discusses lenitions and fortitions from an introductory point of view. Lass (1984: ch. 8), presents a rather more detailed summary of the different types of phonological process. For more details on the morphophonology of reduplication see Katamba (1993: ch. 9), Spencer (1991: ch. 5).

EXERCISES

2.1 Using the English phoneme inventory, check off which sounds
     have been sampled in 2.10 and which haven't. Then find nouns
     ending in the sounds which haven't been sampled and use them
     to determine whether the generalizations about plural allomorphy
     given in the text hold up.

2.2 The formulation of the phonological rules required to derive the
     plural allomorphy depends on our decision as to what the under-
     lying form of the plural suffix is. Formulate a set of rules on the
     assumption that the UR is (a) /s/ (b) /əz/. Would your rules need
     to apply in a specific order?

2.3 The 3sg present tense agreement ending on verbs and the pos-
     sessive marker (orthographically 's or s') bear considerable re-
     semblance to the plural affix. Investigate their allomorphic
     variation. Do you need different URs from that of the plural
     ending, and are different phonological rules needed? If so, what
     URs and what rules?

2.4 The past tense ending (orthographically -(e)d) shows character-
     istic phonologically conditioned allomorphy. State the nature of
     the allomorphy and provide a UR and set of rules to account for
     it.

2.5 Nouns in the Western Nilotic language, Dholuo (or Luo) have a
     special form in the plural and a similar form when the noun is
     possessed. Thus, the word for 'pot', *agulu,* in the expression *aguc
     mon,* 'the woman's pot' appears in a special construct form. For
     many nouns the plural/construct is marked by a change in the
     final consonant of the stem. Assuming the basic form is the sin-
     gular, the plural/construct form may show evidence of lenition or
     of fortition. Determine for the data below which type of process
     we are dealing with. Try to formulate the changes as a single
     process or set of process (for some of the examples this will not
     be possible). [*mb, nd, ɲʤ, ŋg* represent prenasalized stops, other-
     wise the examples are transcribed broadly into IPA]:

	singular	construct	
A	lep	lew	'tongue'
	jaθ	jað	'tree'
	ot	od	'house'
	tiʧ	tiʤ	'work'
	guok	guog	'dog'

B	kitabu	kitap	'book'
	ʧiewo	ʧiep	'porcupine'
	mbiði	mbiθ	'wild pig'
	udo	ut	'ostrich'
	agaʤa	agaʧ	'chair'
	ŋgaji	ngaʧ	'paddle'
	agulu	aguʧ	'pot'
	rawera	raweʧ	'boy'
	ʧogo	ʧok	'bone'

C	jam	jamb	'hurricane
	ten	tend	'neckrest'
	opuɲ	opuɲʤ	'heel'
	koŋo	koŋg	'beer'
	pala	pand	'knife'

2.6 Dissimilatio lateralium latinorum. What accounts for the allomorphy in the Latin adjective suffixes in column B?

A		B	
floːr-is	'flower'	floːraːlis	'floral'
luːna	'moon'	luːnaːris	'lunar'
later-is	'side'	lateraːlis	'lateral'
lati-um	'Latium'	lati-aris	'of, from Latium'
litter-a	'letter'	litteraːlis	'literal, pertaining to letters'
miːlit-is	'soldier'	miːlitaːris	'military'
mort-is	'death'	mortaːlis	'mortal'
naːtuːr-a	'nature'	naːturaːlis	'natural'
naːw-is	'boat'	naːwaːlis	'naval'
pluːr-eːs	'many'	pluːraːlis	'plural'
popul-us	'people'	populaːris	'of the people'
reːgul-a	'rule'	reːgulaːris	'regular'
sepulcr-um	'grave'	sepulcraːlis	'sepulchral'
soːl	'sun'	soːlaːris	'solar'
woːk-is	'voice'	'woːkaːlis'	'vocal'

The following noun forms, which have suffixes in *-al/ar*, illustrate the same phenomenon:

animal	'animal'	kalkar	'spur'
koklear	'spoon'	exemplar	'copy'
lakuːnar	'type of ceiling'	luperkal	'cave on Palatine hill'
pulwiːnar	'type of couch'	toral	'valance (of couch)'
torkular	'wine press'	tribuːnal	'tribunal'

chapter 3

Syllables and Syllabification

3.0 Introduction

In the earliest forms of generative phonology the syllable played no role. Thus, in the monumental *The Sound Pattern of English* (Chomsky and Halle 1968: SPE), a study which consolidated and established the methodology of the field for some time, the term 'syllable' doesn't even appear in the index. Instead, words were held to consist of sequences of consonants and vowels.

However, in chapter 1 we saw that syllables can be viewed as hierarchical structures, represented by means of a tree diagram. This was not in keeping with the approach of SPE, which endeavoured to capture all relevant phonological information about a word in a representation consisting of a string which formed a single line of structure. However, a syllable tree diagram is not a single line. The strings of segments are grouped together, in much the same way that words are grouped together in syntax to form phrases. Because syllabic theory rejects the single-line or **linear** approach, it is often referred to as a type of **non-linear phonology**.

Why are syllables important in phonological theory? There are three main reasons. First, when we look at the word stock of languages we find that they conform to certain organizational principles. For instance, in English there are no words which begin with the sequence /kn/. A name such as the monosyllabic Scandinavian *Knut* /knuːt/ is unpronounceable in English. An English speaker trying to pronounce it would most likely introduce a schwa and pronounce the word as /kənuːt/ (much as in the name *Canute*). Such sequences are possible in other languages, of course, but it is part of what an English speaker knows about English that /kn/ is not a possible way to begin an English syllable.

The general term for the type of constraint which governs the possible sequences of sounds is **phonotactic constraint** (phonotactic meaning roughly, 'the way in which sounds are arranged or ordered'). Some constraints apply to the level of morphemes, while others apply to the level of whole words. However, a great many constraints in a given language will tend to apply at the level of syllable structure. This is true of the /kn/ constraint, for instance. This is one of the major reasons why syllable structure is of such importance in phonology. Appeal to syllable structure will help us to understand why words and morphemes are constrained to take the forms they take.

Syllable structure also plays an important role in the organization of the phonological processes of a language. This often occurs through the operation of syllabically based phonotactic constraints. Many of the processes we saw in chapter 2 are motivated by the need to respect constraints. For example, epenthesis is generally found precisely where the morphology of the language combines morphemes in such a way as to result in a violation of the phonotactics, creating, say, an illicit consonant cluster, or when the underlying form of a morpheme violates the phonotactic constraints and has to be 'repaired' before it can be pronounced. Consider again the case of Koryak, introduced briefly in chapter 2, section 2.4.3. There we saw that a number of morphemes have no vowels in underlying representation, e.g. those illustrated in 2.36, repeated here as 3.1.

3.1   a.   //t-pŋlo-n//
       b.   //mt-pŋlo-n//
       c.   //na-pŋlo-n//

These give rise to the words in 3.2:

3.2   a.   təpŋəlon   'I asked him'
       b.   mətpəŋlon   'we asked him'
       c.   napŋəlo-n   'they asked him'

I argued that these surface forms can be considered the result of a rule of epenthesis which applies from left-to-right and inserts a schwa whenever one is needed. Let us investigate this in a little more detail.

The maximal syllable permitted in Koryak is CVC – onset-nucleus-coda. Consider the UR //tpŋlon//. We will try to fit it to our template step by step. The first consonant /t/ is a possible onset. However, the sequence /tp/ is not an onset. Therefore, we have to epenthesize a schwa after /t/ in order to form a possible syllable. This gives us the intermediate form /təpŋlon/, in which /təp/ is a possible syllable. The next sequence is /təpŋ/. This is not a permissible syllable, but it could become so if the next sound is a vowel, when /ŋ/ would form the onset to the second syllable. Proceeding, we find that the next member of the sequence is /l/: /təpŋl/. This can only be syllabified by resort to another schwa to give /təpŋəl/. Finally, we add /on/ to get the surface form /təpŋəlon/.

What we have illustrated here is a simple example of a syllabification procedure (usually known as a **Syllabification Algorithm**). Clearly, if our analysis is correct, the epenthesis process of Koryak cannot be stated without reference to such a procedure. This illustrates one of the major roles that the syllable plays in contemporary phonology.

Finally, it is sometimes the case that a phonological process can best be understood as operating at the level of the syllable or some constituent of the syllable. For instance, a rule might affect a consonant but only if it is in the onset of a syllable. In other cases, it may be the rhyme constituent which is the locus of a phonological process. We will investigate this in more detail in chapters 5 and 6.

In short, an understanding of syllable structure is essential for an understanding of the phonological organization of a language. This chapter is therefore devoted to the way syllables are structured and the way that they help determine phonotactic constraints.

3.1   Quantity vs. Quality

In section 1.3.2 we were introduced to the basics of syllable structure. In this section we will examine syllables in rather more detail and see what principles underlie the division of words into syllables. We have seen that the syllable can be represented as an onset followed by a rhyme, and the rhyme itself may be made up of a nucleus followed by a coda. An important aspect of this type of representation is the fact that the syllable is regarded as made up of smaller units hierarchically arranged, as illustrated in the tree diagram for *strengths*, repeated here as 3.3

3.3

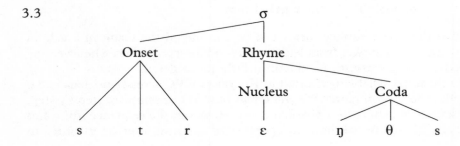

One distinction which turns out to be very important is that between a simple constituent containing just one element, and a constituent containing several elements. Compare the tree in 3.3 with those in 3.4:

3.4   a.   b.   c.   d.   e.   f.

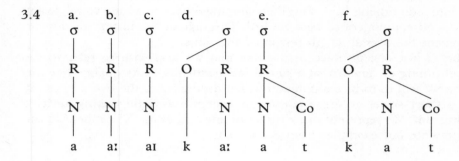

In 3.4a we have a maximally simple syllable, akin to the first syllable of the word *acid*. This syllable cannot, of course, exist as a separate word in its own right in English, because it consists of a short vowel. There is a single nucleus, forming the unique element in the rhyme, which is the only constituent of the syllable. In 3.4b, c, the syllable is slightly more complex in that the nucleus is a long vowel or a diphthong. In 3.4d we see a simple example of a syllable with just an onset but no coda. In 3.4e, the syllable has a coda but no onset. Thus, these examples tell us that neither the onset nor the coda is an essential or obligatory part of the syllable in general. This level of freedom is not permitted to all languages, as we will see later. Finally, in 3.4f we have a syllable with both onset and coda.

We will discover that the number of sounds occupying a given constituent can be extremely important for the organization of the phonological system of a language. In particular, the number of sounds which make up the nucleus or the coda can be of importance for a variety of phonological phenomena, especially stress placement. Many languages distinguish between two types of syllable. In the first there is a short vowel in the nucleus and no coda. In the second type, there is a long vowel or diphthong in the nucleus, or there is a coda (or both). A syllable of the first type, of the form CV, is called **light**, while a syllable of the second type, CVː, CVV or CVC (or CVVC, CVCC etc.) is called **heavy**. The property of being light or heavy is, naturally enough, referred to as syllable **weight**. For this, and a variety of other reasons, it turns out to be very useful to distinguish between the sounds themselves and the number of segments in a syllable.

Now, long vowels usually behave phonologically like diphthongs. For instance, a long vowel often develops into a diphthong. In many accents of English, the vowel I have transcribed as [iː] is pronounced more like [ɪi] or even [ij]. In British RP, the [eɪ] diphthong developed from an earlier long [eː], which is how the vowel is still pronounced today in many dialects, including General American. On the other hand, it is also common for diphthongs to turn into long vowels in historical change. For instance, in South African English the [aɪ] diphthong has become a long vowel [ɑː]. In Czech we find both processes taking place at different times. Thus, the word [duːm] 'house', corresponds to an earlier form [dɔːm]. The long vowel then split into a diphthong [u̯o]. This then simplified back to a long vowel, losing the second component to become [uː]. Throughout the history of this development the overall length remained the same.

This is just one instance of the way that we may wish to refer to the overall timing or quantity of a sound independently of its quality. For this reason we will introduce a notation which distinguishes the two. Let us say that a short vowel or single consonant occupies a single **timing unit** or **timing slot**. We represent this abstract timing unit as an 'X' symbol. We can then rewrite our examples from 3.4 as 3.5:

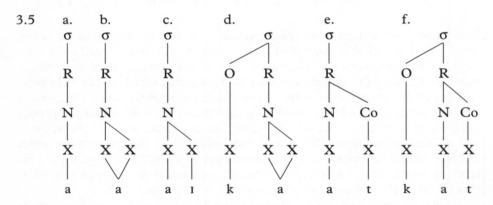

3.5   a.   b.   c.   d.   e.   f.

The different levels in such a hierarchical representation are known as **tiers**. Of particular importance are the lower two. The level at which we distinguish just timing units is referred to as the **timing tier** (or more colloquially, the 'X-tier'). The level at which we characterize the quality of the sound is called the **melody tier**. The sound qualities represented by the symbols /a k t/ and so on in 3.5 are called **melodies**. This unusual terminology derives from the earliest studies of tier structure which involved tone languages. It makes much more sense to speak about a tonal melody than a melody consisting of vowels and consonants, but the terminological extension has stuck.

This additional level of structure allows us to give a more parsimonious characterization of the difference between a light syllable and a heavy one. The syllable illustrated in 3.5a is a light syllable, while the others are all heavy. In 3.5b, c, d the nucleus constituent consists of two timing slots. When discussing tree diagrams of this sort in linguistics, we can say that the nucleus constituent branches. In addition, we can say that the whole of the rhyme constituent branches in 3.5e, f, because the rhyme is comprised of two constituents, a nucleus and a coda. Since the nucleus is a subconstituent

of the rhyme, if the nucleus branches, then we can also say that the rhyme
of which it is a constituent branches. Thus, we can say that a syllable is
heavy if it has a branching rhyme and light otherwise.

Having separated the melodic tier and the timing tier we can talk about
the melodic content of a syllable independently of quantity. As a consequence, we can represent a long vowel (or a geminated consonant) as a
single melodic element attached to two timing slots, as in 3.5b. This makes
a long vowel look rather similar to a diphthong. This helps bring out the
similarities between the two types of vowel. It means, for instance, that we
can represent the two Czech sound changes mentioned above as in 3.6:

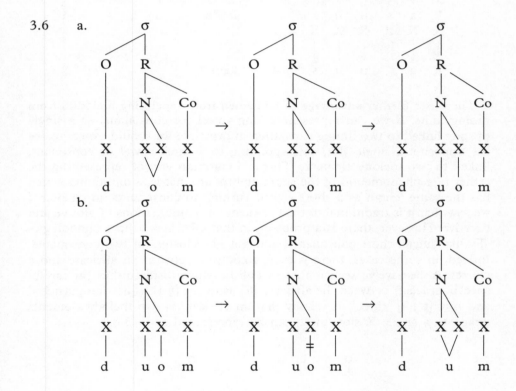

In 3.6a, the long vowel is reanalysed as a sequence of two identical short
vowels and the second component then raised to [u]. In 3.6b, the link
between the /o/ melody and its timing slot is severed. This is **delinking** or
dissociation, shown by a symbolic cut. The /u/ melody element is then associated with the vacated timing slot. This is **relinking** or **reassociation**.

A related advantage to this separation comes from a common phonological process of compensatory lengthening introduced in chapter 2. In many
languages the loss of a coda consonant leads to a lengthening of the nucleus
of that syllable. The two components of this process are linked rather than

being just two independently operative processes which accidentally occur together, because in those languages that exhibit it we do not generally find the lengthening without the coda deletion. Moreover, compensatory lengthening is a frequent phenomenon in the world's languages. We can represent the process very simply by virtue of separating the timing tier from the melody. Consider the change in Latin shown in example 2.44 from chapter 2, *kasnus → ka:nus* 'grey'. This can be represented as in 3.7:

3.7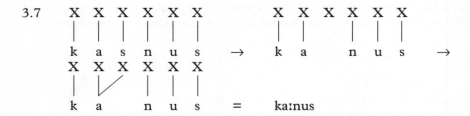

There is a further advantage to be gained from separating melodies from timing units. If we can represent a long vowel (or consonant) as a single melody linked to two timing slots, then in principle we should expect to see the opposite: a single slot, corresponding to a short vowel or consonant, linked to two melody elements. This is a common way of representing the rather rare phenomenon of the short diphthong, that is, a diphthong which has the same length as a short vowel. Turning to consonants, in chapter 2 we saw that it is traditional to treat affricates as combinations of plosive and fricative. However, there is a problem, in that affricates behave phonologically like single, short consonants, and not like clusters of two consonants. Indeed, in some cases, there is even a contrast between an affricate and a cluster. A case we've seen is that of Polish, which distinguishes (in careful speech, at least) between the affricate [ʧ] as in *czy* [ʧ ɨ] '(question particle)' and *trzy* [t ʃ ɨ] 'three'. If we say that an affricate is two melody elements linked to a single X slot, these can be represented as in 3.8:

3.8   a.   b.

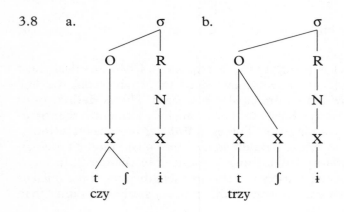

Finally, in languages that have both true geminates and fake geminates the two types often behave differently. A common pattern, for instance, is to find that fake geminates can be broken up by epenthesis, while true geminates cannot be. Thus, we need some way of representing the two types which will distinguish them. The simplest assumption to make is that a true geminate is effectively like a long vowel, that is, a single melody element linked to two timing slots. On the other hand, a fake geminate arises when a morpheme ending in a given consonant happens to be combined with a morpheme beginning with the same consonant. In that case, it makes more sense to assume that each consonant is linked to its own timing slot, and the fact that they are identical is then purely accidental.

Returning to our Archi geminates (p. 25) we can then propose the representations in 3.9a, b for the two forms [ʔasˢas] and [kʼossas]:

3.9   a.   X   X   X   X   X   X
            | | \ / | |
            ʔ   a   s̄   a   s

      b.   X   X   X   X   X   X
            | | | | | |
            kʼ   o   s   s   a   s

3.2   Syllable Types

Much of this chapter will be concerned with English syllable structure. However, to begin, we'll briefly survey the sorts of syllable structure that we find across the world's languages, to see what place English occupies. We've seen that the only obligatory constituent of the syllable is the nucleus, the head of the rhyme. In English no further constituent is necessary, as we saw in 3.5. However, this degree of freedom is not enjoyed by all languages. In Hawaiian, for instance, and a number of other languages of the Pacific, no codas at all are allowed, that is, the language only permits open syllables and prohibits closed syllables. Here are some English loans into Hawaiian (note that Hawaiian has no /t s/ phonemes):

3.10   welaweka   'velvet'
        wekekeː   'whiskey'
        halaki   'Charlotte'
        maːkeke   'market'
        kikiki   'ticket'
        kolokeː   'croquet'
        kilipaki   'Gilbert'

(Elbert and Pukui 1979: 28)

Hawaiian does, however, permit onsetless syllables: *aloha* 'love', *iwi* 'eel'. Thus, all the syllables of the language have the form V or CV (where V = vowel, C = consonant). More succinctly, we can say that there is a **template** for syllables in Hawaiian which can be represented as (C)V. The parentheses indicate an optional element in the template.

In some cases we find that an onset is an obligatory constituent of a language's syllables. This is true, for instance, of Modern Standard Arabic. There are words in Arabic which behave phonologically as though they began with a vowel in certain contexts, for example when combined with certain sorts of other words. However, in other contexts, for instance, in isolation, these apparently vowel-initial words always begin with the glottal stop phoneme. A similar picture emerges from German. Although it might appear from the orthography that German has words (hence syllables) beginning in a vowel, these are always pronounced with a glottal stop. The glottal stop isn't a phoneme in German, it merely indicates the beginning of an otherwise onsetless syllable. Moreover, in Arabic and German we never find two vowels together in adjacent syllables not separated by a consonant. The conclusion is that, in these languages an onset is obligatory.

Interestingly, when children are acquiring the phonological system of their language, a great many begin by going through a phase which seems to include both the Arabic/German constraint and the Hawaiian constraint, so that all syllables for such children consist of exactly one consonant followed by one vowel. Moreover, there are no languages in which the CV type of syllable is not found. For these reasons, we may regard the CV syllable as a basic type, often referred to as the **core syllable**.

The vast majority of languages permit syllables which are rather more complex than the core CV syllable. In English, very nearly the most complex syllable type is illustrated by our earlier example *strengths*, which has a structure CCCVCCC. The Slav languages permit rather more complex clusters, a number of which are quite impossible in English, e.g. Czech /fsplanout/ 'to flare up', /tkviːt/ 'to consist of', /ftʃlenit/ 'to include', /msta/ 'vengeance', while Polish adds examples such as /krnombrnɪ/ 'unruly' (two syllables only!). The Siberian language Itel'men (spoken in Kamchatka) provides splendid examples of consonant clusters both in onset and coda position (Volodin 1976): *tksxqzukitʃen* 'I wanted to eat', *ktwelʲknen* 'he brought it', *ktimplʲx* 'bring it', *k'anʲtʃpx* 'teach him'.

There is a strong tendency for languages to show an asymmetry in the choice of segments permitted in onsets and codas, so that typically a greater variety of consonants or consonant clusters is permitted in the onset than in the coda. For instance, in German there is a restriction which disallows voiced obstruents in coda position. In many languages of the Pacific, codas are limited to a nasal consonant followed by a consonant sharing the same place of articulation (**homorganic consonant**). In other languages, only nasals (e.g. /m n ŋ/) are permitted.

In general we find that a greater variety of consonant sequences is possible between syllables in polysyllabic words than at the beginning or end of a monosyllable. This is because the language treats each syllable as a separate entity. For instance, Japanese permits no codas at all except for /n/. However, we find plenty of words with CC 'clusters', where the first C is a nasal: *sinbun* 'newspaper', *honda* '(surname)', *tenki* 'weather'. These are possible because the initial portions *sin*, *bun*, *hon*, *da*, *ten*, *ki* are themselves possible syllables. Thus, *honda* is made up of *hon* + *da*, giving a sequence that is only possible between separate words or within a word. It would be impossible in Japanese to have a syllable **nda* or **hond*. Interestingly, in actual pronunciation these sequences respect the restriction that the final nasal of the first syllable is always homorganic with (pronounced with the same place of articulation as) the following consonant: [simbun], [teŋki].

Another twist, which is fairly commonly found in such languages, is that it is possible to have a geminated consonant between vowels. For instance in Japanese we have *rippa* 'splendid', *batta* 'grasshopper', *reʃʃa* 'train', *bukka* 'prices'. Such gemination is only possible in Japanese if the consonant is an obstruent, it is not possible with, say, /r/ or /m/. Notice that both in the nasal plus stop sequences and in the geminates there is still a prohibition against the two abutting consonants having *different* places of articulation, so even where a cluster is permitted there are still severe restrictions on its nature.

There is an additional, theoretically very important point to be made about syllable structure in the world's languages. For although there is a good deal of variation in the types of syllables permitted across languages, certain restrictions can be discerned. I have said that some languages have a constraint which states that all syllables must begin with an onset. Other languages, on the other hand, have a constraint which says that no syllable may have a coda (or may have only a very restricted set of coda types). In other languages, such as English, the syllable is free to exist with or without onset and with or without coda. This means that we can say that essentially the types of languages pictured in table 3.1 are permitted:

Table 3.1 Types of syllables

Onset obligatory	Coda prohibited	
Yes	Yes	(a)
Yes	No	(b)
No	Yes	(c)
No	No	(d)

Type (a) is the CV only type of language (perhaps exemplified by the speech of a good many children at certain very early stages). I don't know of any adult languages of this type. Type (b) is the German type. Type (c) represents Hawaiian. Type (d) represents English. Now, what is interesting about this typology is that there are certain types of language which we might otherwise expect to find, but which do not seem to be attested. These are languages in which (1) the onset is prohibited or (2) the coda is obligatory. Thus, there are no languages in which, say, the only syllable types are V and VC. This indicates that onsets have a certain primacy over codas, and this observation will be incorporated in due course into our discussion of syllable structure and the way it is computed.

Another way of talking about such facts is to make use of a concept of **markedness**. This is not a particularly well understood notion, though it is one which is regularly appealed to and discussed. The idea is that certain types of structure (e.g. syllables or segments) are relatively common and expected. These are referred to as **unmarked**. Other types of structure are relatively rare and unexpected. These are called **marked.**

As I mentioned in chapter 1, section 1.4, when we try to formulate general principles governing the world's languages as a whole, we speak about language universals. Thus, it is one of the universals of syllable structure that every language has core (CV) syllables. A statement such as this, which is supposed to be true of all languages, is an **absolute universal**. Another universal statement we can make about syllables is that if a language permits complex onsets (i.e. onsets consisting of a consonant cluster) then it permits simple onsets, consisting of just one consonant. As we learnt in chapter 1, a universal such this, of the form 'if A, then B', is called an implicational universal. Implicational universals are important in linguistics because they help reveal deeper patterns of structural organization which are common to all languages and hence to human language as a whole. The 'A' property of the implication is generally then the marked property, and the 'B' property the unmarked property. Both absolute and implicational universals are consequences of the organization of Universal Grammar (UG).

Where a structure is common throughout the world's languages we can say that it is **universally unmarked.** The core syllable can be regarded as the universally unmarked syllable type because it occurs in all languages, whereas all the other types are banned in some languages. Thus, a syllable with an onset containing five consonants is impossible in all but a small number of languages. We could call such a syllable type **universally marked**. The CVC syllable type is very common in the world's languages, even though it is not permitted or highly restricted in some. We can say that, at the universal level, it is relatively unmarked. In a few languages, the closed syllable is actually a favoured one. This is true of Itel'men, for example. In that language we would say that closed syllables are relatively unmarked. However, in Japanese, which only permits a limited set of closed syllables, we would say that the closed syllable is a relatively marked phenomenon. Finally, we can say that onsets are unmarked with respect to codas. This is implicit in the notion of core syllable and the universal which we deduced from table 3.1. While there are languages which prohibit codas, there are no languages which prohibit onsets, and although there do not seem to be any languages which require that all syllables have a coda (even Itel'men!), there are a good many which require onsets.

3.3   English Syllable Structure and Phonotactic Constraints

3.3.1   Consonant clusters

We will now explore some of these themes by examining English syllable structure in more detail. We begin with the onset. The first observation is that not all the sounds which are often regarded as consonantal phonemes can appear in an onset (at the beginning of a word, at least). There are three interesting cases in English, that of /ʒ/, /ŋ/ and /ð/.

The marginal phoneme /ʒ/ never appears word initially in native English words, though it can be heard in words (especially proper names) borrowed from languages such as French and Russian. Thus, we may hear *gendarme* and *Zhivago* pronounced /ʒɔndɑːm/ and /ʒɪvɑːgou/. In a sense, then, this sound is foreign to English onsets. On the other hand, the /ŋ/ sound is simply unpronounceable in absolute initial position. A word such as /ŋato/, which means 'man' in the Nilotic (East African) language, Dholuo, can only be pronounced properly by an English speaker after phonetic training. We'll see that there is a principled difference between these two cases. The sound /ð/ is an intriguing case of a phoneme with a defective distribution: it occurs word-initially, but only in grammatical (function) words such as *the, this, then, there, thee*. Content words borrowed from other languages (predominantly Greek) spelt *th-* are always pronounced with a voiceless /θ/: *thesis, theodolite, thalassaemia*. Hence, in a certain sense, /ð/ is not permitted initially.

When we look at two-membered clusters we see that there are significant constraints. Consider the list of words in 3.11a and compare them with the sequences in 3.11b, which are impossible to pronounce in English:

3.11   a.   play   b.   lpeɪ
              pray   rpeɪ
              puce   jpuːs
              dry   rdaɪ
              dwell   wdɛl

Clearly, the difference between each item in the list is the order of the first consonants. Notice, that each of the initial clusters consists of plosive (P) plus an approximant, either liquid (L) or glide (G). The sequences P+L or P+G are possible but the orders L+P or G+P aren't. More generally we can say that the order Sonorant + Obstruent is disallowed. This restriction on the distribution of plosives and approximants is not universal: there are some languages in which such combinations are permitted. However, it is very common to find such a constraint against the order Sonorant + Obstruent in the world's languages, and while there are a great many languages which, like English, would permit, say, P+L or P+G clusters but not

L+P or G+P clusters, there are none which permit L+P or G+P clusters while ruling out plosive + approximant clusters. In other words, the clusters of 3.11b are marked with respect to those of 3.11b. This observation can be couched in the form of an implicational universal, namely 3.12:

3.12   If a language has onset clusters of the type glide/liquid + plosive, it will also have onset clusters of the type plosive + glide/liquid.

The question now arises why approximant + plosive sequences should be marked in onsets relative to plosive + approximant sequences. However, before we address that issue, let's consider some further types of phonotactic constraint governing English onsets. Examine the two lists in 3.13 and 3.14:

3.13	twin	3.14	*tlip
	trip		*tnip
	tube		*srip
	snip		*pnip
	slip		*knip
	swim		
	suit [sjuːt]		

In 3.14 we find that certain combinations are impermissible even if they don't violate the markedness ban on Sonorant + Obstruent combinations. In particular, the clusters /tl/ and /sr/ are unpronounceable in English, as are combinations of a plosive and nasal. Again, I should emphasize that there is no universal ban on such combinations. In 3.15 we see a number of perfectly respectable words in Czech exhibiting these clusters:

3.15	/tliːt/	'to rot'	/tnout/	'to hit'
	/sriːpat/	'to scrape off'	/pnuciː/	'tension'
	/knedliːki/	'dumplings'		

However, it is noteworthy that even in Czech such clusters are rare compared with clusters such as *tr-*, *st-*, *pl-*, or *kl-*.
    Finally, consider the following words:

3.16	pueblo	[pweblou]
	Buenos (Aires)	[bwenos]
	fois (gras)	[fwa]
	voilà	[vwala]

These words all consist of /p b f v/ followed by /w/. They are all pronounceable in English, in the sense that English speakers can pronounce them. On the other hand, careful consideration will reveal that the only examples of such words are obvious foreign borrowings. There are no native words with these clusters initially. In a sense, then, we can say that clusters such as /pw/, /vw/ are impossible in English, even though they can be pronounced by native speakers and actually occur in a handful of words.

We thus have three types of impossible clusters. One type violates a very general markedness principle, (e.g. *rt-), the second violates some constraint more specific to English (e.g. *tl-), while the third seems to violate a principle of English, even though the result is pronounceable to English speakers, e.g. ?pw-. (The ? here indicates a form which is not entirely acceptable but less unacceptable than one marked *.). There is no generally accepted terminology for the distinction between *rt-/*tl- type restrictions on the one hand, and ?pw- types on the other (though some writers speak of impossible and non-occurring, as opposed to impossible and occurring forms). Let us therefore say that the clusters such as *rt- or *tl- are ruled out by **strong constraints**, while clusters such as ?pw- are excluded by **weak constraints**. We saw that the *rt- type clusters are excluded by a general markedness principle which leads to the prohibition of sonorant + obstruent clusters, while the *tl- type clusters are prohibited because of the identity of the particular sounds in the cluster (i.e. tl- as opposed to kl- or tr-). We can say that the constraints of the former kind are **structural constraints**, because they will ultimately be couched in terms of the constituent structure of the syllable. The latter type will be referred to as **collocational constraints** (cf. Fudge 1969).

There remains one final point to make about onsets. In English it is possible to have onsets with three consonants, as in *strength, spring, square*. However, it is interesting that only one particular consonant, /s/, is permitted at the beginning of such a three-membered cluster. Moreover, the only way to form such a cluster is to add the /s/ to a legitimate two-membered cluster, such as tr-, pr- or kw-. This behaviour makes /s/ special. Suppose we say that /s/ has the special property of attaching itself to *any* onset (though this is a slight oversimplification). Then, we will predict that it can form clusters with all singleton onset consonants as well as two membered clusters. In this way, we predict the existence of the clusters *sm-, sn-, sw-, sl-, sp-, st-, sk-* (though not *sr-, which has to be ruled out by a special collocational constraint). The problem of *s-* clusters will re-emerge in section 3.3.2 when we discuss the role of sonority in syllable structure.

We now turn to codas. The first thing to note is that consonant clusters are permitted in coda position. We start with clusters of two consonants. It will be important to consider just monomorphemic items first, ignoring, for example, all plurals and past tenses. This is because in English, at least, the situation changes radically when we look at such polymorphemic words. In 3.17 we see a representative (though not exhaustive) set of words with two-membered coda clusters (the examples with /r/ in 3.17c are only clusters in rhotic dialects, of course):

3.17   a.   lamp month land want sponge mince lens sink
        b.   help bulb elf film wealth melt cold pulse kiln milk
        c.   carp herb carve worth heart word horse marsh search barge
             work erg
        d.   grasp last risk apt lapse act axe

The first thing to notice is that coda clusters are somewhat more complex
than onset clusters. There is a large group formed from a nasal + obstruent
or a liquid + obstruent. Then there is a smaller group ending in two
obstruents. It turns out that there are severe collocational restrictions on
which obstruents can combine with each other in this way. However, for the
present notice that in the first three groups we find the order sonorant +
obstruent. In English it is quite impossible to reverse this order in a coda.
Thus, examples such as 3.18 would be unpronounceable:

3.18   *lapm *lezn *sikn *hepl *codl *pusl *capr *wodr *hosr

If we include morphologically complex words, then we see that the possibilities are greatly increased. The additional combinations include those
illustrated by the words of 3.19:

3.19   rubbed   watched   judged   rigged
        loved   loathed   raised   rouged
        jammed   hanged
        rubs   loves   jams   rigs   hangs
        depth   eighth   fifth

English also has three membered clusters, such as *prompt, against, next,* and
even four membered clusters from plurals or past tenses, such as *prompts,
glimpsed, sculpts, twelfths, texts, sixths* and *thousandths*). It is noticeable that these
all involve the addition of some sort of coronal obstruent (/s z t d θ/).
   These additional combinations are produced by addition of the plural and
3sg. agreement morpheme /s, z/, the past tense morpheme /t, d/ and the
denominal morpheme and ordinal number morpheme /θ/. Notice that this
produces an interesting effect, in that any word ending in certain clusters
will automatically be perceived as morphologically complex. Thus, we know
that the words *depth, fifth, watched, hanged,* and especially such cases as *texts*
or *twelfths* must consist of at least two morphemes (*deep + th, five + th, watch
+ d, hang + d, text + s, twelve + th + s*) solely from the phonology. Very few
languages seem to have this sort of property.
   In discussing syllable structure I have simply stipulated that a syllable
consists of onset followed by rhyme. However, we haven't yet seen any
strong evidence favouring the existence of a rhyme constituent. One of the
reasons why many phonologists argue for rhymes (as opposed to, say, a

constituent consisting of onset + nucleus) is that a language will often have collocational restrictions between nucleus and coda, but seldom between onset and nucleus. This is explicable if we assume a special connection between nucleus and coda. We can then borrow a concept from syntax and say that a syllable head 'selects' (or fails to select) particular types of codas, much as a transitive verb selects an object, while an intransitive verb fails to select one. An example from English is the restriction on the codas possible after the diphthong /aʊ/. Consider the data in 3.20:

3.20   a.   dine   dime
              tight   type   tyke
              bride   bribe
              nice   knife
              rise   drive

        b.   down   */daʊm/   */daʊŋ/
              tout   */taʊp/   */taʊk/
              proud   */praʊb/   */praʊg/
              nous   */naʊv/
              rouse   */raʊv/

What these data suggest is that it is impossible for /aʊ/ to be followed by a coda whose place of articulation is other than coronal. In other words, /aʊ/ cannot be followed by labial or velar consonants.[1] This is a weak constraint, since English speakers do not seem to experience any great difficulty saying things like /daʊm/, it is just that such sequences sound very un-English.

Another constraint that has been discussed in structural terms concerns the rhyme as a whole, not just the coda. Compare the examples of 3.21 with those of 3.22:

3.21   a.   wind /wɪnd/   tent   ant   fund
        b.   wide   Tate   art   loud
        c.   wind /waɪnd/ taint   aunt   found

3.22   a.   wimp   kemp   bank   hunk
        b.   wipe   cape   bake   hawk
        c.   /*waɪmp/   /*keɪmp/   /*bɑːnk/   /*hɔːnk/

Sequences such as /aɪmp/ and /ɔːnk/ in 3.22c do not form permissible rhymes. The problem is that in these examples the rhyme consists of four segments in all, two in the nucleus and two in the coda. We can say that we get an illicit rhyme if (1) the final segment is non-coronal (i.e. labial or velar in English), and (2) both the nucleus and the coda are branching (see section 3.1 for the notion of 'branching'). This is illustrated in 3.23:

3.23   a.   b.

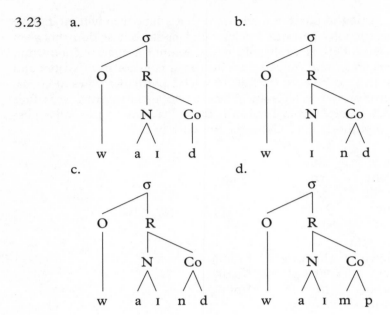

c.   d.

As you can see, 3.23d is excluded because N and Co branch, and /p/ isn't a coronal.

The point of this example is that, in order to be able to state such a constraint we need some way of saying 'the rhyme cannot contain more than four elements', which means that our constraint has to make direct reference to the rhyme constituent. The technical way phonologists do this is to speak of the **rhyme projection** of a word. 'Projection' in this context means just those specifically referred to structures that we are interested in. Thus, the rhyme projection of a word like 'context' will be /ɔn ɛkst/, i.e. the word minus the onsets of all its syllables. However, we can only refer to genuine constituents in this fashion. Hence, the phonotactic constraints offers some support for the notion of a rhyme. The notion of rhyme projection is of particular importance, as we shall see, in defining stress patterns, because in the overwhelming majority of cases it is only the nature of the rhyme which determines the position of stress in a given language, English included.

3.3.2 The Sonority Scale

I suggested in the previous section that there were universal principles governing some of the structural constraints on syllable structure. The most important such principle is based on the phonetic notion of sonority discussed briefly in chapter 1. There we distinguished between essentially sonorant sounds (vowels, liquids, glides and nasals) and essentially non-sonorant sounds (the obstruents: plosives, fricatives and affricates). However, sonority (sonorance or resonance) is a matter of degree. For instance, the vowel /a/ is clearly more sonorant than the consonant /m/. Indeed, /a/ is more sonorant than the vowels /i/ or /u/.

As a rough approximation we may say that Universal Grammar provides for a **sonority scale** for sounds, shown in 3.24, ranging from least to most sonorant:

3.24   obstruents < sonorant consonants < vowels

It has been known since at least the end of the last century that relative sonority is related to syllable structure (though in generative phonology it has been generally recognized for only about a decade). The peak or nucleus of a syllable is always the most sonorant element, while the onset tends to increase in sonority towards the nucleus and the coda tends decrease in sonority away from the nucleus. This tendency has been called by a variety of terms, but we will follow Selkirk (1984a: 116) in calling it the **Sonority Sequencing Generalization** (SSG):

3.25   In any syllable, there is a segment constituting a sonority peak that
         is preceded and/or followed by a sequence of segments with pro-
         gressively decreasing sonority values.

The SSG is another of our principles of UG, and the most important of the principles governing syllable structure.

We can see this tendency illustrated in syllables such as *plump* and *quilt*. In 3.26 I have represented these words using a **sonority grid** to represent the relative sonority of each segment in the word. The abbreviations are O = obstruent, N = nasal, L = liquid, G = glide, V = vowel:

3.26   a.   b.

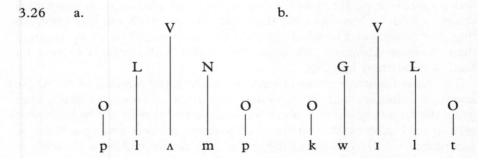

On the other hand, the sonority scale together with 3.25 rules out a number of the impossible onset types we mentioned in the last section, such as *lpeɪ, rpeɪ, jpuːs, rdaɪ, wdɛl jduː,* not to mention *ndeɪ, lmeɪ, wleɪ, jmeɪ,* and *pteɪ, tpeɪ, mneɪ, nmeɪ, lreɪ, jweɪ.* Likewise, it rules out a good many types of coda which aren't attested in English, such as those in 3.18. These are all sequences which are ruled out by a strong constraint. We can now see that the constraint in question is that embodied in the Sonority Sequencing Generalization.

The scale shown in 3.24 and the associated SSG can't account for the whole of syllable structure, even in one language such as English. This is because excluded onset clusters such as /pw/ or /tl, ml, rw, kn/ and so on respect the SSG. However, it is interesting to note that onsets such as *tl-, ml-, rw-* or *kn-* tend to be rare in the world's languages (cf. my remarks about the Czech examples in 3.15). In all likelihood the reason for this is that the sounds are too 'close' in sonority to make comfortable bedfellows. Recall that we decided in the previous section that it is only obstruents that happily coexist with other consonants in the onset. We can perhaps say that obstruents are sufficiently far from liquids and glides to form onsets, but that they are too close to nasal stops and that nasals themselves are too close to approximants to form onsets.

To make this idea buy us any advantage we need to refine the scale somewhat, to take into account finer degrees of difference. One influential suggestion is due to Selkirk (1984a). She proposes an index of sonority, with classes of sounds being given a numerical sonority value. A simplified version of her scale is provided in 3.27:

3.27   sonority scale
        vowels   /a, ɔ, eɪ, i, u/   6
        glides   /j, w/   5
        liquids   /r, l/   4
        nasals   /m, n, ŋ/   3
        fricatives/affricates   /v, ð, z, ʧ/   2
        plosives   /p, b, t, d, k, g/   1

Strictly speaking we could define a scale with finer gradations in which high vowels would be less sonorous than mid vowels which are less sonorous than low vowels, and in which voiced obstruents would be more sonorant than voiceless. However, this scale makes all the distinctions needed for English (and most languages).

The most notorious problem with this scale is the position of /s/. As we know, /s/ combines with more or less any onset to create a cluster, even when the following sound is a plosive, and we saw that /s/ has to be treated as a special case in this regard. But plosives are less sonorous than /s/ according to 3.27. Therefore, any *sp-, st-, sk-* cluster will be a violation of the Sonority Sequencing Generalization. Even if there were some clever way around this problem, we would still have to explain why English permits *sp-, st-, sk-* clusters but not *ps-, ts-, ks-.* We will just say that /s/ behaves exceptionally in English (as in many other languages).

Our brief discussion of syllable structure in English boils down now to the following: English permits two-membered onsets and codas, with exceptional provision for *s*C- onsets and a variety of special types of -CCC and -CCCC coda. This means that we can regard 3.28 as a kind of basic English syllable template.

3.28

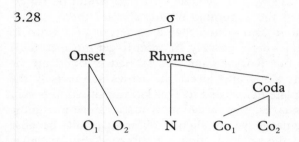

We can now state some of our structural constraints in terms of the sonority scale. For instance, O_2 must have an index of 4 or greater. Notice that the whole point of using the sonority scale is that these are all continuous intervals. The scale would have little meaning if we were obliged to set up restrictions such as 'the onset must have an index of 1 or 3–4'.[2]

Although the SSG represents a universal tendency in syllable structure, and although there are many languages that adhere to it in an exceptionless fashion, it is not an absolutely valid statement about all syllables in all languages. We have already seen the problem posed by *s*- initial clusters in English. Other languages present us with much more serious violations of the SSG. The examples of 'difficult' clusters from Itel'men given at the beginning of the chapter illustrate this. In the Slavic languages we frequently find consonant clusters violating the SGG (as you can tell from the Czech and Polish examples). Here are some further examples from (the conservative variety of) Literary Czech, in which we find words such as /rtuts̪/ 'mercury', /lbi/ 'of a skull', /jsem/ 'I am', /jdu/ 'I go'. In Arabic, we enounter a great many codas violating the SSG:[3] /misr/ 'Egypt', /daxl/ 'income, /d̪axm/ 'huge', /ħibr/ 'ink', /rubʕ/ 'four', /nut̪ʕ/ 'pronunciation'. Despite these exceptions, the SGG is an important generalization. When we consider principles of syllabification in section 3.4 we will see that considerable use is made of it even in languages which seem to violate it.

3.4   Syllabification Principles

3.4.1   The syllabification algorithm

Although we have spent some time discussing syllable structure, there is a sense in which this structure is redundant. For in English, as in most languages, the syllable structure of a word can be determined from knowing the segmental composition of the word. Thus, confronted with a sequence /kæt/ a speaker of English will know automatically that the correct syllable structure of the word specifies /æ/ as the nucleus, /k/ as the onset, and /t/ as the coda.

If this were all there were to say, then syllable structure would be superfluous. However, as we saw at the beginning of this chapter there are occasions when it is important to know the syllable structure of a word in order to apply phonological rules appropriately. In order to get the epenthetic schwas in the right place in our Koryak example, we had to build up the syllable structure as we went along and insert the schwa at precisely the points when the syllable template demanded it. This kind of situation is very common in the world's languages. The situation is made more intriguing by the fact that in some languages we get slightly different results because of differences in the way that the syllabification is performed. For instance, take examples 3.1a, 3.2a and apply the process from right-to-left. From 3.1a, repeated here as 3.29, we would then get the incorrect form 3.30 (check this step-by-step to make sure you understand why):

3.29   //t-pŋlo-n//   'I asked him'

3.30   *təpəŋlon

If all languages worked from left-to-right there would be no problem, but things aren't that simple. Itô (1989) points out, for instance, that we can distinguish the slightly different epenthesis rules of two different dialects of Arabic by assuming that in one dialect it operates from left-to-right while in the other it operates from right-to-left.

This means that Universal Grammar must provide for a foolproof, mechanical way of computing the syllabic structure of a word. In mathematics, a procedure with these properties is known as an 'algorithm', and that is the reason we referred to the syllabification process for Koryak as a 'syllabification algorithm'. The algorithm works in essentially the same way for all languages: we scan the string of phonemes and compute the syllable structure which best fits. Although phonologists are largely in agreement on the importance of the syllable there is less agreement as to how syllables should be represented and analysed and how syllabification works. I shall therefore present one influential way of looking at syllable structure, which has the great virtue of being relatively easy to understand. In section 3.5 I very briefly discuss an important alternative view which has been rapidly gaining currency amongst phonologists. You should be prepared to encounter further theoretical approaches to syllable structure, though most of them can be viewed as elaborations of the two approaches discussed in this and the next section.

To illustrate the principles we'll begin with the simplest case, that of a monosyllabic word, even though it may seem pretty obvious how the syllabification is supposed to work for such words. The basic idea is very straightforward: first, we scan the word for the most sonorous element, and identify this as the peak or nucleus. Then we assign consonants to the left of the peak to the onset position. Finally, we assign consonants to the right of the peak to coda position.

In fact, we can be a little more specific. As I mentioned in section 3.2, all languages have onsets, though some lack codas. Moreover, in a given language, codas are frequently more restricted in type than onsets. This is related to the notion of core syllable. This suggests that onset formation takes precedence over coda formation. Therefore, let's assume that we syllabify our word *cat* in three separate stages: Nucleus Formation, Onset Formation, and Coda Formation, as in 3.31:

3.31   a.   b.   c.

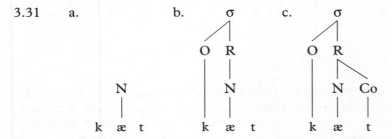

What are we doing in 3.31? First we identify the nucleus of the syllable and label it 'N'. We know that the nucleus must be the vowel /æ/ in this word because it is the most sonorous element of the word and hence, by the Sonority Sequencing Generalization, must be the peak or nucleus of the syllable. (Check that you understand how the SGG works for this case by drawing a sonority diagram for *cat* along the lines of 3.18). This process is Nucleus Formation. Next, we identify the onset (Onset Formation). Since an onset is a sister constituent to a rhyme this requires us to label the nucleus as (part of) a rhyme constituent. Simultaneously we can label the larger constituent consisting of onset followed by rhyme as the syllable. All this is shown at one fell swoop in 3.31b. Finally, we need to syllabify the final consonant by labelling it as a coda and attaching it as a daughter constituent to the rhyme (Coda Formation).

Cat is an easy case. Consider something slightly more complex: *catkin*. Here we have two vowels, each surrounded by consonants. In 3.32 we see the sonority grid for this word:

3.32

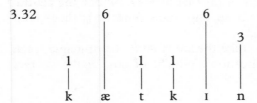

The Sonority Sequencing Generalization tells us that a single syllable (with certain exceptions) only has one peak. The word *catkin* has two peaks, therefore it consists of two syllables. Moreover, the two peaks are the two vowels /æ, ɪ/, as we would expect.

Having identified *æ, ɪ* as nuclei, we can identify the two *k*'s as onsets, giving us 3.33:

3.33.

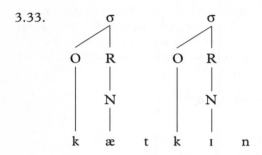

This leaves us with the *t* and *n* to syllabify. The *n* must form the coda of the second syllable. In principle, the *t* could either attach to the *k* to form a complex onset or form the coda of the first syllable. But since in English we can't have an onset consisting of two plosives, this only leaves the latter solution, giving us 3.34:

3.34.

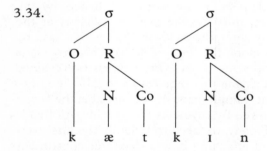

In fact, this is the solution we would have arrived at no matter what order we applied the separate stages of syllabification. This is because not only is *tk*- an impermissible onset, but -*tk* is an impermissible coda. Therefore, the only legitimate syllabification for the word is that of 3.34. Notice the central role of the phonotactic constraints. In an important sense it is these constraints which govern syllabification.

Things are not always this simple. Take the word *misty*. In principle, each of 3.35 could be legitimate syllabifications. Which, of any, is the correct one?

3.35   a.

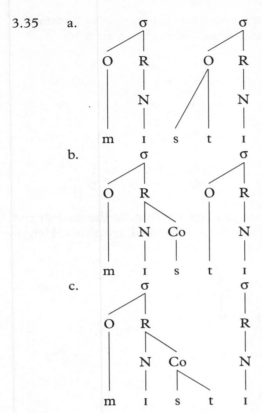

By recognizing the primacy of the onset, however, our algorithm can given us a determinate answer by selecting just 3.35a as correct. This will be true if we interpret the algorithm to mean that we associate consonants to the onset position as many times as possible until we run out of consonants, or we encounter a cluster which can't form an onset (such as -*tk*-). This seems to be the way syllabification is effected in all languages, and so we may assume that it is the result of a principle of Universal Grammar. The principle is important enough to have earned a special name: the **Maximal Onset Principle**. This can be stated very succinctly: maximize onsets.

Why should it be so useful to assign *misty* the syllable structure of 3.35a? The reason is that there are phonological processes which are sensitive to this type of syllable structure. We know that in English voiceless plosives /p, t, k/ are aspirated initially. Thus, the word *pear* is pronounced [pʰɛː]. On the other hand, this fails to happen when the plosive is preceded by /s/. Hence, *spare* is pronounced [spɛː]. Now, this happens in non-initial syllables, too, when they are stressed. Thus, in *repair* we have aspiration, [rɪpʰɛː], while in *despair* there is none, [dɪspɛː]. On the other hand, in a two word phrase such as *this pear* we again find aspiration. This is easy to understand if the syllable structure for *repair* and *despair* is as shown in 3.36:

3.36

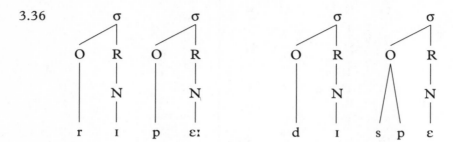

The aspiration is found in the phrase *this pair* because, in the normal run of events, two separate words will always be syllabified separately. Hence, they will give us 3.37:

3.37

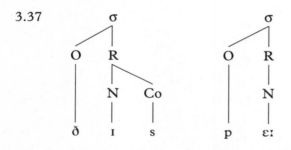

Finally, I said earlier that syllable structure can be determined just from the segmental composition of a word. However, I also said that it makes sense to think of a glide as segmentally the same as a high vowel in a non-nuclear position. But this means that when we encounter the segments /ɪ ʊ/ in a word we won't know whether the melody is to be interpreted as a vowel or a glide until we know whereabouts it appears in the syllable. But we can't determine that until we know whether it's a vowel or a glide. To see this consider the minimal pair *aeon* and *yon*. In 3.38 we see the two words syllabified:

3.38   a.

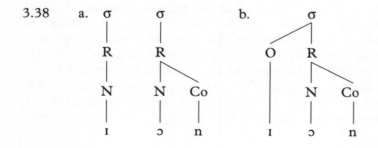

From this we see that the segmental composition of the two words is identical, namely /ɪɔn/. Clearly, there has to be some extra information provided to ensure that the two words surface with distinct syllable structures. The simplest way to do this (and one that has its analogues in descriptions of other languages), is to use the device of **prespecification**. We prespecify the /ɪ/ of *aeon* as a nucleus, as in 3.39a:

3.39   a.   N   b.
             |
             ɪ   ɔ   n   ɪ   ɔ   n
             'aeon'   'yon'

Notice that the syllabification algorithm, guided by the SGG, will compute a sonority grid for /ɪɔn/ in 3.39b in which both /ɪ/ and /n/ are less sonorous than /ɔ/. (Recall that we defined glides and high vowels as being slightly less sonorous than other vowels.) The simplest interpretation of this situation will be one under which /ɪ/ is a consonant. In other words, the algorithm will only interpret /ɪɔn/ as a disyllabic, rather than a monosyllabic sequence if it is expressly told that it is disyllabic (as in 3.39a).

Prespecification is only required in a handful of cases, namely, when /ɪ ʊ/ appears before a vowel. If a high vowel melody appears between two consonants then the only syllabification consistent with English phonotactics will be one in which the melody is linked to a nucleus. Thus, the syllabification algorithm will not give us the unpronounceable monosyllable [kætkjn] from //kætkɪn//, *catkin*.

Cases such as *aeon* are the only cases in which the syllable structure cannot be predicted directly from the segment structure. In other languages this indeterminacy between glide and high vowel is more widespread and it is possible to construct arguments in favour of the prespecification analysis (Guerssel 1986 offers one such example from Berber). Some phonologists would prefer to be able to predict syllable structure for all cases, however. For them it is therefore necessary to distinguish glides from high vowels in underlying representations. We will see how this can be done in the next chapter when we look at phonological features.

3.4.2 Ambisyllabicity

Thus far we have examined cases in which the syllable structure is relatively straightforward, because only one syllabification is compatible with the phonotactics or with other aspects of the phonology such as aspiration of voiceless plosives. However, matters are not always so clear cut. Moreover, although naive (non-linguist) speakers can usually tell very easily how many syllables there are in a word, in general they have very few reliable intuitions about the correct syllabification of polysyllabic words (and all too often when a

group of speakers does show strong preferences they are influenced by
irrelevant considerations such as orthography). Therefore, unless there are
straightforward phonological tests for syllable structure, it can be very difficult to arrive at a definitive syllabification.

The problem is exemplified by a simple case such as *happy*. It is far from
clear that the syllable structure for this word has to be [ha] [py]. Indeed,
there are actually good reasons for doubting this structure. Recall from
chapter 1 that English short vowels are generally unable to appear at the end
of a word without a coda consonant. Now, short /æ/ is just such a vowel.
Therefore, it is impossible to have a word /*hæ/ in English. Yet we have just
said that *happy* consists of exactly this syllable followed by /pɪ/.

One interesting way around this problem is to say that the second syllable
of *happy* has /p/ as an onset, but that the first syllable is also closed, by the
same /p/. In other words, we make /p/ simultaneously both the coda of the
first syllable and the onset of the second, as in 3.40:

3.40

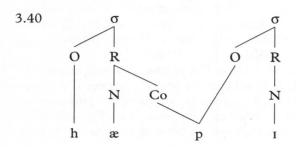

The property of belonging simultaneously to two syllables is called
ambisyllabicity. It is somewhat controversial, and by no means all phonologists accept the idea. However, the concept has been used by a number
of linguists to explain a variety of phenomena in which syllable structure is
implicated in phonological processes, including stress placement and the
aspiration of voiceless plosives in English. A defence of ambisyllabicity in
English can be found in various parts of Giegerich's (1992) overview of the
phonology of English.

3.4.3   Appendices to codas

We left our earlier discussion of syllable structure without deciding what to
do about the final clusters of words such as *against, text, midst,* and so on.
We noted that the number of such words, if we restrict ourselves to monomorphemic cases, is rather low. Moreover, it turns out that there are no
monomorphemic words with four final consonants. All of the cases cited
earlier are cases such as *sculpts, twelfths,* and *texts,* which are inflected forms.
However, if we include inflected words then we found that it was reasonably

common to encounter words ending in three consonants. The suffixes involved are the regular plural, 3rd sg. agreement, and the past tense. These
surface phonologically as [s, z] or [t, d] in such clusters. A small number
of other clusters are formed from the suffix /θ/, e.g. *sixth*.

There is clearly some sort of generalization to be captured here. The
simplest way of handling these data is to say that English permits any
number of coronal obstruents to be tagged onto the end of a syllable. This
would seem to make the coda rather a complicated animal. We need not
necessarily say that these extra consonants are part of the coda, however.
Since the majority of such clusters are formed as a result of suffixation
(indeed, usually inflection), they will only appear at the end of the word
itself. Some linguists have therefore suggested that they should be thought
of as special **appendices** to the final syllable as shown in 3.41 for the word
fifths (morphologically *five* + *th* + *s*):

3.41

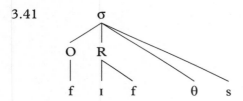

This treatment can then be extended to any coronal which appears after
another consonant in a word final coda, as in *convicts*:

3.42

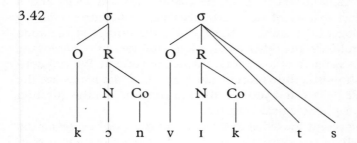

It is a feature of English that complex word final coronal clusters almost
always signal an inflectional (or occasionally derivational) suffix. Moreover,
when we consider the etymology of many of the 'monomorphemic' exceptions to this generalization we find that historically they derive from inflected forms. Thus, *midst*, which has a very unusual sequence of voiced
plosive followed by *-st*, is clearly a superlative form of *mid*. Similar remarks
hold of *next*, *whilst*, *against*. Moreover, while it is possible to find monomorphemic words ending in clusters of plosive + coronal obstruent following
a short vowel, such as *apt*, *apse*, *act*, *axe*, when the vowel is long, this is
only possible if the coronal obstruent is an inflectional suffix. Thus, *aped*

can only be the past tense of *ape, apes,* the plural/3sg of *ape, ached* the past tense of *ache, aches* the plural/3sg of *ache.*

There are further advantages to assuming that the final consonant of words like *apt, act,* and so on is a syllable-final appendix rather than part of the coda. One of the cooccurrence restrictions on English syllable edges is that a syllable may not end in two obstruents unless the second is a coronal. Thus, while *lift* is fine, **lifk* is not a possible word, nor are **atp, *atk* and so on. If the structure of *lift* is that shown in 3.43, then we can maintain a strong structural constraint on codas: the coda cannot contain two obstruents:[4]

3.43

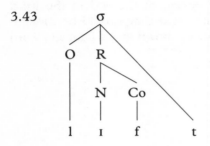

3.5   Moras

We have been assuming a hierarchical structure which splits syllables into an onset and a rhyme, and which splits the rhyme into a nucleus and a coda. It turns out that neither of these articulations is uncontroversial. In Government Phonology, for instance, (Kaye 1990) the notion of the coda plays a very limited role. On the other hand, a large number of phonologists have questioned the existence of a separate rhyme constituent. We will consider this latter question in a little more detail here, since the issues are the centre of considerable debate and you are likely to come across the question whenever you look at phonological research.

If we wanted to represent the syllabic structure of the word *cat* using the fewest assumptions about structure we would assign it the representation in 3.44:

3.44

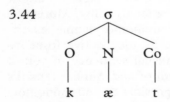

This is still a hierarchical representation, but minimally so. There is no further level of organization at which the onset/rhyme distinction is drawn. We often refer to such as structure, in which there are no intermediate constitu-ents, as 'flat'. Other things being equal, we would normally want to assume the simplest structures possible. This is a corollary of Occam's Razor, a principle attributed to the fourteenth-century English philosopher William of Occam, which states, roughly translated, 'don't postulate more theoreti-cal machinery than is absolutely necessary'. On the face of it, provided that a representation such as 3.44 is adequate, it should therefore be preferred over the 'standard' representation including the rhyme constituent.

Now, as it happens, this representation is sufficient for most purposes. For example, we can represent the word *catkin* as 3.45 and *misty* as 3.46:

3.45

3.46

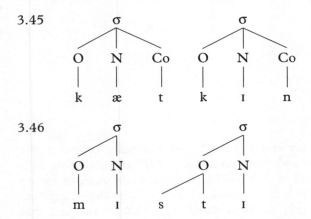

Why then does anyone imagine that we need a rhyme constituent? The main reason is that certain phonological phenomena, especially stress placement, can be easily stated if we adopt the notion of rhyme (or rhyme projection) whereas we have to make further assumptions of some kind if we adopt the flat structure of 3.44–6.

Representations such as 3.44–6 were adopted by one of the first phono-logists to study syllables within a generative framework (Kahn 1976) and in the extremely influential monograph of Clements and Keyser (1983). A summary of the ideas can be found in Katamba (1989). However, in this section I will briefly describe a related approach to syllable structure which makes use of the notion of syllable weight.

Recall that we distinguished between light (CV) syllables and heavy (CV:, CVV CVC) syllables. As we will discover, this distinction is of cru-cial importance to the understanding of a great many stress systems. With the rhyme constituent we can easily capture the distinction: a light syllable is one whose rhyme at no place branches, a heavy syllable is one whose rhyme branches. Without the rhyme constituent it is difficult to reconstruct this idea using the flat syllable structure, unless additional machinery is found. The additional machinery is the notion of a unit of weight or **mora**. We have already made use of the notion of timing slot. The mora is a rather

similar notion, except that a mora is a timing slot for any part of the syllable
other than the onset. We usually notate a mora with the symbol μ (Greek
letter 'mu'). If we return to the examples of quantity with which we began
this chapter, 3.4, we can represent the moraic structure of those syllables as
in 3.47:

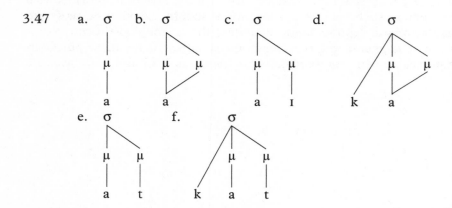

The distinction between heavy and light syllables is readily coded as the
distinction between a syllable with just one mora (3.47a) and a syllable with
more than one mora (the rest of 3.47). This is done without need for an
intervening level of X-slots, such as we provided in 3.5. Note that the onsets
in 3.47d, f are attached directly to the syllable. This reflects the fact that
onsets do not play any role in determining syllable weight and hence cannot
be constituents of a mora.

The moraic theory and the theory of syllable structure in which the
rhyme is a constituent make subtly different predictions about the behaviour
of syllables in certain phonological contexts. However, for many practical purposes they are identical in their effects. The crucial point about each is to
recognize the distinction between onsets and the rest of the syllable, a distinction which is central to all contemporary theories of syllable structure.

FURTHER READING

An introduction to English syllable structure is provided by Hogg and McCully
(1987), and by Giegerich (1992). Goldsmith (1990) discusses English syllable structure and sets this in a wider theoretical perspective. Fudge (1969, 1987) provides
a wealth of information about syllable structure and phonotactics. An introduction
to the Kahn/Clements and Keyser CVC model of the syllable is given in Katamba
(1989). A very good advanced introduction can be found in Roca (1994). Kenstowicz
(1994) provides an extremely detailed advanced survey of the issues. For a discussion from a rather different theoretical perspective see Lass (1984). Ladefoged
(1993) discusses syllabicity and sonority from the phonetic point of view.

EXERCISES

Phonotactic Constraints

3.1 Collect other examples of words such as *Vladimir, vroom!* What type of restrictions are there on such clusters?

3.2 Construct a complete list of English words with *s*OL/G- initial clusters (where O stands for 'obstruent' and L/G stands for 'liquid or glide'). What types of gaps are there? Is there a principled reason for each of these gaps?

3.3 It has sometimes been claimed that the English palato-alveolar affricates are really clusters consisting of a stop + fricative (i.e. [tʃ dʒ] rather than [ʧ ʤ]). Use the phonotactic regularities of English to mount an argument against this analysis.

3.4 Compare the kinds of onset and coda clusters permitted in English with those of any other language familiar to you. How can you most parsimoniously describe the difference between the two languages?

3.5 List other examples of monomorphemic words with four rhyme segments (ending in a coronal), whose codas begin with consonants other than nasals. Check that the generalization works with these other cases too. (If you speak a rhotic dialect, try substituting /r/ for the nasal.)

Sonority Scale

3.6 List the types of codas excluded in English by the Sonority Sequencing Generalization, giving sample non-words. Can you think of violations of these coda restrictions in languages with which you're familiar?

Syllabification

3.7 Transcribe each of the words below into your dialect of English (or the dialect of a friend if you are not a native speaker of English). Apply the syllabification algorithm to the words, showing each of the stages separately. Be careful to justify your choices at each stage. For some of these words special provision has to be made outside the syllabification algorithm proper. Discuss these special provisions:

craftier   funnelling   divulged   attempts   neofascism
withstands   syllabify   astringent   incriminate   kayak
re-align

Timing tier

3.8   In Tongan (Churchward 1953) there are ten vowels /a e i o u aː eː iː oː uː/. The normal position for stress is the penultimate syllable: *móhe* 'sleep', *mohéŋa* 'bed', *fetúʔu* 'star', *fetuʔúa* 'starry'. A word final long vowel is stressed: *kumáː* 'rat', *haŋéː* 'to be like', *kotokóː* 'to cackle'. A long vowel cannot be in a non-final stressed syllable. Thus, a form such as **húːfi* would be impossible.

When a suffix consisting of a single light syllable is added to a word ending in a long vowel, the long vowel is in penultimate position and hence the position where stress is assigned. This is an illicit position. What happens is the the long vowel 'expands into a double vowel, with the stress on its second element' (Churchward 1953: 11). Thus, adding the suffix *-fi* to *huː* 'to go in' gives *huúfi* 'to open officially'. This word has three syllables, not two. Likewise, from *fakaháː* 'to show' we get a nearly synomous verb by suffixing *-ʔi* to give *fakahaáʔi*.

Tongan has a phenomenon of 'definitive accent', in which the stress is displaced to the final vowel of any word at the end of a definite nominal phrase (e.g. a nominal phrase headed by the definite article). Thus, 'house' is *fále*, 'in the house' is *i he falé*, 'school building' is *fale áko*, 'in the school building' is *i he fale akó*, 'in the old school building' is *i he fale ako motuʔá* (from *motúʔa* 'old'). Vowel splitting occurs when a word ending in a long vowel is given definitive accent: *fakuháː* in the definitive accent form gives *fakuhaá*, while *poː* 'night' gives *poó*. When a word such as *huúfi*, which has undergone long vowel splitting, gets the definitive accent the long vowel is restored (because it is no longer stressed): *huːfí*.

Provide a description of these facts making use of the notion of timing tier. For these purposes you can assume that assigment of stress consists of adding a mark [stress] to some element of the syllable.

chapter 4

Distinctive Features

4.0 Introduction

In our discussion of assimilation processes in chapter 2 we saw how in connected speech a voiced fricative may become devoiced under the influence of a voiceless sound immediately after it, as when *five past* is pronounced [faɪfpɑːst]. What we need to say to describe this situation is that an aspect of the pronunciation of the voiceless plosive, a property of voicelessness, has been acquired by the preceding fricative. Phonological theory has developed a simple way of representing such a process. To begin with we can represent the situation before assimilation as in 4.1:

4.1

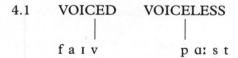

    VOICED   VOICELESS

       f a ɪ v   p ɑː s t

In this diagram, I have separated out the specific properties of being voiced or voiceless. I have shown this very informally for the time being by attaching the labels 'VOICED' and 'VOICELESS' to the relevant phonemes. The assimilation can now be described as the spread of the voicelessness property from the /p/ to the /v/, displacing the 'VOICED' label for the /v/, as in 4.2:

4.2   VOICED   VOICELESS

       f a ɪ v   p ɑː s t

This gives us 4.3, in which the former /v/ sound is now labelled as 'voice-less', and hence has become /f/:

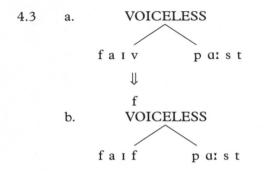

4.3   a.   VOICELESS

              f a ɪ v   p ɑː s t

                    ⇓

                    f
       b.   VOICELESS

              f a ɪ f   p ɑː s t

The first point about this sort of diagram is that we are talking about just one phonetic property, that of being voiced or voiceless. The next point is that we have assumed that this property has a life of its own and can be manipulated independently of any of the other phonetic properties of the sound. This is an important assumption which we will discuss in much more detail later in the book. For the present it doesn't matter too much exactly how this 'spreading' process works, the important point is that voic-ing assimilation clearly involves one sound giving its voicelessness to the previous sound.

There are a number of other processes involving other phonetic proper-ties which behave in a similar fashion. Instead of speaking of a 'label' or 'phonetic property', we will use the term **feature**. We will see that the idea of separating out features of sounds and allowing them to behave independ-ently in this fashion is very important for the description of a number of phonological processes, especially those involving assimilation. We can call this the **autonomy of action** property. A feature will be motivated in part to the extent that it fulfils this kind of autonomy function. Conversely, by examining the types of assimilation process which languages have helps us to identify which features show autonomy of action and which have to be postulated by phonological theory. Later in this and the next two chapters we will see a number of other examples in which phonological rules have to be stated in terms of assimilation processes involving individual features or groups of features. However, autonomy of action in assimilation pro-cesses is not the only justification for the concept of the distinctive feature, nor was it the first, historically. In this chapter I will devote most of the discussion to examining the second motivation for the feature concept.

4.1 Distinctive Features and the Classification of Sounds

4.1.1 The classificatory function of features

We have seen only a brief example of one feature in operation. However, phonologists claim that a sound can be completely decomposed into features. These features then give a complete characterization of the linguistically relevant aspects of the sound. Much research effort is currently being expended trying to ascertain precisely what set of features is needed to adequately describe any sound system in the world's languages. The traditional description of sounds given in chapter 1 presupposes that sounds fall into groups or classes. We will see that by identifying all of the relevant features of a sound we will thereby obtain a classification system for sounds. In addition, we will find that we can capture the notion of a natural class using features. We will call this the **classificatory function** of features. *→ natural class*

In earlier structuralist theories of phonology which prevailed in the 1920s to 1950s, the classificatory function was very important, since classifying sounds was one of the main goals of that theory. The most influential structuralist approach to features was that of the Prague School of linguists in the 1930s, and in particular the theories of two Russian émigrés, Trubetskoy and Jakobson. The principal motivation for feature theory at that time was to capture the contrastiveness of phonemes. Trubetskoy (1939) developed a carefully articulated theory of the notion of contrast or opposition, and much of his reasoning has been incorporated into contemporary theory. Jakobson (1939) first proposed formally the idea of features.

To take a concrete example of one of Trubetskoy's types of opposition, consider English obstruent phonemes. These fall into two classes, voiced and voiceless. Each member of the pair /f v/ or /p b/ is identical apart from this feature. Since such a sound may only have one or the other property, we can say that there is a **binary opposition** between the two classes of sound. The way that binary oppositions are notated is to say that there is a feature [voiced] and that it has two **values** or **specifications**, a 'plus' value and a 'minus' value. Sounds such as /f p/ are labelled [–voiced] while sounds such as /v b/ are labelled [+voiced]. A feature such as [voiced] which takes exactly two such values is called a **binary feature**. Sometimes, in order to stress that we have a binary feature, it will be referred to as the feature [±voiced] (read 'plus or minus voiced'). Using this notation we can rewrite the representations in 4.1 as 4.4:

4.4   [+voiced]   [–voiced]
            | |
      f a ɪ v   p ɑː s t

Because the features serve to distinguish one phoneme from another, they were called **distinctive features**. It is one the important claims of phonological theory that all speech sounds are not indivisible wholes but must be decomposed into sets of such features, or **feature bundles**, in an exhaustive manner. One of the main goals of phonological theory is to identify precisely the set of distinctive features required to describe the sounds of any language and to understand the phonologies of the world's languages.

The concept of the distinctive feature is of central importance to generative phonology. An influential system was devised by Chomsky and Halle in SPE. However, the only real role accorded to the distinctive feature in SPE was the classificatory role. The autonomy function of features played no part. In this chapter we will describe more recent developments in which the feature system fulfils both the classificatory and autonomy roles. This, it turns out, will also serve as a more sophisticated interpretation of the IPA classification. We will discuss a fair number of the consonants on the standard IPA chart, though we will concentrate on the relatively familiar by looking in some detail at the English sound system. For reference, a full set of the features used is given in appendix 4.3.

4.1.2   Major class features

The first set of features we will discuss are those required to partition sounds into their major classes. We start with the (true) consonants, vowels, liquids and glides. By 'true consonant' I mean obstruents and nasal stops. The most basic binary opposition is that between consonants and vowels. We can make this distinction by simply using one feature, [±consonantal]: consonants are [+consonantal] and vowels are [−consonantal]. In our discussion of the IPA classification, I pointed out that it is traditional to distinguish approximants from other consonants. This can be achieved by another major class feature [±approximant]. The value [+approximant] characterizes liquid sounds /l r/ and glides /j w/. The true consonants will, of course, be [−approximant]. On the other hand, vowels bear some resemblance to the liquids and glides, in that they don't involve a narrow stricture. Therefore, we can allow vowels to be marked [+approximant], too. How do we distinguish glides from liquids? We saw in chapter 3 that we can best think of a glide as a vowel in a non-nuclear syllabic position. However, the liquids behave like consonants. Therefore, we can easily distinguish the two classes by labelling liquids [+consonantal] and glides [−consonantal]. This leaves us with glides and vowels. These are identical in their feature composition so far, but glides only appear in the margins of syllables (onsets and codas) and vowels only appear in syllable nuclei, so the two types of sound are in complementary distribution. Given that we have a way of indicating syllable structure, there is no need to distinguish vowels from glides featurally. The major classes derived from [consonantal, approximant][1] are shown in table 4.1.

Table 4.1 Major classes from [cons, approx]

	cons	*approx*
true consonants	+	−
liquids	+	+
glides/vowels	−	+

The next distinction is that between obstruent consonants (plosives, affricates and fricatives) and other sounds (sonorant consonants and vowels). As I pointed out in chapter 1, there is a good deal of controversy surrounding the precise phonetic characterization of this property. In our discussion of syllabification in chapter 3 we saw that sounds can be placed on a sonority scale. The version I described had five values. Clearly, this is not a binary feature. However, in many respects phonological systems behave as though there were a simple two-way distinction between sonorants and non-sonorants (obstruents). We can therefore speak of a binary feature [sonorant]. Any sound with a value 3 or more on our sonority scale will be [+sonorant] and other sounds will be [−sonorant].

The sonorant consonants are those which are naturally voiced. In obstruents there is a stricture in the oral tract which reduces the resonance of the cavity, but which also tends to prevent the sound from being voiced. Thus, the 'natural' state for an obstruent is voicelessness. We often say that a sonorant is a sound which is spontaneously voiced. Any stricture which inhibits this spontaneous voicing therefore gives rise to an obstruent. Another way of saying this is to refer to a theory of markedness for segments. We introduced the idea of markedness in connection with syllable structure. Historically, however, the notion goes back to the structure of segments. The unmarked value for voicing for a sonorant is [+voiced] and the unmarked value for an obstruent is [−voiced]. Conversely, of course, the marked values for these sounds are [−voiced] for sonorants and [+voiced] for obstruents. It may seem slightly odd to a speaker of English to think of /b/ as marked compared to /p/. However, the testimony of the world's languages bears this out: if a language has no voicing contrast in the obstruents (a common situation) then the obstruents will almost always be voiceless. Lass 1984: 148ff discusses voicing in consonant systems in some detail.

These three features, [consonantal, approximant, sonorant], divide the sounds of a language into obstruents, sonorant true consonants, liquids, glides and vowels. The sonorant true consonants are the nasals. This classification is shown in table 4.2.

Table 4.2   Major classes from [cons, approx, son]

	cons	approx	son
obstruents	+	−	−
nasals	+	−	+
liquids	+	+	+
glides/vowels	−	+	+

Liquids and glides are usually sonorant. However, these sounds may sometimes lose their voicing. In practice, this means that the sound reverts to a kind of voiceless fricative. This leads to an interesting situation in the case of glides, since such fricatives will be very similar to genuine fricatives marked [+cons, −approx, −son], so that a change in the voicing would cause a change in all three of the major class feature values. In fact, it is quite common for real fricatives such as [v] [ʒ] to develop from glides [w], [j].

The binary features we have introduced each divide the set of sounds into two disjoint classes. In principle, all sounds are either voiced or voiceless, sonorant or obstruent, etc. What this means is that we have used binary features to **cross-classify** the set of sounds. In the earliest models of phonology based on distinctive features all features were thought to be binary, and so all features had this function of imposing a cross-classification. This is still true of many features, though we will modify that assumption for some of our features later.

4.2   Consonant Features

To aid our further consideration of distinctive features we will examine selected portions of the IPA chart of consonants. In table 4.3 we see a representative sample, grouped according to the place of articulation classes introduced in chapter 1 (labial, coronal, dorsal, guttural).

4.2.1   Manner features

We start with the classification implied by the rows labelled 'stop' (which for the time being I take to include affricates), 'fricative', 'nasal' and 'approximant', which we can broadly refer to as 'manners of articulation'. A

— unary features. (handwritten)

Table 4.3 Selected consonants

LABIAL		CORONAL			DORSAL			GUTTURAL		
p			t	ʧ	c	k	q	ʔ		stop/affricate
b			d	ʤ	ɟ	g	G			
ɸ	f	θ	s	ʃ	ç	x	χ	h		fricative
β	v	ð	z	ʒ	ʝ	ɣ	ʁ	ɦ		
	m		n		ɲ	ŋ	N			nasal
w			lr		j					approximant

major distinction is that between stops and continuant sounds. Recall that a stop sound is one in which air is prevented from passing through the oral cavity. This is true of plosives, and also of nasals, in which the air is obliged to pass through the nasal passages. In the case of fricatives and approximants the air can pass through the mouth. The feature distinguishing these two classes of sounds is [continuant]: stops are [−continuant], fricatives are [+continuant].

Depending on exactly how we define 'passes through the oral cavity' a lateral sound /l/ may or may not be defined as continuant. In some definitions a continuant is produced only when the passage through the midline of the mouth is free. On this definition a lateral would be a stop, because the air can only pass along the sides of the tongue, it can't go down the midline. However, on a more liberal definition of continuance, we might say that a continuant is produced whenever air can pass through any part of the mouth unobstructed. On this definition, laterals would be continuants. It doesn't matter for our purposes which solution we adopt (and it might even be the case that laterals behave as stops in some languages and as continuants in others). For English I shall arbitrarily assume that laterals are [+continuant]. Rhotic sounds will also be [+continuant], as will glides. This means that for English we can say all the approximants are continuants. Finally, we may ask whether affricates count as continuants or stops. In a sense, the answer is 'both'. The IPA transcription of affricate effectively treats them as a single segment whose first half is a plosive and whose second half is a fricative. This idea is pursued in greater detail in appendix 4.1.

When considering the formation of English regular plurals in chapter 2 (section 2.2) we found we needed to distinguish between those coronal fricatives which produce a relatively high level of turbulent noise (such as /s z ʃ ʒ/) from those that do not (e.g. /θ ð/). The simple way of drawing this distinction is to appeal to a feature [strident], defining [+strident] sounds as those which produce the higher noise levels. This feature is only of relevance to fricatives, so only those sounds marked [−sonorant, +continuant] will be marked for it. For other classes of sounds marking for [strident] will

Table 4.4 Major classes and subclasses of consonants (including glides)

	cons	approx	son	cont	nas
plosives(stop)	+	−	−	−	−
fricatives	+	−	−	+	−
nasals	+	−	+	−	+
liquids	+	+	+	+	−
glides	−	+	+	+	−

be undefined (i.e. it will have no meaning).[2] Notice that we are departing from our tendency to propose features defined in terms of the actions of the articulators. The feature [strident] is defined in terms of the *acoustic* properties of the sounds which bear it. Other [+strident] fricatives are the labiodentals [f v] and the uvulars [χ ʁ]. Other [−strident] fricatives are the bilabials [ɸ β], palatals [ç ʝ], velars [x ɣ], and glottals [h ɦ].

Phonologists are generally agreed on the need for a feature [nasal] to distinguish nasal sounds from others. Sounds marked [+nasal] have the velum lowered so that air can pass through the nasal passages, giving rise to nasal resonance. Non-nasal [−nasal] sounds have the nasal port closed off by raising of the velum. In fact, the distinction between nasal consonants and other consonants can usually be captured by distinguishing between obstruents, approximants (liquids and glides) and stop sonorants (nasals). However, the feature [nasal] seems to behave independently in phonological processes (just like [voiced] does in English Fricative Devoicing). For example, the vowel /æ/ in the US pronunciation of /kæn/ *can* is nasalized ([kæ̃n]), which can be readily thought of as the spreading of the [+nasal] feature from the consonant to the vowel. It is also usual to distinguish between /l/ and /r/ by appeal to a feature [lateral], so that /l/ is [+lateral] and /r/ is [−lateral]. A lateral sound is one made by passing air down the side of the tongue rather than over it.

Using the features introduced so far we can distinguish the classes of sounds shown in table 4.4.

4.2.2 Place of articulation features

Now we turn to the problem of place of articulation. We begin with the basic set of plosives, /p t k/.[3] The simplest way of distinguishing these would be to set up three features [labial], [coronal] and [dorsal]. However, it has become clear that the place of articulation contrasts do not lend themselves to analysis in terms of binary contrasts. When we consider place of articulation, we are considering a particular dimension of pronunciation which has several different points along it, and for the straightforward examples these different points are mutually exclusive. (Ladefoged 1993 has an extended discussion of this problem.) This means that, other things being equal, a simplex consonant cannot be simultaneously labial and velar, or coronal and glottal. This is not to say that it's impossible to have *secondary* articulations. There is no problem in imposing secondary features such as labialization or palatalization on another sound. However, to say that a labial stop has been palatalized, for instance, is not the same as saying that the stop is simultaneously a labial stop and a palatal stop.[4]

The upshot of these considerations is that labels such as [labial], [coronal] or [dorsal] do not make very good binary features. Another way of thinking of this is that the characterization of sounds as labials, coronals, velars (and uvulars, pharyngeals and glottals) does not involve a cross-classification. The way we will deal with this descriptive problem is to depart from the tradition of classical generative phonology as enshrined in *The Sound Pattern of English* (Chomsky and Halle 1968).

In the SPE classical generative approach all features were assumed to be binary, so that coronal sounds were marked [+coronal] and non-coronals were marked [−coronal]. That system involved a rather clever way of defining labials, without actually using a feature [labial]. It used a feature [anterior]: sounds made further forward in the mouth than palato-alveolars such as [ʃ] were [+anterior] while those made at the palato-alveolar level or further back were [−anterior]. Velars were therefore [−coronal, −anterior], and labials were [−coronal, +anterior]. This proved to be an ingenious way of classifying places of articulation, though one which departed radically from the more traditional descriptions such as that of the IPA. However, it was later realized that a feature [labial] is needed because labiality can spread in assimilations (as we will see in more detail in chapter 5). Thus, the classificatory criterion for features conflicted with the autonomy of action criterion. As a result phonologists introduced the feature [labial].

Adopting a binary feature [labial] doesn't solve the conceptual problem with place features, which is that places of articulation don't readily form binary oppositions. The most direct way of capturing a place of articulation is to simply label the place and leave it at that. Thus a labial sound can be marked just [labial]. We do not mark it [+labial], because there is no [−labial]. A non-labial sound is given some other place feature, such as [coronal] or [guttural]. Such features, which in effect only have one value, are called **unary features**. We can think of them as specifying a particular point along the dimension of place. This means that we can regard the descriptive place labels in table 4.3 as the unary features. In order to make it easier to distinguish this type of feature from the binary one, I shall write them in capitals: LABIAL, CORONAL, DORSAL, GUTTURAL. These features have the interpretation expected from our descriptions in chapter

— place features are UNARY

1. LABIAL sounds are made by means of a stricture involving at least one of the lips. CORONAL sounds involve a stricture made by raising the front part of the tongue, that is, the blade of the tongue or the tongue tip. In DORSAL sounds the stricture is made with the dorsum of the tongue, and GUTTURAL sounds involve a stricture produced by retracting the tongue root or by means of a laryngeal gesture.

We still need to make finer distinctions among the coronal consonants. The most distinctions are made in the fricative series, so we may compare /θ s ʃ ç/. The place of articulation of /θ s/ is very similar (in some languages, in which /s/ is a dental sound rather than an alveolar sound, the difference would be even smaller). The two sounds can be differentiated by appeal to the feature [strident], just introduced. Another feature often used to make this distinction is called [distributed]. A sound marked [+distributed] is one which involves a constriction down the central line of the oral cavity which extends for a relatively long stretch. Sounds made by the blade of the tongue have this effect, compared with sounds made by the tip or apex of the tongue. /θ/ has a laminal articulation, which means it is produced by bringing the blade of the tongue against the teeth. It therefore counts as [+distributed]. On the other hand /s/ is made with the tongue tip (whether against the gum ridge as in English or against the teeth as in French or Russian) and is therefore [−distributed].

To distinguish [s] and [ʃ] we must distinguish those sounds which (essentially) involve the hard palatal in their articulation (i.e. palato-alveolars and palatals proper) from those which do not. This can be done by differentiating between sounds made in the anterior part of the cavity and those made in the more posterior part. The latter involve articulation with the palate. Therefore, we need the original SPE feature [anterior]. However, unlike the SPE feature, our [anterior] is only needed for making a distinction between CORONAL sounds. We will say that a specification for [anterior] on any sound other than one marked CORONAL will be undefined. The phonemes /θ s/ will be [+anterior] while /ʃ ç/ will be [−anterior].

Finally, it is worth asking how uvular sounds can be represented. In chapter 1 I described these as a type of DORSAL sound. How, then, do they differ from velars? A velar is made by bringing the tongue body against the soft palate, which means keeping it fairly high. The uvula is placed lower in the oral cavity than the soft palate, so the tongue body doesn't need to be raised in order to reach it. Anticipating discussion of vowel features in the next section, we can adopt the traditional generative description and say that the velars are [+high] while the uvulars are [−high].

4.2.3 Laryngeal features

In addition to features referring to manner and place of articulation it is necessary to assume a set of features relating to the operation of the larynx, and the vocal cords. These features distinguish the different phonation types found in speech sounds. The most important of these for English is the contrast between voiced and voiceless sounds. Here we can simply use the binary feature with which we opened this section, [voiced]. However, in chapter 1 I mentioned that many languages use other types of airstream mechanism in the production of consonants, giving rise to glottalized or ejective sounds, and implosives. Other sounds, too, can be glottalized, including, in some languages, vowels, by closing the vocal cords and giving them a 'creaky voice' quality (though such sounds are not then referred to as ejectives). Another type of phonation found in a good many languages is aspiration.

Clearly, in order to describe this situation in distinctive feature terms we need to have a way of describing different states of the larynx in featural terms. Two features are commonly employed to capture these phonatory distinctions, following the analysis of Halle and Stevens (1971). For the present, let's just consider voiceless stops. The feature [constricted glottis] (often abbreviated to [constricted]) distinguishes glottalized from plain sounds. It refers to a gesture in which the vocal folds are drawn tightly together, preventing normal phonation, and causing the creakiness referred to earlier. It is the gesture required to make a glottal stop. The feature [spread glottis] (or [spread]) involves opening out the vocal folds so that air can pass through without causing them to vibrate. Aspirated sounds and /h/ are positively specified for this feature. Since the vocal cords can't be simultaneously constricted and spread it is impossible to have both positively specified at once, i.e. [+constricted, +spread] is an impossible combination. The combination [−constricted, −spread], of course, simply refers to plain sounds without any special phonation type.

By increasing tension in the vocal folds we obtain a voiceless sound. By decreasing that tension we get a voiced sound. This can easily be described using just the binary feature [±voiced]. In a number of languages of India we have voiced aspirated stops. These can most easily be analysed as the [+voiced] counterpart of a voiceless aspirate. There are no voiced ejectives, because this would require us to put the larynx in two incompatible states. However, the implosives (which are all voiced) involve a constriction in the larynx, just like ejectives. Therefore, we can use the feature [constricted] for implosives. This means that the features [constricted glottis], [spread glottis] and [voiced] can cross-classify the major types of stop system found in the world's languages. The resulting picture is shown in table 4.5.

In this table I haven't bothered to provide a value where the feature system disallows it, so that there is no value for [constricted glottis] if the sound has the marking [+spread glottis] and vice versa.

4.2.4 Distinctive features for English consonants

The picture so far can be summarized in tabular form, as in table 4.6 (ignoring certain features which are not necessary for making phonemic

Table 4.5 Laryngeal features for plosives

	constricted glottis	spread glottis	voiced
p	−	−	−
pʰ		+	−
b	−	−	+
bʰ		+	+
p'	+		−
ɓ	+		+

Table 4.6 Distinctive feature matrix for English consonants

	p	b	t	d	k	g	f	v	θ	ð	s	z	ʃ	ʒ	h
cons	+	+	+	+	+	+	+	+	+	+	+	+	+	+	+
approx	−	−	−	−	−	−	−	−	−	−	−	−	−	−	−
son	−	−	−	−	−	−	−	−	−	−	−	−	−	−	−
cont	−	−	−	−	−	−	+	+	+	+	+	+	+	+	+
strid							+	+	−	−	+	+	+	+	−
nas	−	−	−	−	−	−	−	−	−	−	−	−	−	−	−
voiced	−	+	−	+	−	+	−	+	−	+	−	+	−	+	−
[PLACE]	L	L	C	C	D	D	L	L	C	C	C	C	C	C	G
ant			+	+					+	+	+	+	−	−	

Table 4.6 (Cont'd)

	m	*n*	*ŋ*	*w*	*l*	*r*	*j*
cons	+	+	+	−	+	+	−
approx	−	−	−	+	+	+	+
son	+	+	+	+	+	+	+
cont	−	−	−	+	+	+	+
nas	+	+	+	−	−	−	−
lat	−	−	−	−	+	−	−
voiced	+	+	+	+	+	+	+
[PLACE]	L	C	D	L	C	C	C
ant					+	+	−

distinctions in English). The place features are abbreviated to L, C, D, G. A tabulation of this sort is often called a **distinctive feature matrix**.

4.3 Vowel Features

English vowels constitute one of the more complex of the world's vocalic systems, and we will not attempt a detailed description of it at this stage. Instead, we will look at some typical systems found world-wide and consider them in order of increasing complexity. One of the simplest, but still relatively common, vowel systems has just three members. By far the commonest variant seems to be the triangular system shown in 4.5:

4.5   front   central   back
       i   u   high
              a   low

A system of this sort is found in such diverse languages as Classical Arabic, pre-conquest Quechua, Aljutor (a paleosiberian language spoken in Kamchatka) and most of the Australian languages.

As we know from chapter 1, the crucial dimension of articulation which determines vowel quantity is the position of the tongue body. This helps define the acoustic properties of the vowel in terms of its formants. In a three-membered system of the sort shown in 4.5 there is sometimes a certain amount of phonetic leeway in the actual pronunciation of the sounds. However, /i/ is generally front and high, /u/ is back and high, while /a/ is low and often neither front nor back but central (though it may have a genuinely front or back articulation). Naturally, in many languages with such a frugal vocalism there is a great deal of rule-governed vowel allophony as vowels are influenced by neighbouring consonants, especially if the language has a rich set of consonants, such as the Eskimo languages.

The vowel triangle in 4.5 can be thought of as defining in the ideal case the extremities of an articulatory 'vowel space'. We will forebear from analysing such an unpopulated system in distinctive feature terms until we have some more vowels at our disposal. Let's embellish our triangular system by the addition of further sounds, inserted within the basic triangle. One of the commonest vowel systems in the world's languages has five vowels arranged roughly as in 4.6:

4.6   front   back
       high   i   u
       mid   e   o
       low   a

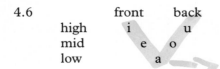

This type of system (ignoring length contrasts) characterized Classical Latin (which forms the basis of the spelling system of a great many languages as well as the transcriptional system of the IPA) and is the system found in a good many languages including Spanish, Greek, Czech, Tagalog, Swahili, as well as many contemporary varieties of Quechua, and many colloquial forms of modern Arabic (so-called dialects).

Normally in such systems /a/ behaves phonologically like a back vowel (though phonetically it is frequently pronounced rather as a central vowel or even as a front vowel (IPA /a/ or even /æ/). For instance, in Czech the vowel is phonetically front, /a/. The two phonological front vowels, /i e/ participate in lexical (morphophonemic) palatalization processes. For instance, a suffix beginning with /i/ or /e/ usually causes the velar consonants /k g/ to alternate with /ʧ ʒ/. However, suffixes beginning with /a/ never induce such palatalizations.

I have also shown the traditional descriptive labels for these vowels. We can easily translate these labels into binary distinctive features, by making reference to the body of the tongue. These tongue body features work in two dimensions: up-down and front-back. Ignoring for the present the problem presented by central vowels, we can say that there is a single feature [back] distinguished /i e/, which are [−back], from /u o a/ which are [+back]. Notice that [back] refers to the position of the tongue body. It is important not to confuse the [+back] sounds with the posterior (i.e. [−anterior]) sounds. The feature [anterior] refers to a region of the oral cavity, not a portion of the tongue (and in fact [−anterior] sounds are frequently [−back] in articulation).

In the height dimension we have a three-way contrast. Therefore, we need more than one height feature. The usual solution is to assume two features, [high] and [low]. Mid-vowels are neither high nor low, so they are given the feature specification [−high, −low]. (It is impossible for the tongue body to be simultaneously raised and lowered, so there is no class of sounds [+high, +low].)[5]

These three features are sufficient to distinguish our five vowels. In fact, in theory we could distinguish a sixth vowel, with the featural representation [−back, −high, +low], or a front counterpart to the back vowel /a/. Conservative (Literary) Slovak provides an example of such a six-vowel system:

4.7

	front	back
high	i	u
mid	e	o
low	æ	a

It might be noted that /u o/ are rounded vowels. Now, we don't actually need to use a separate feature for our five- or six-vowel systems to distinguish these vowels from others. However, there are more complex systems in which pairs of vowels occur contrastive solely in a feature [round]. For instance, it is not uncommon to find in a given language that non-low front vowels may be either rounded or non-rounded (German, French, Finnish and Hungarian are examples). This would give us the system shown in 4.8, which can be thought of as a schematic version of the Finnish system:

4.8

	front	back
high	i y	u
mid	e ø	o
low	æ	a

In order to account for such as system we need to characterize /i e æ a/ as [−round] and /y u ø o] as [+round].

Finally, another common distinction found in vowel systems is illustrated in the set 4.9:

4.9

	front	back
high	i	u
	ɪ	ʊ
mid	e	o
	ɛ	ɔ
low	æ	a

Here in the non-low vowels we see illustrated the distinction I discussed in chapter 1 between 'tense' vowels [i u e o] and the 'lax' vowels [ɪ ʊ ɛ ɔ]. I pointed out that this distinction, which is very important for the vowel harmony systems of many language groups, is generally analysed in terms of advancement or retraction of the tongue root, so that the tense vowels have the tongue root advanced somewhat, while the lax vowels lack this gesture. We can therefore assume a feature [Advanced Tongue Root] or more commonly, [ATR].

The vowels in the systems we have seen so far have fallen into a front or a back series. However, a good many languages distinguish central vowels, too. A very common six-vowel system is shown in 4.10a and a somewhat less common one in 4.10b:

4.10	a.	front	back	b.	front	back
high		i	ɨ u		i	u
mid		e	o		e	ə o
low			a			a

In 4.10b the sixth vowel is the schwa. Such a system is found in Chukchee and Archi. In 4.10a the additional vowel is a high unrounded central vowel. Such a system is found in Polish and (in stressed syllables) in Russian, amongst a good many other languages. How can we characterize the vowels /ɨ ə/?

The simplest and most obvious ploy would be to assume a feature [±front] in addition to [±back]. Then we would be able to define the central vowels as neither front nor back, i.e. [−front, −back]. However, there are two problems with this. The first is similar to the problem we noted with the features [high], [low], namely, that it would be physically impossible for a sound to have the specifications [+front, +back]. The second problem is that the front-back dimension differs from the height dimension in a crucial way: whereas it is very common to have a three-way height contrast between high, low and mid-vowels, we seldom, if ever, seem to get a pure three-way contrast along the front-back dimension. Thus, where we have, say, three high vowels /i ɨ u/ or /i u ɯ/ we almost always find that there is some other feature (typically lip rounding) which distinguishes one of the pairs. Thus, it is not clear that there is ever a purely *phonological* need for the contrast between front, back and central sounds.

For this second reason phonologists are reluctant to introduce an extra [front] feature. Instead, central vowels are generally treated as back vowels, since this is the way they tend to pattern. For example, both the /i/ and /e/ vowels of Russian and Polish are associated with lexical palatalizations (much like Czech), but not /ɨ/, which thus behaves like a back vowel. This leaves us with the thorny problem of how the feature system captures the phonetic differences between, say, the central [ɨ] of Russian and the back [ɯ] of Japanese, which I shall not discuss.

A particularly tricky vowel sound is the familiar schwa, [ə]. The problem with this is that it seems to be best characterized as lacking any features at all: it is neither high nor low, front nor back, and phonologically it will sometimes behave as though [+ATR], sometimes as though [–ATR] depending on the language. I will suggest a way of handling English schwa at the purely phonological level in a later chapter, but for the present it must be admitted that this sound is one of the least well understood sounds in phonology.

We have now seen how we may classify sounds into broad, descriptively sanctioned groups. Later in this chapter we will see how to organize the features for consonants and vowels in such as way as to allow us to formalize phonological processes in the maximally elegant fashion. In the next section we see how distinctive feature theory allows us to capture general aspects of sound systems in a satisfying way.

4.4 Redundancy and Underspecification

4.4.1 Redundancy rules and underspecification

So far we have assumed that all sounds are always specified for all the features that are deployed in the language. However, if we continue with this practice we will be allowing ourselves to repeat information about the nature of any given sound which is predictable from other features. In chapter 2 I briefly mentioned the notion of *redundancy*, in which certain properties of sound are predictable from its other properties. For instance, in English all nasals are voiced, sonorant stops. Thus, if we have specified a phoneme as [+nasal] we also know, automatically, that it will bear the specifications [+voiced, +sonorant, –continuant]. We say that the features [voiced], [sonorant] and [continuant] are **redundant** for nasals. In general, linguists eschew redundancy, and many phonologists in particular assume that phonological theory should permit such redundancies to be extracted from the lexical representations of words and morphemes, so that the redundant feature values can be specified by means of a general rule. Such a rule is called a **redundancy rule**. Since we are defining conditions on the featural structure of individual segments, these particular types of redundancy rule are sometimes called **segment structure conditions**.

I shall illustrate the notion of redundancy rule by consideration of the standard five-vowel system introduced in the previous section. Here it is shown in table 4.7.

The first, most obvious point is that given a specification [+high] we automatically know that the segment is also [–low]. Similarly, if a vowel is specified [+low] we know that it must be [–high]. We can capture this redundancy by means of a pair of rules such as 4.11:

Table 4.7 A standard five-vowel system

	i	e	a	o	u
back	–	–	+	+	+
high	+	–	–	–	+
low	–	–	+	–	–
round	–	–	–	+	+

4.11   a.   [+low]   ⇒   [–high]
       b.   [+high]   ⇒   [–low]

These rules tell us that whenever we have a sound marked [+low] we can also mark it [–high], and whenever the sound has been characterized as [+high] we can automatically mark it [–low]. These relationships are implicit in the very definitions of the features themselves. Moreover, they are universally valid, in the sense that, given the definitions of [high] and [low], it is logically impossible for any language to violate these rules. We may call such statements *implicit* redundancy rules, since they are immanent in the architecture of phonological theory itself, and not a specific property of any particular language.[6]

Redundancy rules are somewhat different in status and function from phonological rules proper and I have indicated this by using a slightly different notation (with a double arrow ⇒ instead of the single arrow →). The difference is that a phonological rule proper has hitherto been conceived of as a process which *changes* certain feature specifications or other aspects of structure. Such a rule is not unnaturally called **structure changing**. However, the redundancy rules *add* structure, without changing one specification into another. Such rules are generally called **structure building**.

If we consider just our five-vowel system, then it is also plain that other redundancies can be extracted, which are different in nature from the implicit redundancies captured in 4.11. For example, if we consider {i e} we can see that they are the only front vowels in the system. This means that there are no front low vowels in this inventory. Hence, we don't need to specify either sound as [–low] because this information is predictable given that they are both [–back]. In other words, [–low] is a redundant feature specification for these sounds. We can capture this fact by means of rule 4.12:

4.12   [–back]   ⇒   [–low]

It is important to appreciate that [low] is redundant for front vowels only when certain inventories are considered. This means that it (like any feature) may be redundant in one language but distinctive in another. For example, if we had the inventory in table 4.8, matters would be rather different.

Table 4.8   Table 4.7 +/æ/

	i	e	æ	a	o	u
back	–	–	–	+	+	+
high	+	–	–	–	–	+
low	–	–	+	+	–	–
round	–	–	–	–	+	+

Now, we can't say that [low] is redundant, because it is the only feature which distinguishes /æ/ from /e/. Thus, by changing the overall system, we change what is predictable and what is not. This means that the redundancy rule in 4.12 is very different in status from those in 4.11, in that such a redundancy rule will only hold of those languages with a vowel inventory such as that in table 4.6, in which [low] is redundant and not distinctive. In other words, this is a language-specific redundancy rule. ‖

Let's continue to extract redundancies from our five-vowel inventory. The vowels {o u} are the only [+round] vowels here, and both of them are back and non-low. Thus, from the joint specification [+back, –low] we can set up another redundancy rule, 4.13:

4.13   [+back, –low]   ⇒   [+round]

At the same time we can predict that any front vowel will be [–round]. Hence, we can add 4.14 to our list:

4.14   [–back]   ⇒   [–round]

We have already seen that all the [–back] vowels are also [–low]. This means that we can modify 4.14 to take this into account, as in 4.15:

4.15   [–back]   ⇒   [–round, –low]

Finally, we can observe that /a/ is the only vowel in the system marked [+low]. Therefore, once this specification is fixed we can predict the values of all the other features, since there is no contrast with any other type of [+low] vowel. This means that we can say that low vowels are [+back] and also that they are [–round]. We can therefore add 4.16 to predict the rounding and backness specifications of the low vowel:

4.16   [+low]   ⇒   [–round, +back]

There is an obvious implication from the fact that some sounds have redundant specifications: such sounds need not be specified for their redundant features in the first place. Depending on the membership of the

Table 4.9   Underspecified version of table 4.7

	i	e	a	o	u
back	–	–		+	+
high	+	–		–	+
low		–	+	–	
round					

Table 4.10   Table 4.9 after rules 4.11

	i	e	a	o	u
back	–	–		+	+
high	+	–	–	–	+
low	–	–	+	–	–
round					

Table 4.11   Table 4.10 after rule 4.13

	i	e	a	o	u
back	–	–		+	+
high	+	–	–	–	+
low	–	–	+	–	–
round				+	+

inventory, we can therefore leave certain feature values without any specification at all. This is indicated by leaving the appropriate cell in a matrix
such as table 4.6 blank, and we often speak of a **blank specification** or
blank value for such features. A matrix with all the redundancies extracted
in this way is called an **underspecified** matrix. The notion of underspecification has become very important in current phonological theory. These
underspecified entries are found in the underlying representations of words.
When a word is ultimately uttered, of course, all the different aspects of its
pronunciation have to be specified. Thus, we can think of the redundancy
rules as filling in predictable values of features when we finally come to characterizing the exact pronunciation of a given sound.

One intriguing consequence of our discussion of the vowel features is
that, given these rules we can predict all the specifications of [round] for
these vowels. In other words the entire feature [round] is redundant for this
system. If we extract the redundancies captured in rules 4.11–16 we can
replace table 4.7 with table 4.9.

The redundancy rules, as I have said, will fill in these blanks when we
come to specify the final pronunciation of a word. For instance, after the
application of rules 4.11 we will obtain table 4.10.

After further application of rule 4.13 we will obtain table 4.11.

Likewise, the other redundancy rules will fill in all the blanks to reconstitute our original fully specified matrix.

We have seen two conceptually distinct types of redundancy rule, the implicit type and the language-specific type. Despite the important difference in conceptual status between the two, there is a tendency to lump them together and refer to them all as **default rules**. Such rules apply 'by default', that is, when there is no other overriding characterization. Thus, other things being equal, in our five-vowel system, the front vowels {i, e} are always going to be [–low], and this is therefore the default value for such vowels. However, in the six-membered system shown in table 4.8, one of the vowels, /æ/, is unusual in being both front and low. Therefore, it must be specially marked as [+low], overriding what would otherwise be the default setting for the [low] feature.

Default rules are regarded as part of Universal Grammar, even when they are capable of being violated. The idea is that a language learner would normally assume that such a default rule applied to his/her language and would require some kind of evidence to the contrary in order to change that assumption. Another way of thinking of this is to say that systems which involve a violation of one of the universal defaults is in some ways more complex or unusual than a more well-behaved language. In other words, violation of defaults results in a marked phoneme system. The theory of markedness for segments is rather slippery and controversial. However, this is a fairly straightforward way of capturing the basic idea behind markedness, which is that certain sorts of system are more frequent, easier to learn and so on than others.

Having seen how underspecification works for a simple vowel system, let's see how it might be applied to the rather more complex case of the English consonants. If we look at the distinctive feature matrix for consonants in table 4.1 we notice at once a number of redundancies as well as a number of minimally contrastive features.

The [voiced] feature is a clear example of a contrastive feature, since /p b/, /t d/ and so on differ solely in voicing. However, even this is not contrastive for all sets of consonants. The sonorants, for instance, are all [+voiced] underlyingly (English lacks, say, a voiceless lateral of the kind found in Welsh, or voiceless nasal phonemes such as those found in Burmese). On the other hand, specification for [sonorant] itself can be predicted on the basis of feature specifications such as [+nasal], [+approximant] and [–consonantal]. This means that this feature itself is redundant.

In table 4.12 I have presented one way of underspecifying the English consonant system. (Recall that English has vowels so that some of these consonants need specifying for major class features that are not required to distinguish them from other consonants.)

There are certain subtleties in this underspecification. First, notice that we don't need to specify that a [+anterior] sound is CORONAL because only coronals can be anteriors. However, we don't even need to specify

Table 4.12 Underspecified matrix for consonants

	p	b	t	d	k	g	f	v	θ	ð	s	z	ʃ	ʒ	h
approx							–		–					–	
cont	–	–	–	–	–	–	+	+							
strid									–	–	+	+			
nas		–		–		–									
voiced	–	+	–	+	–	+	–	+	–	+	–	+	–	+	
[PLACE]	L	L	C	C	D	D	L	L							G
ant											+	+	–	–	

CORONAL for the non-anteriors, because the [anterior] feature is only defined for coronals. Therefore, if a sound has any marking at all for the feature [anterior] we know it must be CORONAL. Likewise, if a sound is marked either [+strident] or [–strident] we know that it must be a fricative and hence [+continuant].

4.5 Underspecification and Structure Preservation

It might be asked what the point is of extracting these redundancies and drawing up distinctive feature matrices with holes in them, such as table 4.12 rather than leaving all the specifications intact. There are two reasons for stating redundancies in a grammatical description.

The first is the less important and is essentially conceptual. A grammar has to have a **lexicon**, that is, a list of representations corresponding to words (and morphemes). For most linguists it is important that all the regular (i.e. rule-governed) aspects of a representation be removed from the lexical representation and derived by means of a rule. This includes regularities about pronunciation (or phonological structure more generally). This is what it means to capture linguistically significant generalizations in a grammar. Now, the sorts of featural redundancies just described are generally

Table 4.12 (Cont'd)

	m	*n*	*ŋ*	*w*	*l*	*r*	*j*
cons						+	
approx				+		+	+
nas	+	+	+				
lat					+	−	
[PLACE]	L	C	D	L		C	
ant							−

regarded as linguistically significant generalizations. Therefore, it would be improper to leave all this information in each lexical entry, where it will just be repeated for item after item. By far the most parsimonious course to take is to extract out these regularities and state them in the form of redundancy rules or conditions.[7]

The second motivation for redundancy rules is empirical. It turns out that in many cases a better grammar can be written if we extract these redundancies and 'fill in' the relevant feature specifications after other phonological rules have had a chance to apply. Russian provides a particularly intriguing illustration of this. Russian has (essentially) a five-vowel system: {i e a o u}. It also has phonemically contrastive palatalization of consonants, so that *brat* (with plain /t/) 'brother' contrasts with *brat^j* 'to take' (with palatalized /t^j/). Now, in certain circumstances we observe an alternation between /o/ and /e/: when underlying /o/ is surrounded by palatalized consonants, it is replaced by /e/. This can be seen from the following examples (cf. Hamilton 1980: 129–31, a useful introduction to these matters for those who read some Russian):

4.17   a.   p^jok   '(he) baked'   p^jetʃ^j   'to bake'
           b.   deʃovɨj   'cheap'   deʃev^jl^je   'cheaper'
           c.   ʒon   'women (gen.)'   ʒen^jit   'he gets married'
           d.   p^jotr   'Peter'   p^jet^ja   'Pete'

This only affects the sound /o/ (not, for instance /u/) and it applies to by no means all cases. Indeed, the majority of words fail to undergo the process. This is partly because modern /e/ in Russian stems from two different sounds (at least), only one of which underwent the original sound change in the medieval period giving rise to the present alternations. Moreover, loan words (such as *g^jote* 'Goethe') don't undergo it. Russian speakers tend to be conscious of the change and it is reflected in the spelling system (the alternating /o/ is actually written as 'ë', reflecting its historical source). Finally, the rule is badly motivated from a surface phonetic point of view, because some of the 'palatalized' consonants which condition it (such as /ʃ ʒ t͡s/), although they were palatalized at the time of the original sound change, have now become 'hardened', i.e. they have lost their palatalization. Thus, the rule has all the hallmarks of a lexical rule.[8]

If we assumed that all vowels are fully specified for all vowel features (i.e. at least [back, high, low, round, ATR]) then we would have to write a rule which turned /o/ into /e/. We can write such a rule informally as 4.18:[9]

4.18 $[-\text{high}] \rightarrow \begin{bmatrix} -\text{back} \\ -\text{round} \end{bmatrix} \quad / \; C^j ___ C^j$

However, if we make use of our redundancy rules and the underspecified matrix in table 4.9 we can rewrite this rule more simply as 4.19:

4.19 $[-\text{high}] \rightarrow [-\text{back}] \quad / \; C^j ___ C^j$

This effects the change on the underspecified matrix illustrated in 4.20:

4.20

	o		'?'
back	+		–
high	–	→	–
low	–		–

The new vowel '?' has a feature composition which is not **distinct** from that of /e/. This doesn't mean it is exactly the same as /e/ – this isn't possible, since the '?' phoneme has no specification for [round]. However, '?' doesn't contain any specification which would contradict any of the feature values for a fully specified /e/.

Given the way the redundancy rules work, the phonological system will interpret '?' as identical to /e/. This is because a redundancy rule will specify the derived vowel, '?', as [–round]. This is a reflection of the fact that the phoneme inventory of Russian doesn't contain any rounded front vowels. Recall, that '?', which started out as a back vowel, has become [–back] by rule 4.19. The consequence is that we don't have to stipulate the change in rounding in rule 4.19 itself. This may seem a small saving (obviating the need to refer to one distinctive feature in a rule), but in more complex cases, of the kind we encounter with consonants, for instance, the savings are more significant. Moreover, where there are several rules which change one type of phoneme into another, we would find that the redundant information (e.g. about the roundedness of front vowels) would have to be included in each of those rules. By extracting the regularity as a redundancy

Table 4.13 Underspecified matrix for standard five-vowel system

	i	e	a	o	u
back	–	–	+	+	+
high	+	–		–	+
round			–	+	

rule we only have to state it once. This correctly captures the fact that the redundancy is systematic, and that it is not just a coincidence that it recurs throughout the phonology.

The kind of situation just illustrated occurs when one set of underlying phonemes is converted into another set of sounds *which are also underlying phonemes*. In these circumstances the overall inventory of sounds is not increased by the phonological process. Instead what we have is a process of neutralization of a contrast in certain contexts, much like the neutralization in voicing in the phrase *five past*. For instance, rule 4.19 essentially says that the front-back distinction is suspended or neutralized between palatalized consonants. A neutralizing rule of this sort which doesn't create novel sounds is called **structure preserving**. Structure preservation is an important property of the class of phonological rules we referred to as lexical rules in chapter 2. In effect, underspecification helps us to formalize the notion of structure preservation without having to incorporate redundant information into the formulation of the rule.[10]

The Russian case also illustrates another aspect of underspecification. I have given table 4.9 as the underspecified matrix for Russian vowels. However, this is not the only theoretically possible underspecification. In table 4.13 we see another underspecification, this time using the feature [round] to predict values for [low].

You should be able to provide redundancy rules to fill in the blanks to table 4.13 yourself. Notice that table 4.13 uses as many feature specifications and features as table 4.7, so in that respect they are equally concise and efficient representations. However, if table 4.13 represented the Russian system we would no longer have such a straightforward explanation for the o-fronting process. For if /o/ is fronted now it will give a rounded front vowel /ø/ rather than /e/. This would mean that we would have to write in a derounding processes, which in the present context would not be motivated independently. Arguably, a child makes use of such information when setting up underlying underspecified matrices.

Not all processes are structure preserving, of course. Again, let's consider the Russian vowel system, and this time we will look at allophonic variation in vowels when surrounded by palatalized consonants. The important cases concern the vowels {ɛ a ɔ u} (something related but more complex happens with /i/). When such a vowel immediately follows a palatalized consonant its initial part is slightly palatalized; when the vowel precedes a palatalized consonant the final part is slightly palatalized. However, when flanked by palatalized consonants, the vowel is fronted (/ɔ u a/) and/or raised (/ɛ a/). Phonetically, we have the alternation between (roughly) [ɛ a ɔ u] and [e æ œ y] (though these transcriptions exaggerate the extent of fronting of the back vowels). For instance, the words /pʲɛtʲ/ 'to sing', /pʲatʲ/ 'five', /lʲɔtʃʲik/ 'pilot', /tʃʲutʃʲ/ 'a little' have narrow transcriptions [pʲetʲ], [pʲætʲ], [lʲœtʃʲik], [tʃʲytʃʲ]. This means that there is a rule similar to 4.19 but affecting (almost) all vowels <u>at the level at which their features are fully specified</u>. Therefore, /ɔ/ alternates, for example, with a non-phoneme [œ]. The change induced in the case of /ɔ u/ is identical to that of rule 4.19, except that it applies over a fully specified representation and hence can only change the value of one feature, [back], leaving the specification for [round] untouched. This creates a new segment which is not part of the underlying inventory.

This process has all the hallmarks of a postlexical process. Speakers tend not to be aware of it, it is automatic and exceptionless and it is not reflected in the orthography. This means that, given underspecification, one and the same rule can operate in two distinct ways, depending on whether it applies before or after all the redundant values have been specified. In general, if a rule applies after all redundant values are filled in then it will create new sounds, not part of the underlying inventory of phonemes, and hence non-structure preserving. This in practice generally means the automatic rules of the phrase phonology (which frequently give rise to allophonic variation).

4.6 Natural Classes and Phonological Rules

4.6.1 Characterizing natural classes

An obvious point about the fricative voicelessness assimilation process introduced in chapter 2 is that it applies to a particular group of sounds, namely, voiced fricatives, which can be given a simple phonetic description. Now, this observation conceals an extremely important methodological point. Consider how we might characterize the set of targets for Fricative Devoicing. In principle, there are two ways we can set about this. The first method would be to list all the sounds undergoing the process and state what happens to them individually. Adopting this notational convention and characterizing the assimilation as the spreading of the voiceless feature, we will have a rule such as 4.21:

4.21   {v ð z ʒ}
              |
          X   X
           ＼   ＼   ⌟
              [−voiced]

The alternative is to give an overall description to the set of targets. This would give us something like 4.22:

4.22   {voiced fricative}

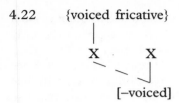

[−voiced]

In fact, the formulation in 4.22 is much superior to that in 4.21, even though they may appear identical in their effects. This is because behind these two notations lie different theoretical presuppositions.

If we just list the set of sounds undergoing a process, as in 4.21, then the question arises what other kinds of sets of sounds might undergo such a rule in other languages or dialects. The notational conventions presupposed in 4.21 treat individual sounds as equals. Therefore, we might expect to find other processes (perhaps in other languages) in which some arbitrarily different list of sounds underwent a similar devoicing. For example, we might see a process such as 4.23:

4.23   {v a r m}

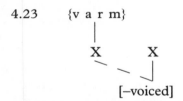

[−voiced]

Now a process such as this would be highly unlikely. In 4.23 the devoicing applies to a group of sounds which has no natural description beyond listing of its members. In other words, there is something unnatural about such a set of sounds behaving as a unified group. We would like our notation to make it difficult for us to write rules such as 4.23, while making it easy to write rules such as 4.22. The key is to define our rules in terms of *classes* of sounds rather than just lists.

We can use distinctive features to define classes of sounds very easily. Consider the set of voiced fricatives. These can be defined in an unambiguous fashion using the feature chart of table 4.6. Firstly, they are all, of course, [+voiced]. Secondly, being fricatives, they are obstruents, and hence [−sonorant]. Finally, all fricatives are [+continuant] sounds. These three feature specifications are shown in 4.24:

4.24   [+voiced, −son, +cont]

They serve to define precisely the voiced fricatives and no other sounds.

An important fact to notice from 4.24 is that in constructing this characterization we have omitted any mention of certain redundant feature specifications, for example, [+consonantal] or [−nasal]. This point will be amplified later in this section.

Now consider what we would have to do to define a set of sounds such as {v a r m} for English using distinctive features. As it happens the only feature specification common to all four members of this set (other than [+voiced]) is [−lateral], and this is because /l/ is the only phoneme of English which is positively specified for this feature. We couldn't actually use the characterization [−lateral] to try to define the class {v a r m} because [−lateral] defines all the sounds in English except /l/, and not just the small subset we are interested in.

Therefore, to define the sounds using feature notation we would have to provide an unambiguous feature characterization for each sound. These are shown in 4.25:

4.25   distinctive feature characterization
         a.   /v/:
         [+voiced, −son, −cont, LAB]
         b.   /a/:
         [+low, −round, −ATR]
         c.   /r/
         [+cons, +approx, −lat]
         d.   /m/
         [+nas, LAB]

From a purely notational point of view there is an impressive difference between the distinctive feature characterization of the set of target segments in 4.21 and that in 4.23. In 4.21 the entire set of targets can be defined using just three feature specifications. However, just in order to define one sound /v/ in 4.23 we need to specify a total of *four* features. Add to this the extra eight specifications needed to distinguish /a r m/ and it is clear that the notation distinguishes the two cases starkly. Moreover, the set of 4.23 illustrated in 4.25 has to be further defined with the help of a connective with the meaning of OR, that is, the set is defined as 'either 4.25a or 4.25b or 4.25c or 4.25d'. This type of definition of a set, relying on the use of 'or', is often referred to as a **disjunction** (a term borrowed from logic). The point here is that it is undesirable to define sets in terms of a disjunction since this means denying that there is any real homogeneity to the set: they are just a collection of unrelated individuals. This isn't the case with the feature set in 4.24, where we have a genuine class of related sounds. In this case we have a simple **conjunction** of features.

We can say that the set of sounds defined in 4.24 is a natural class of sounds. Intuitively, this is a class of sounds that 'belong together' in some sense. It is a fundamental precept of phonological theory that (regular) phonological processes apply to natural classes and not just any old assemblage of sounds. Distinctive feature theory gives us a simple way of characterizing this notion, and this is one of the most important aspects of the classificatory function of distinctive features.

The precise characterization of a natural class in a given language in general depends on what other sounds there are in the language. Suppose there were a dialect (let's call it dialect X) in which the set of fricatives included /s z/ but in which the fricative devoicing rule for some reason failed to apply to /z/. In this dialect, then, the process would be defined over the sounds /v ð ʒ/. How would we characterize this set? We can't use our previous analysis because this includes /z/. We would therefore need to find a way of specifying /v ð ʒ/ in such a way as to exclude /z/. It should be clear that there is, in fact, no way of doing this. But this means that we have reached an intriguing conclusion: /v ð ʒ/ is not a natural class in English, because it can't be defined using a single set of feature specifications, without also including our unwanted sound /z/. In the unlikely event of finding a genuine dialect X we would have to define this depleted class undergoing fricative devoicing by means of a disjunction.

The other side of this coin is that if it turned out that in dialect X there were no /s z/ sounds at all (for example, if everyone spoke with a lisp and therefore failed to contrast /s z/ and /θ ð/) then we would be able to use our original distinctive feature characterization for the set /v ð ʒ/. In this sense, then, naturalness is relativized to the underlying sound inventory of the language/dialect.

This discussion suggests a way of using the distinctive feature notation to provide a technical definition of 'natural class'. Recall that the problem with our 'unnatural' classes is that in order to define them we need to define a disjunction of the form 'sound x or sound y or . . .', while a natural class is defined as a conjunction of features. This means that if we count up the number of feature specifications needed to characterize the entire set in an unnatural class it will inevitably be greater than the number required to characterize just a single one of its members. For instance, in the set /v a r m/ we need just four specifications for /v/ but twelve for the whole set. Therefore, an unnatural class can be defined as one which requires more feature specifications than does any one of its members. A natural class is one in which this situation doesn't obtain. Hence, the total number of feature specifications needed for the whole class does not exceed that needed for the most complex member.

4.6.2   How to compute natural classes

Before we leave this topic we will examine a simple phonemic system (or rather, portion of a system) and see how we compute whether a given set of sounds constitutes a natural class in that system. We will take for illustration the familiar five-vowel system discussed earlier, repeated in table 4.14.

Table 4.14 A standard five-vowel system

	i	e	a	o	u
back	–	–	+	+	+
high	+	–	–	–	+
low	–	–	+	–	–
round	–	–	–	+	+

Consider the set of vowels {i e}. Is this a natural class? First we must identify which features this set has in common. They are given in 4.26:

4.26

	i	e
back	–	–
low	–	–
round	–	–

Our first approximation to the solution is then 4.27:

4.27   [–back, –low, –round]

Next we check that no other sounds share exactly these specifications. This is true for our system, because /a/ is [+low, +back], and /o/ and /u/ are [+back, +round].

This is therefore a satisfactory solution, in the sense that we have adequately identified the set as a natural class. However, it is apparent that some of these features are redundant. In particular, we know that all front vowels in this system are [–low] and [–round]. Therefore, the most parsimonious definition of the class is simple: [–back]. In other words, {i e} are the (only) two front vowels in the inventory.

It might seem that we could have arrived at the same solution a little more directly by considering an already underspecified matrix. If we consult table 4.9, we will see that the features for which the two sounds are distinctively specified are just [high] and [back]. The sounds differ on values for [high], but they have the same value for [back]. However, we can't just assume that the class is defined as [–back], since we then have to check that none of the other sounds is specified redundantly as [–back]. This means, in effect, consulting the fully specified matrix. To see this, consider the set {a o u}. By now it should be clear that this is simply the set of back vowels. This natural class therefore needs no other specification than [+back]. This is precisely the answer we will get from inspection of the fully specified matrix in table 4.7: [+back] is the only common feature, while it is proper to none of the other vowels, outside the set we are describing. However, from table 4.9 we encounter problems, because /a/ isn't specified for [back] in that matrix.

4.6.3 Features and rules

The concept of natural class allows us to sharpen up what we mean by a phonological rule. Specifically, where a rule formalizes a natural phonological process, we expect to find: (1) that the set of targets is a natural class, and (2) that the environment, where it is defined in terms of sets of sounds, is defined in terms of natural classes.

We have also seen that splitting off features and considering their phonological behaviour separately from the rest of the sound of which they are a part allows us to capture notions like 'voicelessness assimilation' very straightforwardly, though not all phonological processes involve the spreading of a feature. One case in point which illustrates this is the devoicing of obstruents in word final position which is found in a good many languages, for instance, Russian. Many Russian nouns form their genitive plural by deleting the vowel ending of the nominative singular. If this leaves a voiced consonant then that consonant is devoiced. Some examples are given in 4.28:

4.28   nom sg   gen pl
          fraza   fras   'phrase'
          beseda   beset   'conversation'
          doroga   dorok   'road'
          golova   golof   'head'

The rule can be stated informally as in 4.29:

4.29   voiced obstruent $\rightarrow$ voiceless /____ (end of word)

To formalize this kind of process we need to say that a sound changes its feature composition in the given context. This means that we need to be able to write a rule which has the effect of 4.29 but which is couched in terms of distinctive features. Before we can do this, it will help to have a way of expressing the notion 'end of a word'. We will use a parenthesis, labelled 'word'. The result will be 4.30:

4.30 $\begin{bmatrix} +\text{voiced} \\ -\text{son} \end{bmatrix} \rightarrow \begin{bmatrix} -\text{voiced} \\ -\text{son} \end{bmatrix} / \underline{\quad})_{\text{Wd}}$

In fact, this formulation contains more information than is required, for all we need to say is that one feature specification, [+voiced], changes to another, [−voiced], in the requisite context. Since the specification for [−son] doesn't change we don't need to mention it in the structural change of the rule. Therefore, we can rewrite 4.30 as 4.31:

4.31 $\begin{bmatrix} +\text{voiced} \\ -\text{son} \end{bmatrix} \rightarrow [-\text{voiced}] / \underline{\quad})_{\text{Wd}}$

Linguists, like other scientists, like to provide the most general statement of a rule or principle. In distinctive feature terms, this usually means the formulation which appeals to the least number of feature specifications. In this connection notice what would happen if we removed the [+voiced] specification from the target, as in 4.32:

4.32   [–son]   →   [–voiced]   /____)$_{\mathrm{Wd}}$

In 4.31 we are saying that a voiced obstruent devoices at the end of a word, while in 4.32 we are saying that any obstruent will be voiceless in that position. It may seem as though these are different rules. The two formulations are identical in their effects, however. If a word ends in an obstruent that is already voiceless, then 4.32 will simply rewrite '[–voiced]' as '[–voiced]'. When a rule applies in this fashion to a form which already conforms to the change introduced by the rule, we say that the rule applies **vacuously**. By omitting the specification [+voiced] in our fricative devoicing rule, we would obtain the same effect. Vacuous application of a rule is not any indication that something is wrong with the formulation. On the contrary, it means we have achieved the most general statement possible, which usually means we have captured the real generalization. The only reason why vacuous application might seem conceptually problematic is if we insist on thinking of rules as processes which change one thing into another. This is a useful, but sometimes misleading, metaphor. In fact, the function of the rules is to code the constraints on the distribution of sounds. Thus, we should really think of Russian obstruent devoicing as establishing those contexts in which a voiced obstruent is not allowed to appear and where a voiceless obstruent must appear instead. In other words, instead of reading 4.32 as saying 'devoice a voiced obstruent word finally' we should read it as saying 'any word final obstruent must be voiceless'.

Finally, to illustrate the way that contexts can be written using natural classes, consider the process of vowel shortening in English. Long stressed vowels are shortened somewhat when they are found in a syllable closed by a voiceless consonant. Again, we can use a labelled parenthesis to indicate 'end of a syllable'. Let's assume for the sake of argument a feature [long] to represent vowel length, and a feature [stress]. Then we can represent this process very simply as 4.33:

4.33 $\begin{bmatrix} +\text{long} \\ -\text{cons} \\ +\text{stress} \end{bmatrix}$ →   [–long]   /____ [–voiced])$_{\sigma}$

Here, the natural class of voiceless sounds is very simply represented as just a single feature (a more narrowly defined class, e.g. the voiceless fricatives, would have required more features, of course).

The two types of rules just illustrated involve strings of segments arranged in a single line, so to speak. In other words, we are dealing here with linear rules. However, in our discussion of Fricative Devoicing, we saw a more articulated way of picturing a phonological process, involving representations in more than a single, linear, dimension. All phonological rules were linear in earlier varieties of generative phonology (and in informal descriptions it is still common to see rules written in such a format). However, most phonological processes are now couched in the multi-dimensional (or non-linear) terms of our Fricative Devoicing rule. In a sense, then, the linear formulations are of essentially historical interest in the development of phonological theory. However, they can be thought of as a simplified version of the rules we will be postulating elsewhere in the book. In the next chapter we investigate in rather more detail the way that a more articulated view of feature representations helps us to formalize recurrent types of phonological process.

Finally, we are now in position to return to a problem which often puzzles people when first introduced to phoneme theory. I cautioned in chapter 1 against the common fallacy of confusing the notion of 'phoneme' with that of 'allophone'. The conceptual problem is this: what we actually hear are the allophones of a phoneme. The phoneme itself is an abstract concept which cannot be identified with any single allophone. Thus, if we say that English voiceless stops have two allophones, a plain form [p t k] and an aspirated form [p^h t^h k^h], we are not, strictly speaking, saying that either of these forms is the 'real' phoneme. However, there is a strong tendency to make this assumption, which is exacerbated by generative theory. For in generative descriptions we regularly speak of an allophone (e.g. [p^h]) being derived from an underlying form such as /p/. (We even tend to use the slash notation for underlying forms, mimicking the slash notation for phonemes.)

Given the theory of distinctive features we can resolve this conceptual confusion rather straightforwardly. We no longer need to say that a given *sound* is the basic or underlying form. Rather, what we need to ask is 'what features are distinctively specified for the underlying form of a given surface phone (in a given context)?' For instance, suppose we follow tradition and regard the aspirated allophone as derived.[11] The task is to account for the distribution of the two allophones, [p p^h]. Let's assume for the sake of simplicity that we are just talking about the onset types {p sp} and no other occurrences of the /p/. All we need to say is that both allophones are represented by a common underlying form and that this form has the specifications [−voice, −cont, LAB]. On its own this feature characterization doesn't define any sound at all, of course. It is only in conjunction with the various redundancy rules and any phonological rules which might apply to a given token of /p/ that we finally specify the full feature set and hence the actual pronunciation of the word. If the /p/ occurs in a syllable such as *pat* then an aspiration rule will add the (non-distinctive) feature [+spread glottis], thereby ensuring the sound will be aspirated. Then, both representations will be subjected to various redundancy rules (one of which will specify the [p] in *spat* as [–spread glottis]).

This means that we have a clear interpretation of the notion 'underlying phoneme' as an abstract concept – it is simply the distinctive feature representation of a sound without any redundant feature specifications. The concept 'surface phone' then refers to a representation in which all the features required for pronunciation are specified. Clarifying the concept of 'phoneme' in this fashion is one of the great theoretical advantages of distinctive feature theory.

APPENDIX 4.1   CONTOUR SEGMENTS

One set of sounds which we have so far ignored is those sounds which appear to be made up of two (or more) sounds, produced as a single segment. There is quite a variety of such sounds in the world's languages, but in English and the more familiar European languages the main representatives of this type are diphthongs (a single segment consisting of two distinct vowel gestures) and the affricates.

In chapter 2, section 2.5, I suggested that the simplest way of representing diphthongs was as a sequence of two vowels each with its own X slot. We then account for the fact that the diphthong tends to behave like a single segment by associating it with only a single nucleus position in syllable structure. In this way a diphthong has more or less the same representation as a long vowel. By analogy with tone we call a diphthong a **contour segment**.

However, not all contour segments behave like a lengthened segment. An affricate, for instance, is essentially a composite of a plosive followed by a homorganic fricative, but produced in roughly the same time it takes for a single ungeminated consonant. One way of representing this situation would be to say that we have a plosive and a fricative attached to a single timing slot in the order plosive + fricative (thereby mimicking the IPA notation). However, this would not be entirely satisfactory. For one thing we would not have an explanation for why it is that in true affricates the place of articulation of the plosive and fricative phases is always identical. A better solution is therefore to say that we can alter our model slightly to allow contradictory values of certain features (in the present case [continuant]) to be simultaneously attached to a given segment. Thus, an affricate has the feature specifications [–cont, +cont].

An advantage of this way of representing affricates is that any rule which applies to a preceding [+continuant] sound will apply to the affricates and any rule which applies to a following [–continuant] segment will also apply to them. Thus, it is straightforward to represent the fact that affricates behave in some respects like stops and in other respects like fricatives. If we are not interested in most of the other features of an affricate we can simplify this kind of representation by indicating both values of the feature [continuant] but on separate tiers in the representation. Thus, the distinction between plosive [t], fricative [s] and affricate [t͜s] could be diagrammed as in 4.34, where T is a cover symbol for all the features of [t s t͜s] except continuance:

4.34

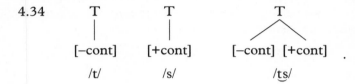

APPENDIX 4.2   AN ALTERNATIVE APPROACH TO VOWEL FEATURES: ELEMENTS

I earlier pointed out a problem with regard to binary features, particularly those used to describe vowels. The features [+high], [+low] are mutually exclusive, since it's impossible for the tongue body to be in two places at once. However, this is not adequately reflected in the formalism of binary features. In order to reflect this exclusion we have to appeal to a redundancy rule (or rather, two such rules). Yet this seems very messy, particularly since redundancy rules are usually intended to code relationships which the speaker can in principle override (for instance, vowels are redundantly voiced in most languages, but this specification can be overridden by speakers of those languages like Japanese which have devoiced vowels).

Usually when awkwardnesses of this sort arise, the theory itself is blamed. Many phonologists have therefore argued that there is a fundamental flaw in the binary feature system inherited from Prague School structuralism. One influential solution to this problem is to adopt unary features throughout the system. I shall illustrate this proposal by briefly discussing the vowels.

In section 4.3 I pointed out that a common three-vowelled system comprised just the vowels of 4.35:

4.35   i   u

             a

I then pointed out that this type of system often changes into a five-membered system by the addition of /e o/. This frequently comes about as the result of the fusion of two vowels in a diphthong (as we saw in chapter 2). Two of the commonest diphthongs in the world's languages are /ai/ and /au/, and in language after language, it is these diphthongs which develop into /e/ and /o/.

Suppose we regard the three basic vowels of 4.34 as the primitive building blocks of all vowels, in effect, treating them as a kind of feature, or **element**. The |i| element is associated with the phonetic property of palatality, the |u| element with labiality (and secondarily with a high, back articulation) and the |a| element is associated with openness (and secondarily with a low articulation). Next we can say that a mid-vowel is a combination of these elements. Thus, we will have the following representations for a familiar five-vowel system (indicating elements between | |):

4.36
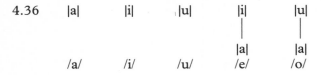

The representations for /e o/ are intended to be interpreted as '|i/u| modified by the |a| element'. This produces a high vowel which has been lowered (to mid). At the same time we can modify |a| by the |i/u/| elements to get low vowels with palatal or labial colouring, while a combination of |i| and |u| (in any order) will surface as [y], as in 4.37:

4.37
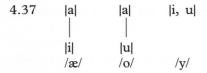

To get these distinctions from the elements we have been tacitly using a notion of **dependency** or **government**. Thus, we can say that in /e/ |i| governs |a| or |a| is a dependent of |i|. A convenient way of writing this on one line is |i > a|. In some versions of this approach we can have mutual government, such that neither element predominates. In such a theory (favoured by Dependency phonologists; see Lass 1984, Durand 1990) we can distinguish [e] from [ɛ] in this way: in [e] |i| predominates so that we have the representation in 4.36, while in [ɛ], neither element predominates so we can represent this sound as |i,a| (or, indeed, |a,i|). The distinction between [o] and [ɔ] can be handled correspondingly using |u|. Not all phonologists working with elements would accept this analysis, however, and Kaye, Lowenstamm and Vergnaud (1985), for instance, distinguish [e/ɛ] in terms of an element |I| which corresponds roughly to [+ATR]. Thus, in a language distinguishing the two types of sound, [ɛ] would be |i > a| while [e] would be something like |(i > a) > I|. Somewhat different proposals are made by van der Hulst (1989). It would take us too far afield to delve into these possibilities in greater detail. Suffice it to say that element theory in one form or another is becoming increasingly influential and, because of some of the inherent defects in binary feature theory (and, indeed, underspecification) must be taken very seriously by phonologists.[12]

APPENDIX 4.3   LIST OF DISTINCTIVE FEATURES

consonantal

[±cons]   Consonantal sounds are made with a constriction in the vocal tract which is either complete (in the case of stops) or sufficient to cause friction (as in the case of fricatives). Obstruents, nasals, liquids are [+cons], glides and vowels are [–cons].

approximant

[±approx]   Approximant sounds are made with an oral tract constriction which is less than that required to produce friction. This therefore excludes the fricatives and stops, including nasal stops. Vowels, glides and liquids are [+approx], other sounds are [–approx]

sonorant

[±son]   Sonorant sounds are those which resonate and hence do not involve turbulent noise (as found with fricatives and plosives). In sonorant sounds the pressure inside and outside the vocal tract is roughly equal (while in obstruents there is a pressure build up in the oral tract caused by a constriction). Obstruents (plosives, affricates and fricatives) are [–son], other sounds are [+son].

continuant

[±cont]   In continuant sounds the air is permitted to pass through the vocal tract (this includes around the side of the tongue in the case of laterals). In non-continuants (stops) there is an occlusion which prevents this (even though the air may escape unhindered through the nose, as in the case of nasal stops). Plosives and nasal stops are [–cont], other sounds (including laterals) are [+cont]. (In some definitions the air must be permitted to pass through the *midsaggital* region of the oral tract, i.e. down the centre of the mouth; this would then exclude the laterals.)

strident

[±strid]   A strident sound is one which includes a component of high-frequency noise ('white noise'), caused when the airstream is forced through a narrow gap, and directed onto a hard surface (such as the gum ridge or the teeth). Stridency is only defined for fricatives and affricates. Labiodentals, sibilants and uvular fricatives/affricates are [+strid]; all other fricatives/affricates are [–strid].

nasal

[±nas]   Nasal sounds are produced by lowering the velum and allowing air to pass through the nasal passages. Nasal stops, (pre-) nasalized consonants, glides or vowels are all [+nas]. Other sounds (oral sounds) are [–nas].

lateral

[±lat]   In a lateral sound the tongue obstructs the centre of the oral tract, forcing the air to flow by the side of the tongue. It is thought by many that all laterals are coronal sounds.

distributed

[±distr]   In a distributed sound there is a constriction down the central line of the oral cavity which extends for a relatively long stretch. The feature is generally only used to distinguish different types of fricative or affricate, though under most definitions it also applies theoretically to stops. The feature applies to coronal sounds, and, depending on the author, may or may not include the labial region. Under the narrower definition (restricted to coronals) interdentals, palato-alveolars, and palatals are [+distr] ([θ ʃ ç ç]. Under the broader characterization this would also include [ɸ]. (In Halle and Clements 1983 the feature is defined so as to apply to the midsaggital region, which would exclude the laterals.)

[PLACE]

This is a cover term for the next four features.

LABIAL

LAB   A unary feature. Sounds marked with this feature involve a constriction of the lips to give either a labial (labiodental) consonant or a rounded vowel/glide.

CORONAL

COR   A unary feature. In a coronal sound the tongue blade is raised from its notional resting position. This is found with dentals, alveolars, palato-alveolars, retroflex and palatal sounds; labials, velars, uvulars, pharyngeal and laryngeal sounds are not marked with COR.

DORSAL

DOR   A unary feature. Sounds bearing this feature are made by raising the dorsum (tongue body) towards the hard palate, the soft palate (velum) or the uvula. The dorsal consonants are the velars and uvulars.

GUTTURAL

GUTT   A unary feature. Sounds bearing this feature are produced in the pharyngeal or laryngeal (glottal) region, e.g. [ʔ h ɦ ʕ ħ].

anterior

[±ant]   This feature is defined only for COR sounds. An anterior ([+ant]) sound is made with a constriction at or forward of, the alveolar ridge. Posterior ([–ant]) sounds are produced behind the alveolar ridge. The anteriors are the dentals and alveolars, the posterior sounds are the retroflex, palato-alveolar and palatal sounds.

high

[±high] A high sound is made by raising the dorsum (tongue body). The palatals, velars, palatalized, velarized consonants, together with the high vowels and glides are all [+high]; other sounds are [–high].

back

[±back] In front ([–back]) sounds the dorsum (tongue body) is brought forward, while in back ([+back]) sounds it is retracted. Central as well as back vowels/glides are [+back], as are velars, uvulars, and pharyngeals and velarized and pharyngealized consonants.

low

[±low] Low sounds are made by bringing the dorsum (tongue body) down towards the floor of the mouth. Low vowels, pharyngeals and pharyngealized consonants are all [+low]; other sounds are [–low].

round

[±round] Rounded sounds are produced by contracting the muscles around the lips so that they form a ring. Rounded consonants (such as [kʷ, pʷ sꟷ] and rounded vowels are [+round]; all other sounds (including labial consonants which lack a rounded secondary articulation, such as [p m ɸ]) are [–round].

ATR

[±ATR] 'Advanced Tongue Root'. This feature applies predominantly to vowels. [+ATR] vowels are made by drawing the root of the tongue forward, thus enlarging the pharyngeal cavity, tending to raise the tongue body, and tending to give the sound a more tense articulation, e.g. [i e o u]. [–ATR] sounds lack this gesture, e.g. [ɪ ɛ ɔ ʊ a ɑ].

voiced

[±voiced] In voiced sounds the vocal folds can vibrate to produce a periodic sound; in voiceless sounds the configuration of the larynx doesn't permit this.

constricted glottis

[±constr] or [±constr gl] Constricted glottis sounds are glottal or glottalized. Any ejective, implosive or glottalized vowel/glide is [+constr]. All other sounds are [–constr].

spread glottis

[±spread] or [±spr gl] Spread sounds are aspirated, with the vocal folds drawn apart to allow a 'breathy' articulation and often a longer VOT. Aspirated (voiceless) consonants, breathy or murmured voiced consonants and voiceless vowels/glides are [+spread]; other sounds are [−spread].

FURTHER READING

For readings on distinctive features see further reading to chapter 5. For a very interesting, though rather advanced, discussion of the relationship between sonority and major class features see Clements (1990) (whose views are also discussed in Clements and Hume 1994). I have taken over the essential idea of 'approximant' from Clements (1990) (and the earlier tradition he was basing himself on) including the non-traditional claim that vowels are approximants. A useful survey of distinctive features is found in Halle and Clements (1983). They provide a helpful reference list of features and their definitions, which I have availed myself of in appendix 4.3.

A good survey of underspecification, arguing for a different type of underspecification from the one presented here, namely, Radical Underspecification, is given in Archangeli (1988). Her arguments are summarized in Roca (1994) and summarized and extended by Durand (1990). Kenstowicz (1994), as ever, is the most up to date and exhaustive textbook survey. A more advanced discussion of the relative merits of Radical Underspecification and other types, with a very detailed exposition of the rationale behind underspecification, is given in Steriade (1994).

EXERCISES

4.1. Use the chart of table 4.5 to describe the following sounds not found in English:

[ç] [dz] [x] [ʒ] [ɸ] [ɟ] [ʁ]

4.2. Consider a hypothetical dialect of English which is identical to normal English except that it lacks /s z/ phonemes. Prove that the set /v ð ʒ/ constitutes a natural class in this dialect.

4.3. Here is (one interpretation of) the vowel phoneme inventory of Archi:

	i	e	ə	a	o	u
high	+	−	−	−	−	+
back	−	−	+	+	+	+
low	−	−	−	+	−	−
round	−	−	−	−	+	+
ATR	+	−	−	−	−	+

Compute two underspecifications for this inventory. Your two under-specifications are indistinguishable if we just consider their function as classifying the vowel inventory. Explain why this is so.

4.4. Take the vowel inventory for Archi given in Exercise 4.3 and list all the possible subsets consisting of three vowels (e.g. {i e ə}, {a o u} and so on). You should be able to find ten distinct sets. Then determine which set is a natural class and which set is not.

4.5 Provide a set of redundancy rules to fill in the blanks in table 4.13.

4.6. Take the set of Archi consonants presented in table 1.3 in chapter one. Provide a distinctive feature analysis for as many of these consonants as you can using the features already discussed. What other features might you need to describe this system?

chapter 5

Rules and Domains

5.0   Introduction

So far we have looked almost exclusively at the representational aspect of phonology: how sounds and syllables are to be described. In this chapter we turn to the more dynamic aspects of the subject and ask how to describe and analyse phonological alternations and processes. We will start with a summary of the type of system proposed in the classical theory of generative phonology. This has certain important drawbacks, and we will see how phonologists have tried to eradicate these. A crucial component of this will be a more articulated description of individual sounds, in which we ask what the relationships are between the individual features that go to make up a sound. Next we will look at the interactions between rules which come about by virtue of the order in which they apply relative to one another. We then turn to the way that phonotactic constraints can be called upon to motivate the operation of rules. Finally, we look at the phonological domains in which rules apply and find that this is a further aspect of phonological structure that can restrict the operation of phonological processes.

5.1 Phonological Rules in a Linear Framework

5.1.1 The SPE system

In the last chapter we examined the classificatory function of distinctive features and the role of distinctive features in characterizing natural classes. In this chapter we will extend that discussion and develop a more articulated way of looking at the relationship between the individual features of a sound. This will help us to examine the second function of distinctive features, that of autonomous units in phonological processes. We will see that the nature of feature representations is crucial to the way we formulate phonological rules.

However, before we turn to such things we need to devote a little time to discussing the historical development of generative phonology and especially the way that rules have been notated. We will start with our old friend, Fricative Devoicing. A simple and transparent way of notating the Fricative Devoicing process without recourse to distinctive features would be as in 5.1, in which we see the conventions introduced in chapter 2:

5.1   {v ð z ʒ}   →   voiceless / ____ voiceless

In this notation we simply state the target class on the left of the arrow and the structural change and the environment on the right of the arrow. However, we have not represented the process as one of spreading or sharing of a particular feature. Rather, the notation in 5.1 simply says that a particular change occurs in a particular environment.

In the original ('classical') version of generative phonology, as codified in SPE, all phonological rules were written in essentially the format of 5.1. This format differs from the one used in chapter 4 principally in that the entire process is notated, so to speak, along a single line. However, in chapter 4 I introduced a very different notation, in which the crucial feature of voicing was represented on its own line of representation, and hence could be treated as an independent property, capable of autonomous behaviour such as spreading. In fact, such a multilinear style of representation (often, rather misleadingly, referred to as 'non-linear') is a relatively recent innovation in generative phonology. Until the mid-1970s rules were only written in the format seen in 5.1.

In this section we will look in a little more formal detail at the older 'linear' style of rule. This is a format which is still used, especially for more informal or descriptive presentations of data, and, of course, it is the format found in a good deal of earlier literature which is still of importance. It is therefore necessary to be familiar with that format, even if a number of the rules we will discuss in this chapter are notated differently. In the next section we will see why that format had to be abandoned as a general characterization of phonological processes.

The general format for a 'linear' rule is given in 5.2:

5.2   Generalized phonological rule (as in SPE)
       A X B   →   A Y B

This rule states that a segment X is replaced by a segment Y in the context or environment defined by A____B. Using the notation introduced in chapter 2, we then write this as 5.3:

5.3   X   →   Y   /A____B

It is important to realize that the environment may be anything: a segment, a string of segments, or a boundary symbol indicating the edge of a syllable, a morpheme, or a word, and so on. In addition, either or both of the symbols A, B, may null, i.e. they may stand for nothing. When A or B are null we get 5.4a, b, respectively:

5.4   a.   X   →   Y   /____B
       b.   X   →   Y   /A____

Thus, in the example of Fricative Devoicing in 5.1, there is no context specified to the left of the target, so the rule has the shape of 5.4a. This means that any sound at all can appear there in principle (or even no sound at all).

Rules such as 5.3 are referred to as **rewriting rules**. This is because the 'X's' get rewritten as 'Y's'. If either A or B is non-null we have a **context-sensitive rewriting rule**. If both A and B are null, then we get 5.5, in which there is no context at all. This type of rule is called a **context-free rewriting rule**:

5.5   X   →   Y   /____

In effect a context-free rule such as 5.5 states that an X always turns into a Y, no matter what the environment.[1]

In chapter 2 we saw a process under which /t/ in Russian is deleted when flanked by consonants. We can represent this process as in 5.6:

5.6   t   →   ∅   / [+cons] ____ [+cons]

Recall that the feature [+consonantal] identifies consonants (as opposed to vowels and glides). The idea of deletion is notated in a rewriting format by saying that the deleted segment is 'rewritten' (or 'replaced by') zero, ∅.

We can handle insertions in a similar fashion. Earlier in chapter 2 I discussed at some length allomorphy of the plural morpheme in English. We noted that when the stem ends in a sibilant (e.g. *walrus, ostrich*), a schwa is epenthesized. This process was written as in 5.7:

5.7 $\emptyset$ $\rightarrow$ ə   / sibilant ____ z

This rule 'rewrites' nothing as a schwa (providing that the 'nothing' is sandwiched between a sibilant and the plural ending).

5.1.2   The problem of assimilations

This, in a nutshell, was the SPE theory of rule formalization. The full theory included a variety of conventions for abbreviating complex rules. These are briefly discussed in appendix 5.1. (Some of these conventions are no longer needed because of the changes in the way phonological rules are written in the multilinear format.)

However, this is not the format we used for describing Fricative Devoicing in chapter 4. The reason for this is that this linear format has turned out to be insufficiently expressive to be able to capture the essential character-istics of commonplace phonological processes. This is especially true of assimilation processes such as Fricative Devoicing. The most striking illus-tration of the deficiency of linear rules comes when we consider straightfor-ward place of articulation assimilation processes, one of the commonest phonological processes in the world's languages. A standard example of this is provided by English. In ordinary casual speech the coronal nasal /n/ will tend to be pronounced with the same place of articulation as an immedi-ately following obstruent (provided the nasal is in the same word or at the end of a word which is 'closely knit' to the following word). This is illus-trated in the data of 5.8:

5.8

in pairs	[im]	⎫	bilabial
in Brighton	[im]	⎬	
in fact	[iɱ]	⎭	labiodental
in these	[in]		dental
in turn	[in]		alveolar
in church	[iɲ]	⎫	palato-alveolar
in German	[iɲ]	⎬	
in shares	[iɲ]	⎭	
in York	[iɲ]		palatal
in Kent	[iŋ]		velar

What is happening here is very simple: the nasal shares its place of articula-tion features with the following obstruent. However, it turns out to be rather difficult to capture this insight using just a list of features to characterize

each separate segment and using just the linear rule format of 5.1. The
problem is that the notation as developed thus far doesn't afford a simple
way of saying 'X has the same feature specifications as Y'.

The way SPE solved this problem was to introduce a new notational
device, the **Greek letter variable**. This notation uses a letter of the Greek
alphabet to stand for a feature value, i.e. + or −. To say that two segments
have the same value for a feature we simply have to use the variable and
make sure they are the same. Thus, whatever value, + or −, we give to one
sound will automatically be assigned to the other.

In the case of our place of articulation assimilation processes, let's assume
for the sake of argument that we have the following set of binary features:
[±labial], [±coronal], [±anterior], [±high]. The binary features [±labial],
[±coronal] can have the same function for our purposes as the LABIAL and
CORONAL features introduced in the previous chapter. Now, to capture
the idea that, say, /n/ becomes /m/ before a labial we can formulate a process
5.9:

5.9 $\begin{bmatrix} +\text{nasal} \\ +\text{coronal} \end{bmatrix}$ →   [αlabial]   /____ [αlabial]

What this says is that the alveolar nasal will have the same specification for
[labial] as the following segment. This is because, by the Greek letter variable notation, if α in the environment is '−', then the nasal will be specified
as the same, i.e. [−labial], and if α is '+', then the nasal will be specified as
[+labial]. Similarly, to achieve assimilation for the other features we can add
those features, together with a different Greek letter variable, β, γ and so on.
(We can't use one and the same variable for all the features, of course,
otherwise they would all end up with the same specification, which would
produce nonsense). The result would be something like 5.10 (simplifying
somewhat):

5.10 $\begin{bmatrix} +\text{nasal} \\ +\text{coronal} \end{bmatrix}$ → $\begin{bmatrix} \alpha\text{labial} \\ \beta\text{coronal} \\ \gamma\text{anterior} \\ \delta\text{high} \end{bmatrix}$ /____ $\begin{bmatrix} \alpha\text{labial} \\ \beta\text{coronal} \\ \gamma\text{anterior} \\ \delta\text{high} \end{bmatrix}$

Now, this type of formulation does its job. However, it has a serious,
indeed fatal, drawback. For it is impossible to rule out, in a principled way,
all sorts of potential processes which are never observed, but which are just
as easy to write using such a format. The main problem is that there is no
particular reason why the value of, say, [labial] acquired by the target segment should be identical to that of the [labial] feature of the next segment
as opposed to any other feature. For instance, if we simply consider the
notational device irrespective of what we know is natural about phonological
processes, we might expect a rule like 5.10 to be no more common that a
rule such as say, 5.11:

5.11 $\begin{bmatrix} +\text{nasal} \\ +\text{coronal} \end{bmatrix} \rightarrow \begin{bmatrix} \alpha\text{labial} \\ \beta\text{coronal} \\ \gamma\text{anterior} \\ \delta\text{high} \end{bmatrix} / \underline{\quad} \begin{bmatrix} \beta\text{labial} \\ \gamma\text{coronal} \\ \delta\text{anterior} \\ \alpha\text{high} \end{bmatrix}$

To the extent that such a process would give phonetically interpretable
results, this would produce a labial (of some sort) before a velar, a coronal
before a labial, and so on. This would be bizarre and nothing so odd is
found in segmental assimilations. Even if such a process did crop up as a
highly idiosyncratic part of some language or other, we would still be at a
loss to explain why the assimilation type in 5.9 is so common while the
process shown in 5.11 is vanishingly rare.

5.2 Feature Geometry

The conclusion from the last section is that the linear notation for assimilation using the Greek letter variables fails to account for why assimilations
are phonetically <u>natural</u> phenomena. This failing is one of the principal
reasons for abandoning this approach and adopting the alternative which we
implicitly appealed to in our description of Fricative Devoicing. What we
need is a theory of rules which can treat assimilations as a process in which
a feature or set of features from one sound is acquired by a neighbouring
sound. This will require a change from the SPE way of looking at rules, but
also a change in our perception of segments as just an unordered bundle of
features.

5.2.1 Features, nodes and spreading

We have seen Fricative Devoicing treated as a type of spreading process: the
feature [–voiced] spreads from the voiceless segment to the next segment on
its left. We can solve some of the notational problems with rules like 5.9 by
making use of our place of articulation features, LAB, COR, DOR. Suppose we formalize the assimilation found in *in Kent* in terms of spreading
of the DOR feature onto the /n/ of *in*, displacing the COR feature. This is
shown in 5.12:

5.12

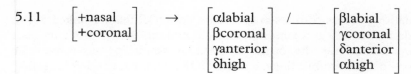

The assimilation process consists in spreading the DOR feature linked to the /k/ leftwards to the /n/, and simultaneously delinking the /n/ from its own place feature, COR. Thus, the former /n/ comes to be interpreted as the velar /ŋ/, by virtue of the double linkage with DOR. This captures in a rather direct way the idea that the two consonants <u>share</u> their place of articulation.

Clearly we can propose the same process for the labial assimilation shown by *in Paris*. All we need do is replace the DOR feature with LAB in 5.12. However, there is a problem here. We would like to say that place of articulation assimilation is a unitary phenomenon. In other words, we would like to say that the process illustrated by 5.8 is just one process. However, our feature notation, with its three separate features LAB, COR, DOR, seems to be treating it as three distinct phenomena. We are therefore failing to capture the true nature of the process. In the terminology of linguistics, we are failing to capture a linguistically significant generalization about the nature of place of articulation assimilation.

What we need is a way of spreading one feature in such a way that this will give rise to all the separate subprocesses of 5.8 in one fell swoop. Now, at present we don't have such a feature. This is, in fact, a general descriptive failing in the system we have developed so far. In chapter 4 section 4.2.1 we grouped the place of articulation features into larger classes, labelled LABIAL, CORONAL, and DORSAL, but we said nothing which explicitly states that LAB, COR and DOR are all features of the same type, namely, place of articulation features. What we need is a kind of 'superfeature' representing <u>any</u> place feature. Let's therefore assume such a feature, and call it PLACE. This will have four values: LABIAL, CORONAL, DORSAL, GUTTURAL. In other words, the place features themselves are values of a larger feature. This straightforwardly captures the obvious phonetic fact that sounds have essentially one basic place of articulation but there is a large choice ranging from bilabial to pharyngeal. Now we are in a position to formalize the whole of 5.8 at one go. We simply say that the PLACE feature spreads, as in 5.13:

5.13

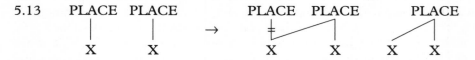

We can see how this works in detail from 5.14. Thus, we can represent *in Paris* as 5.14a, and *in Kent* as 5.14b:

5.14   a.

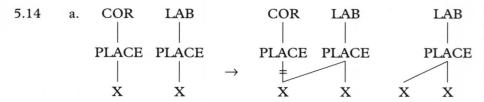

b.

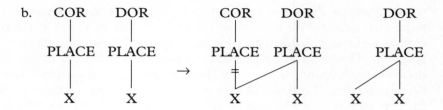

The case of palatals, as in *in York*, is a slightly more complex instance of this idea. Notice that a palatal sound is one which is coronal, but [–anterior], while the coronal sound of /n/ is [+anterior]. We could, therefore, have specified /n/ as [+anterior] (though this feature specification is redundant for nasals). The [–anterior] feature specification is nonetheless acquired by the /n/ as a consequence of spreading. This is illustrated explicitly in 5.14c:[2]

5.14 c.

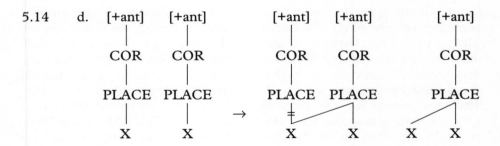

A similar account can be given of *in fact, in these, in church, in German, in shares*, where additional subtleties of articulation are treated as features dependent on the LAB and COR features.

Finally, notice that even when the assimilation produces no discernible effects, as in *in turn*, we can still treat this as an instance of the same assimilation. The result is 5.14d:

5.14 d.

[+ant]	[+ant]		[+ant]	[+ant]		[+ant]
COR	COR		COR	COR		COR
PLACE	PLACE	→	PLACE	PLACE		PLACE
X	X		X	X		X	X

Thus, we have achieved our goal of providing a single, unified account of place of articulation assimilation.

Although we've been able to represent assimilations rather easily and naturally using these notational devices, there are several aspects which require elucidation. First, we must ask why it is that we are able to represent certain features independently, by placing them on separate 'levels' in our diagrams. This is an important observation. Let's recall the traditional IPA description. A sound such as /t/ is given a three-term description specifying voicing (laryngeal), place and manner features: voiceless alveolar plosive. In the feature system we have been adopting, the description 'plosive' is effectively split up into major class features (obstruent) and manner (stop). Thus, we can describe /t/ as a voiceless alveolar obstruent stop. By bunching all the features of a particular kind together we get a feature matrix such as that in figure 5.1 (ignoring certain irrelevant features):

Figure 5.1   Feature specifications for /t/

	t	
cons	+	
approx	–	major class features
son	–	
cont	–	manner features
nas	–	
voiced	–	voicing (laryngeal) features
PLACE	COR	place features
ant	+	

What we will say is that the four bands into which the features are grouped should be given theoretical status. Instead of considering a sound to be simply an unstructured bundle or list of features, a sound will be regarded as consisting of a set of features arranged hierarchically into our four groups. The way that hierarchies are represented in linguistics is generally through tree diagrams. We will therefore replace the simple column of feature specifications in figure 5.1 with a tree diagram in which the nodes correspond to groupings of features. The first of these nodes dominates the whole tree and is referred to as the ROOT node. Subordinate to this node there are two other classes of feature: laryngeal features and other features. The 'other' features are those that correspond to aspects of articulation determined by the oral and nasal cavities above the level of the larynx. These are thus the supralaryngeal features. This basic division is represented as a separation between the LARYNGEAL and SUPRALARYNGEAL nodes. Finally, there are two basic types of supralaryngeal feature as we have seen, and these are represented as the MANNER and PLACE nodes. Because features are now articulated into tree structures, we often refer to the theory of features as the theory of **feature geometry**. The overall picture is shown in figure 5.2:

Figure 5.2   Basic geometry for features

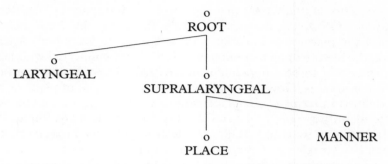

These nodes are often referred to as **class nodes** or **class tiers**, since they help define classes of features. It should be stressed that this is just one way of organizing these nodes (essentially that suggested by Clements 1985 in his original paper on feature geometry). There is a good deal of very active debate as to how best to organize these tiers. However, for our purposes a diagram such as figure 5.2 will be sufficient.

The ROOT node has a number of functions in this theory. One of them is to be the class node for the major class features. Likewise, the LARYN-GEAL, MANNER and PLACE nodes are generally held to dominate (mainly binary) distinctive features. If we add this information we get the rather more complex diagram shown in figure 5.3. However, this is no more than figure 5.2 with all the distinctive feature names added:

Figure 5.3   Partial feature geometry

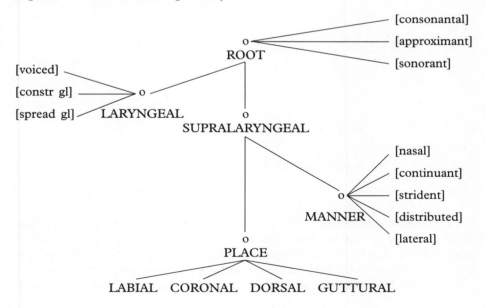

In chapter 4 I pointed out that the [anterior] feature is only relevant for coronal sounds. It doesn't make any sense to ask whether a labial or a velar sound is anterior or not. We say that [anterior] is a **dependent** of CORONAL. In this way CORONAL has a double role, in functioning both as a specification of the place of articulation and as a separate 'mini-tier' of its own. Likewise, the feature of lip rounding, which is clearly connected with labiality, is frequently said to be a dependent of LABIAL. These features principally apply to consonants. However, vowels also involve a type of place of articulation, defined in terms of the placement of the body of the tongue. We can therefore identify a set of TONGUE BODY features, namely, [high], [back], [low]. In addition, we could include the feature [advanced tongue root] here (although it is strictly speaking a misnomer to refer to this as a tongue body feature). The resulting picture is that of figure 5.4, which, though not actually complete, is sufficient for the description of a good many languages:

Figure 5.4   'Complete' feature geometry

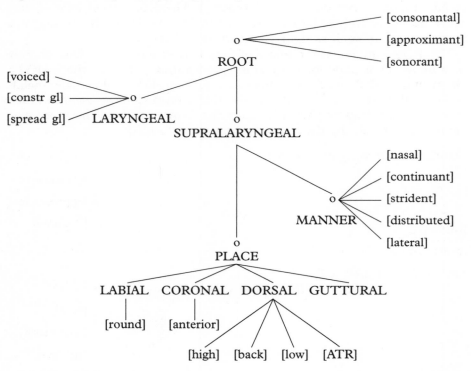

The feature geometric representation for the sound /t/ corresponding to figure 5.1 will now be that of figure 5.5 (where for simplicity I continue to omit irrelevant features). Armed with this more articulated theory of feature structure we can return to the formulation of assimilation processes. By now it should be easy to see that we have been implicitly assuming that it

Figure 5.5 Feature geometric representations of /t/

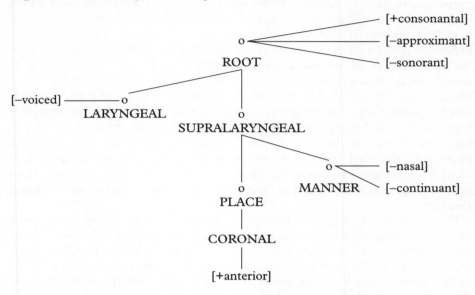

is not only features but whole class nodes that can behave autonomously and spread from one segment to another. Thus, when a consonant assimilates to another in place of articulation, the two consonants come to share one and the same PLACE class node. How exactly is this to be represented using feature geometry?

The idea we wish to capture is that the sound undergoing assimilation comes to share its PLACE node with the following sound. In other words, where we have, say, a cluster /mp/ arising by assimilation from /np/ we wish to say that the /m/ is identical to the /p/ in all its supralaryngeal features except for the manner features. We can represent this if the PLACE node of the /p/ is attached to the SUPRALARYNGEAL node of the /n/ and the old link between that node and the PLACE node of the /n/ is severed. This is shown schematically in figure 5.6 I am ignoring manner, laryngeal and root features here, and using the abbreviations S-L for SUPRALARYNGEAL and PL for PLACE. It's usual to label the whole tier just once per diagram:

Figure 5.6 Place assimilation

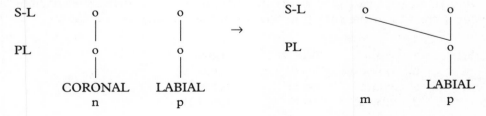

The technical term for the links between the nodes in such diagrams is **association line**. In figure 5.6 we see a process in which an association line, between the PLACE and the SUPRALARYNGEAL nodes of /n/, is cut. This process is known as dissociation or delinking. The subsequent joining of the PLACE node of /p/ to the SUPRALARYNGEAL node of /m/ is a process of reassociation or relinking (cf p. 77). When a link is severed by delinking, then one of two things happens to the stranded bit of feature tree. Either another rule in the language applies and attaches the severed portion somewhere else, or no such rule is applicable and nothing happens. If nothing happens then we end up with an unattached set of features and nodes at the end of the derivation. This is the case with the PLACE-CORONAL bit of tree which is detached from /n/ in figure 5.6. Such left over pieces of tree are simply deleted at the end of the derivation by a general convention or principle called **Stray Deletion** or **Stray Erasure**.

It is not just the PLACE node which can spread to an adjoining segment to give rise to assimilations. In principle, this can happen with any of the class nodes. Indeed, if there is no good evidence for such spreading, then there is little justification for the class nodes in the first place. It is difficult to find good examples of the whole of a MANNER node spreading (and for this reason a number of phonologists have proposed revising the system so as to account for manner features in a different way. We will retain Clements's (1985) original framework, however, because it brings out the similarity with the traditional descriptions rather better and because nothing crucial hangs on this. What about the LARYNGEAL node. Such a node will be justified if a language has a spreading process which affects any of the laryngeal feature specifications under that node. An example of this is Russian voicing assimilation in obstruents. In 5.15–16 we see some examples of this pervasive process. In 5.15 we see a variety of words followed by the conditional particle *bɨ* (which essentially turns the verb in the sentence from a 'do' form to a 'would do' form):

5.15	a.	sup	'soup'	[subbɨ]
	b.	ʃkaf	'wardrobe'	[ʃkavbɨ]
	c.	pros^{j}it^j	'to ask'	[pros^{j}id^{j}bɨ]
	d.	nas	'us'	[nazbɨ]

In 5.16 we see a variety of words and their diminutives, formed by attaching the suffix -*ka* to the root (the final -*a* in these examples is a suffix):

5.16	a.	rɨb-a	'fish'	[rɨpka]
	b.	golov-a	'head'	[golofka]
	c.	vod-a	'water'	[votka]
	d.	glaz-a	'eyes'	[glaska]

What is happening here is that the first member of a consonant cluster acquires the same voicing specification as the following consonant. This is different from English Fricative Devoicing, where only a voiceless consonant affected the previous sound. To capture the Russian process we therefore need to ensure that both values, [+voiced] and [−voiced] spread. However, this is clearly a single, unitary process. Therefore, we don't want to write two distinct rules, one for voicing the other for devoicing, since that would misleadingly imply that the two aspects of voice assimilation were distinct. We can easily capture this unity, however, by saying that it is the LARYN-GEAL node which spreads. Thus, we can represent 5.15a, 5.16a as 5.17, 5.18 respectively:

5.17

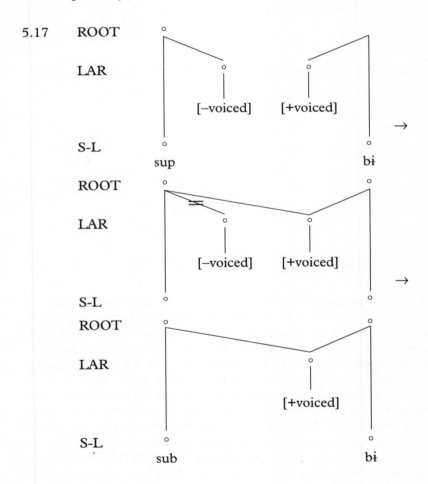

5.18

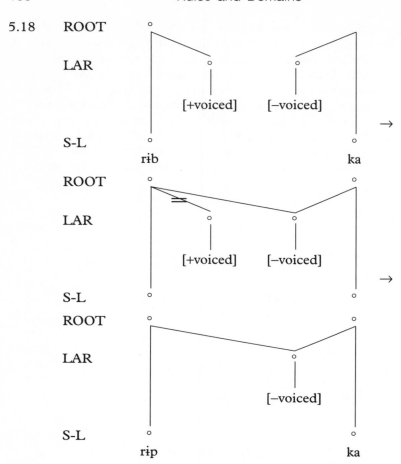

Before we leave this example there is one aspect of the feature geometric representation which we have not yet clarified, but which is very important. Unfortunately, it is one which cannot be captured easily on the printed page. The different classes of features reflect different aspects of the articulators. These are largely independent of each other. Thus, we can change the voicing of a sound (almost) completely independently of the place or manner of articulation. This means, in particular, that the separate class nodes can undergo spreading (association and reassociation) independently of each other. The way this is usually pictured is to imagine that the feature tree is not a two-dimensional representation, but rather a three-dimensional object, like a hanging mobile. Thus, we might imagine the SUPRALARYNGEAL and PLACE tiers in the plane of the page, the LARYNGEAL tier sticking out in front of the page, and the MANNER tier protruding out of the back of the page. In this way, it is possible for the LARYNGEAL node to reassociate to the ROOT node of the previous sound without crossing over

the line between the ROOT and SUPRALARYNGEAL tier. I have attempted
to illustrate this in figure 5.7:

Figure 5.7   Three-dimensional representation of feature geometry

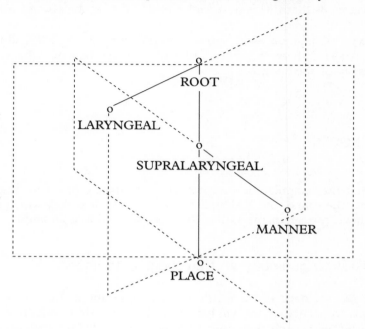

At present this observation is essentially just a clarification, but in the next
subsection we will see that it is of some theoretical importance.

The other node which has been implicated in spreading is the ROOT
node itself. If spreading originates at the root of one phoneme then all the
features of the target segment will be replaced by all those of the first. This
phenomenon is known as **full** or **total assimilation**. A striking illustration
of this phenomenon is found in the Austronesian language, Toba Batak (as
reported by Hayes 1986b). Here /n/ assimilates to a following consonant, as
illustrated in the examples in 5.19:

5.19   a.   mañan baoa an   →   maña[b] baoa an
            eat man that
            'That man is eating'
       b.   baoa an peddek   →   baoa a[p] peddek
            man that short
            'That man is short'
       c.   lean lali   →   lea[l] lali
            give hen-harrier
            'Give a hen-harrier'

    d. soñon gottina   →   soño[g] gottina
       as replacement
       'in exchange'

Hayes assures us that this is observed no matter what the second consonant might be.

    This type of phenomenon can be diagrammed as in 5.20, illustrating example 5.19a (where 'n', 'b' stand as cover symbols for the complete feature array of the sounds):

5.20

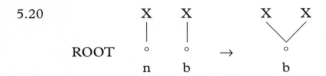

Notice that the assimilation is represented as sharing of a root node. This means that the role of the X slots in 5.20 is crucial. It is they which indicate that we have two segments rather than one after the assimilation.

5.2.2   Feature geometry and autosegmental theory

At this point we need to be a little more precise about the nature of such operations. In particular, we will have to impose certain restrictions on what can be done with such diagrams, otherwise, we will find that we can describe both natural processes, such as place of articulation assimilation, and a whole host of completely unnatural processes with equal ease. This would be a highly undesirable situation, for then our model would have no explanatory content, and wouldn't form the basis of a serious theory of the phonological events it describes.

    An important example of the kind of phenomenon that doesn't seem to be attested, whether in English or any other language, is illustrated by the hypothetical example in 5.21:

5.21   . . . n k p . . .   →   . . . m k p . . .

The reason 5.21 looks odd is that it is a case of assimilation at a distance, which, moreover, has skipped over a consonant which is nearer to the target. In general, assimilation processes don't behave in this fashion. Rather, they are local processes, in the intuitive sense that the target and the source of the assimilatory feature have to be adjacent to each other.[3]

    The key to understanding how to rule out such illegitimate processes is to see what they would look like in feature geometric terms. Consider figure 5.8 (a representation of 5.21):

Figure 5.8 Illicit assimilation

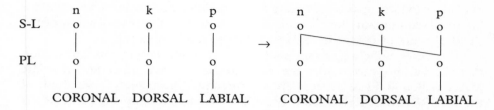

The crucial point about figure 5.8 is that the association line drawn between the PLACE node of the /p/ and that of the target, /n/, crosses over the PLACE association line of the /k/. This phenomenon of crossing association lines violates a basic principle of phonology, first formulated within the theory known as Autosegmental Phonology by John Goldsmith (1976). He proposed a well-formedness constraint on representations according to which any derivation in which lines cross is ruled out automatically. In many respects it is parallel to the constraint in syntactic theory against crossing of lines in a phrase structure grammar (cf. Radford 1988). In both cases the main theoretical motivation is to maintain a straightforward hierarchical structure. This seems to be a fundamental principle of linguistic organization, though it is perfectly possible to imagine things being otherwise. A constraint like the one barring the crossing of association lines thus reflects an important truth about language.

At this point, the attentive reader may well raise the objection that perfectly ordinary cases if assimilation result in crossing association lines once we take the full feature geometry into consideration. Consider a full representation of the perfectly ordinary . . . n p . . . → . . . m p . . . labial assimilation process, as shown in figure 5.9, with all the nodes included:

Figure 5.9 Labial assimilation

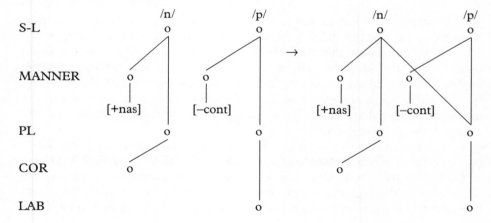

From the way these diagrams are drawn it would seem as if we have crossing association lines after all, since the lines indicating manner of articulation (which at the very least must include specifications [+nasal] for /n/ and [−continuant] for /p/) will get in the way of the reassociation of the PLACE node of /p/ to the SUPRALARYNGEAL node of /n/.

This ceases to be a problem once we recall from the previous subsection that the various class nodes are autonomous of each other and that the MANNER and PLACE tiers are in different dimensions. If we think of the SUPRALARYNGEAL and PLACE nodes as sitting in the plane of the paper, and the MANNER node projecting perpendicular to the paper, then the reassociation of the PLACE node will not encounter any associations to the MANNER node.

5.3 Rule Ordering

In chapter 2 we looked in some detail at the phonological alternations undergone by the plural morpheme in English. One of the conclusions we came to was that there were two processes involved, one of devoicing and the other of schwa epenthesis, and that the order in which they applied was crucial. The essential details are repeated in 5.22–3:

5.22	//kæt + z//	//dɔg + z//	//wɔːlrʌs + z//	
			wɔːlrʌs ə z	Epenthesis
	_____	_____	_____	Devoicing
	kæt s			
	[kæts]	[dɔgz]	[wɔːlrʌsəz]	

5.23	//kæt + z//	//dɔg + z//	//wɔːlrʌs + z//	
	kæt s		wɔːlrʌs s	Devoicing
			wɔːlrʌs ə s	Epenthesis
	_____	_____		
	[kæts]	[dɔgz]	*[wɔːlrʌsəs]	

As is clear from 5.23, if we apply Devoicing before Epenthesis to an underlying form such as //wɔːlrʌs + z// we get an incorrect output *[wɔːlrʌsəs]. Thus it would appear that the two rules have to be applied in a stipulated order. Now, the idea that an ordering can be imposed on rules by the analyst has played an important role in the development of phonological theory within the generative tradition. However, it has also been one of the more controversial aspects of generative phonology. In this section, we will examine the principal issues.

The question of rule ordering doesn't necessarily arise for every given pair of rules. There are many rules in a language which simply don't interact with each other in any way. For instance, if a language has a rule which devoices an obstruent at the end of a word (as in Russian) this is not likely to interact with a rule which reduces an unstressed vowel to schwa. Such

rules are often called **mutually non-affecting**. However, there are a good
many ways in which pairs of rules can interact with each other, and a number of these have assumed theoretical importance for a variety of reasons.

To begin with we will consider a rather simple type of interaction. Suppose a rule A creates a new segment of some sort, and there is a rule B
which converts that new segment into a different segment. Clearly, rule
A has to apply before rule B if this is to happen. This is a very frequent
interaction. An interesting example of the type is provided by certain Slavonic languages such as Polish or Russian. As I noted in chapter 4, Slavicists
generally argue that the Slavonic languages have a phonological rule of velar
palatalization. The effects of such a rule in Polish are to transform /k g x/
into /tʃ ʒ ʃ/. This happens when a stem ending in a velar receives a particular
type of suffix, for instance, one beginning with the high front vowel /i/. This
occurs regularly when a noun stem receives the verb suffix -ić. Some examples are given in 5.24:

5.24   a.   menk-a   'torment'   mentʃ-ić   'to torment'
       b.   wag-a   'scale'   waʒ-ić   'to weigh'
       c.   strax   'fear'   straʃ-ić   'to frighten'

However, this is not the whole story. For after these sibilants (nearly) all
/i/ sounds are backed to the central/back vowel, /ɨ/. Thus, examples 5.24b,
c should really be 5.25:

5.25   a.   menk-a   'torment'   mentʃ-ić   'to torment'
       b.   wag-a   'scale'   waʒ-ɨć   'to weigh'
       c.   strax   'fear'   straʃ-ɨć   'to frighten'

Now, we know that /ić/ (and not /ɨć/) is the basic or underlying form of the
suffix because that is the form which is found with the majority of stems.
Moreover, it is quite impossible in Polish to pronounce /tʃ ʃ ʒ/ before the
front vowel /i/; we only find the central (back) vowel after those sounds.

We can analyse this situation very simply by saying that there are two
rules, Velar Palatalization and i-Backing. Clearly, Velar Palatalization creates
the conditions under which i-Backing can apply, so the two rules must apply
in that order, as shown in 5.26–7:

5.26   //strax + ić//
              ʃ   Vel Pal
                   ɨ   i-Backing
         [straʃɨć]

5.27   //strax + ić//
         _____   i-Backing
              ʃ   Vel Pal
         *[straʃić]

When one rule creates the conditions for another to apply in this fashion we say that the rules are in a **feeding** order. In this case we can say that Velar Palatalization **feeds** i-Backing.

This state of affairs can be contrasted with the curious behaviour of a small number of diminutive and augmentative suffixes in Polish. Let us consider just the augmentative suffix-*isko*. This is added to nouns to give a word meaning 'large (possibly ugly) . . .'. When added to a word ending in /ʃ/ it conditions a shift from /ʃ/ to /ç/ ([ç] is a typically Polish sound midway between /ç/ and /ʃ/). Some examples are:

5.28   a.   kapeluʃ   'hat'   kapeluç-isko   'great big hat'
        b.   arkuʃ   'sheet'   arkuç-isko   'great big sheet'

Rubach (1984: 148) refers to this process as Nominal Strident Palatalization (which we will call NSP). Notice that the new /ç/ segment doesn't trigger i-Backing.

Now, the question arises as to what happens when -*isko* is added to a noun stem ending in a velar. Since -*isko* begins with /i/ we would expect it to trigger Velar Palatalization. This should then feed NSP, bypassing i-Backing. Such a derivation is illustrated in 5.29 for the stem *gmax* 'building':

5.29   //gmax + isko//
            ʃ   Vel Pal
            ç   NSP
         _____   i-Backing
            *[gmaçisko]

However, the correct pronunciation is [gmaʃisko]. This can be understood if we assume that NSP is constrained to apply before Velar Palatalization. Then we obtain 5.30:

5.30   //gmax + isko//
         _____   NSP
            ʃ   Vel Pal
                  ɨ   i-Backing
         [gmaʃisko]

Velar Palatalization and NSP apply in such a way that Velar Palatalization is prevented from feeding NSP. This situation is referred to as **counterfeeding** and we say that NSP **counterfeeds** Velar Palatalization. Any rule B counterfeeds a previous rule A if rule B would have fed rule A had it applied before rule A. This type of interaction is not as common as feeding. The effect, as can be seen from 5.30, is to preserve on the surface a contrast which would otherwise be neutralized between those words which end in /ʃ/

underlyingly, and those which end in a velar which gets palatalized to /ʃ/ by certain suffixes.

For the next type of interaction we can reconsider English plurals. If derivations 5.23 had been observed we would have had a situation in which Devoicing applies to all three different types of underlying form. However, one type of underlying form (//wɔːlrʌs + z//) is deprived of this privilege because Epenthesis applies beforehand, thereby pre-empting Devoicing. Where a rule narrows the range of application of a subsequent rule in this fashion we speak of a **bleeding** order. In this case we say that Epenthesis **bleeds** Devoicing.

In Russian we encounter an intriguing situation in which two rules simultaneously bleed each other. Russian verbs form their past tense by adding -*l* to the stem. In the masculine singular form no other affixes are added, but in the feminine and neuter singular and in the plural form we add, respectively, -*a*, -*o*, -*i*. Most past tense stems end in a vowel, but a small number end in a consonant. Now, for the majority of these consonant stems, the -*l* of the masculine singular (i.e. when there is no following vowel) is dropped, by a process we can call L-Deletion. This is illustrated for a selection of verbs in 5.31–5:[4]

5.31	a.	pʲok-	'bake'
	b.	pʲok	past masc sg
	c.	pʲoklʲi	past pl

5.32	a.	lʲog-	'lie'
	b.	lʲog	past masc sg
	c.	lʲoglʲi	past pl

5.33	a.	grʲob-	'row'
	b.	grʲob	past masc sg
	c.	grʲoblʲi	past pl

5.34	a.	nʲos-	'carry'
	b.	nʲos	past masc sg
	c.	nʲoslʲi	past pl

5.35	a.	vʲoz-	'drive'
	b.	vʲoz	past masc sg
	c.	vʲozlʲi	past pl

However, a subtly different picture emerges when we consider consonant stems ending in /t d/. Here what happens is that the /l/ of the past tense suffix is preserved and it is the final consonant of the stem that gets deleted, as seen in 5.36–7:

5.36   a.   mʲot-   'sweep'
        b.   mʲol   past masc sg
        c.   mʲolʲi   past pl

5.37   a.   vʲod-   'lead'
        b.   vʲol   past masc sg
        c.   vʲolʲi   past pl

We can account for this state of affairs by assuming a rule of T/D-Deletion in addition to L-Deletion. T/D-Deletion is easy to state, since it just deletes the dental plosives from a stem before the past tense suffix. Clearly, if we apply T/D-Deletion first, then we can formulate L-Deletion in a maximally general fashion, by saying that it deletes the past tense /l/ after any consonant. Since the /t d/ of stems such as *mʲot, vʲod* will already have been deleted those stems will not interfere with this generalization. This gives us sample derivations 5.38:

5.38   //vʲoz + l//   //vʲod + l//
                              vʲol   T/D-Del
        ‾‾‾‾‾‾‾‾‾
        vʲoz   ‾‾‾‾‾‾‾‾‾   L-Del
        [vʲoz]   [vʲol]

An interaction such as this, in which each rule bleeds the other, is known as **mutual bleeding**. To see how this works, note that, given the ordering in 5.38, T/D-Deletion bleeds L-Deletion on words such as *vʲol*. However, if we had had the opposite order, as in 5.39, then L-Deletion would have bled T/D-Deletion to give the (non-existent) word *vʲod*:

5.39   //vʲoz + l//   //vʲod + l//
        vʲoz   vʲod   L-Del
                                         T/D-Del
        ‾‾‾‾‾‾‾‾‾   ‾‾‾‾‾‾‾‾‾
        [vʲoz]   *[vʲod]

This would have rather serious consequences for T/D-Deletion, because now the rule would never get the chance to apply. In a sense, the system represented by 5.39 is 'simpler', since it involves one rule less. On the other hand, given the way we have couched the rules, the order represented in 5.38 is the only one possible if we are to retain both rules in the grammar.

In the same way that we can speak of counterfeeding, so we can ask what happens when a rule would bleed another rule if they applied in a different order. In a sense we have already seen this, of course, because the two rules of T/D-Deletion and L-Deletion have this property. Thus, L-Deletion in 5.38 would have bled T/D-Deletion had they applied in the opposite order, so we can say that L-Deletion **counterbleeds** T/D-Deletion. Likewise, in 5.39, T/D-Deletion would have bled L-Deletion, so in that case we would have said that T/D-Deletion counterbleeds L-Deletion. However, we also encounter situations of counterbleeding where mutual bleeding doesn't obtain. Slavic provides another simple example.

On p. 65 we saw examples of the Russian adjectivizing suffix -*n*. This is common throughout Slavic and it triggers velar palatalization. In addition, it is traditional to assume that the underlying form of this suffix contains a vowel. This is one of a particular class of famous Slavic vowels, known as 'yers', which alternate with zero (i.e. which are deleted) whenever a lexical vowel appears in the following syllable. Otherwise, it surfaces as a full vowel. I shall represent a yer as an ordinary vowel in capital letters. Thus, the underlying form of the adjective suffix in a language like Bulgarian will be //-En//. This suffix will have two surface allomorphs, -*n* and -*en*. It is commonly assumed that this yer is a front vowel and it is responsible for triggering the Velar Palatalization (e.g. Scatton 1976).

Now, Bulgarian (like a number of Slav languages) exhibits an adjective form with special suffixes found when the adjective is used predicatively (that is, following the verb 'to be'). In the masculine singular form the suffix is itself null, while in the feminine singular it is -*a*. Thus, from a root *mrak* 'darkness, gloom', we obtain the masc sg predicative adjective form *mratʃen* 'dark'. In the fem. sg form the stem is followed by a vowel and we obtain *mratʃna* (morphologically, *mratʃ-n-a*). Notice that the yer vowel, /E/, has dropped in this form.

We can summarize all this by saying that there is a rule of Yer Deletion which deletes a yer when there is a 'real' vowel in the following syllable. In addition, we have our rule of Velar Palatalization. The derivations of *mratʃen* and *mratʃna* are shown in 5.40:

5.40   //mrak + En//   //mrak + En + a//
          mratʃ   En   mratʃ   En   a   Vel Pal
        _____   mratʃ   n   a   Yer Del
        [mratʃen]   [mratʃna]

Now, it is the yer in //mrakEna// which triggers Velar Palatalization. Therefore, if Yer Deletion had applied before Velar Palatalization it would have bled the palatalization rule and we would have obtained **mrakna* as the fem sg form. Hence, Velar Palatalization and Yer Deletion apply in a counterbleeding order.

As I have said the concept of rule ordering is not uncontroversial. First, it must be pointed out that it is not always necessary to impose a specific ordering on rules, if we accept certain other principles. For instance, we might say that a rule can apply at any stage in the derivation provided its structural description is met. Such a rule is referred to as an **anywhere rule**. For instance, other things being equal we don't actually need to impose an ordering on the Polish rules of Velar Palatalization and i-Backing discussed above. Suppose we simply allowed each rule to scan the derivation continually and apply whenever it could. Then at the very outset, when the suffix and stem are combined in the example in 5.26, only Velar Palatalization is applicable. After it has applied it creates the conditions which trigger i-Backing. Thus, there is a natural ordering implicit in the formulation of the two rules. Such an implicit relationship is referred to as **intrinsic ordering**. All phonologists who work with phonological rules accept that rules may apply in such an intrinsic order.

.However, this will not work for the case of, say, English plural allomorphy. This is because, given complete freedom, both Epenthesis and Devoicing could apply to a form such as //wɔːlrʌs + z/. If both were allowed to apply we would then get the unwanted order (that would be a counterbleeding order – check that you understand why). In general, if two rules have to apply in a counterfeeding order, as is the case with Polish Velar Palatalization and NSP, or a counterbleeding order, such as Epenthesis and Devoicing, then that order has to be stipulated and we speak of **extrinsic ordering**.

A crucial question in phonological theory has been whether extrinsic rule ordering is necessary to linguistic theory. One of the theoretical problems which extrinsic ordering poses concerns language acquisition: given that phonological rule systems tend to be quite complex, how would a child be able to figure out the right order in which to apply all the phonological rules? This learnability problem is rendered particularly acute when we appreciate what a child has to do to learn a phonology. All the child is presented with is the surface forms of various morphemes, appearing in various alternative allomorphs depending on morphological and phonological environment. From this array of surface forms the child has to compute: (1) the underlying forms, (2) the rules. But the shape of the underlying forms will depend on which rules are postulated, and contrariwise, the form of the rules will depend on which underlying forms are posited. This already constitutes a sizeable learnability problem. If the child also has to work out the correct order of all the rules, the task becomes truly immense.

Of those who accept the notion of ordering a good many phonologists have tried to develop theoretical principles which will predict which order a rule will apply in. In the most optimistic case we might be able to predict the ordering relationships of all rules simply by inspecting the form of the rule and applying certain universal principles. Early proposals along these lines were put forward by Kiparsky (1973) and Koutsoudas et al. (1974). However, these proposals related to the earlier, linear, SPE rule types. Many of the cases they discussed (especially those to do with stress) are simply no longer relevant because stress is handled by a different type of theory nowadays (see chapter 7 on Metrical Phonology), which appeals to very different formal devices. Likewise, a good many rules are now known to be sensitive to prosodic domains such as the syllable, and this means that such rules, which in the SPE model would stand in an ordering relationship, are now mutually non-affecting because they apply in different domains. Finally, phonologists now widely recognize that there are at least two types of segmental phonological rule, the lexical rule and the postlexical rule. Pretty well all contemporary theories of phonology have been influenced by the proposals advanced within the theory of Lexical Phonology (Kiparsky 1982, 1985) that lexical and postlexical rules apply in separate components. The lexical rules apply just to lexical items while the postlexical rules apply across syntactic boundaries and thus apply only after the syntactic component has constructed surface forms of sentences. This means that postlexical rules are automatically ordered after lexical rules. In some models of Lexical Phonology, the lexical rules are further stratified, which imposes an additional ordering. Thus, there is increasingly less need for stipulated extrinsic ordering of rules.[5]

5.4   Rules and Phonotactics: 'Conspiracies'

In chapter 3 we saw that part of what a speaker knows about his/her language is what types of syllable are well formed. The conditions on syllable structure form part of the phonotactic constraints of the language. Now, in many languages we find that syllable structure constraints are violated when we combine morphemes to form words. We saw a fairly typical case of this in chapter 2, section 2.4.3, when we discussed Epenthesis in Koryak.

Let's review those examples and see exactly how syllable structure can play a role in the operation of epenthesis. The crucial examples from the root //pŋlo// 'ask' are repeated as 5.41:

5.41   a.   təpŋəlon   //t-pŋlo-n//   'I asked him'
        b.   mətpəŋlon   //mt-pŋlo-n//   'we asked him'
        c.   napŋəlon   //na-pŋlo-n//   'they asked him'

In chapter 2 we said that the function of Epenthesis was to break up illegal consonant clusters. However, given what we know about syllable structure and the construction of syllables by the syllabification algorithm we can regard Epenthesis as part of the algorithm itself. Koryak has a simple syllable template, essentially CVC, that is, a syllable can have at most one onset consonant and one coda consonant. Syllabification of an underlying form proceeds from left to right. When we reach a sequence which can't be syllabified we perform the minimal epenthesis operation needed to obtain a legal syllable structure. We can see how this operates by starting with 5.41a, b. We will assume that the algorithm works its way along the word, trying to fit the melody elements to the CVC syllable template. When it comes to an impasse it epenthesizes a schwa.

Each of 5.41a, b begins with a cluster. Only the first of these consonants can be syllabified, therefore, and it becomes the onset. Then we have to epenthesize a schwa to give the first syllable. The algorithm continues along the words, and again comes to a halt because it encounters two consonants, only the first of which can form an onset. The result is shown in 5.42a, b:

5.42   a.

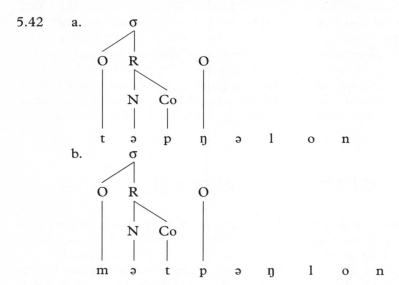

The algorithm again has to epenthesize, after which the whole of the rest of the words can be syllabified normally:

5.43   a.

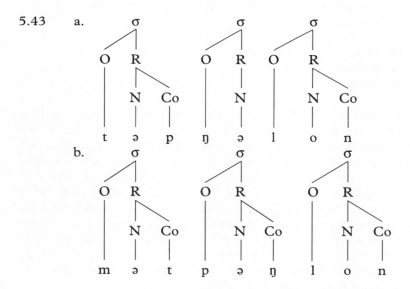

Example 5.41c can be handled in a similar fashion (try it for yourself to check you understand how the system works).

A good many languages have a set of rules which are designed to maintain

a particular type of syllable. How would the Koryak situation be described
in the SPE framework? Recall that SPE had no recourse to syllable structure as such, and didn't have any mechanism to permit phonotactic constraints to govern the operation of rules. The main problem is posed by
the word initial clusters such as *#mt-* and the word internal clusters such
as *-pŋl-* in words such as *təpŋəlon* from //tpŋlon// (where # represents a
word boundary). In the first case, the schwa is inserted immediately after
the first consonant, whereas in the second case it is inserted after the second. From the point of view of syllable structure this is obvious: we don't
need to add a schwa immediately after /p/ in 5.41a because the /p/ will be
the coda of the previous syllable, and won't need the support of the schwa.
However, without appeal to syllable structure, it is not so easy to capture
this.

Let's see what kind of rule system we would need in the SPE framework
to handle this. What we need is one rule to break up a word initial cluster
by epenthesizing immediately after the first consonant of the word and
another to epenthesize after the second of a cluster of three consonants.
These rules are shown schematically in 5.44. For simplicity we can represent consonants of any sort as 'C':

5.44   a. ∅   →   ə   /#C _____ C   Initial Epenthesis
        b. ∅   →   ə   /VCC _____ C   Medial Epenthesis

Derivations for 5.41a, b are shown in 5.45:

5.45   a. //t-pŋlo-n//   b.   //mt-pŋlo-n//
            təpŋlon   mətpŋlon   I. Epenthesis
            təpŋəlon   mətpəŋlon   M. Epenthesis
            [təpŋəlon]   [mətpəŋlon]   Output

The problem with this solution is that we require two distinct (though
clearly rather similar) rules to account for one process. Moreover, when we
look at the purpose behind the rules, they are clearly fulfilling the same sort
of function, namely, maintenance of phonotactics. This sort of situation is
quite common in the world's languages.

A classic case of this type is the Yawelmani dialect of the Californian
language, Yokuts, which was discussed by Kisseberth (1970), who first raised
this type of problem for the SPE approach. Kisseberth referred to assem-
blages of rules which all have the same phonotactic function as **conspiracies**. Within the SPE framework the problem of conspiracies was never
satisfactorily resolved. Nowadays, the relationship between rules and
phonotactic constraints has been the arena for considerable debate. Some
phonologists have argued that all or most rules should actually be triggered
by constraints so that the rules themselves are seen as 'repair strategies' for
fixing up violations of constraints (e.g. Paradis 1988–9). Other phonologists

have gone even further and argue that we can abandon the whole concept of 'rule' and allow phonological alternations to be decided entirely in terms of constraints (as in Optimality Theory: McCarthy and Prince 1994). This latter development promises to be an extremely important and influential approach to phonological theory. However, these issues go beyond the scope of an introduction such as this. We will now proceed to other types of domain which influence the operation of rules.

5.5   Prosodic Domains and Rules

In section 5.1 we discussed the ramifications of a place of articulation assimilation process that affects /n/ in English. As we saw, this happens across word boundaries. However, there are situations in which it fails to apply. For instance, consider the difference in pronunciation between 5.46 and 5.47:

5.46   They want to live in Boston.

5.47   Of all the towns they want to live in, Boston is the nicest.

While place assimilation would be quite normal in 5.46, it would be very strange in 5.47. The reason is that it is not possible for assimilation to take place if the target and the source of the assimilation are separated by a pause (recorded in 5.47 by the comma). In effect, we pronounce the first clause (ending with 'in') as one intonational unit, and the second clause as a second intonational unit, and the assimilation is not permitted across such a unit. This sort of situation is commonplace. The question we will address in this section is how we capture the idea that a pause, i.e. the boundary of an intonational unit (or any other such boundary) can govern the operation of phonological processes.

The general term we will use for such units is **phonological domain** or **prosodic domain**. The prosodic domains we will discuss are the syllable, word, phrase, and the whole utterance. In recent years it has become apparent that regular postlexical phonological processes may be restricted in their application by domain type. Processes typically apply either within a particular domain (for instance, at one edge of the domain), or between the boundaries of certain domains. In this section we will look briefly at a number of such cases.

5.5.1   Syllable-based processes

A number of cases have been reported of rules applying within the domain of the syllable. A very simple example of this is a rule which turns an alveolar nasal into a velar in certain varieties of Spanish (Harris 1983: 46ff; cf. also Nespor and Vogel 1986: 74ff). This is illustrated in 5.48:[6]

5.48   a.   kantan   →   ka[ŋ]ta[ŋ]   'they sing'
              ramon entró   →   ramo[ŋ] entró   'Ramon entered'
              instituto   →   i[ŋ]stituto   'institute'
        b.   poner   →   po[n]er   'to put'
              jo no soj   →   jo [n]o soj   'I am not'

Velarization takes place in the 5.48a examples but not in the 5.48b examples. We can easily understand this behaviour if we recognize that the process takes place when the /n/ is in the rhyme. This can be stated very simply as 5.49:

5.49   Velarization

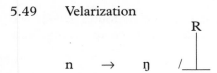

This is read as stating that the rule affects any /n/ at any position within a rhyme.

   Harris (1983: 57ff) points out that all dialects of Spanish exhibit an alternation between the /j/ glide component of diphthongs such as /jo/ or /oj/, and a consonant of some kind. In the Porteño dialect of Buenos Aires, the glide alternates with the voiced alveopalatal fricative [ʒ]. This is an example of a fortition process, and Harris refers to the process as 'Glide Strengthening'. It is illustrated by alternations such as 5.50:

5.50   a.   konvo[j]   'convoy'   konvo[ʒ]es   'convoys'
        b.   le[j]   'law'   le[ʒ]es   'laws'

In addition, the endings /-jendo/ and /-jó/ show an alternation:

5.51   a.   kom[j]endo   'eating'
              lam[j]ó   'licked'
        b.   kre[ʒ]endo   'believing'
              le[ʒ]ó   'read'

Harris assumes that the glide element /j/ of these diphthongs is part of the nucleus, and hence part of the rhyme. He then notes that the /ʒ/ alternant occurs when the glide is at the left edge of the syllable (though not, interestingly, in onset position, since the glide is still part of the nucleus). This is illustrated in 5.52:

5.52

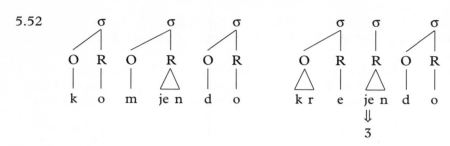

(This glosses over certain details concerning syllabification, but the general idea is fairly straightforward.) Glide Strengthening is formulated in 5.53:

5.53   Glide Strengthening

$$j \quad \to \quad 3 \quad /\ _\sigma(\underline{\qquad}$$

A variety of other syllable-based rules in Spanish can be found in Harris's monograph. Other cases of syllable-based rules are given in Nespor and Vogel (1986).[7]

5.5.2 Foot-based processes

We will see in chapters 7 and 8 that word stress defines an important domain in the characterization of stress rules, the **foot**. Although we will see that there is some controversy over the definition of the foot, the basic idea is that it consists of a stressed syllable together with any adjacent unstressed syllables if there are any, either on the left, or on the right. Thus, in an English word such as *còmpartmèntalizátion* we have a main stress at the end and two secondary stresses. These define three feet, of the form (compart)$_F$ (mentalize)$_F$ (ation)$_F$. Each of these feet consists of a stressed syllable followed by one or more unstressed syllables.

It is still a matter of controversy whether this or any similar notion of 'foot' plays a role in the segmental phonology of a language. This is because many cases of sensitivity to foot structure can be reanalysed in different terms, and because in any case a number of phonologists feel that the notion 'foot' is redundant even when analysing stress systems (e.g. Selkirk 1984). However, to illustrate the sort of thing that people mean when they speak of foot-based processes, I'll discuss one of the more convincing examples from the literature.

The best cases seem to involve phonology that is also morphology, such as reduplication processes (a detailed discussion of this can be found in Broselow and McCarthy 1983). A simple example has been provided by Poser (1989), who considered the Australian language, Diyari. The basic stress system of this language is that main stress falls on the first syllable and then secondary stresses fall on odd numbered syllables. This is illustrated in

5.54 (where an acute accent indicates main stress and a grave accent indicates secondary stress):

5.54   a.   (dáka)_F   'to pierce'
        b.   (wáka)_F (rì)_F   'to break'

One rule of Diyari which appeals to this structure is a process of reduplication, illustrated in 5.55 (Poser 1989: 132):

5.55.   stem   reduplication
        a.   daka   dakadaka   'to pierce'
              yata   yatayata   'to talk'
              dunka   dunkadunka   'to emerge'
              kanku   kankukanku   'boy'
        b.   kanini   kanikanini   'mother's mother'
              wakari   wakawakari   'to break'
              kulkuŋa   kulkukulkuŋa   'to jump'

What is clearly happening here is that the first foot of the word is reduplicated. This means the whole word in the case of *daka* or *dunka*, and the first two syllables in the case of *kanini* or *wakari*.

5.5.3   Phonological words

In chapter 2, section 2.4.1, I introduced Hungarian Vowel Harmony. Recall that in a Hungarian word the vowels have to be either all [+back] or all [–back] (with certain systematic exceptions). The examples are repeated here as 5.56:

5.56   a.   teːrkeːprøːl   'map'
              føldrøːl   'land'
              yɟrøːl   'business'
              siːnrøːl   'colour'
        b.   laːɲroːl   'girl'
              uːrroːl   'gentleman'
              fogroːl   'tooth'

Unfortunately, the generalization doesn't always work. Here are some violations of it:

5.57   a.   føːvaːroʃ   'capital (city)'
        b.   uːrnø ː   'lady'
        c.   yɟbuzgoː   'eager'
        d.   ønjaːroː   'self-propelled'

What is common to these is that they are all morphologically compound words. They have the structure given in 5.58:

5.58   a.   føː + vaːroʃ
             head + town
        b.   uːr + nøː
             gentle + woman
        c.   yɟ + buzgoː
             matter + eager
        d.   øn + jaːroː
             self + moving

Compounds such as these are rather frequent in Hungarian, and it is clear that they are words rather than phrases. Firstly, they are always stressed on their first syllable, just like all other words in the language, and secondly, they often have partly or entirely idiosyncratic meanings. Thus, *føːvaːroʃ* means specifically capital city, not just any important town.

In order to understand the workings of vowel harmony, then, we need a more refined notion of 'word'. Although *føːvaːroʃ* is a single word morphologically in the sense that it is a single compound word, for the phonological purposes of Vowel Harmony it behaves as though it still consisted of two words. The Vowel Harmony process is then confined to each one of those two words, and does not cross over those boundaries. We will therefore say that *føːvaːroʃ* is made up of two **phonological words**. The domain of Vowel Harmony is then 'within a phonological word'. This is shown in 5.59 where the subscript *w* stands for 'phonological word':

5.59   a.   (føː)$_w$ (vaːroʃ)$_w$
        b.   (uːr)$_w$ (nøː)$_w$
        c.   (yɟ)$_w$ (buzgoː)$_w$
        d.   (øn)$_w$ (jaːroː)$_w$

In this Hungarian example, the phonological words happen to coincide with the original morphological words which make up the compound. A slightly different sort of case can be found in Italian (Nespor and Vogel 1986: 124ff). There are two sorts of prefix in Italian. One type is productive with a transparent meaning and it attaches to words, while the other type is morphologically and lexically restricted, often has an opaque meaning (or no meaning at all) and may attach to bound stems which are not in themselves free-standing words. Italian also has a constraint against voiceless /s/ in intervocalic position, only /z/ is found there. Thus, words spelt with a single 's' between vowels (reflecting what was historically /s/) have these pronounced as /z/: *rosa* [roza] 'rose', *resistenza* [rezistentsa] 'resistance'. One systematic exception occurs when /s/ appears immediately after a productive preposition, such as *ri-* 'to do again': *risuonare* 'to ring again' (from *suonare* 'to ring'), *a-* 'not' as in *asociale* 'asocial' (from *sociale* 'social'). The form *presentire* is a minimal pair in this regard. With the meaning 'to have a presentiment' the word is pronounced [prezentire], but with the meaning 'to hear in advance' it is pronounced [presentire]. In the latter meaning it is formed from the regular, productive prefix *pre-* 'before, in advance', attached to the word *sentire* 'to hear'. However, it is impossible to give any meaning to the formatives *pre-* and *sentire* in the meaning 'to have a presentiment' (any more than this can be done to the English *presentiment*).

We can readily account for this behaviour by assuming that the productive prefixes form a separate phonological word of their own. Then we simply formulate a rule of s-voicing which voices underlying /s/ between two vowels, <u>inside a phonological word</u>. This will apply to cases like *rosa* and *resistenza* but not to *risuonare* or *asociale*, as shown in 5.60, 61:

5.60   a.   (rosa)$_w$
         b.   (resistenza)$_w$

5.61   a.   (ri)$_w$ (suonare)$_w$
         b.   (a)$_w$ (sociale)$_w$

The difference between the two pronunciations of *presentire* is reflected in 5.62:

5.62   a.   (presentire)$_w$ 'to have a presentiment'
         b.   (pre)$_w$ (sentire)$_w$ 'to hear in advance'

In these examples a phonological word is seen to be less than a morphological word. However, we also find cases where a phonological word seems to encompass more than a single morphological word. The commonest situation where this arises is with **clitics**. A clitic is a word which cannot exist in isolation, but which needs to be attached to another word. A simple example from English would be the *'s* of *Tom's* in *Tom's a linguist*, where the clitic is actually the main verb of the sentence. It is thus like an affix, in that it is a bound form, and, indeed, many clitics are called bound words. However, in many cases we find that clitics are entirely different from affixes in that they can attach to any kind of word irrespective of its syntactic or morphological category. Affixes, on the other hand, always attach to words or stems of a particular morphosyntactically definable type. It is customary to distinguish between clitics and affixes when writing representations of morphologically analysed words by separating affixes by means of a dash or a plus sign, e.g. *dog–s* or *dog+s* and separating clitics by means of an equals sign, =, e.g. *Tom='s*.

Finnish is an example of a language with clitics which attach to words of all categories. One clitic in particular, *=ko*, has the function of turning a sentence into a question focusing on the word it is attached to, which is always the first word in the sentence. Finnish has a vowel harmony system rather similar to that of Hungarian. When =*ko* is cliticized to a word, it undergoes harmony. This can be seen from examples 5.63 (note that Finnish has rather free word order):

5.63   a.   hæn laulaa
             he   sings
             'He is singing.'
        b.   hænkø laulaa?
             he=KO sings
             'Is HE singing?'
        c.   laulaako   hæn?
             sings=KO he
             'Is he SINGING?'

In 5.63 we see =*ko/kø* attaching to a pronoun and a verb, showing it can't be an ordinary suffix. When the word it attaches to (the **host**) has front vowels (5.63b) we get =*kø* and when the host has back vowels (5.63c) we get =*ko*.

As in Hungarian, we can assume that the domain for Vowel Harmony is the phonological word, w. However, that means that the clitic forms a single phonological word with its host. Thus, we have the representations of 5.64 for the cliticized words in 5.63:

5.64   a.   (hæn=kø)$_w$
        b.   (laulaa=ko)$_w$

5.5.4 Phonological phrases

Phonologists have uncovered a number of cases in a variety of languages in which the operation of a phonological process seems to be governed by syntactic structure. Thus, a process may apply only within a particular type of phrase, or only at the boundary between phrases of a particular type. Frequently, such phrases correspond to syntactically defined phrases such as English *black cat, a black cat,* or *has already left*. However, in other cases the relationship is rather more complex. We saw in the last subsection that a phonological word may not necessarily correspond exactly with a morphological word, but may be either smaller or larger. Likewise, we often find that we need to appeal to a unit called a **phonological phrase**, and that this doesn't always coincide with the syntactic phrase on which it is based.

An example of a phonological process which makes reference to the phrase is a phenomenon in Italian known as Raddoppiamento Sintattico (RS), which means 'syntactic doubling'. I shall base my description on Nespor and Vogel (1986: 165ff). The basic process has the following effects: it lengthens the first consonant, C, of a word provided that (1) the immediately preceding word ends in a stressed vowel and (2) the sound immediately after C is a vowel, glide or liquid (i.e. is a non-nasal sonorant). Some examples are given in 5.65, where the ligature ‿ means that the next consonant is doubled, and a stressed syllable is marked with an acute accent ´:

5.65.   a.   Avrátrovato   il pescecane.
                (he) would-have found the shark
                'He must have found the shark.'
      b.   E appena passato con trécani.
                is just   passed with three dogs
                'He has just passed by with three dogs.'
      c.   Era venuto con trépiccoli cobra.
                was come with three little cobras
                'He came with three little cobras.'

In 5.65 the RS process applies to a target word (*trovato, cani, piccoli*) which is in the same phrase as the immediately preceding vowel-final stressed word (*would have found, with three dogs, with three little cobras*). In 5.66 we see comparable examples in which the first consonant of the word is not doubled, even though the previous word ends in a stressed vowel. The double slashes // indicate that the words concerned are in separate phonological phrases:

5.66   a.   Devi   comprare delle mappe di cittá //molto vecchie.
                you-must buy   of-the maps of city very old
                'You must buy some very old city maps.'
      b.   Ne   aveva   soltanto tré // di bassotti.
                of-them he-had only   three of dachshunds.
                'He only had three dachshunds.'
      c.   Guardó //piú attentamente e   vide che era un pitone.
                he-looked more carefully   and saw that was a python
                'He looked more carefully and saw that it was a python.'

Now, in 5.66 we seem to have the right sequence of trigger and target for RS, so what rules out RS must be the fact that the crucial words straddle distinct phonological phrases. How can we determine what constitutes a phonological phrase? The answer depends in part on the language, though there are general principles which seem to be true of all languages. One such universal property of the phonological phrase is that it must contain the syntactic head of the phrase. Additionally, in Italian, if modifiers of a head (e.g. adjectives modifying nouns or adverbs modifying verbs) are to the left of the head, they can be incorporated into the phonological phrase containing that head. However, if the modifiers are to the right of the head, then they can't be so incorporated and have to form a phonological phrase of their own. The result is that the examples of 5.63 form the phonological phrases shown in 5.67 (where ϕ = 'phonological phrase'):

5.67   a. (avrá_trovato)$_\phi$ (il pescecane)$_\phi$
          b. (con tré_cani)$_\phi$
          c. (con tré_piccoli cani)$_\phi$

Let's look at this in more detail. In 5.63a the main verb, *trovato*, is the most important part of the verb phrase 'must have found the shark'. In other words, it is the head of the phrase. Likewise, in 5.63b, *cani* 'dogs' is the head of the noun phrase. In 5.63c, *piccoli* 'little' is not the head of the phrase; however, it is to the left of the head, and can therefore form a phonological phrase with that head. We can see this more clearly if we represent the syntactic structure using traditional tree diagrams.[8] (We'll depart from some of the assumptions adopted by Nespor and Vogel to simplify the explanation, but we'll maintain the essentials of their account).

In 5.68 I give the structure for the whole of 5.63a. The important point to note here is that the Auxiliary verb, *avrá* 'would have', is attached to the left side of the main verb *trovato* 'found' and can thus form a phonological phrase with it. The phrase, VP, which determines the domain of the RS process and the head of that phrase, V, are boxed:

5.68

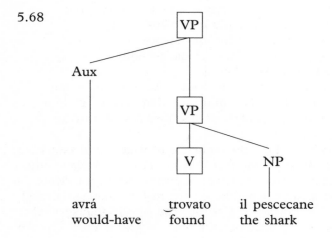

In 5.69 we see the prepositional phrase in 5.63b. The crucial phrase and its head are boxed. Here notice that the numeral (Num) *tre* 'three' is a pre-modifier of the head of the noun phrase, *cani* 'dogs':

5.69   PP

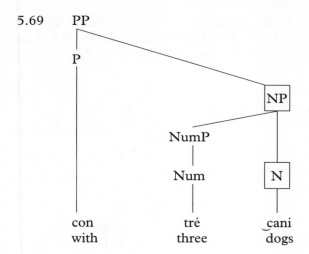

| con | tré | cani |
| with | three | dogs |

In 5.70, corresponding to 5.63c, we see that the doubling takes place between the numeral and the adjective which modifies the head of the noun phrase. In Italian it is usual for an adjective phrase to follow the noun it modifies. However, on occasions we find the adjective appearing as a premodifier, as in 5.63c. Therefore, the adjective (and any other premodifiers) can form a single phonological phrase along with the head noun. Again the noun phrase and its head are boxed:

5.70   PP

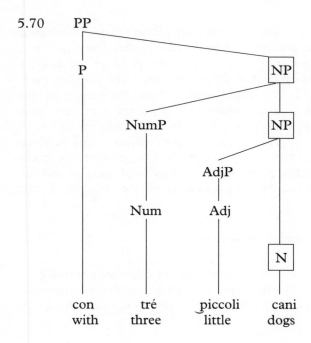

| con | tré | piccoli | cani |
| with | three | little | dogs |

Now compare the situation with the examples in 5.66. In 5.71 we can see that the would-be target, *molto* 'very, is an adjective phrase acting as a post-modifier of the head noun *mappe* 'maps' (the normal position for adjective phrases):

5.71.

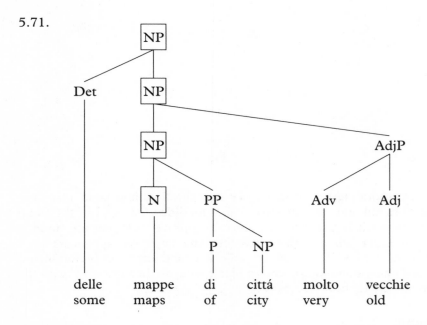

delle	mappe	di	cittá	molto	vecchie
some	maps	of	city	very	old

The point here is that *cittá* and *molto* are not part of the same phonological phrase. This is because the adjective phrase *molto vecchie* 'very old' is a postmodifier of *mappe* 'maps' (i.e. it appears to the right of the head it modifies). In addition, it is separated from that head by another post-modifying phrase, *di cittá* 'of the city'. Under these circumstances the adjective phrase can't form a single phonological phrase with the head noun it modifies. Nor can *di cittá* 'of the city' form a single phonological phrase with the noun head, because it too is a postmodifier, and hence is on the wrong side of the head it modifies. It is as though the syntactic structure introduces a kind of slight pause between 'city' and 'very'. (and between 'maps' and 'of'). The resulting phonological phrase structure is that of 5.72:

5.72   (delle mappe)$_\phi$ (di cittá)$_\phi$ (molto vecchie)$_\phi$

Clearly, the trigger, *cittá*, and the target, *molto*, are in different phonological phrases and so RS is blocked. A similar picture can be found with the other two examples. In 5.73 we see the syntactic structure of the crucial part of 5.66b:

5.73

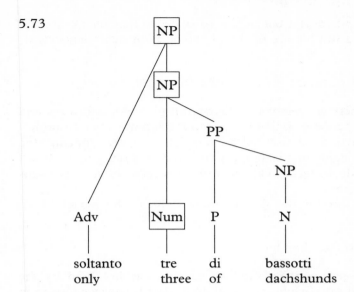

Here, the head of the whole noun phrase is the Numeral *tre* 'three'. Again, the modifier 'of dachshunds' appears to the right of this head, and therefore can't form a phonological phrase with it. The result phrasal structure is 5.74:

5.74   (soltanto tre)$_\phi$ (di bassotti)$_\phi$

Finally, in 5.66c, we have an adverbial phrase which postmodifies a verb. Again, because the modifier comes to the right of its head, it can't form a phonological phrase with it. (You should be able to draw a plausible tree diagram to represent this). The phrase structure is therefore that of 5.75:

5.75   (Guardó)$_\phi$ (piú attentamente)$_\phi$

There are important reasons why it can be rather difficult to investigate the behaviour of phonological phrases and rules which refer to them. As was the case with phonological words, we find that there is often a discrepancy between syntactically defined phrase structure and phonologically defined phonological phrases. Indeed, this is the whole point behind the notion. This means that it is necessary to find sometimes rather subtle evidence which will help establish exactly what the criteria are in a given language for constructing phonological phrases. Another indeterminacy is brought about by the fact that different syntactic theories will provide very different surface syntactic structures for one and the same construction in a given language. There has been relatively little collaboration between phonologists and syntacticians in trying to establish common ground here, and the study of the phonological phrase as a domain for phonological processes is still in its infancy. Nonetheless, there is a fair degree of evidence that such a domain is necessary to gain a full picture of the phonologies of many languages.

5.5.5   Intonational phrases and the phonological utterance

We have seen that there are reasons to distinguish phonological words and phonological phrases, corresponding broadly, but not perfectly, to morphological words and syntactic phrases. Also important are larger domains, the first corresponding roughly to a clause in syntax (or sometimes to a phrase) and second to a whole sentence. The most obvious reflex of such domains is in intonation patterns.

We can illustrate this for the first of these domains by means of an example such as 5.76:

5.76   By the sea-shore, they found an old cave.

The natural way of pronouncing such an example, as indicated by the comma, is to divide it into two intonational units. As I briefly mentioned in chapter 1, intonation is characterized by a variety of 'tunes' or tone contours. In languages like English these are fixed on the most prominent or accented syllable of a phrase. In the case of 5.76 we would normally find a tonal contour on the word *sea* which falls then rises (on the word *shore*). The second part of the sentence would then have a falling tone on the word *cave*. We can thus delimit two intonational units, as in 5.77, in which each accented syllable is in capitals, and the intonation is shown schematically as a set of tone marks:

5.77   (by the SEA - shore)   (they found an old CAVE)

The two intonationally defined units in 5.67 are referred to by a variety of terms in the literature on rhythm and accent. We shall call them **intonational phrases** (after Nespor and Vogel 1986), and notate them by means of a bracket labelled 'I': (by the sea-shore)$_I$.

There are often several different ways of breaking up an utterance into intonational phrases, depending on speech rate, emphasis and even syntactic structure. For instance, a sentence such as 5.78 would often be pronounced as 5.79:

5.78   They found an old cave by the sea-shore.

5.79   (they found an old cave by the sea-shore)$_I$

On the other hand, 5.80 seems to require the phonological structure 5.81:

5.80   They found an old cave, by the sea-shore.

5.81   (they found an old cave)$_I$ (by the sea-shore)$_I$

In 5.79 we have a single intonational phrase. However, in 5.81 we have two intonational phrases (as indicated in orthography by the comma). Neither variant is more 'correct' than the other, they are simply appropriate in slightly different contexts.

Finally, we can say that the whole of sentence 5.76 constitutes a phonological domain. This is the smallest span that would normally constitute a complete utterance (on the assumption that people are well-behaved and speak in nicely completed sentences). We therefore refer to such a domain as the **phonological utterance**. It is notated by a bracket labelled 'U': (by the sea-shore they found an old cave)$_U$.

The precise delimitation of the intonational phrase is still a matter of some controversy. For instance, when we consider wider stretches of utterance, and in particular, when we consider the role of intonation, there are grounds for saying that intonational phrases can be grouped into larger domains, which are still intonational phrases themselves and not phonological utterances proper (e.g. Ladd 1986). However, it would require a specialist text on intonation to investigate these ramifications properly so we will content ourselves with a relatively simplified account.

In one rather famous case a difference in intonational phrasing corresponds to a difference in grammatical structure. Consider sentence 5.82:

5.82   Phonologists who know dozens of fascinating languages are universally admired.

This can be pronounced as 5.83 (corresponding to 5.84) or as 5.85 (corresponding to 5.86):

5.83   Phonologists who know dozens of fascinating languages, are universally admired.

5.84   (Phonologists who know dozens of fascinating languages)$_I$ (are universally admired)$_I$.

5.85   Phonologists, who know dozens of fascinating languages, are universally admired.

5.86   (Phonologists)$_I$ (who know dozens of fascinating languages)$_I$ (are universally admired)$_I$.

Example 5.83–4 tells us that those phonologists who know dozens of fascinating languages benefit from everyone's admiration, though it doesn't say anything about the phonologists who don't know many languages. On the other hand, examples 5.85–6 presuppose that phonologists are admired by everyone, and adds as an incidental piece of information the fact that they (we?) know all these languages. In 5.83 *who know dozens of fascinating languages* is a restrictive relative clause, serving to delimit more precisely the class of phonologists under discussion. In 5.85, however, the clause is an appositive relative clause, which serves to add extra information about the noun it modifies, without delimiting the reference. Appositive relative clauses are a type of parenthetical phrase, rather like expressions such as *in fact, as you know,* or *of course* when found in the middle of a sentence. As such they are set off intonationally, forming their own intonational phrase.

In chapter 6 we'll see that there are rules in English which make reference to the domains of intonational phrase and phonological utterance, so I shan't give any detailed examples here. We will also touch upon these domains in our discussion of the rhythm of English in chapter 8.

5.5.6 The prosodic hierarchy and Strict Layer Hypothesis

We have said that phonological rules may refer to the domain of syllable (or part of the syllable, the rhyme), the foot, the phonological word, the phonological phrase, the intonational phrase and the phonological utterance. These domains form a hierarchy, with each domain being included in the next domain higher up. Put another way, each domain down to the level of the syllable comprises instances of the next domain down. This hierarchy is illustrated in figure 5.10:

Figure 5.10 Schematic representation of the prosodic hierarchy

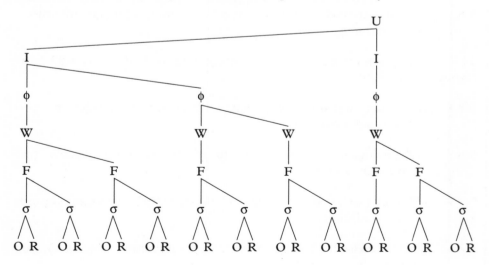

Implicit in this type of representation of things is the claim that each level in the hierarchy consists only of elements from the next level down. Some phonologists argue that this is an important aspect of phonological organization and that analyses should not be proposed which violate it. There are two sorts of violation possible in principle: we could have a situation in which a unit at one level contains a unit from a higher level, or we can have a situation in which a unit at one level contains a unit two levels down, thus skipping a level. The first possibility is shown hypothetically in figure 5.11:

Figure 5.11   Hypothetical violation of Strict Layer Hypothesis

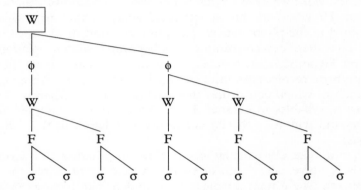

Here we see a situation in which a phonological word, the boxed W in figure 5.11, consists of two phonological phrases. Analyses which would require this kind of structure are not generally proposed in the literature, because there is no need for them and in any case it is not obvious how they could be interpreted. However, there is a way of relaxing the strictest interpretation of the Strict Layer Hypothesis which is regularly suggested by phonologists. For we could allow a given unit to consist of smaller tokens of the same kind of unit. For instance, phonologists regularly suggest that there may be 'major' and 'minor' intonation phrases and that a (major) intonational phrase may therefore itself consist of two (minor) intonational phrases. This situation is diagrammed in figure 5.12:

Figure 5.12   Minimal relaxation of Strict Layer Hypothesis

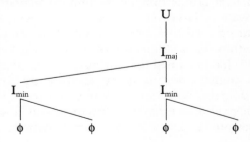

Figure 5.13   Hypothetical violation of Strict Layer Hypothesis

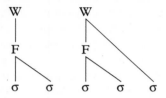

Figure 5.13 shows two feet consisting of two syllables each and then at the end of the word we have a syllable left over. This kind of situation is not uncommon. However, in this hypothetical analysis, the stray syllable has been adjoined to the phonological word, not to a unit on the next layer up, the foot. This therefore constitutes a rather more subtle violation of the Strict Layer Hypothesis. In practice, most of the debate about the validity of the hypothesis revolves around cases such as figure 5.13. We have already seen an analysis which constitutes this kind of violation when we looked at appendices to syllables in chapter 3 (check over those examples to ensure you understand why they should constitute a violation of the Strict Layer Hypothesis).

We will not take a particular stand here on whether the Strict Layer Hypothesis is universally valid, or merely a guiding principle that should only be broken where unavoidable, or a complete red herring. Suffice it to say that in general it holds, and that as a point of methodology it would be desirable, other things being equal, to have such a principle to adhere to since it arguably offers us a more constrained and hence more interesting theoretical framework.

5.5.7   Prosodic domains: final remarks

This section has given a number of examples of rules whose application is governed by prosodic units such as syllables, feet, words and phrases. In addition, some authors (e.g. Nespor and Vogel 1986) argue for a domain between the phonological word and the phonological phrase which they call a **Clitic Group**. I have not discussed this here, because it is somewhat controversial, and it is rather difficult to find particularly clear examples which would motivate it. However, in chapter 8 we will see the way that a Clitic Group might be used to analyse certain phenomena relating to English stress and rhythm. In addition to these domains, Condoravdi (1990) and Kanerva (1990) have claimed that further prosodic domains are needed, with less obvious counterparts in syntactic structure. In fact, the whole question of what domains there are, how they are to be defined, how they relate to morphological and syntactic structure, and how they determine phonological behaviour is a matter of intense debate. A further set of questions concerns the relationship between these domains and the rhythmic processes discussed in chapters 7 and 8. We can't delve into such matters in an introductory text such as this, but any reader who has persevered this far should be in a position to look at some of the research literature dealing with those questions.

APPENDIX 5.1   ABBREVIATORY CONVENTIONS IN PHONOLOGICAL RULES

In the classical SPE model of phonology, in which rules applied in a 'linear' fashion, in which the featural content of segments had no internal structure and in which no reference was made to prosodic categories such as the syllable, it was necessary to develop a formal notation which would allow generalizations to be captured which would be captured in rather different ways in more contemporary theories. These conventions concern the environments of rules. The abbreviatory conventions are still in use (technically) though they are used rather sparingly nowadays.[9] But it is necessary to be at least passively familiar with them in order to understand much of the earlier literature on phonology. In this appendix I therefore present a brief overview of the most important of these conventions. A more detailed discussion is provided by Kenstowicz and Kisseberth (1979: 339ff).

The parenthesis notation

Parentheses (or 'round brackets' colloquially) are used to indicate that material may appear in a given context for a rule, but doesn't have to, in other words, parentheses enclose material which, in a sense, is optional for the operation of the rule. Kiparsky (1973: 95) (cf. Kenstowicz and Kisseberth 1979: 342) discusses a palatalization process in Karok, under which /i/ palatalizes a following /s/, as in examples 5.87 (the dashes indicate morpheme boundaries):

5.87   ʔu-skak   'he jumps'   ni-ʃkak   'I jump'
        mu-sara   'his bread'   nani-ʃara   'my bread'

However, this process also applies if a consonant intervenes between /i/ and /s/:

5.88   ʔu-ksah   'he laughs'   ni-kʃah   'I laugh'
        ʔu-ksup   'he points'   ni-kʃup   'I point'
        mu-psiːh   'his leg'   nani-pʃiːh   'my leg'

The basic rule, illustrated by the data in 5.87, is palatalization of /s/ after /i/. We would normally regard this as an assimilation process, involving spreading of a feature such as [−back], but I will follow the linear analysis of Kiparsky, and Kenstowicz and Kisseberth to make the notational point clearer. The rule is 5.88:

5.89   s   →   ʃ / i_____

However, we also have to allow for the interposed consonant, to account for the data in 5.88, so we need to say that a consonant (which we can notate simply as C) can optionally intervene. This is recorded by putting the optional consonant inside parentheses:

5.90   s   →   ʃ / i (C) _____

Given the conventions which Kenstowicz and Kisseberth observe, this rule is interpreted as applying either to the data of 5.87, or to those of 5.88. The abbreviation is interpreted as meaning that it applies both when there is just the /i/ vowel but no consonant and also when there is an intervening consonant. In other words we define the environment as a conjunction (*both . . . and*).

The brace convention

Braces are used to combine two sounds or groups of sounds in an environment, when either of them can appear but not both. Such an *either. . . or* environment is a disjunction. Before the advent of syllable structure in generative phonology it was common for phonologists to refer to processes which occur either before a consonant or before the end of the word (i.e. before a word boundary #). This is how nasal velarization in Spanish would have been couched:

$$5.91 \quad n \quad \rightarrow \quad \eta / \_\_\_ \quad \begin{Bmatrix} C \\ \# \end{Bmatrix}$$

We know now, of course, that this is a syllable based process, and that the disjunction 'either before a consonant or before a word boundary' is just a convoluted way of saying 'in the coda'.

An example of the use of braces in a different context is found in Rubach's (1984) analysis of Polish. Rubach argues that there is a rule which deletes /j/ after a coronal consonant. This is illustrated by the data of 5.92:

5.92   a.   kop-atç   'to dig'   kopjẽ   'I dig'
              gʒeb-atç   'to bury'   gʒebjẽ   'I bury'
              wam-atç   'to break'   wamjẽ   'I break'

b. pis-atç   'to write'   piʃẽ   'I write'
    maz-atç   'to smear'   maʒẽ   'I smear'

Rubach argues that the /j/ element seen in the 1sg forms in 5.92a is responsible for the alternations s/z ~ ʃ/ʒ in 5.92b. After the coronals [ʃ ʒ] but not
after the labials in 5.92a, the /j/ then deletes. This is represented in 5.93:

5.93   j   →   ∅   / COR _____

The data of 5.94 illustrate another set of environments in which /j/ deletes:

5.94 a. mɨj-ẽ   'I wash'   mɨj-õts   'washing'
      b. mɨ-w   '(he) washed'   mɨ-tɨ   'washed
                                                  (participle)'

5.95 a. pomagaj-õ 'they help'   pomagaj-õts 'helping'
      b. pomaga-mɨ 'we wash'   pomaga-tç   'to wash'

These verb stems end in a /j/ which, however, only surfaces when the next
sound is a vowel (5.95a) not a consonant (5.95b). Moreover, the /j/ element
disappears at the end of a word, too:

5.95 c. pomaga   '(he) helps'

Rubach does not treat this last set of alternations in terms of syllable structure. He therefore assumes rule 5.96 to handle these cases of j-deletion:

5.96   j   →   ∅   /_____ $\begin{Bmatrix} C \\ \# \end{Bmatrix}$

Finally, he collapses rules 5.93 and 5.96 to get 5.97:

5.97   j   →   ∅   / $\begin{bmatrix} COR\_\_\_\_\_ \\ \_\_\_\_\_ \begin{Bmatrix} C \\ \# \end{Bmatrix} \end{bmatrix}$

The braces device has long been rather controversial. Indeed, some linguists
(e.g. McCawley 1972) have felt that braces actually hide generalizations
rather than capture them, or, indeed, capture non-existent generalizations.
This is certainly the received view on the use of braces to 'capture' the
notion of syllable boundary.

Angled brackets

On occasions phonologists have wished to express the idea that one part
of the environment of a rule is only relevant or valid if another part is. In

Polish velars alternate with alveolar affricates or fricatives in certain morphologically determined environments. This is illustrated by examples 5.98,
99:

5.98   a.   kozak   'Cossack (nom sg)'   kozatsɨ   'Cossacks
                                                          (nom pl)'
        b.   norveg   'Norwegian (nom sg)'   norvedzɨ   'Norwegians
                                                          (nom pl)'

5.99   a.   ʒeka   'river (nom sg)'   ʒetse   'river (dative sg)'
        b.   noga   'leg (nom sg)'   nodze   (dative sg)'

Rubach assumes that these alternations are the result of a rule which he
calls Second Velar Palatalization. This applies at the stage in the derivation
when the velars have already been turned into palato-alveolars [tʃ dʒ]. He
therefore formulates the rule as 5.100 (I have slightly altered Rubach's
notation):

5.100 $\begin{bmatrix} +\text{strident} \\ -\text{high} \\ -\text{continuant} \end{bmatrix}$ →   [+anterior]   /   _____ $\begin{bmatrix} \text{V} \\ -\text{back} \end{bmatrix}$

This, however, isn't the whole story, because the velar fricative /x/ also
undergoes the alternation, to give [s]:

5.101   tʃɛx   'Czech (nom sg)'   tʃɛsi   'Czechs (nom pl)'[10]

The problem is that in the environments illustrated in 5.99 the velar fricative produces a different output from the expected [s]. Instead, we get
[ʃ]:

5.102   patriarxa   'patriarch (nom sg)'   patriarʃe   'patriarch (dat sg)'

This is the result of a distinct palatalization rule (First Velar Palatalization,
the palatalization rule we discussed in section 5.3). The Second Velar Palatalization rule only applies to /x/ when the following vowel is /i/, not /e/.
   Rubach solves this descriptive problem by using a device which allows
him to say that if the input velar segment is a fricative, then the following
vowel is [+high]. This device is the **angled bracket**. Thus, we can rewrite
the rule as 5.103:

5.103 $\begin{bmatrix} +\text{strident} \\ -\text{high} \\ <+\text{continuant}> \end{bmatrix}$ →   [+anterior]   /   _____ $\begin{bmatrix} \text{V} \\ -\text{back} \\ <+\text{high}> \end{bmatrix}$

'Greek letter' variables

Earlier in the chapter I introduced the notational device of variables taking
feature specifications (+ or −) as values in order to describe place of articulation assimilation. However, I then rejected that type of solution on a
variety of theoretical grounds. However, there are occasions when the 'Greek
letter variable' notation, arguably, can be used to capture genuine phonological generalizations. A possible case is provided by Rubach (1993) in his
description of Slovak. Slovak has a distinction between short vowels and
long vowels, as well as a number of shortening and lengthening processes
sensitive to this distinction. It is easy to prove that the alternations affect the
pairs of vowels shown in 5.104:

5.104   i   iː   u   uː
         e   i̯e   o   u̯o
         æ   i̯a   a   aː

The symbols [i̯e], [i̯a], [u̯o] represent rising diphthongs, so that the [i̯], [u̯]
elements are very much like glides. Rubach presents persuasive evidence to
the effect that we must regard these diphthongs as essentially long vowels,
which then undergo a diphthongization process. It is easy enough to see
how this works in the case of lengthened [e o], since it is essentially the
same process found in Old Czech mentioned in chapter 3, section 3.1. We
simply assume a process under which the first element of a long mid-vowel
is replaced by the corresponding high vowel:

5.105

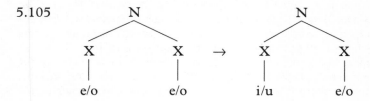

In featural terms this is:

5.106

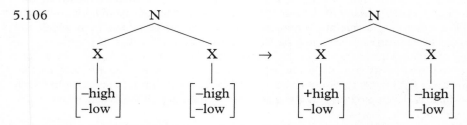

The problem arises when we consider the behaviour of /æ/ vis-à-vis /a/. We
need to be able to diphthongize the former without affecting the latter.

Rubach first points out that we can consider the high vowels to undergo diphthongization vacuously (the [+high] specification on the first component will be 'changed' into [+high] so nothing will happen and the vowels will remain [iː uː]). Next, he points out that, using the traditional set of binary features, the generalization is that a vowel diphthongizes if it is a front unrounded vowel or a back rounded one. In feature terms this means the vowels affected have the specifications in 5.107:

5.107   [−back, −round]   [i e æ]
            [+back, +round]   [u o]

We can capture this as a natural class if we use the Greek letter notation: [αback, αround]. Clearly, when α = '−' we get [i e æ] and when α = '+' we get [u o].

FURTHER READING

Any contemporary textbook on phonology will provide discussion of distinctive feature theory. However, beware! Each author will be obliged to develop a particular version of whatever theory s/he is summarizing in order to get it to work properly and this will mean that you will encounter a whole host of descriptions which will look unfamiliar. There is no introductory text which deals with feature geometry in any detail, though there is some discussion in the final chapter of Carr (1993). A good survey of the issues is provided by Roca (1994). Kenstowicz (1994) provides by far the most up-to-date, detailed, and exhaustive discussion of the issues. Clements and Hume (1994) is a very good survey of recent developments. A beginner wanting to take up these questions further can do a lot worse than starting with Clements's very clear (1985) paper. McCarthy (1988) is also an extremely lucid survey of the issues, with a different set of proposals. Halle (1992) is a very clear and succinct exposition of one way of looking at features. Broe (1992) is a very helpful summary. Ladefoged and Halle (1988) puts modern theory and earlier tradition into an interesting perspective. An influential new approach to phonetic primes, which sees them from much more of a phonetician's perspective, is that of Browman and Goldstein (1986). Many of their analyses of certain types of assimilation, deletions and epenthesis in terms of overlapping articulatory gestures have been widely accepted by mainstream phonologists which means that a number of popular examples of 'phonological' processes, including one or two or my pedagogic favourites, are now treated as essentially phonetic phenomena. It is beyond the scope of an introduction like this to discuss such questions in detail, but it is one area in which the field is developing and in which our understanding of the issues seems to be deepening.

Many texts deal with rule ordering and the formal notation for rules in one fashion or another. Hyman (1975) and Kenstowicz and Kisseberth (1979) can be recommended for earlier theoretical stances. Kenstowicz and Kisseberth (1977) presents a number of the earlier arguments for the basic SPE position in monograph form.

On prosodic domains, the standard reference is Nespor and Vogel (1986). The papers of the journal, *Phonology Yearbook*, vol. 4 (1987), deal specifically with this issue. Inkelas and Zec (1990) is a collection of papers on this topic. A concise overview of Nespor and Vogel's work is given by Roca (1994).

A summary of Lexical Phonology can be found in Spencer (1991: ch. 4), Katamba (1993), Carr (1993) and Kenstowicz (1994). A very good survey is given in Kaisse and Shaw (1985).

EXERCISES

5.1   Provide full feature geometric representations of the following consonants of English:

l   ʧ   ʒ   j

5.2   Examine the three forms in 5.46. For any of these forms, is it necessary that the two rules of Epenthesis 5.47 must apply in a particular order?

5.3   The syllable algorithm for Koryak breaks down when confronted with examples such as ʔənnəŋəjtəgəjŋən 'catch of fish' or pəl'həl'həgəjŋən 'river flow'. Explain exactly what goes wrong.

The reason for this discrepancy is that some schwas none-theless have to present in underlying structure in Koryak. Where are the lexical schwas in these words? Present an analysis both in terms of the syllabification algorithm and in terms of the rejected SPE solution.

5.4   Below are data from Komi-Permjak (taken from the dictionary of Batalova and Krivoshchekova-Ganthan 1985). These illustrate a phonemic neutralization. Which phonemes are neutralized and under which circumstances? Which of the two neutralized phonemes is basic? [[ɤ] is a back unrounded mid vowel].

vem	'brain'	petavnɨ	'to germinate'
petalɤm	'germinated'	subtnɨ	'to get up'
lem	'glue'	vɤv	'horse'
vonɨ	'to mature'	lonɨ	'to be present'
vadɤr	'shore'	lador	'side'
pivsʲivlɨnɨ	'to steam oneself'	tavo	'this year'
talun	'today'	petavtɤm	'ungerminated'

	'horse'	'field'
Nominative	vɣv	ɨb
Genitive	vɣvlɣn	ɨblɣn
Instrumental	vɣlɣn	ɨbɣn
Approximative	vɣlaɲ	ɨblaɲ

	'to hear'	'to go'
infinitive	kɨvnɨ	munnɨ
1sg pres.	kɨla	muna
imperative	kɨv	mun

5.5 Some rules of Lardil (Australia)

Lardil nouns in object position agree in tense with the verbs that govern them and hence take an uninflected form, a Non-future and a Future form (Hale 1973, Kenstowicz and Kisseberth 1979). Study the following sets of examples. From the A examples determine the UR of the two tense affixes. The B examples show the effects of phonological alternations affecting stems and the suffixes. Identify two rules to account for the suffix allomorphy. [Approximate IPA equivalents to orthographic symbols: *th* = [θ], *tj* = [c].]

	Uninflected	Non-future	Future	Gloss
A	kentapal	kentapal-in	kentapal-uɽ	'dugong'
	yaraman	yaraman-in	yaraman-uɽ	'river'
	kethar	kethar-in	kethar-uɽ	'river'
B	mela	mela-n	mela-ɽ	'sea'
	wanka	wanka-n	wanka-ɽ	'arm'
	tjempe	tjempe-n	tjempe-ɽ	'mother's father'
	wiʈe	wiʈe-n	wiʈe-ɽ	'interior'
	kenʈe	kenʈi-n	kenʈ-wuɽ	'wife'
	ŋiɲe	ŋiɲi-n	ŋiɲi-wuɽ	'skin'
	pape	papi-n	papi-wuɽ	'father's mother'
	ŋuka	ŋuku-n	ŋuku-ɽ	'water'
	kaʈa	kaʈu-n	kaʈu-ɽ	'child'

[The *e ~ i* and *a ~ u* alternations in the last five examples are the result of a process which you can ignore: assume the underlying form ends in *-i, u* respectively.]

The data in set C, D show further stem alternations. Write two further rules to account for these alternations:

	yalul	yalulu-n	yalulu-ɽ	'flame'
C	mayar	mayara-n	mayara-ɽ	'rainbow'
	wiwal	wiwala-n	wiwala-ɽ	'bush mango'
	karikar	karikari-n	karikari-wuɽ	'butter-fish'
	yiliyil	yiliyili-n	yiliyili-wuɽ	'species of oyster'

D	yukar	yukarpa-n	yukarpa-ɽ	'husband'
	wulun	wulunka-n	wulunka-ɽ	'species of fruit'
	wuʈal	wuʈaltji-n	wuʈaltji-wuɽ	'meat'
	kantukan	kantukantu-n	kantukantu-ɽ	'red'
	karwakar	karwakarwa-n	karwakarwa-ɽ	'species of wattle'

Finally, the examples of E show one further stem alternation, requiring a further rule:

E	a.	ŋalu	ŋaluk-in	ŋaluk-uɽ	'story'
	b.	putu	putuka-n	putuka-ɽ	'short'
		murkuni	murkunima-n	murkunima-ɽ	'nullah'
		ŋawuŋa	ŋawuŋawu-n	ŋawuŋawu-ɽ	'termite'
		tipiti	tipitipi-n	tipitipi-wuɽ	'species of rock-cod'
		thapu	thaputji-n	thaputji-wuɽ	'older brother'
	c.	muŋkumu	muŋkumuŋku-n	muŋkumuŋku-ɽ	'wooden axe'
		tjumputju	tjumputjumpu-n	tjumputjumpu-ɽ	'dragon-fly'

Do your rules have to apply in an extrinsically specified order or can they be applied whenever their description is met (intrinsic ordering)?

5.6   Turkish vowel harmony

Turkish (Clements and Sezer 1982, Lewis 1967) has a vowel harmony system reminiscent of that of Hungarian (cf. chapter 2). It is possible to analyse this as the rightward spreading of certain vowel features to underspecified vowel positions. On this assumption, analyse the following Turkish noun forms. Assume all the vowels of the language are represented. Isolate those vowels and provide a fully specified distinctive feature matrix for them. Then formulate a vowel harmony rule. Be careful to identify the underlying form of the suffixes.

Nom sg	Gen sg	Nom pl	Gen pl	gloss
akʃam	akʃam-in	akʃam-lar	akʃam-lar-ɨn	'evening'
ev	ev-in	ev-ler	ev-ler-in	'house'
gøz	gøz-yn	gøz-ler	gøz-ler-in	'eye'
gyl	gyl-yn	gyl-ler	gyl-ler-in	'rose'
ip	ip-in	ip-ler	ip-ler-in	'rope'
kɨz	kɨz-ɨn	kɨz-lar	kɨz-lar-ɨn	'girl'
kol	kol-un	kol-lar	kol-lar-ɨn	'arm'
orman	orman-in	orman-lar	orman-lar-ɨn	'forest'
pul	pul-un	pul-lar	pul-lar-ɨn	'stamp'
vapur	vapur-un	vapur-lar	vapur-lar-in	'steamer'

chapter 6

Postlexical Processes in English

6.0 Introduction

In this chapter we will illustrate the principles developed in the previous chapters by examining a number of common processes in English in some depth. As we proceed, we will introduce a number of refinements and extensions to those theoretical ideas. Although my description will be largely based on traditional generative accounts of the phenomena, I shall have to depart from conventional wisdom on a number of occasions. The theoretical points which will be illustrated include

- the use of distinctive features to capture natural classes;
- the use of features and feature geometry to state processes of assimilation;
- the importance of syllable structure for the formulation of processes;
- the role of prosodic domains generally.

Postlexical processes are phonological processes which are triggered solely by phonological structure, and which thus do not have lexical exceptions or morphological conditions. For this reason they are sometimes called

automatic processes. Many of these processes operate across word boundaries or are affected by the phonological structure of a whole phrase, so they
are also often referred to as **connected speech** processes or phrasal phonology. We will divide the postlexical processes (somewhat arbitrarily) into
three groups: assimilations, syllable-based processes, and insertions and
deletions. The syllable-based processes act over the domain of the syllable,
of course, but in several cases it will be of interest to ask how the process
is influenced by the broader phonological domain.

6.1 Assimilation Processes

6.1.1 Assimilations as spreading processes

Consider the data in 6.1, based on Gimson (1980: 296):

6.1   a.   What you want   [wɔtjuːwɔnt]   [wɔtʃuːwɔnt]
       b.   Would you   [wʊdjuː]   [wʊdʒuː]
       c.   In case you   [ɪŋkeɪsjuː]   [ɪŋkeɪʃʃu]
       d.   Has your . . .   [hæzjɔː]   [hæʒʒɔː]

The examples in the second transcription represent reasonably careful pronunciations, though not the hyper-careful pronunciations shown in the first
column of transcriptions. There are several points to notice here. First, there
is a process affecting sequences of coronals, /t d s z/ + /j/. Second, in each
case the coronal sound is turned into an alveopalatal. Third, the /j/ disappears. Fourth, the alveopalatal is long (note that a long affricate will tend
to sound rather like a plosive followed by an affricate, as in 6.1a, b).

The core process is again a type of assimilation. The coronal sounds are
turned into a type of palatal, hence we can call this process Coronal Palatalization. This is a slight misnomer, since the coronals are turned into
alveopalatals, and not genuine palatals (i.e. not /c, ɟ, ç, ʝ/). Moreover, the
plosives are turned into affricates, not alveopalatal stops. However, this is
natural, in that affricates universally tend to behave like a kind of plosive
and there is a very strong tendency for palatal or alveopalatal stops to be
affricated. We can summarize the process as in 6.2:

6.2   coronal obstruent   →   alveopalatal /____ palatal glide

In addition, the process clearly involves ancillary processes, notably consonant lengthening and the loss of /j/. What seems to have happened is that
the affricate or fricative has 'taken the place' of the /j/ which conditioned the
original process. This is an example of compensatory lengthening, introduced in chapter 2, section 2.4.4. The overall number of segments is main-
tained, even if one of the phoneme melodies is lost.

One of the surrounding melody elements then spreads into the vacated position. We can represent this by making use of our distinction between melody elements and skeletal slots. The basic idea is illustrated in 6.3:

6.3   a.
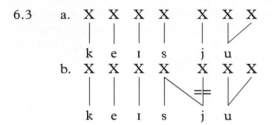

b.

In 6.3b I've delinked or dissociated the /j/ melody from its own skeletal slot and associated it to that of the /s/ slot. The result is a kind of complex segment, /sj/. This could correspond to a number of sounds, depending on the language, but in English it corresponds to a kind of /ʃ/. We are left in 6.3b with an unassociated X slot. In English (though not necessarily in other languages or under other circumstances), such a slot can be the target of a relinking process which attaches the /ʃ/ melody element, newly formed from /s+j/, to the vacated X slot, as in 6.4:

6.4

We now have the result desired: a long alveopalatal fricative. The reassociation in 6.4 represents the process of compensatory lengthening.[1]

Now let's consider the process in more detail, at the level of features. What distinguishes /s/ from /ʃ/ is the feature [anterior], which in chapter 5 we assumed to be a dependent of the CORONAL subnode of the PLACE node. The phoneme /s/ is [+anterior], while /ʃ/ and /j/, are [−anterior]. A reasonable assumption, then, is that this type of palatalization involves spreading to the left of the feature [−anterior]. This is illustrated in 6.5:

6.5   Coronal Palatalization
ROOT

PLACE

CORONAL

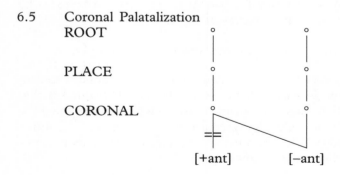

[+ant]   [−ant]

There is a phenomenon which bears some superficial resemblance to Coronal Palatalization. If we listen carefully to the pronunciation of words such as *huge* or *hue* then we find that the initial segment is not a glottal fricative as we would expect. Rather it is a voiceless palatal (not alveopalatal) fricative [ç]. This process looks rather like the palatalization of /s/ to /ʃ/. In fact, we don't need a special rule for this process. If you try whispering a series of vowels you'll find that in effect you are producing a series of 'h' sounds with different vowel colourings. Thus, we can think of the /h/ consonant as a devoicing of the following vowel. Now, in a word like *huge* or *hue*, it looks as though the /h/ is followed by an approximant, the glide /j/, rather than a vowel. However, this is probably not the case. The [juː] sequence that we find in words like *pew* or *cue*, or in many British dialects, *new*, is rather unusual, in that only the vowel [uː] can follow a cluster of consonant + /j/ of this sort. For this reason it makes sense to treat this sequence as a rising diphthong, /iu/. This will gives us 6.6 as the representation for *hue*.

6.6

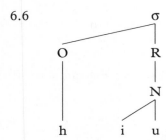

Now, the [u] component of the [iu] diphthong is always a long vowel, [uː]. This is rather unusual behaviour. We can account for it, however, by assuming that in words like *pew, cue, hue*, the [i] component moves leftwards to join the X-slot of the previous consonant, to form a kind of contour segment. That way we can account for the fact that the consonant seems to be no longer that a single consonant, and not a genuine cluster. The 'u' melody then spreads into the vacated nuclear X slot. This is shown in 6.7 for *cue*:

6.7

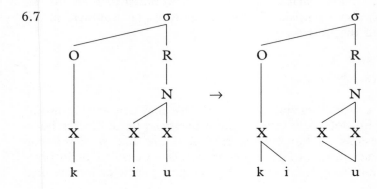

When this happens to *hue* we end up with a sequence [hi] attached to one onset X slot. A high vowel in a consonant position is always interpreted as a glide, in this case [j]. Since /h/ is essentially a devoicing of the next segment, this means we can represent the sequence as a devoiced [j], i.e. [ç]:

6.8

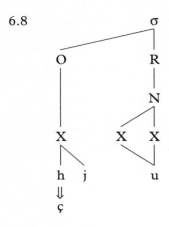

Another assimilation processes which resembles Coronal Palatalization is illustrated in 6.9:

6.9   this shop   [ðɪsʃɔp]   →   [ðɪʃʃɔp]
      his shop   [hɪzʃɔp]   →   [hɪʒʃɔp]
      this genre   [ðɪsʒɔnrə]   →   [ðɪʃʒɔnrə]
      his genre   [hɪzʒɔnrə]   →   [hɪʒʒɔnrə]

Here, an alveolar fricative is turned into an alveopalatal by a following alveopalatal. For the present we will call this Sibilant Palatalization.

The last assimilation process is found with *tr-/dr-* onsets, in words such as *train*, *drain*. The retroflex articulation of the /ɹ/ affects the /t d/ with the result that we have an alveopalatal (or even retroflex) rather than an alveolar plosive. We will call this Alveopalatalization. The precise environment of this rule is discussed in the next section.

6.1.2   Domain of application

Having seen how Coronal Palatalization works we may ask what prosodic domain it applies in. Relatively little research has been done on this question, so our conclusions will be tentative. It is often said that an assimilation such as Coronal Palatalization fails to occur 'before a pause'. This in practice often means 'fails to occur across a phonological phrase or intonational phrase boundary'. This is shown in 6.10 (where (. . .)$_I$ represents an intonational phrase and (. . .)$_Φ$ represents a phonological phrase):

6.10   a.   If you just wait, you can have one.
              (if you just wai[t])$_I$ (you can have one)$_I$

        b.   Pete used a hammer.
              (Pe[t]e)$_Φ$ (used)$_Φ$ (a hammer)$_Φ$

        c.   Jeremy bought used cars.
              (Jeremy)$_Φ$ (bough[t])$_Φ$ (used cars)$_Φ$

In 6.10b, c the noun phrases *a hammer* and *used cars* come after the head of the verb phrase *used* and *bought* and so form their own phonological phrases.

Since a phonological phrase boundary is smaller than an intonational boundary and contained completely within one, we would normally just say that the process is blocked across the Φ boundary. However, in 6.11 it appears that it nonetheless takes place across a phonological phrase boundary:

6.11   a.   If you just (wai[ʧ])$_Φ$ (your turn)$_Φ$, you can have one.
        b.   You can (do i[ʧ])$_Φ$ (yourself)$_Φ$.

Moreover, it is not just the pronoun *you* or its derivatives that give rise to the palatalization (though these account for the majority of tokens of /j/ which trigger the rule). In 6.12 we see examples in which content words beginning with /j/ condition the process:

6.12   a.   You can cite Yevtushenko.
              You can ci[ʧ] Yevtushénko.
        b.   Can you find Yerevan?
              Can you fin[ʤ] Yereván?

What seems to be happening in 6.11a, 6.12a, b is that the word ending in /t d/ is stressed but the following syllable, beginning with /j/ is unstressed: *wáit your, cíte Yevtu . . . , fínd Yere . . .* In 6.11b, the word preceding it is stressed but the following word is still unstressed: *dó it your . . .* Now, a unit consisting of a stressed syllable followed by a sequence on unstressed syllables is a foot and we know that some phonological processes are conditioned by foot structure (see chapter 5, section 5.4.2). The intriguing aspect of this foot-based process, however, is that the foot spans more than one word. We will discuss this in more detail in chapter 8. We can represent the domain as in 6.13:

6.13   a.   You can (cíte Yevtu)$_F$ (shénko)$_F$.
        b.   Can you (fínd Yere)$_F$ (ván)$_F$.

In the transcriptions given in 6.12 neither *Yevtushenko* (the name of a Russian poet) nor *Yerevan* (the capital of Armenia) are stressed on the first syllable. However, this is true only for relatively relaxed speech. In more careful speech the first syllables of these words are given secondary stress, as in 6.14. A secondary stress is still a stress, so this creates a new foot boundary and hence blocks the Coronal Palatalization rule:

6.14   a. You can (cíte)$_F$ (Yèvtu)$_F$ (shénko)$_F$.
         b. Can you (fínd)$_F$ (Yère)$_F$ (ván)$_F$

6.2   Syllable-based Processes

We know from chapter 3 that the syllable is a very important domain for the statement of phonotactic constraints. At the same time, this turns out to be a domain in which a number of phonological processes can be defined. Given the importance of some of these processes for the phonology of English, and given the general interest of the syllable as a phonological domain, it is worth devoting special attention to this domain.

6.2.1   Aspiration

The first syllabically conditioned process we'll look at is one of the most famous cases of allophonic variation in English (though one which still poses interesting problems for phonologists and phoneticians), the aspiration of voiceless stops. I shall first of all outline what has come to be the standard story about this process, and then suggest a radical alternative, which seems to me to fit the facts better and to make more phonological sense.

In chapter 1 I pointed out that a set of sounds such as the voiceless plosives would be pronounced in a variety of ways depending on whereabouts in the word they appeared. In particular, at the beginning of a stressed syllable, such as *pat*, a plosive such as /p/ will be pronounced with aspiration, as [pʰ]. It's now time to investigate this process in more detail. First, we need to ascertain where aspiration occurs. This is when we encounter the first of our problems. There are two difficulties. Firstly, the facts seem to be slightly different for different dialects (especially where Britain and America are concerned). Secondly, aspiration is not an all-or-nothing phenomenon: voiceless plosives are subject to different degrees of aspiration depending on their position, so it is not possible to speak about a simple distinction between aspirated and unaspirated sounds. (This type of gradient quality is common with postlexical processes.)[2]

Consider the data in 6.15, which represent a fairly standard British pronunciation:

6.15	pip	pʰɪp	task	tʰæsk/tʰɑːsk	cusp	kʰʌsp
	pest	pʰɛst	talk	tʰɔːk	keep	kʰiːp
	pot	pʰɔt	toot	tʰuːt	kite	kʰaɪt
	put	pʰʊt	take	tʰeɪk	quoit	kʰɔɪt
	park	pʰɑː(ɹ)k	tout	tʰaʊt	coke	kʰouk

From these transcriptions we conclude that /p t k/ get aspirated at the beginning of a monosyllable but not at the end. We will see that things are a little more complex than this in final position, but the aspiration of the initial consonant is uncontroversial in all dialects (except for some Northern English and Scottish varieties, see Wells 1982b).

The data of 6.15 contrast strongly with those of 6.16, which show that /p t k/ must be in absolute syllable initial position:

6.16	a.	spy	[spaɪ]	[*spʰaɪ]
	b.	sty	[staɪ]	[*stʰaɪ]
	c.	sky	[skaɪ]	[*skʰaɪ]

Finally, note that the aspiration is found with polysyllabic words, too:

6.17	a.	Perry	[pʰɛrɪ]
	b.	Terry	[tʰɛrɪ]
	c.	Kerry	[kʰɛrɪ]

These data are often summarized by saying that the voiceless plosive is aspirated when it is at the beginning of a syllable and is unaspirated when final or when there is a preceding /s/. What happens, however, in the middle of a word? Consider the data of 6.18:

6.18	a.	slipper	[slípə]
		fitter	[fítə]
		quicker	[kwíkə]
	b.	whisper	[wíspə]
		blister	[blístə]
		whisker	[wískə]

Here it seems that the intervocalic plosive remains unaspirated whether or not it is preceded by /s/. However, consider the data in 6.19:

6.19	a.	report	[rɪpʰɔːt]
		retort	[rɪtʰɔːt]
		record	[rɪkʰɔːd]
	b.	despair	[dɪspɛː]
		restore	[rɪstɔː]
		discard	[dɪskɑːd]

In these examples we see that the stop is again aspirated (6.19a) provided it is not preceded by /s/ (6.19b).

What this suggests is that the voiceless stop is aspirated in a stressed syllable provided it is not preceded by /s/. This is generally accepted as the standard account of the variation. However, it is an oversimplification in a number of respects. Although the strongest degrees of aspiration are undoubtedly heard in syllables bearing primary stress, a certain degree of aspiration is also found in the initial /t/ in 6.20a–c:

6.20   a.   temperamental   [tʰɛmprəmɛ́ntl]
        b.   tomorrow   [tʰəmɔ́rou]
        c.   to borrow   [tʰəbɔ́rou]
        d.   stochastic   [stɔkʰæstɪk]
        e.   starvation   [stɑːveɪʃn̩]

Admittedly, the aspiration in cases such as 6.20b, c is rather weak. Yet as Kahn (1976: 32) points out, there is a noticeable contrast between the /t/ of *tomorrow*, where there is weak aspiration, and that of *sty*, where aspiration is completely out of the question. Again, where the plosive is preceded by /s/ as in 6.20d, e there is no possibility of aspiration.

These are generally taken to be the crucial facts about aspiration in English. I have summarized them in 6.21:

6.21   Aspirated:
        (1)   beginning of stressed syllable not preceded by /s/
        (2)   beginning of word initial unstressed syllable not preceded by /s/
        Unaspirated: elsewhere

Thus, the generalization seems to be that the plosive is aspirated at the absolute beginning of a stressed syllable or at the absolute beginning of a word, and is unaspirated elsewhere. This forms the basis of the most usual formulation of the process, informally stated in 6.22:

6.22   {p t k}   →   [+spread glottis] $\left\{\begin{array}{l} / \ \sigma[\underline{\hspace{2cm}} \ \text{+stress}] \\ / \ \# \ \underline{\hspace{2cm}} \end{array}\right\}$

The way to interpret this rule (or more accurately, pair of rules) is to read σ as a syllable boundary and # as a word boundary. Thus, the rule states that {p t k} become aspirated (signalled by the feature [+spread glottis]) when a syllable or word boundary immediately precedes. Hence, if the syllable or word begins with /s/ this condition will not be met and the rule will not apply. This syllabic condition essentially means that the /s/ and the plosive are in the same onset position. The feature specification [+stress] indicates that the syllable is stressed. This is just an informal notational device we will use for the present to indicate a stressed syllable (though one which derives from earlier theories of generative phonology). The proper way to treat stress will be discussed in chapter 7.

This approach to the problem presupposes that the unaspirated variant is the basic form of the phoneme and that the aspirated allophone is derived. This makes sense in that the aspiration is gradient and seems to depend on stress. We can therefore think of the stress as being somehow responsible for the aspiration process (but to varying degrees). Though this is the standard story, there are important problems with it. The first is a simple omission, easily remedied. Most commentators (Kahn 1976 being an exception) fail to point out that the voiceless affricate /ʧ/ behaves rather like a plosive with respect to aspiration. It is perfectly possible to pronounce an affricate as plain or aspirated, and the usual pronunciation in English, especially in a stressed syllable, is with aspiration. This can be easily accommodated provided we have a way of ensuring that plosives and affricates are treated as a natural class. In fact, we can make use of our multidimensional analysis of affricates for this purpose. We simply need to ensure that the rule applies to a sound bearing the features [−continuant, −sonorant]. Since an affricate bears both values of [continuant], it will therefore fall under this definition. Hence, we can regard the affricate as a kind of plosive. In fact, it would require some complication to a rule such as 6.22 to prevent it from applying to an affricate.

The second problem is more serious, in that it concerns the class of environments in which aspiration occurs. Kreidler (1989: 116), for example, gives a rather different pattern of aspiration, which strikes me as rather more accurate (for contemporary British speech at least). He points out that in word final position voiceless plosives may be aspirated. This is true of British RP according to Wells (1982b) and it is true of my (slightly modified) RP. Moreover, he claims that where a word ends in /s/ followed by a plosive, aspiration is obligatory. This seems to me to depend on dialect and speech style. However, it is clear that there is fair likelihood of aspiration in final s-clusters. Thus, the words of examples 6.15 should really be transcribed as in 6.23:

6.23	pip	pʰɪpʰ	task	tʰæskʰ/tɑːskʰ	cusp	kʰʌspʰ
	pest	pʰɛstʰ	talk	tʰɔːkʰ	keep	kʰiːpʰ
	pot	pʰɔtʰ	toot	tʰuːtʰ	kite	kʰaɪtʰ
	put	pʰʊtʰ	take	tʰeɪkʰ	quoit	kʰɔɪtʰ
	park	pʰɑː(ɹ)kʰ	tout	tʰaʊtʰ	coke	kʰoukʰ

Moreover, if we ignore cases in which preglottalization of the stop has occurred (or flapping of /t/ in many American and some British and Australian dialects), we find that aspiration is also possible (in certain accents at least) in an unstressed syllable after the tonic. This is more likely where the speaker is being particularly careful or emphatic, but in many accents

(including my own, for instance) there is a fairly clear distinction between
the words of 6.18a and 6.18b. In the latter there is no possibility of aspiration in any speech style, while in the former it is possible to impose a
small degree of aspiration, in, say, emphatic speech. Furthermore, my impression is that there is a noticeable difference between the voiceless stops
in 6.18a and those of words of similar structure (i.e. containing a voiceless
stop before an unstressed vowel) in, say, Russian. Russian has no significant
degree of aspiration for any of its stops and suppression of aspiration is one
of the key skills an English speaker has to learn in order to acquire a good
Russian accent. Thus, apart from immediately after /s/, it seems that pretty
well any voiceless stop may be aspirated but that in certain positions the
degree of aspiration is very slight (though detectably different from absolutely no aspiration). In some cases these facts are obscured somewhat by
the fact that the stop will be preglottalized in some of these positions (e.g.
syllable finally before a word boundary or another consonant). However, the
overall picture seems to be that summarized in 6.24:

6.24   Impossible: onset of a syllable preceded by /s/
        Possible: elsewhere

Now, this suggests a radical reappraisal of the aspiration phenomenon. For
if we distinguish positions of potential aspiration from positions where aspiration is absolutely excluded, we find that the former, where aspiration is
possible, form the 'elsewhere' case. This means that we must treat the plain,
unaspirated sound as the derived variant. What does this tell us about the
underlying representations?

Here it is worthwhile pausing to consider exactly how underlying forms
of sounds are determined. Let's consider the two allophones of /p/ in relatively simplistic terms. We have two allophones, [p, pʰ]. What is the basic
underlying form? There are three logically possible answers: (1) [p], (2)
[pʰ], (3) something else. Previously, phonologists have tended to assume
answer (1). This entails setting up a rule to aspirate the underlyingly plain
sound in various contexts. However, normally we chose as the basic variant
the default sound, that is, the sound which occurs in the 'elsewhere' case.
Given our reasoning so far, this would imply solution (2), in which the
underlying form is /pʰ/. This would then necessitate a rule of Deaspiration
which would turn /pʰ/ into [p⁼] in *sp*- clusters in onsets, but would leave the
aspiration unaffected elsewhere.

Now, many students of English phonology would find it rather strange
that English should have underlyingly aspirated plosives. In fact, given the
theory of distinctive features which we have been assuming, it is rather
misleading to say that English voiceless stops are underlyingly aspirated
phonemes. Recall that an aspirated stop is distinguished from an unaspirated
one by the feature specification [+spread glottis]. However, this feature is
completely redundant for stops in English (which is equivalent to saying

that aspiration is not contrastive). Therefore, the underlying representations of our voiceless stops will bear no specification for [spread glottis]: they will be marked [0spread glottis]. We must then assume that there is a rule which specifies the value as [–spread glottis] in an *s*- cluster in onsets. In addition, there has to be a default rule which states that [0spread glottis] is specified as [+spread glottis] for voiceless stops. The two rules are given in 6.25:

6.25   a.   [0s.g.]   →   [–s.g.] /   [$_\sigma$s $\begin{bmatrix} \underline{\qquad\qquad} \\ -son, -cont \end{bmatrix}$

       b.   [0s.g.]   →   [+s.g.]

Rule 6.25a fulfils the function of a rule of Deaspiration. The default rule 6.25b is a redundancy rule, which is required in order to supply a non-contrastive phonetic feature specification, in much the same way that we need to have a redundancy rule specifying nasals as [+voiced].

Clearly, it is important to ensure that the rule specifying [–spread glottis] in *s*- clusters applies before the default rule, otherwise, all voiceless stops will end up aspirated indiscriminately. This is achieved by a general convention on rule application relating to rules which have the characteristics of rules 6.25, in which one rule could apply to all the forms that the other rule applies to. If 6.25b were to have precedence then we would never even know that 6.25a existed, because all of its forms would undergo 6.25b. When two rules, A and B, can apply to a particular set of forms, and B applies to all the forms that A applies to, but A does not apply to all the forms that B applies to, then we can say that A is the more specific of the two rules, and B is the more general. The general convention states that the more specific rule has to apply first. This is called the **Elsewhere Condition**.

By adopting this solution we find that the underlying form of the voiceless labial stop, /p/, is neither aspirated nor unaspirated, but rather is neither: it is unspecified for the aspiration feature, which is just as it should be, given that aspiration is non-contrastive. In effect, the solution to the puzzle on p. 210 about underlying forms for consonants is that (3) is correct.

One final detail needs to be mentioned. There are words in which a voiceless plosive in word medial position is preceded by /s/ but is still aspirated. Some examples are given in 6.26:

6.26   a.   ricepaper   [raɪspʰeɪpə]
       b.   horsetail   [hɔːstʰeɪl]
       c.   housecoat   [haʊskʰout]

The crucial point about the examples of 6.26 is that they are all compounds (*rice* + *paper* etc.) Clearly, what is happening here is that the rule of Deaspiration fails to apply across compound words. We can account for this very simply given the principles already discussed. Recall that syllabification operates over single words. This is the reason for the existence of (near) minimal pairs such as *des[p]air* vs. *this [pʰ]ear*, discussed in chapter 3 section 3.4.1. Therefore, all we have to assume is that the syllabification principles of English are sensitive to the morphological structure of compounds and treat each component as a separate word for the purposes of syllabification. Thus, *ricepaper* is treated like *this pear* and not like *despair*.

6.2.2   Approximant Devoicing

In some descriptions of English a special process of Approximant Devoicing is described. In this, an approximant in the onset of a syllable is devoiced when the preceding consonant is voiceless. Examples are:

6.27   pray   [pr̥eɪ]   train   [tr̥eɪn]   crane   [kr̥eɪn]
        fresh   [fr̥eʃ]   thresh   [θr̥eʃ]   twin   [tw̥ɪn]
        quick   [kw̥ɪk]   swim   [sw̥ɪm]   play   [pl̥eɪ]
        clay   [kl̥eɪ]   sleep   [sl̥iːp]   pure   [pju̥ə]
        queue   [kju̥ː]   few   [fju̥ː]

Now, recalling that /h/ in English is effectively a devoicing of the following vowel (or glide in the case of /hj/), we might wish to say that the devoicing of the approximants in 6.27 was an instance of the same process. The aspiration borne by the initial plosive would then affect any sonorant which wasn't a stop (i.e. all the sonorants, excluding the nasals, but including the vowels, of course). In this case our approximant devoicing is just an aspect of aspiration (itself a redundant feature of voiceless stops). If this is so then approximant devoicing should fail to be observed exactly where aspiration is impossible, i.e. in an onset when the plosive is preceded by /s/. This appears to be the case, as seen in examples 6.28:

6.28   strain   [streɪn]   sprain   [spreɪn]   scream   [skriːm]
        destroy   [dɪstrɔɪ]   display   [dɪspleɪ]   disclose [dɪsklouz]

This formulation may appear at odds with received wisdom, however. One of the questions which was discussed in great detail in the American structuralist tradition of phonemics was how to handle the difference in pronunciation between words such as 6.29a and 6.29b:

6.29   a. nitrate   b. night rate

The puzzle posed by these words is that they seem to consist of identical phonemes, yet they are distinguishable. In most descriptions we find that one difference between the two words is in the devoicing of the /r/. This is found in 6.29a, but not 6.29b:

6.30   a.   [naɪt̬r̥eɪt]   b.   [naɪtreɪt]

This is certainly true in those accents or speech styles where the /t/ of *night rate* is preglottalized. However, in my speech (and that of a number of British accents, I suspect) the contrast is not so strong as to be definitive. Although the /r/ of *nitrate* is definitely devoiced, there is also slight devoicing of the /r/ in *night rate*, as a direct consequence of the residual aspiration of the final /t/ of *night*. However, all this would simply serve to strengthen the assumption that Approximant Devoicing is part and parcel of aspiration.

Matters seem to be a little more complex than this, however, in that Approximant Devoicing seems not to be limited to a position immediately after a voiceless stop. We also find it after voiceless fricatives, even though these are not normally considered aspirated in English, as in the case of *swim, sleep* from 6.27. However, we can't simply say that the approximant gets devoiced in all positions immediately following a voiceless obstruent. Consider the following examples (taken from Kiparsky 1979: 440):

6.31   a.   Is[l̥]ip   (I)$_\sigma$ (slip)$_\sigma$
         b.   eye-s[l̥]ip   (eye)$_\sigma$ (slip)$_\sigma$
         c.   ice-[l]ip   (ice)$_\sigma$ (lip)$_\sigma$

Here we find that the /l/ is devoiced when it occurs in the same onset as /s/ (examples 6.31a,b) but not if the /s/ is part of the previous word and hence not part of the onset (6.31c). The examples in 6.32 illustrate the same phenomenon:

6.32   a.   midwifery   [mɪdwɪfr̥ɪ]
              fried   [fr̥aɪd]
              rough rider   [rʌfraɪdə]

         b.   shrimp   [ʃr̥ɪmp]
              mushroom   [mʌʃr̥uːm]
              fish roe   [fɪʃrou]

It is hardly surprising that this Devoicing process should be so similar to that found after aspirated stops. After all, aspiration is simply a period of voicelessness following the release of the stop, and hence, in effect, is akin to the addition of an /h/ sound, itself a voiceless fricative. Thus, we may think of both aspiration and Approximant Devoicing as essentially the same process, that of devoicing whatever sonorant follows the obstruent in the same onset. On the other hand, the fact that Approximant Devoicing is also conditioned by fricatives and not just stops shows that the two rules are distinct.

For the purposes of this subsection the important aspect of these processes is the fact that they are found within the onset of a syllable. Thus, syllable structure plays an important role here in the allophonic variation shown by consonantal segments. Since, syllabification depends in part on morphological structure, and in particular, where word boundaries fall, we can see that the aspiration/devoicing phenomenon is the result of the interaction of several aspects of phonological structure.

6.2.3 Clear/dark /l/

In chapter 1 we looked briefly at the allophony of the /l/ phoneme. I pointed out that there are two main pronunciations of /l/ in standard accents of British English (including RP) as well as a number of US dialects, the so-called 'clear l', [l] and 'dark l' [ɫ], a velarized alveolar lateral. What governs this allophony? In 6.33 we see a number of crucial cases from my (British) speech:

6.33   a.   mill   [mɪɫ]
             milk   [mɪɫk]
             milking   [mɪɫkɪŋ]

        b.   limb   [lɪm]
             climb   [klaɪm]

        c.   miller   [mɪlə]
             yellow   [jɛlou]

It is fairly easy to see that [l ɫ] are in complementary distribution and that [ɫ] appears in unambiguous coda position, while [l] appears elsewhere. Particularly important here is the contrast between *mill* and *miller*, given that the second is derived by suffixation from the first. The alternation is obligatory, applying at all rates of speech and with all speech styles in the dialects in question. The question which arises next is which form of lateral is basic, [l] or [ɫ].

   In discussing aspiration of voiceless stops I pointed out that it is usual to take one of the allophones as the underlying form. Which allophone is chosen depends on what gives the most simple and elegant description. The traditional account takes the velarized *l* [ɫ] as a secondary, derived variant of the plain *l*. In other words, it is generally assumed that the plain form is the underlying allophone and that the allophony takes the form of adding a secondary articulation, velarization, to this plain underlying variant. Given this assumption we could state the rule as 6.34:

6.34   Coda

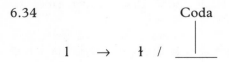

Notice that the formulation of this rule indicates that velarization takes place whenever the /l/ is some part of a coda. This doesn't necessarily mean that the /l/ will appear in absolute final position. Hence, 6.34 will apply to *milk* as well as to *mill*.

This account of the velarized *l* is what you will find in a good many descriptions of English. However, it is somewhat incomplete. First, consider what happens when a word such as *tell* is followed by an unstressed syllable beginning with a vowel, as in *tell a story*. Here we find that the /l/ is no longer velarized. This is easy to account for. In ordinary speech this phrase will consist of two phonological words:

6.35

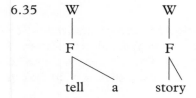

Assuming *tell a* is syllabified just like *teller* we get 6.36 for both forms:

6.36

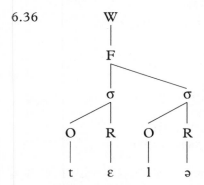

This contrasts, of course, with a phrase such as *story to tell* in which the /l/ must be velarized.

The second point to make concerns syllabic /l/. As we know /l/ is often the sole occupant of the rhyme. Now, syllabic /l/ is always pronounced 'dark'. This is illustrated in 6.37:

6.37   bottle   [bɔtɫ]   bubble   [bʌbɫ]
        tickle   [tɪkɫ]   tunnel   [tʌnɫ]

How does our rule cope with this? If we assume that such a rhymal /l/ is in some sense part of the coda then nothing more need be said. However, this is rather an odd way of thinking of a syllabic liquid, which we generally think of as occupying a nucleus position. Moreover, if the syllabic /l/ were solely a coda we would end up with a syllable without any nucleus at all. By minimally modifying our statement of the generalization we obtain the correct rule: /l/ is velarized iff (if and only if) it is part of the rhyme. We therefore amend 6.34 by replacing Coda with Rhyme.

6.38

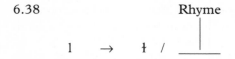

$$l \quad \rightarrow \quad ɫ \; / \; \underline{\hspace{2cm}}$$

6.2.4 Retroflection

In the previous section I mentioned the process of Alveopalatalization, by which /t/ followed by /ɹ/ acquires a retroflex or alveopalatal articulation. I will represent the sound as a retroflex plosive, /ʈ/. This process is found in the cases illustrated in 6.39, but prohibited in the examples of 6.40 (taken from Nespor and Vogel 1986: 80):

6.39	treat	[tʰ]reat	(treat)$_\sigma$
	street	s[t]reet	(street)$_\sigma$
	retrieve	re[t]rieve	(re)$_\sigma$ (trieve)$_\sigma$
	citrus	ci[t]rus	(ci)$_\sigma$ (trus)$_\sigma$
	destroy	des[t]roy	(de)$_\sigma$ (stroy)$_\sigma$
	nitrate	ni[t]rate	(ni)$_\sigma$ (trate)$_\sigma$
6.40	night rate	*nigh[t] rate	(night)$_\sigma$ (rate)$_\sigma$
	rat race	*ra[t] race	(rat)$_\sigma$ (race)$_\sigma$
	cut rate	*cu[t] rate	(cut)$_\sigma$ (rate)$_\sigma$
	tight rope	*tigh[t] rope	(tight)$_\sigma$ (rope)$_\sigma$

The third column indicates the syllable structure of these words. It is clear from these data that the precondition for Alveopalatalization is that both /t/ and /ɹ/ must be in the onset of the syllable.

6.2.5 Vowel shortening

In our discussion of the vowel phonemes in chapter 1 I noted that it was very difficult to know whether vowel length or vowel quality is what distinguishes pairs such as [iː/ɪ] or [uː/ʊ]. In fact, the situation is complicated somewhat by a length alternation. Before a voiceless plosive any vowel, short, long or diphthong, is subject to a rule of Vowel Shortening (cf. Gimson 1980: 94ff). Thus, the words *bee, bead, beat, bid, bit* might be transcribed [biː, biːd, bit, bɪd, bɪ̆t], where [ɪ̆] represents an ultrashort [ɪ]. Gimson points out that this is only occurs in accented syllables.

6.2.6   Glottal Reinforcement

The final set of processes are clearly governed to a certain extent by syllable structure, though the precise details of what conditions them is not entirely clear as yet. They all involve some kind of glottalization of a consonant, and they occur with different frequency and under slightly different conditions in various dialects of English. The first, and in a sense basic, process is that of preglottalization of the voiceless stop or affricate. Because this serves to make the pronunciation of the stop more emphatic, this is often called Glottal Reinforcement. In some accents of the North of England this can even take the form of an ejective.

In American English, glottalling mainly seems to affect /t/ (see Kahn 1976: 48), so we'll limit ourselves to consideration of that case. Consider the examples in 6.41 (slightly adapted from Nespor and Vogel 1986: 77):

6.41   a.   wait   [weɪʔt]
             report   [rɪpɔːʔt]
             giant   [ʤaɪənʔt]
        b.   atlas   [æʔtləs]
             witness   [wɪʔtnəs]
        c.   wait patiently   [weɪʔtpeɪʃn̩ʔtlɪ]
             wait reluctantly   [weɪʔtrɪlʌktn̩ʔtlɪ]

These examples all illustrate possible sites for preglottalization. On the other hand, there are other positions where this reinforcement is impossible:

6.42   a.   take   [*ʔteɪk]
             steak   [*sʔteɪk]
        b.   matter   [*mæʔtə]
             master   [*mɑːsʔtə]
             attack   [*əʔtæk]
        c.   night owl   [*naɪʔtaʊl]
             heartache   [*hɑːʔteɪk]
        d.   wait a minute   [*weɪʔtəmɪnɪʔt]
             wait eagerly   [*weɪʔtiːgəlɪ]

How can we distinguish the contexts in which Glottal Reinforcement does and does not take place? From 6.41a and 6.42a we can say initially that reinforcement is found at the end of a syllable and prohibited at the beginning. Do we need to say more than this? In 6.41b we see reinforcement word medially. However, this is only possible when the phonotactics of English demand that the /t/ be syllable final. When this condition isn't met, as in 6.42b, no reinforcement is possible. (Recall that no English syllable can begin *tl-* or *tn-*.) There is an interesting contrast between 6.41c and the examples of 6.42c, d. In, e.g., *wait patiently* we have reinforcement at the end of a word. In 6.42c, d the /t/ is in word final position, either absolutely, in 6.42d, or at the end of a word within a compound in 6.42c, yet there is no reinforcement. Clearly, the reason is that in 6.42c, d the /t/ is followed immediately by a vowel.

How can we explain this patterning? Assuming all these examples, including 6.42d, to be pronounced as single phrases, without any break between the words, we might wish to say that syllabification can occur across the word boundary and hence put the /t/ into the onset of the next syllable in the examples of 6.42c, d. This would mean that 6.42c, d would have essentially the same structure as 6.42a, b. We could then claim that a single generalization is at work: /t/ may only be reinforced with glottalization if it is unambiguously in the coda position. For example, *night owl* and *wait eagerly* would have the structure shown in 6.43:

6.43   a.

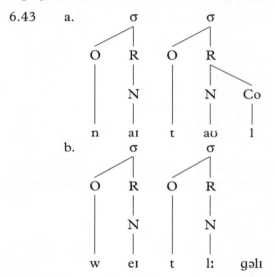

However, this solution is unsatisfactory. In general, we do not assume syllabification across word boundaries in English (though this is attested in other languages, e.g. Spanish). Indeed, in comparing examples such as *this pear* and *despair* in chapter 3 it was vital that we assumed that resyllabification across word boundaries did not take place. In the present case we can tell that the /t/ of examples 6.43 cannot be the onsets of the second syllables because such a single voiceless onset in a stress-bearing syllable could be reasonably heavily aspirated (or rather, given our earlier discussion, would be more resistant to deaspiration), especially in the case of 6.43b, where the first syllable of *eagerly* bears the main accent). However, this doesn't happen. To confirm this, compare the pronunciation of a phrase such as *book a telephone call* with that of, say, *look at elephant calls*. If we pronounce these carefully and emphatically we will hear heavy aspiration on the /t/ of *telephone*, but heavy aspiration on the /t/ of *at* in *at elephant* would sound comical in most dialects of English. Another problem is that we would have no explanation for the pronunciation of the phrase *wait reluctantly*. In this example we get preglottalling, but the cluster *tr-* is a possible onset. Therefore, if trans-word resyllabification were possible we would expect to be able to syllabify the /t/ with the /r/, and this would pre-empt the glottalling process.

However, we can solve these problems at a sweep by making use of a notion which I introduced in chapter 3 (though without discussing it in great detail). What we would like to be able to say is that preglottalling takes place whenever the voiceless plosive comes at the end of the syllable, or in other words, when it is in a coda. The explanation for the failure of preglottalization in 6.43 hinges on the idea that the consonant is somehow too closely attached to the following vowel to permit it to be considered properly within the coda of the previous syllable. Yet we have seen that we cannot simply say that the consonant shifts from the coda position to the onset slot of the next syllable.

In order to gain the best of both worlds we can assume that those plosives which fail to undergo glottalization are both in the coda of the first syllable and in the onset of the following syllable, in other words, they are ambisyllabic. This makes a good deal of phonetic sense. After all, it is very difficult, or indeed impossible, at the phonetic level to distinguish syllable boundaries. These boundaries can only really be established as a result of the phonological behaviour of sounds. Therefore, by linking the consonant simultaneously to the two syllables we have a simple representation of this phonetic property, and at the same time a way of distinguishing representationally between the two conditions. We can therefore propose 6.44 as representations for *night owl* and *wait eagerly*:

6.44   a.

b.

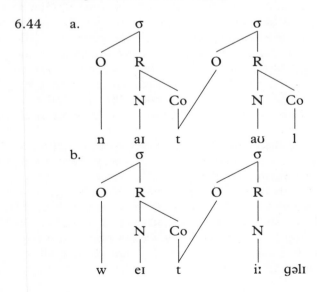

We can conclude, therefore, that Glottal Reinforcement in American English is a rule which inserts a glottal stop before a voiceless plosive when it is contained exclusively within a coda. This can be formulated as in 6.45:

6.45   Coda
                               |
                               |
     ∅   →   ʔ / _____ $\begin{bmatrix} -\text{cont} \\ -\text{voiced} \end{bmatrix}$

There is an interesting notational question here. As it stands it would seem that the rule as formulated in 6.45 would still apply to the representations in 6.44 because the consonants are still in a coda even though they are also in an onset. However, it seems to be a universal property of rules of this sort that they fail to apply if a single segment is linked to two separate prosodic units. This point was first made in the context of the behaviour of true geminates. As we know from chapter 2, these are single melody elements linked to two timing slots. In general, no rule can affect only one half of such a geminate. This is known as **Inalterability** (after Hayes 1986a).[3] Here, a single melody element is linked to two different nodes in a syllable (indeed, in different syllables). Therefore, by a universal convention the rule doesn't apply to such cases. Another way of thinking of this is to say that the association between melody elements and prosodic structure (i.e. skeletal slots, syllable constituents etc.) is interpreted by a rule exhaustively. That is, the rule assumes that the associations mentioned in the rule are the only associations it will encounter. If it meets additional associations, as in the case of 6.43, then it fails to apply.

The glottal stop insertion process is the standard account of Glottal Reinforcement. However, given our more recent perspective on the nature of features and segments, it's worthwhile delving into the process a little further. For while a rule of the shape 6.45 is descriptively adequate, in the sense that it captures the basic alternation, it is puzzling in that we have no particular explanation for why it should be that such an insertion takes place. If we can have a glottal stop inserted, why not a [b] or a [x]? One way of approaching this problem is to ask whether we really have an insertion process here.

Let's consider the theory of distinctive features developed in chapter 5. There, we saw that it makes sense to think of features as governed by a type of geometry. In particular we distinguished between laryngeal features of a sound (such as its voicing features) and its supralaryngeal features (such as manner or place features). I also suggested that a glottal sound such as [h] or [ʔ] could be thought of as a sound lacking supralaryngeal feature specifications. Now, the glottal stop is phonetically a voiceless sound. Suppose we take the representation of a voiceless stop, say [t], and remove all the supralaryngeal features. This is shown in 6.46:

6.46   a.

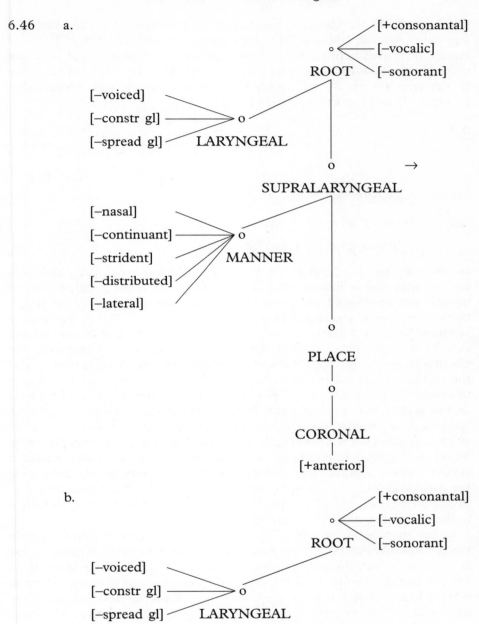

Now, this is almost the representation we would assume for the glottal stop.
However, many phonologists assume that [ʔ] is effectively a glide, and thus
[−consonantal], and in SPE the glottal stop is claimed to be a sonorant
(though this decision has been strongly criticized on phonetic grounds).
On the other hand, if [ʔ] really is a stop in any sense, it is presumably a

consonant. Let's therefore assume that the root features of [ʔ] and voiceless stops are identical, and that [ʔ] is effectively a voiceless obstruent. The only feature mismatch between 6.46b and a genuine [ʔ] is that glottal stops are generally characterized as having a constricted glottis (this is what gives rise to the stop effect). So we simply need to alter the feature specification [–constr gl] to [+constr gl], to give 6.47:

6.47

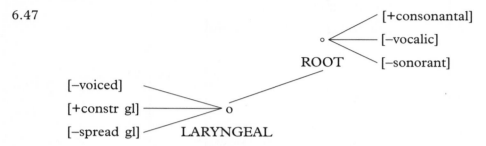

In this way we can 'derive' [ʔ] from any voiceless stop. Let's therefore assume that this is indeed what is happening. Then the preglottalization process can be thought of as one in which we split the articulation of [p t k] into two parts, creating a kind of contour segment. Recall that such a segment has two different melody representations attached to one timing tier. In the first part, we have just the glottal closure (anticipating the closure phase of the stop) without any supralaryngeal involvement. Thus, the melody is marked [+constricted glottis] but left unmarked for features of manner or place. This is the glottalling effect. In the second part we have all the appropriate supralaryngeal features, but [constricted glottis] has the specification [–constr gl]. (If this were not the case we would have an ejective stop, which is phonetically quite possible, but doesn't happen to be found in English.) Interestingly, we could in principle have constructed a similar contour segment but with the specification [+spread glottis] during the preglottal phase instead of [+constricted glottis]. This would have produced an aspirate glottal, i.e. [h]. This isn't observed in English, though it is found, for instance, in Icelandic.

In British dialects, including RP, we also find a process of glottalling with voiceless plosives and /tʃ/. As in American, the glottal closure is more or less simultaneous with the stop closure, or just before it. Very frequently, however, in British accents the supralaryngeal element is lost altogether, leaving behind just a glottal stop (something which is not unexpected given the discussion of feature structure and glottalling). Total glottalling, of course, is frowned upon in RP, because it's associated with the dreaded 'Cockney dialect' and other sociolinguistic abominations. However, it's frequently found in the speech of all but the most fanatically fastidious speakers.

A detailed summary of the conditions under which preglottalization occurs in British speech is provided by Wells (1982a: 260). The main contexts in which it is found are given in 6.48:

6.48   a.   sto[ʔp] talking   qui[ʔt]e good   loo[ʔk] down
        b.   sto[ʔp] worrying   qui[ʔt]e likely   loo[ʔk] worried
        c.   stopped   [stɔʔpt]   capsule   [kæʔpsjuːl]
              nights   [naɪʔts]   curtsey   [kəːʔtsɪ]
              looks   [lʊʔks]   picture   [pɪʔktʃə]

From these data it would seem that the basic process inserts a glottal stop before the voiceless consonant provided that consonant is in the coda. In *stopped* we have two voiceless consonants, but only the /p/ is preglottalized. This can be understood if we assume that the /t/ is actually an appendix to the syllable (as discussed in chapter 3). In that case only the /p/ is, strictly speaking, in the coda. Thus, British Glottal Reinforcement seems to be identical to the American rule.

A further point of similarity is the fact that the process fails to occur (for most speakers) if the word is followed by a vowel-initial word, just as in American. Thus, we don't find glottalling in 6.49:

6.49   a.   stop over   b.   quite ordinary   c.   look away

We can account for this in exactly the same way we accounted for the equivalent restriction on American Glottal Reinforcement.

However, there is something of a puzzle with words ending in a voiceless plosive uttered in isolation, as in the exclamations *Stop!*, *Quite!* or *Look!* For many speakers preglottaling is less preferred or even unattested in such cases. Yet we have a straightforward case of syllable-final stop in such words, so we would expect preglottalling to occur if it were conditioned in purely syllabic terms.

Just to show that not everything in phonology can be neatly accounted for, I will briefly mention a curious fact about preglottalling, which defies straightforward explanation. Wells (1982a) reports another set of data from certain RP speakers who permit preglottalling in the contexts shown in 6.50:

6.50   a.   ho[ʔp]eless   b.   ma[ʔt]tress   c.   e[ʔk]ual

Here, the normal syllabification principles of English (specifically the Maximal Onset Principle) would give us the syllable structure *ho.peless, ma.ttress, e.qual* (with a dot indicating the syllable boundary). But in that case the stop would definitely be in the following onset, and not in a coda.[4]

There are two main situations in which preglottalization seems never to occur. One is when the voiceless stop is a single medial consonant, as in *happy, dotty, lucky*, the other is when the syllable after the voiceless stop is the one which receives stress, *apply, attain, account*. This suggests that the preglottalling is a type of reinforcement of the coda at the end of the stressed syllable. The data of 6.50 could, perhaps, be accounted for if we assumed that the speakers who accept such pronunciations operating with a slightly different syllable structure, in which the first syllable is closed by the plosive. This would be rather similar to a frequent phenomenon in other languages in which a consonant in such a position is geminated (as a way of reinforcing the stressed syllable). But this is rather speculative.

6.3 Deletions, Lenitions and Insertions

6.3.1 Deletions

6.3.1.1 Consonant elisions   Connected speech frequently has fewer segments in it than one might imagine. Both vowels and consonants are elided (deleted) especially in rapid speech. In very fast and casual speech entire syllables can be lost. This process affects some types of word more than others. In particular, function words, such as *the*, *of*, auxiliary verbs and so on, tend to be prone to this kind of simplification. However, these have rather special properties which need to be treated separately. All the examples cited in this section will involve lexical words.

Recall from chapter 2 that Russian has a process in which a sound such as /t/ disappears when surrounded by 'too many' consonants. Thus, the root *mest-* 'place' (as in the word *mesto*) combines with the adjective suffix *-nij* to give a word pronounced as *mesnij* 'local'. This sort of behaviour is common in the world's languages, and is a well-known feature of connected speech in English. Consider the data in 6.51, some of it taken from the corpus of British English collected by Brown (1977: 61ff) from television newscasters:

6.51	a.	first three	[fəːstθriː]	[fəːsθriː]
		last night	[lɑːstnaɪt]	[lɑːsnaɪt]
		the fact that	[ðəfæktðət]	[ðəfækðət]
		aspects	[æspɛkts]	[æspɛks]
		interest of the	[ɪntrɛstəvðə]	[ɪntrɛsəðə]
	b.	discharged prisoners	[dɪstʃɑːdʒdprɪzənəz]	[dɪstʃɑːdʒprɪzənəz]
		hurled twenty (yards)	[həːldtwɛntɪ]	[həːltwɛntɪ]
		sandwich	[sændwɪdʒ]	[sæmwɪdʒ]
		nothing stands still	[nʌθɪŋstændzstɪl]	[nʌθɪŋstænstɪl]
		World Wild Life Fund	[wəːldwaɪldlaɪffʌnd]	[wəːlwaɪlaɪffʌnd]
		banned for life	[bændfəlaɪf]	[bæmfəlaɪf]

These examples illustrate the dropping of the coronal plosives /t d/ in clusters, an extremely common occurrence. I shall refer to the general process as Cluster Simplification. Even where the coronal is the past tense/participle morpheme it is likely to be elided (e.g. *discharged, hurled* in 6.51b). Normally the simplification takes places when the coronal is flanked by consonants. Occasionally, however, we see a cluster being simplified even when the next word begins with a vowel (e.g. *interest of the*), though I suspect that this is lexically restricted or applies only in rather rapid speech. Notice also that in some cases we see assimilations applying to the output of the consonant deletion process (e.g. *sandwich*).

A further type of consonant elision occurs very frequently to the output of some of the assimilation rules discussed in section 6.1.1. Recall that assimilations and palatalizations produce such pronunciations as [hæmbːæg], [ðɪʃːɔp] and [wʊdʒːʊ] from *handbag, this shop* and *would you*. However, in casual speech these are much more likely to be pronounced [hæmbæg], [ðɪʃɔp] and [wʊdʒʊ]. What is happening here is that a geminated consonant is being simplified to a single consonant (a process we can call Degemination).

Degemination doesn't apply in all cases, however. Geminate consonants are not found in monomorphemic English words. However, they can be created when words are compounded (6.52) or affixed with the certain morphemes (essentially the 'stress neutral' affixes) as in examples 6.53:

6.52   rat tail   [rætːeɪl]
        milkcrate   [mɪlkːreɪt]
        house sale   [haʊsːeɪl]

6.53   unknown   [ʌnːoun]
        ill-looking   [ɪlːʊkɪŋ]
        solely   [soulːɪ]
        leanness   [liːnːəs]

Degemination in these cases is much less likely than in the case of the assimilation examples above.

6.3.1.2   Vowel Reduction and elision   English vowels are subject to a good deal of variation, notably Vowel Reduction. In many languages with stress, vowels retain more or less the same quality whether they are stressed or not. This is true of Spanish, Italian, Polish, Czech, Hungarian and a whole host of other languages. However, in many other instances an unstressed vowel is reduced, frequently to schwa. This is characteristic of English, where unstressed vowels frequently reduce to [ə] or [ɪ].

Complete reduction, that is elision of unstressed vowels is extremely common in all but the most careful speech registers. In the examples given in 6.54–6, the reduced version is followed by an alternative, more careful, unreduced pronunciation in parentheses. In 6.54a–d we see examples which have become effectively lexicalized, in that the full pronunciation would be relatively unusual at all speech rates:

6.54   a.   secretary   [sɛkrətrɪ]   ([sɛkrətərɪ])
       b.   promontory   [prɔməntrɪ]   ([prɔməntərɪ])
       c.   veterinary   [vɛtnərɪ]   ([vɛtərɪnərɪ])
       d.   different   [dɪfr̩nt]   ([dɪfərənt])
       e.   chancellor   [ʧɑːnslə]   ([ʧɑːnsələ])
       f.   talkative   [tɔːktɪv]   ([tɔːkətɪv])

Notice that the syllable [rɪ] has been dropped in 6.54c; 6.54f on the other hand goes counter to the tendency not to drop the vowel if the following consonant is an obstruent, and is consequently not such a common alternative pronunciation.

In 6.55–6 we see a variety of consonant clusters created by vowel drop:

6.55   a.   correct   [krɛkt]   ([kərɛkt])
       b.   belief   [bliːf]   ([bɪliːf])
       c.   police   [pliːs]   ([pəliːs])
       d.   saliva   [slaɪvə]   ([səlaɪvə])

6.56   a.   potato   [pteɪtou]   ([pəteɪtou])
       b.   tomorrow   [tmɔrou]   ([təmɔrou])
       c.   malaria   [mlɛːriə]   (məlɛːriə])
       d.   fanatics   [fnætɪks]   ([fənætɪks])

The clusters of 6.56 are noteworthy because they violate the phonotactic constraints we observed in chapter 3. Notice, too, that in examples 6.56a, b the initial plosive (/p t/ respectively) remains (slightly) aspirated, an indication of the 'real' syllable structure of the words. These clusters also have an alternative, indeed, rather common, pronunciation, in which the reduction of the vowel of the first syllable is compensated for by rendering the following consonant syllabic. Thus, there would be a minimal contrast in the onset of words such as *police* and *please*: in *police* we would have a pronunciation something like [pl̩iːs] as opposed to *please* [pliːz]. Under these circumstances, of course, we would not regard the examples in 6.56 as constituting infringements of the phonotactics.

In 6.57 we see examples of vowel drop from function words in phrases (taken from data collected by Brown 1977: 68):

6.57   a.   two to three   [tutθriː]
       b.   to meet   [tmiːt]
       c.   a week or two ago   [əwiːktuːgou]
       d.   over the years   [ouvðəjəːz]

This kind of reduction is much less likely with lexical words. Thus, we would hardly expect the reduction indicated in 6.58:

6.58   the weaker two agreed   [ðəwiːktuːgriːd]

Vowel reduction may not only give rise to the creation of syllabic sonorants, as in 6.55, 56, we may also encounter syllabic obstruents. This is particularly common with phrases begin *it's*. Examples 6.59a–c are again from Brown (1977: 96), while 6.59d is a common fast speech pronunciation:

6.59   a.   it's the way   [ts̩ðəweɪ]   ([ɪtsðəweɪ])
         b.   it's considered   [ts̩kn̩sɪdəd]   ([ɪtskənsɪdəd])
         c.   it's not   [ts̩nɔt]   ([ɪtsnɔt])
         d.   photography   [f̩tɔgrəfɪ]   ([fətɔgrəfɪ])

In addition, we find that syllabic sonorants which are impermissible or unusual lexically are found in abundance in fast speech. The suffix *-en*, while pronounced as syllabic /n̩/ after a coronal obstruent, is generally pronounced with a schwa after a labial or velar. However, in faster speech styles we find examples such as 6.60, especially if the previous consonant has been glottalled:

6.60   a.   broken down   [brouʔn̩daun]
         b.   open today   [ouʔm̩tədei]

Notice how in 6.60b the labiality of the lost /p/ is retained as a feature of the following syllabic nasal.

One of the problems of representation left unresolved in chapter 4 was that of the schwa or 'reduced vowel'. Now, in many languages the schwa vowel seems to disappear under certain conditions, especially when it is unstressed. In addition, it is difficult to know how best to characterize the schwa in terms of features, since it is neither high nor low, front nor back. A number of linguists have argued that, in many cases at least, the simplest solution is to say that the schwa effectively has no articulatory features. What this means is that we can represent the schwa as a vowel slot (so that it has major class features), which simply lacks any supralaryngeal features. Thus, the schwa is the vowel equivalent of a glottal consonant.

The kinds of representation we obtain for *police*, *malaria* and *photography* are shown in 6.61:

6.61   a.

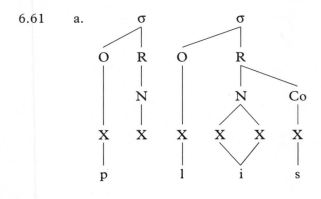

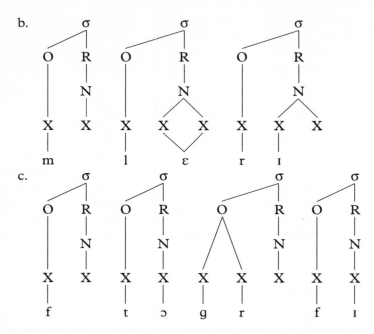

This kind of representation would mean that it would be relatively straight-forward to represent the reductions to syllabic consonants in 6.55, 56, 59. For example, for *police*, *malaria* and *photography* we might envisage processes such as those illustrated in 6.62–4:

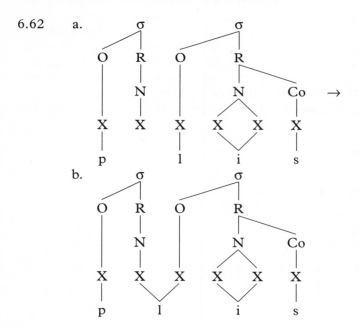

6.63   a.

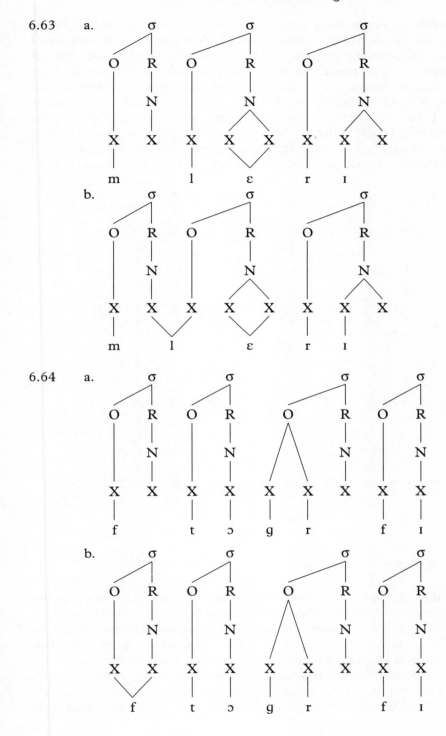

        b.

6.64   a.

        b.

In the 6.64b representations a consonant has occupied the vacant X slot corresponding to the syllable nucleus. In each case there are two consonants which could in principle so spread: *p/l m/l, f/t*. Clearly, it is the most sonorant which wins out. The result is a consonant with two associations. In more rapid speech we might expect that the consonant's former affiliation with the onset position might be lost and the consonant would the become a purely syllabic consonant. In the case of *photography*, in rapid speech, the consonant might itself undergo a kind of 'vowel reduction' by losing its own syllabicity. In that case it would end up adjoined to the following onset and form what to all intents and purposes would be a complex onset, *ft-*:

6.65   a.

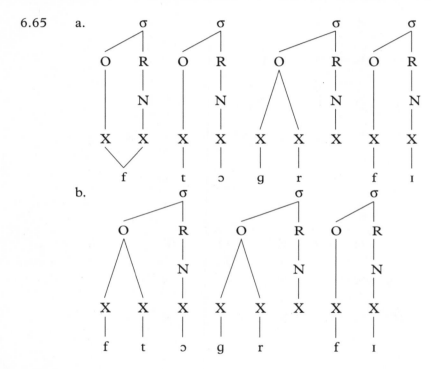

6.3.2   Lenitions

Akin to the deletions are processes of lenition. In these processes a consonant is pronounced with less force and tenseness, and often undergoes other changes as well. We can think of lenitions as being the consonantal equivalent of vowel reduction. Such processes are well known from other languages. Thus, a characteristic of Spanish is that a voiced plosive /b d g/ becomes a corresponding fricative /β ð ɣ/ between vowels. Brown (1977: 74ff) points out that plosives in English are often weakened to sounds reminiscent of fricatives in connected speech in a variety of contexts. In

English there are two well-known lenition processes which I shall mention here, Flapping and Glottalling.

Flapping (sometimes called Tapping) is a process found in General American, certain Irish accents, some varieties of Southern British English, and Australian English. In this process /t/ (and in many accents /d/) is pronounced as a rapid 'flap' of the tongue tip against the alveolar ridge. The result sounds reminiscent of a /d/ though it is of shorter duration, IPA [ɾ]. A detailed description of the process can be found in Nespor and Vogel (1986: 223ff).

Compare the examples of 6.66:

6.66	a.	atone	[t]	e.	atom	[ɾ]
	b.	adore	[d]	f.	adder	[ɾ]
	c.	a tissue	[t]	g.	at issue	[ɾ]
	d.	I describe	[d]	h.	I'd ascribe	[ɾ]

The /t d/ of examples 6.66a–d fail to undergo Flapping, while those of 6.66e–h undergo it. There is variation as to the precise environment of the Flapping rule. In many American accents we also find it applying to words such as *winter, alter, party, hardy*, that is when any sonorant precedes the /t d/. In other accents it is only possible after a vowel. Moreover, Flapping is only possible when /t d/ precedes a vowel. In words such as *petrol, atlas*, or *atmosphere* there is no Flapping.

Examples 6.66c, d suggest that the rule doesn't apply to /t d/ in the onset. How then do we account for the contrast between words such as *atone* and *atom* or *adore/adder*? The principal difference is one of stress: Flapping is impermissible when the second syllable bears (primary or secondary) stress. We can complement the data in 6.66 with those in 6.67, where Flapping is also impossible, to illustrate this (cf. Harris and Kaye 1990: 265):

6.67   a. látèx   b. dáytime   c. sábotàge   d. hábitàt

Notice that these *t*s are precisely those which are likely to surface as aspirated, because they form the absolute onset of a stressed syllable. A near-minimal pair here is shown in 6.68:

6.68   a. sátire   [sætʰaɪɹ]   b. sátyr   [seɪɾɹ̩]

For the present we'll say that Flapping occurs whenever the /t d/ is in the middle of a foot, but not at either edge. This rules out flapped /t/ in the onset of a stressed syllable or word finally.

The rule seems to be delimited only by the phonological domain of the Phonological Utterance (Nespor and Vogel 1986: 224ff). Thus, consider the following examples from Nespor and Vogel:

6.69   a.   A very dangerous wild cat escaped from the zoo
              → ca[ɾ] escaped
        b.   Just the other night a racoon was spotted in our
              neighbourhood.
              → nigh[ɾ] a
        c.   Ichabod, our pet crane, usually hides when guests come.
              → Ichabo[ɾ] our

Notice that the process operates even over Intonational Phrases, as in 6.69b, c. In fact, as Kahn (1976: 102) points out, Flapping can even operate across sentences if they are spoken together as a single utterance. He gives the example 6.70 (cf. Nespor and Vogel 1986: 236):

6.70   Have a seat. I'll be right back   →   sea[ɾ] I'll

The process of t-Glottalling is widespread in a good many accents of Britain, including those of London and the South-East, Scotland, and the North of England. A sample of words in which it occurs is given in 6.71:

6.71   a.   cut   cu[ʔ]
        b.   cutter   cu[ʔ]er
        c.   atom   a[ʔ]om
        d.   water   wa[ʔ]er
        e.   alter   al[ʔ]er
        f.   winter   win[ʔ]er

However, it is impossible with the /t/ at the beginning of the syllable or when an obstruent precedes:

6.72   a.   take   *[ʔ]ake   b.   act   *ac[ʔ]   c.   past   *pas[ʔ]

From this it appears that Glottalling is very similar to Flapping except that it applies at the end of a syllable as well as between a sonorant and a vowel. Like Flapping, Glottalling respects the foot condition, and hence is impossible in the words of 6.69 above (except for the final /t/ of *habitat*). In addition, Glottalling is said to be impossible in words such as *petrol* (though there is vacillation in, for instance, London speech; cf. Harris and Kaye 1990: 269ff).

   To summarize: we have seen rules of Flapping and Glottalling, which take the form of 6.73 and 6.74 in a somewhat informal notation:

6.73   t, d   →   ɾ   / [... [+son] _____ V ...]$_F$

6.74   t   →   ʔ   / [... [+son] _____ $\begin{Bmatrix} V \\ \# \end{Bmatrix}$ ...]$_F$

The [. . .]$_F$ represent the boundaries of a foot.[5] The ' . . . ' in the contextual part of the rule indicates that the target must be properly contained within the foot, i.e. it may not appear at the edge of the foot.

Recall from chapter 5 (appendix) that the braces ('curly brackets') in 6.74 mean that the right-hand environment for the process may be either a vowel or a word boundary. In other words the environment consists of a disjunction of two unrelated contexts. This is an unsatisfactory situation – we would like to be able to say that Glottalling is a unitary process, but this is not really captured by the formulation in 6.74 on account of the disjunction. As we saw in chapter 5, this problem always arises when we have to state part of a rule using the brace notation. A better alternative, therefore, is to seek a characterization of the process which eliminates this disjunction.

I shall be somewhat speculative here. I suggested that the impossibility of Glottal Reinforcement in American English across a word boundary could be understood if we introduced the notion of ambisyllabicity. This notion will also allow us to formulate a context for Flapping and Glottalling. We simply need to say that singleton consonants are ambisyllabic in words such as *better*. Then we say that Flapping is triggered by ambisyllabic /t d/ (provided the foot condition is met). This can be formulated as in 6.75:

6.75

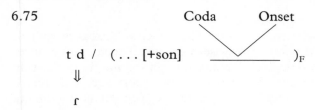

Notice that, since there has to be another syllable after the target /t d/ we don't need to stipulate that the target is followed by a nonempty X in the foot. The operation of the rule is illustrated for *better* in 6.76:

6.76

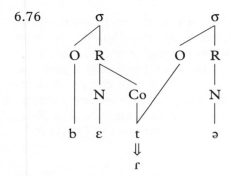

The rule of Glottalling is more complex because /t/ is also a target when it is a pure Coda. Therefore, we have to make the association to the following Onset optional. This is shown in 6.77:

6.77

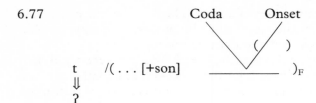

$$t \atop \Downarrow \atop ? \qquad /(\dots [+son] \underline{\qquad})_F$$

This applies to *bet, better* as shown in 6.78:

6.78   a.   b.

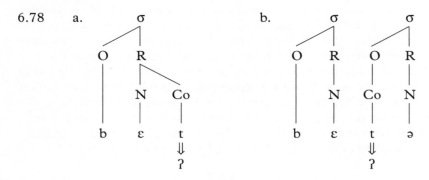

In sum, Flapping occurs anywhere within the Phonological Utterance, though the target must be within the foot. Likewise, Glottalling seems to be unrestricted with respect to phonological domain, though the nature of the rule means that it will be impossible to test whether it occurs across domains. Like Flapping, it is only possible when the target segment is not at the beginning of a foot.[6]

6.3.3   Insertions

While deletions are very characteristic of fast or casual speech, insertions or epenthesis processes, too, are not uncommon in the world's languages. The most usual type of epenthesis is found when a vowel is used to break up a 'difficult' consonant cluster or when a consonant (especially a glide) is inserted between two vowels to break the hiatus. We'll consider a well studied example of vowel epenthesis later in this section. A convenient example of consonant epenthesis is Glide Insertion, found in a number of dialects of English (though not so common in conservative varieties of British RP). It is illustrated in 6.79, 80:

6.79   a.   my other (car)   [maɪjʌðə]
        b.   free a (prisoner)   [friːjə]
        c.   freer (laws)   [friːjə]
        d.   enjoy icecream   [ɛndʒɔɪjaɪskriːm]

6.80 a. few arrests   [fjuːwərɛsts]
      b. fewer rests   [fjuːwərɛsts]
      c. now or never   [naʊwɔːnɛvə]
      d. go away   [gouwəweɪ]

In British English this process is only found when the first vowel of the cluster is high or is a diphthong with a high second component. In other circumstances, we encounter an unusual, though well known phenomenon in which the vowel sequence is broken up by /r/. I shall call this rule R-Epenthesis. It is illustrated in 6.81–2:

6.81 a. law and order   [lɔːrənɔːdə]
      b. Russia and America   [rʌʃərənəmɛrɪkə]
      c. America and Russia   [əmɛrɪkərənrʌʃə]
      d. ma and pa   [mɑːrənpɑː]

6.82 a. over and out   [ouvərənaʊt]
      b. director of   [dərɛktərəv]
      c. fear of   [fɪərəv]
      d. tar and feather   [tɑːrənfɛðə]

In the examples of 6.82 the epenthetic r corresponds to an orthographic r, whereas in 6.81 there is no /r/ at the end of the word, either orthographically or etymologically. In addition to the above contexts we also find /r/ appearing in word formation and inflection when certain vowel final stems are suffixed with vowel initial suffixes, as in 6.83:

6.83 a. star   starry   [stɑːrɪ]
      b. restore   restorer   [rɪstɔːrə]
      c. hear   hearing   [hɪərɪŋ]

For many speakers this applies to suffixed words which do not end etymologically in /r/. This is principally found with the vowel /ɔː/ spelt -aw, as in 6.84:

6.84 a. draw   drawing   [drɔːrɪŋ]
      b. (to) saw sawing   [sɔːrɪŋ]   cf.
      c. saw   saw it   [sɔːrɪt]

For these reasons, it is common to distinguish between the cases in 6.82–83, where the r is referred to as Linking-r and the cases in 6.81 where it is referred to as Intrusive-r.

It would not be surprising to find that the process behaved like two separate rules. It is generally assumed that the Intrusive-r process is a relatively recent phenomenon (having arisen over the last two hundred years

or so; see Wells 1982a: 227). An obvious way of interpreting its rise is to
assume that it is, so to speak, parasitic on the Linking-r process. Thus, if
we consider two favourite examples, *star* vs. *Shah* in the *star is out* and the
Shah(r) is out, we would argue that originally *star* had an underlying and a
surface final /r/, while *Shah* had none. Then, non-rhotic accents lost the
/r/ in coda position, except when the word was followed by a vowel (*sta(r)*
vs. *star is*). Then, the appearance of /r/ in *star is* was reanalysed as a case
of R-insertion (triggering reanalysis of the underlying form of *star* as simply
/stɑː/). Once the rule had been reanalysed expressions such as *Shah is*
became indistinguishable from *star is* with respect to R-insertion and so the
/r/ got inserted in *Shah is* as well as *star is*. Once the process had gone to
completion the two types of /r/ would be completely indistinguishable.
However, it is often the case that changes of this sort don't happen over-
night, but rather occur in a piecemeal fashion, affecting words one at a time
(a phenomenon known as **lexical drift**). Under these circumstances, we
might expect to find vacillation in certain words, as the process drifted
through the lexicon.

Another reason for making a distinction is that the so-called 'intrusive-r'
is stigmatized. RP speakers who in practice apply the process in their own
speech every day of the week are apt to deny vigorously that they would ever
commit such an egregious sin. When asked to produce expressions such
as those of 6.81 they are likely to break up the vowel hiatus with a glottal
stop (though, of course, a glottal stop used to replace a voiceless plosive is
branded by the same speakers as 'ugly' or 'substandard'). This doesn't need
to be the result of linguistic snobbishness, or even, necessarily, a shift to a
more prestigious register. In my own speech, for instance, I have no difficulty pronouncing the examples in 6.81 with their 'intrusive' /r/. However,
the pronunciations in 6.84 are foreign to my accent (which may well mean
that I have generalized the /w/ insertion rule to include a mid-round vowel
as well as a high vowel).

As a result of these sociolinguistic complications, it is perhaps wiser to
distinguish the two processes, noting that the intrusive-r is often avoided in
more careful speech by certain speakers. Without this stigmatization it's
probable that the R-Epenthesis process would become maximally general
and apply everywhere between vowels where Glide Insertion doesn't apply.
The fact that a significant number of speakers go to great lengths to avoid
the process (especially when being observed by linguists!) shows how it is
possible for sociolinguistic variables to confound an otherwise neat linguistic
system.

One reason for believing that R-Epenthesis would normally have generalized but for extralinguistic factors is that there are good reasons for thinking that it is actually essentially the same process as Glide Insertion. Although
we have followed the American structuralist and poststructuralist traditions
and regarded /r/ as a liquid (and hence [+consonantal, +approximant]) there
are grounds for thinking that it is more like a glide, i.e. a [−consonantal,

+approximant] sound. In American English, and other rhotic dialects in which 'r' is not trilled, the 'r' sound postvocalically often represents a rhotic colouring to the previous vowel, almost in the manner of a diphthong. (Kahn 1976 defends the idea that /r/ is a glide in American English.) If this is the correct interpretation, then we can simply say that /r/ is the non-high counterpart to the glides /j w/. On that assumption it is the natural sound to use to break up a hiatus not involving a high vowel.

Finally, what is the domain within which Glide and R-Epenthesis operate? Nespor and Vogel (1986) show that R-Epenthesis operates across an Intonational Phrase, and hence must take the Phonological Utterance as its domain. They provide example 6.85:

6.85   The giant panda[r], as you know, is an endangered species.

Similarly, we can see from 6.86 that insertion of /j, w/ operates in a similar domain:

6.86   a.   The Dead Sea[j], as you know, is really a lake.
         b.   *Ivanhoe* [w], as you know, was written by Scott.

In particularly careful or emphatic speech, another process is like to apply in these examples, however, in which the vowel initial word as is reinforced by a glottal onset. This would then, of course, bleed the glide insertion processes.

FURTHER READING

In addition to the works cited in this chapter, overviews of English segmental phonology can be found in such sources as Gimson (1993), Giegerich (1992), Hawkins (1992). Nespor and Vogel (1986) discuss a variety of English processes in the context of prosodic domains.

EXERCISES

6.1   Place Assimilation in English: check the applicability of place of articulation assimilation in English, illustrated on p. 149. Construct appropriate examples of environments in which it does not apply and targets it does not apply to.

6.2   In which prosodic domain does Place Assimilation apply?

6.3   Formulate the rule of Sibilant Palatalization (6.15).

6.4   I have claimed that vowel shortening before a voiceless consonant is syllabically conditioned. Investigate this claim by constructing a list of words in which the same set of vowels occurs before the same set of consonants, in which the consonant forms (1) the coda of that syllable, (2) the onset of the next syllable. If you are not a native speaker of English, try out your word list on an English-speaking friend. If you are a native speaker, try out your list on a friend who speaks a different dialect from you.

6.5   The l-velarization rule is formulated on the assumption that it is the plain, unvelarized allophone which is basic. This is not a necessary assumption. How would you formalize the process if we were to take the velarized [ɫ] as basic? How would the notion of ambisyllabicity figure in your solution?

6.6   Show how to construct an alternative explanation for the failure of Glottal Reinforcement in cases like *nightowl* and *wait eagerly* using an interaction with the rule of Flapping. What specific assumption do you need to make to get the analysis to work?

6.7   Take one of the following rules and find its nearest equivalent in a language of your choice (e.g. your native language if you are not a native speaker of English). Compare that process with its English counterpart. What are the differences in class of sounds to which the process applies, the environment and prosodic domain it applies in and the phonological change effected?

  • Place Assimilation;
  • Coronal Palatalization;
  • Glottalling;
  • Flapping;
  • Cluster Simplification;
  • schwa deletion.

6.8   Collect and transcribe as many examples of consonant elision of /t d/ (Cluster Simplification) as you can in spontaneous speech, for instance, by recording a radio or TV news bulletin or discussion programme. Using these and other data cited in the literature, determine whether there is a syllabic condition on the elision process. How might you gather negative data (i.e. information about what pronunciations are *im*possible) in order to test your hypothesis?

6.9   *Vowel Reduction*

Each of the following words has at least one reduced vowel ([ə] or [ɪ]). In some cases it is possible to identify a full, unreduced vowel serving as the underlying form of the reduced vowel. For others it is impossible to identify a full form. Indicate which vowels are which and propose and motivate non-reduced forms where possible:

æbəkəs, ædəm, əgeɪn, ætəm, kænəpɪ, kəlaɪd, kəmpiːt, kənaɪv, kɔrəleɪt, dɛfərəns, draɪvə, ɛkspləneɪʃn, fɪnænʃl, ɪnklɪneɪʃn, pəreɪd, prɛpəreɪʃn, prɔvəkeɪʃn, rɛvəleɪʃn, səbsaɪd, səksiːd, səkʌm, səkʌmfərəns, tɛlɪfoun

chapter 7

Stress and Rhythm

7.0 Introduction

In many languages, one or more syllables in a word are singled out for special treatment and given stress. Not all languages have a system of word stress, though in all languages phrases exhibit a characteristic overall rhythm. As is well known, the rhythmic alternation of stressed and unstressed syllables is used in many languages in the organization of poetry. The specific patterns used in poetry are referred to as metres. Many of the analytic tools used by phonologists to study stress and rhythm are derived from the study of metrics and so we frequently speak of the study of such systems as **Metrical Phonology**.

7.1 Lexical Stress

It is notoriously difficult to identify the phonetic (i.e. the physiological and acoustic) correlates of stress and rhythm. Since this book is about phonology, we will simply say that some syllables are phonetically more prominent than others, where prominence is manifested in a number of ways. Firstly, a prominent syllable is generally louder than surrounding ones; secondly, it is often longer in duration than similar, non-prominent syllables; thirdly, the constituent sounds of a prominent syllable, especially its onset consonants, are often more clearly or forcefully enunciated than those in a less prominent one. Finally, a prominent syllable is often the locus of pitch movement (accent), characterizing an intonation contour. This means that a stressed syllable will often be one pronounced on a particularly high (or sometimes particularly low) pitch.

The second important point to bear in mind is that the notion 'stressed syllable' is rather different from 'high vowel' or 'coronal fricative' in that stress, or more generally, prominence, is an inherently relational concept. In other words, we should say that a stressed syllable is more stressed than its neighbours, whereas we do not say that an /s/ sound is more coronal or more fricative than its neighbours. Because of this we do not need to regard all syllables as either stressed or unstressed. In many cases we will encounter syllables in a word or phrase which are stressed, but not to the same degree as the principal stressed syllable. This is known as secondary stress, (as opposed to that falling on the most stressed element, primary or main stress). Not all languages with stress have secondary stress, and in some of those that do have it, it is a rather superficial phenomenon. However, in some languages (to some extent English), secondary stress is no less important for the phonological system as a whole as is primary stress.

There is a variety of transcriptional systems in use for notating stress. In the IPA primary stress is shown by a raised mark before the stressed syllable, and secondary stress is shown by a lowered mark: *entertain* [ˌɛntəˈteɪn]. In many texts you'll see the vowel bearing primary stress marked with an acute accent and that bearing secondary stress marked with a grave accent: *èntertáin*. In other texts, often purely for typographical convenience (for instance, where a good many other diacritics are used with other functions) the vowel of a stressed syllable may be printed in bold face or underlined.

Before we consider individual stress systems in any detail, it is important to gain a feel for the different types of stress system found in languages. The main distinction is between those systems which can be defined in purely (or largely) phonological terms and those in which the stress is determined by morphological principles, or assigned in purely lexical fashion. In the former case we can state phonological rules for the placement of stress, and learners of the language don't need to memorize the stress of a given word separately (apart from exceptional items). We will refer to such systems as **fixed stress systems**. In the latter case, the stress is a distinctive part of the word, just as the first vowel or the last consonant is a distinctive part, and it cannot be determined by any rule. We can call such systems **free stress systems**.

An example of a free stress language is Russian. Russian words can be stressed, in principle, on any syllable. There are no purely phonological constraints on where the stress may fall. Moreover, stress in Russian is often

determined by purely grammatical factors such as morphological class or
the type of suffix a word has. Nouns in Russian show great variation in the
way they are stressed. It is not rare to find words different solely in their
stress, e.g. *múka* 'torment', *muká* 'flour'. Russian nouns appear in two numbers, singular and plural, and several different case forms, generally marked
by suffixes. For a large class of nouns the stress always falls on some syllable
of the stem. In 7.1 we see some examples, illustrated by the genitive sg. and
the nominative and dative pl. of the words *perevorot* 'revolution', *peremena*
'transformation', *učitel´nica* '(female) teacher', *provoloka* 'wire':[1]

7.1		gen sg	nom pl	dat pl
	a.	perevoróta	perevoróty	perevorótam
	b.	peremény	peremény	pereménam
	c.	uč ítel´nici	uč ítel´nicy	ucítel´nicam
	d.	próvoloki	próvoloki	próvolokam

On the other hand, a few nouns are always stressed on the ending (or on
the last vowel of the stem if there is no overt ending), as seen in 7.2 with
the words *stol* 'table', or *statjá* 'article':

7.2		gen sg	nom pl	dat pl
	a.	stolá	stolý	stolám
	b.	statjí	statjí	statjám

However, a large number of nouns shift their stress pattern in the singular
and plural, so that either the ending or the stem is stressed, e.g. *oknó*
'window', *iglá* 'needle', *mésto* 'place':

7.3		gen sg	nom pl	dat pl
	a.	okná	ókna	óknam
		iglý	ígly	íglam
	b.	mésta	mestá	mestám

A smaller group shows stress shift for some cases but not for others. For
example, *golová* 'head', has final stress except for the accusative sg. and nominative pl. where stress is initial: *gólovu, gólovy*. A rather striking example of
this kind of thing is *skovorodá* 'frying-pan', which has final stress throughout
(e.g. genitive sg. *skovorodý*) except for the nom. pl.: *skóvorody*.

Words such as *okno, mesto* end in a suffix *-o* in the nom. sg. which
identifies the word as neuter gender (as opposed to masculine or feminine).
Words in this neuter noun class *regularly* exhibit this alternation between
singular end stress and plural stem stress, or singular stem stress and plural
end stress. One way of thinking of this is to say that the stress is partly
defined in terms of the morphological paradigm. In this case we often speak
of **paradigmatic stress**. (Halle 1973 discusses Russian noun stress from

this perspective.) Also worthy of note is the fact that certain word forms will be distinguished solely by stress, e.g. *ókna* 'windows (nom.)' ~ *okná* 'of a window'. This phenomenon is found in a number of languages with movable stress, for instance, Spanish, Italian, Greek.

Consider the fixed stress languages. In the simplest types, the stress always falls on a particular syllable or set of syllables. Typically, this will be the first syllable of the word (e.g. Czech, Hungarian) or the last syllable (Turkish) or the penultimate (Polish, Swahili). We can call this type of system **positionally fixed stress**.

Let us now turn to some simple examples of positional fixed stress systems to see what kinds occur and how they can be described. Given that stress is a relational phenomenon, we will need to look at whole stretches of syllables in order to understand the nature of stress. An important rhythmic unit is a stretch consisting of exactly one stressed syllable together (possibly) with a group of one or more unstressed syllables. This is called a foot (a term borrowed from classical theories of poetic metre). The stressed syllable may bear primary stress or secondary stress (or even lower degrees of stress) provided it is more prominent than a completely unstressed syllable. The crucial point in the definition of a foot is that there be exactly *one* stress – no more, no less.

To see how the notion of foot fits into linguistic theory, we will examine a variety of foot types found in the world's languages (I shall be following Hayes 1981.) In chapter 8 we will consider how the notion can be extended to English word stress. The best way to see simple straightforward stress systems in action is to look at languages with very regular stress placement (which, alas, excludes English) in which it is possible to construct long polysyllabic words. Languages of this sort abound in areas such as South America, Australia and the Pacific, and so we will take our first examples from these languages.

A common and simple way of representing the foot is as a simple type of tree diagram. The commoner types of foot are given Greek names (derived from the classical Greek traditions of analysing poetic metre). In 7.4 I give examples of the three most frequent foot types using English words. The symbol ° indicates the stressed syllable and the symbol · represents an unstressed syllable:

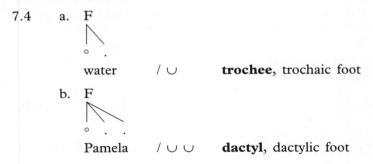

7.4   a.   F

             °   ·

             water   / ∪   **trochee**, trochaic foot

       b.   F

             °   ·   ·

             Pamela   / ∪ ∪   **dactyl**, dactylic foot

c.   F

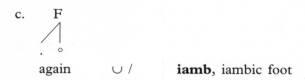

again   ∪ /   **iamb**, iambic foot

In addition you may encounter the anapaest ∪ ∪ / and the amphibrach
∪ / ∪. The feet with two syllables are called binary and those with three
syllables (the dactyl, anapaest and amphibrach) are called ternary.[2]
    Notice the way I have constructed these diagrams. The central, obligatory
component of the foot is the stressed syllable. This can therefore be regarded as the head of the foot (we have to suspend our anatomical pre-
judices here!). Trochees and dactyls are left-headed, while iambs are right
headed. As we know from elementary syntactic theory, a tree diagram can
be rewritten as a string enclosed in sets of brackets. Thus, we could also
represent our example words from 7.4 as 7.5, where the foot is enclosed in
parentheses and the head of each foot (i.e. the stressed syllable) is marked
with an asterisk (this notation is modified slightly from that introduced by
Halle and Vergnaud 1987; see below):

7.5   (* ·)   (* ··)   (· *)
        water   Pamela   again

In 7.6 we see a variety of words from the Australian language Maranungku,
where primary stress on a vowel, v, is marked $\acute{v}$ and secondary stress is
marked $\grave{v}$:

7.6   a.   tíralk   'saliva'
        b.   mérepèt   'beard'
        c.   yángarmàta   'the Pleiades'
        d.   lángkaràtetì   'prawn'
        e.   wélepènemànta   'kind of duck'

This is a very simple system in which every other syllable starting from the
left is stressed, and the initial syllable has the primary stress in the word. We
can therefore say that the stress foot for this language is a binary foot which
consists of a stressed syllable followed by one unstressed syllable (i.e. a
trochee). This is the commonest type of foot. The foot structure for examples 7.6a, c, e, is diagrammed in 7.7:

7.7   a.   F   c.   F   F   e.   F   F   F

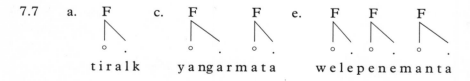

            tiralk   yangarmata   welepenemanta

We will discuss later how to represent the position of primary stress, i.e. the fact that it is the first syllable which bears main stress in Maranungku. Now consider what happens with examples 7.6b, d. The problem here is that the final syllable, though stressed, is not followed by any unstressed syllable, thus violating our characterization of the foot. This sort of thing is going to happen whenever we have a word with an odd number of syllables. However, notice that the singleton syllable still bears stress. Therefore, it is clearly treated as a kind of foot. All we need say, then, is that the unstressed syllables in a foot are optional. A foot of this sort, without unstressed syllables, is called a **degenerate** foot. This is illustrated in 7.8b, d:

7.8   b.   d.

The construction of diagrams such as those in 7.8 effectively provide us with a way of writing stress rules for the language. For if we parse (i.e. analyse) the words into feet then we will know which syllables are stressed and which aren't. All we need is a procedure for assigning feet, what we will call a **stress assignment algorithm**.[3] The algorithm for Maranungku is very simple: construct left-headed binary feet from left to right, the stressed syllable being the first in each foot.

    Now consider a different language, Weri, spoken in South America. In this language we find words such as 7.9:

7.9   a.   nintíp   'bee'
       b.   kùlipú   'hair of arm'
       c.   ulùamít   'mist'
       d.   àkunètepál   'times'

Again, we find a pattern of alternative stresses, but this time the main stress is on the final syllable, and the secondary stresses fall on each alternate syllable working back from it. This suggests that our stress assignment algorithm is essentially the mirror image of that for Maranungku: the feet are iambic and hence have their second, not their first syllable stressed, and the algorithm starts at the opposite end of the word, i.e. the right edge. Thus, the algorithm is: construct right-headed binary feet from right to left, the stressed syllable being the last in each foot. This gives us the representations of 7.10:

7.10

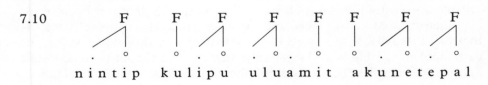

Notice that this time it is the first syllable of odd-syllable words which has the degenerate foot.

It is common to find stress systems similar to these which, however, include minor complications. One of the commonest is illustrated by another South American language, Warao. This has a stress system that looks rather similar to that of Weri, as can be seen from the data in 7.11 (note that each vowel forms a separate syllable, and so two adjacent vowels represent two syllables, not a diphthong):

7.11   a.   yàpurùkitàneháse   'verily to climb'
         b.   nàhoròahàkutái   'the one who ate'
         c.   yiwàranáe   'he finished it'
         d.   enàhoròahàkutái   'the one who caused him to eat'

The main difference seems to be that the stress never falls on the final syllable. It is as though Warao had taken the Weri stress system and shifted it back by one syllable. This is a very simple illustration of a very common and very important phenomenon. For the point is that we can say that the Warao system is identical to that of Weri, provided we ignore the final syllable of every word. Systematically ignored syllables of this kind are called **extrametrical**, or **extraprosodic**. I shall notate this by placing the extrametrical syllable inside angled brackets. This gives us the representations in 7.12 corresponding to 7.11a,c:

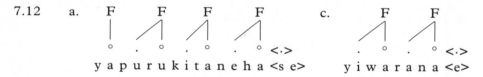

The notion of extrametricality plays a large role in contemporary phonology, especially in the study of lexical stress. However, it is important that the device be constrained. If we were allowed to mark any old syllable extrametrical the device would be so powerful that it would allow us to describe any conceivable pattern, including those which never occur in natural languages. This would mean that we wouldn't have any way of constructing a predictive theory using such a device. However, there is one interesting constraint on the use of extrametricality: an extrametrical element must be peripheral in its domain. What this means is that we can only mark the left or rightmost element of a syllable, foot, word, or whatever extrametrical. It would be impossible to mark, say, the second syllable of a three syllable word extrametrical (unless the final syllable itself also happens to be extrametrical). Moreover, this leads to interesting alternations. If we say that the final syllable of a word is extrametrical, and then add a suffix, the extrametrical syllable is no longer extrametrical and should become visible again to stress rules. This is indeed what happens, as we will see later.

Finally, in our discussions of Maranungku, Weri and Warao, we have developed an algorithm which would put stresses on the right syllables, but we have yet to express the fact that one of these stresses is the main stress. This can be done straightforwardly by reference to the foot. We have analysed a string of stressed syllables as a sequence of feet. To state that one of the stresses predominates over the others we can therefore say that one of the feet in a word is more prominent than the others. In other words we can distinguish one foot which will serve as the head of the word. For Maranungku, this is the first foot constituent, while for Weri and Warao it is the last. Thus, representative examples will take the following form:

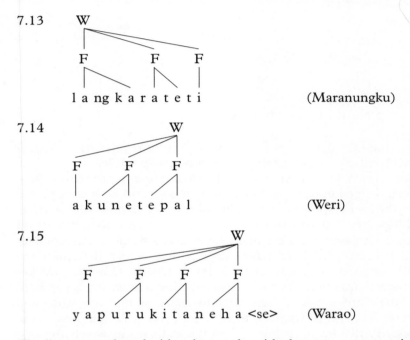

7.13 (Maranungku)

7.14 (Weri)

7.15 (Warao)

Finally, we need to decide what to do with the stray extrametrical syllables. This is part of a broader question of which we will see further ramifications in the next chapter. Recall that in chapter 6 we noted that stray elements which fail to get attached to phonological structure are deleted, by a general process of Stray Erasure (or Stray Deletion). However, this is not typically what happens to elements which have been marked extrametrical. The basic idea behind extrametricality is not that the element concerned be totally lost; rather, it is rendered invisible to certain processes at certain stages in the derivation. This means that we must ultimate find a home in prosodic structure for such elements. In other words, we must ensure that the stray elements are **prosodically licensed**.

In general, in such cases we simply adjoin the stray material to the nearest prosodic constituent which can accept it. In the case of the final syllable in

7.15 there are two possibilities – we could adjoin it to the final foot (to create a novel type of derived foot for this language) or we could adjoin it to the word level. In some cases it is possible to make a principled decision on this score, though given the data we have seen here it makes little difference which solution we choose. However, if we adjoin a syllable to a phonological word, bypassing the foot level, we will be violating the Strict Layer Hypothesis discussed in chapter 5 (section 5.4.6). Let's therefore assume that the stray syllable is adjoined to the 'nearest' suitable prosodic category, in this case the foot. This is accomplished by a general 'cleaning-up' process of **Stray Syllable Adjunction** (SSA). This will give us 7.16 as the final version of 7.15:

7.16

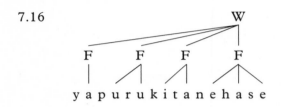

This captures the idea that, from the point of view of regular stress assignment, the final syllable is tacked on to the word as a whole.

   The systems examined so far have had two important properties: first, they have been defined in terms of binary feet, and second, they have placed stresses on syllables irrespective of the phonological content of that syllable. However, things aren't always so simple. In the examples discussed so far we have seen each word bearing a main stress and a number of secondary stresses. It is because of the secondary stresses that we can determine the precise nature of the foot construction in the language. However, we frequently encounter situations in which a language has a main stress per word but no secondary stress. Under these circumstances we find one stress and hence only one foot and so we need to be able to say what happens to the other unstressed syllables. Consider a hypothetical case in which the first syllable of a word is stressed and all the others unstressed. The simplest way to represent this is to say that we have a single foot which takes in the entire word. This is illustrated in 7.17:

7.17

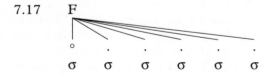

A foot of this sort, which has an indefinite number of elements, is called **unbounded**. The binary and ternary feet discussed hitherto have all been **bounded** feet.

At the same time, it is very common for the quality of the vowel to affect the likelihood of its being stressed. An obvious example is the schwa in English which is prohibited from being stressed. However, one of the most important restrictions is defined in terms of syllable weight (cf. chapter 3, section 3.1). In many languages a syllable will tend to attract stress if it is heavy. A stress system of this sort is called **quantity sensitive**. Conversely, the stress systems we have witnessed hitherto have been **quantity insensitive**. What counts as a heavy syllable may depend on the language. In some cases, a rhyme containing a long vowel, or a short vowel and a coda consonant counts as heavy. In other languages, weight is defined over the nucleus, so that it is only long vowels which count as heavy.

We see a case of both phenomena in the Eastern Meadow-Mari language of Siberia.[4] The language has the following vowels /i y u e ø o a ə/. The full vowels (i.e. all except /ə/) are longer than the schwa and behave phonologically as though they were long. Following Hayes (1981: 57) we will assume the language has no secondary stress. Some examples are given in 7.18, where I denote the difference between schwa and the 'long' vowels as doubling of the full vowels:

7.18   a.   ʃiintʃáam   'I sit'
        b.   ʃlaapáaʒəm   'his hat'
        c.   pýygəlmə   'cone'
        d.   kíidəʃtəʒə   'in his hand'
        e.   tə́ləzən   'moon's'

This stress patterning can be understood if we assume that the foot construction algorithm first looks for the rightmost long vowel (one of our definitions of heavy syllable). It then builds an unbounded left-headed foot over that syllable. This gives us:

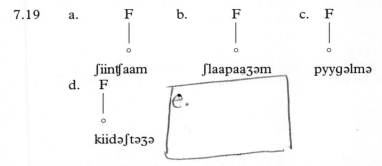

7.19   a.   F   b.   F   c.   F
                  | | |
                  o   o   o

         ʃiintʃaam   ʃlaapaaʒəm   pyygəlmə
        d.   F
             |
             o
          kiidəʃtəʒə

In 7.19e there is no long vowel and so special provision has to be made.

What do we do with the remaining unfooted syllables? Again, the most straightforward way of accounting for them is to say that these syllables are simply attached directly to the foot node by Stray Syllable Adjunction. This

means, of course, that we will obtain a host of derived foot patterns which
are not found phonologically. The result is shown in 7.20:

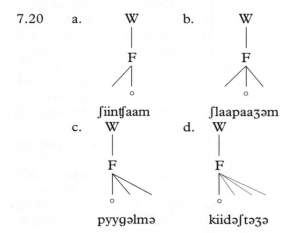

7.20   a.   W   b.   W

                     F   F

                     ∘   ∘

            ʃiintʃaam   ʃlaapaaʒəm

        c.   W   d.   W

             F   F

             ∘   ∘

          pyygəlmə   kiidəʃtəʒə

Finally, what do we do with example 7.18e? Here the stress falls on the first
syllable. Essentially what seems to be happening here is that the stress
algorithm starts from the right edge of the word in search of a heavy syllable
and then stops at the left edge if it doesn't find one. For systems of this sort
we can build a subclause into the definition of the algorithm, which states
that the first syllable is stressed if no other syllable can get stress. Thus, we
can think of *tələzən* as receiving the default stress assignment.

   To conclude this section, we will look in some detail at a system with
bounded quantity sensitive feet. Consider the data in 7.21, forms of the
Latin verb meaning 'to take' (where again doubled vowels are interpreted as
long):

7.21   a.   kápite   2pl imperative active
             kápioo   1sg present active
             kápitis   2pl present active
             kápiunt   3pl present active
             kapíminii   2pl imperative passive
             kéeperant   3pl pluperfect

        b.   kápe   2sg imperative active
             kéepii   1sg perfect active

        c.   keepístii   2sg perfect active
             kapiúntur   3pl present passive
             kapiéebant   3pl imperfect active
             kapiéemus   1pl future active
             keepéere   3pl perfect active (poetic)

As you should be able to see from the data in 7.21, Latin is a classic example of a quantity sensitive language. The stress falls on the penultimate syllable if that syllable is heavy (examples c) and on the previous syllable, the antepenultimate, if the penultimate is light (examples a) and on the first syllable of a disyllabic word (examples b). Notice that Latin treats any rhyme consisting of a vowel (including a short vowel) followed by a consonant as heavy (e.g. *keepistii, kapiuntur*).

However, there is a problem in deciding exactly how the stress algorithm should work. This is because (unlike the case with, say, Eastern Meadow-Mari), the final syllable is never stressed, even if it is heavy (as in *kapioo, kapiminii, kapieebant* or *keeperant*). The notion of extrametricality comes to our rescue here. This is the way we record the fact that a peripheral syllable (commonly the final syllable) nevers receives stress. We therefore make all final syllables extrametrical. The syllabification algorithm for Latin then has three components: (1) final syllables are extrametrical, (2) construct a left-headed foot over the right edge of the word, (3) if the last syllable is heavy, align the head of the foot on that syllable. The algorithm can be seen in operation for the words *kapite, kapimini:* and *kapieebant*:

7.22

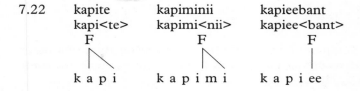

Finally, the extrametrical and the pretonic syllables can be grouped into the foot by Stray Syllable Adjunction (ignoring secondary stress):

7.23

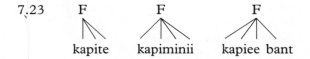

Here, then we have an example of a language which makes use of binary (hence bounded) quantity sensitive feet.

In the next chapter we will see that these concepts are of great value in describing the much more complex stress system of English (though we will see that there is rather more to say about Stray Syllable Adjunction, especially where the pretonic unstressed syllables are concerned). For the present it is of interest to note that the Latin stress rule can be applied to certain types of word in English, too. For example, the nouns *América, aróma, veránda* are stressed on precisely the syllable which would get stressed in Latin. For this reason, many phonologists assume that the foot in English is binary and left-headed (trochaic).

7.2   Compound Stress and Phrasal Accent

We've seen how one of a string of stressed syllables bears primary stress, and we've analysed this by saying that one of the feet in a word is the most prominent (and hence the head constituent of that word). This is realized by making the stressed vowel of the head syllable of that foot more prominent than the rest. Now, when we combine words to form compounds or phrases, we find that some words are more prominent than others. Given some sort of multiword domain, we can therefore identify a particular word as the head of that domain (i.e. the head of a compound or phrase). This helps us to delimit the domains of phonological phrase and intonational phrase briefly introduced in chapter 5. We will begin by investigating the contrasting behaviour of (true) compounds and (true) phrases in English. I shall present a version of the earliest account of this contrast within the framework of Metrical Phonology, since in many respects this is the most straightforward way of viewing the phenomena.

7.2.1   Compound stress

English abounds in compound words, formed by concatenating two other words. The process is recursive, i.e. it feeds itself. Some examples of compounds are given in 7.24:

7.24   coffee table
        coffee table salesman
        finance committee
        finance committee chairman
        finance committee selection panel
        finance committee chairman selection panel
        finance committee selection panel elections

A compound of this kind can be assigned a constituent structure on the basis of its meaning. Thus, a coffee table salesman is a salesman of coffee tables, giving us the structure [[coffee table] salesman]. In 7.25 I've provided constituent structure analyses of some of the examples of 7.24, using both a bracketing and a tree diagram:

7.25   a.

        [[finance committee] chairman]
        (= chairman to the finance committee)

b.

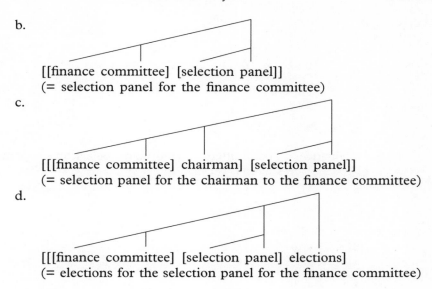

[[finance committee] [selection panel]]
(= selection panel for the finance committee)

c.

[[[finance committee] chairman] [selection panel]]
(= selection panel for the chairman to the finance committee)

d.

[[[finance committee] [selection panel] elections]
(= elections for the selection panel for the finance committee)

Compound words tend to exhibit a characteristic accentual pattern, which is illustrated by the examples of 7.25. In long compounds we get various degrees of stress, partial stress and relative lack of stress, depending on the structure of the compound. Thus, in 7.25b, c, d, *selection* is the most strongly stressed, while *finance* and *elections* are moderately stressed and *committee* and *panel* are relatively unstressed. This can be represented by labelling weak nodes and strong nodes in the constituent structure diagram using the symbols *w* and *s*, as shown in 7.26:

7.26   a.

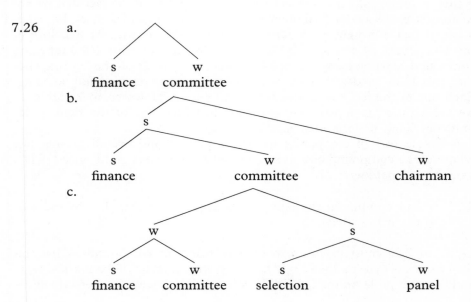

b.

c.

d.

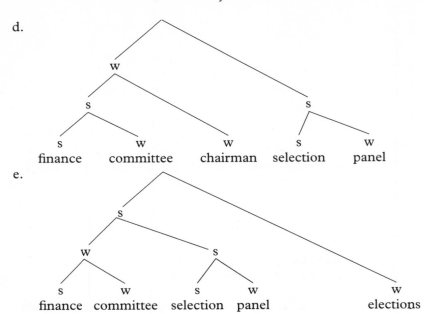

e.

Diagrammatic representations such as these formed the basis of the theory of Metrical Phonology (e.g. Liberman and Prince 1977).

How do these representations come about? According to Liberman and Prince (1977) the basic rule of compound stressing is 'make the first member of the compound strong'. This can be seen from simple cases such as *coffee table* and *finance committee*.[5] The remaining member of the compound is then automatically marked as weak. This is a reflex of the fact that we are treating stress as a relational phenomenon. In more complex cases, however, it seems that the metrical pattern depends on the constituent structure of the compound as a whole. In 7.25a we have a uniformly left branching compound: starting from the top of the tree, every node on the left branches into two lower nodes, but each node on the right remains unbranching. Each one of the leftmost nodes is marked strong. However, in 7.25b, c, d, we see a different constituent structure, in which one of the right nodes branches. That node is then marked strong.

A simple way of computing the stress pattern and overall prominence relations of a compound has been proposed by Liberman and Prince (1977), paraphrased here as 7.27:

7.27   In a compound consisting of [L₁ L₂], L₂ is strong iff (= 'if and only if') it branches.

L₁, L₂ in 7.27 must be taken to refer to words or compounds. What this then means is that if a right node fails to branch then it will be marked weak and its sister node on the left will be strong. This is what happens to all the nodes in 7.26a. However, in 7.26b, c, d, the right node dominating *selection panel* branches and so it gets marked strong. Within that branch there is no further branching of right nodes (i.e. neither *panel* nor *elections* branch), so *selection* gets marked strong. Likewise, in 7.26e, the subtree dominating *selection panel elections* doesn't include any branching right nodes, so the strong nodes are distributed much as in 7.26c. The element which is entirely dominated by strong nodes is the one bearing the main stress of the compound. It is then claimed that the other relative degrees of stress depend on how many strong nodes dominate an element.

This way of analysing compound stress has been very influential in the development of metrical phonology. However, the trees predicted by the theory do not always give the right pattern of non-primary stressing, and this has led many phonologists to propose a variety of alternative ways of handling these facts, one of which is introduced below. Nonetheless, this type of analysis is important because it emphasizes the relational nature of stress and rhythm. It also illustrates clearly the way that phonological (in this case prosodic) organization must often be linked to morphological or syntactic structure in some way (whether directly or indirectly).

7.2.2 Phrasal accent

One of the reasons why compounds are interesting in English, is because, in the standard cases just discussed, their accentual pattern differs from that of ordinary syntactically formed phrases. If we consider a non-compound phrase in isolation and without any special emphasis, then the main accent falls on the rightmost lexical word. This is illustrated in 7.28, where the most accented word is put in capitals:

7.28   a.   a large black CAT
          b.   gave Fido a BONE
          c.   almost as bulky as an elephant in a SPACEsuit

This is true of entire sentences. Thus, the final word of 7.29 is the one which bears the most prominence, when spoken in a 'neutral' context.

7.29   The parcel Tom was carrying seemed almost as bulky as an elephant in a SPACEsuit.

In SPE, the rule which assigns this phrase-final prominence is called the Nuclear Stress Rule (NSR). We'll assume that such a rule is operative in English. This is the most important rule governing the placement of accents in phrases, i.e. phrasal accent.

The effects of the NSR are only apparent when the phrase or sentence is spoken in a neutral or nonemphatic context. It is, of course, possible to put

extra emphasis on pretty well any word in a phrase, especially if it's necessary to establish a contrast between two ideas. For instance, with the right
intonation (a falling-rising pattern), the sentences illustrated in 7.30 could
be followed by the corresponding conclusions in 7.31:

7.30   a.   TOM writes Chinese.
        b.   Tom WRITES Chinese.
        c.   Tom writes CHINESE.

7.31   a.   . . . but Dick doesn't.
        b.   . . . but he doesn't speak it.
        c.   . . . but not Korean.

We won't be much concerned with such special accentuations (though they
are very important for an overall understanding of the nature of rhythm,
accent and intonation). However, once a special accent is placed on a
particular word, the effects on the rest of the rhythmic structure of·the
utterance can usually be predicted straightforwardly using the principles
governing 'normal', unemphatic speech.

7.3   Eurhythmy

Having briefly looked at the way elements of compounds and phrases are
accented, we must now broaden the picture and look at the distribution of
strong and weak accents over longer stretches. Since generative phonologists
first started investigating stress and rhythm from the metrical perspective it
has been realized that in many languages there are principles of rhythmic
organization which serve to keep a roughly even rhythm. This is not to say
that we pronounce prose like poetry; rather, what is found is that there is
a strong tendency to avoid sequences of accents which deviate too far from
this simple rhythmic pattern. Instead, these languages will impose an alternative pattern of strong and weak beats either in duple rhythm (. . . strong
weak strong weak strong . . .) or triple rhythm (. . . strong weak weak strong
weak weak . . .). This general tendency is sometimes called **eurhythmy**. As
a result, such languages will tend to avoid uninterrupted sequences of completely unstressed syllables, or **lapses**, as well as sequences of heavily stressed
syllables, or **clashes**.
    It has been widely observed that different languages seem to impose
different standards of eurhythmy. It is generally said that in a languages
such as English or Russian there is a tendency to keep a constant number
of stressed syllables in a given time stretch. Thus, there is a tendency for a
phrase such as 7.32 to take roughly the same amount of time as those of

7.34 and 7.35, with each 'bar' (indicated by slashes) taking roughly the same amount of time:

7.32 / Which / cats / chase / mice?/

7.33 / Many / voters / wanted / hanging/

7.34 / Competent / managers / readily / innovate/

On the other hand, in languages such as French, Japanese, or Polish, it is said that the overall timing of an utterance depends on the total number of syllables, irrespective of whether they are stressed. Thus, we would expect the Polish sentence 7.35 to take roughly twice as long as 7.36:

7.35 muj brat bɨw tam
my brother was there

7.36 moja çostra bɨwa tutaj
my   sister was   here

This gives rise to a perceived distinction between languages like English, whose rhythmical patterns resemble morse code (a sequence of longer syllables with shorter syllables crammed between them), and languages like Polish whose rhythmical patterns resemble a machine-gun (a sequence of units all roughly the same length). 'Morse-code' languages are often called 'stress-timed' and 'machine-gun' languages are often called 'syllable-timed'. The tendency to maintain a constant number of metrical units (stresses or syllables) in a given time span is called **isochrony**.

It turns out that there is a good deal of controversy over the phonetic facts. However, many phonologists draw roughly this typological distinction. Whatever the phonological and phonetic reasons for it, such rhythmical differences account for an important part of the difference between accents within a language, and the pronunciation differences between one language and another. Failure by students of foreign languages to acquire the rhythmic structures of the language they are studying is one of the commonest sources of a 'foreign accent' (as well as one of the hardest to eradicate fully). Moreover, rhythmic differences of this sort tend to have an effect on other aspects of phonological and phonetic organization, including segmental phonology.

One of the most well-known and well-studied examples of eurhythmic effects is a phenomenon in English known variously as Iambic Reversal, The Rhythm Rule, Stress Retraction and Clash Avoidance. Consider the examples in 7.37:

7.37 DunDEE, TennesSEE, DiANE, unKNOWN.

In each case the main stress falls on the final syllable, indicated by capital letters. Now consider the phrases in 7.38:

7.38   a.   DUNdee MARmalade
        b.   TENnessee WILliams
        c.   DIane KEAton
        d.   UNknown SOLdier

Since these expressions are all phrases and not compounds the principal accent now falls on the second word (the difference between compounds and phrases is discussed below). However, the stress on the words of 7.37 in the 7.38 examples has been shifted back to the next stressable syllable on the left.

The reason for this seems to be to avoid a clash between two adjacent stressed syllables, as shown in 7.39:

7.39   DunDEE MARmalade   →   DUNdee MARmalade

I shall refer to this phenomenon as **Iambic[6] Reversal**. Notice that if we alleviate this clash by combining the words of 7.37 with words stressed on their second syllable or subsequent syllables then there is much less likelihood of Reversal:

7.40   a.   DunDEE preSERVES
        b.   TennesSEE legiSLAtion
        c.   DiANE McINley
        d.   unKNOWN adDRESS

Thus, we see that English tries to maintain an alternative rhythm of a stressed syllable followed by one or two unstressed ones.

It turns out that the tree diagrams we've seen don't lend themselves readily to the investigation of eurhythmic effects. The main reason for this is technical, to do with the fact that the tree diagrams impose a rather complex constituent structure on the phonological representations. In order to capture the effects of Iambic Reversal much of this tree structure has to be destroyed and recomputed. Liberman and Prince (1977) therefore suggested a simpler and more direct way of representing the overall rhythmic structure of a phrase without reference to this gratuitous constituent structure.

The way this is done is to construct from the tree a metrical **grid**. This consists of a series of rows containing marks (here represented as x's) above those units which are given as relatively prominent (i.e. strong) in the tree. Restricting ourselves to the level of words and above, let's return to see how this works for one of the examples of compounds we've seen. In 7.41 I've built a grid for example 7.26c:

7.41
```
                              x
       x                      x
       x           x    x          x
       x x    x    x x  x x  x    x x
```
finance committee selection panel

To construct this grid we first assign a mark to each syllable on the lowest level of the grid. This in effect marks all the potentially stressable units (i.e. syllables). Then, we assign a mark on the second level to each *stressed* syllable. This gives us the partial grid shown in 7.42:

7.42
```
       x                x      x       x
       x x    x    x x  x x  x    x x
```
finance committee selection panel

Now we make use of the tree given in 7.26c to determine where the other marks go. At each of the levels defined by the tree, we place a mark over the most prominent syllable of the most prominent unit. At the third level we have two units, *finance committee* and *selection panel*. Of these the prominent units are *finance* and *selection*. Therefore, the stressed syllables of these words get a mark:

7.43
```
       x                      x
       x           x     x         x
       x x    x    x x  x x  x    x x
```
finance committee selection panel

Finally, at the fourth level, we place a mark over the most prominent member of the entire compound, *selection*, to give 7.41.

How does this type of representation help us to understand the alleviation of stress clashes by Iambic Reversal? In 7.44 we see the grids for the words *Dundee* and *marmalade*:

7.44   a.   x   b.   x
```
              x    x           x      x
              x    x           x    x x
```
              Dundee   marmalade

When we put these together to form a phrase we get 7.45, where *marmalade* has acquired an extra grid mark because it has the principal stress of the whole phrase:

7.45   x
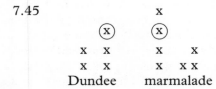

Comparing this with the grid for the phrase *Dundee preserves*:

7.46   x
                      x   x
              x   x   x
              x   x   x x
              Dundee   preserves

The grid in 7.46 shows a pattern of alternating peaks and troughs. Every stressed syllable is followed by a stressless one, in conformity with the tendency towards alternating rhythms (eurhythmy). In 7.45, however, we have a pair of grid marks (those circled) which are not separated by a trough. This constitutes a stress clash. The grid notation provides us with a straightforward way of representing the way this is alleviated by Iambic Reversal. We can simply assume that the leftmost of the two offending marks is moved leftwards to the next column of marks that can support it. This is shown in 7.47 and 7.48:

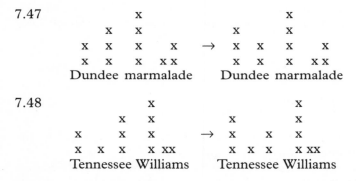

7.47   x   x
              x   x   x   x
         x   x   x   x   →   x   x   x   x
         x   x   x   x x   x   x   x   x x
              Dundee marmalade   Dundee marmalade

7.48   x   x
                   x   x   x   x
         x   x   x   →   x   x   x
         x   x   x   x xx   x   x   x   x xx
              Tennessee Williams   Tennessee Williams

Notice that in *Tennessee Williams* the offending stress mark is moved to the column of grid marks over the first syllable. It is not moved simply to the next syllable on the left. The idea is that it is the next most prominent syllable on the left that gets the extra stress, and this is the reason for insisting on moving the x mark to the next suitable column in the grid. This type of phenomenon is relatively easy to capture with the grid notation.

This concludes our survey of the basic features of stress and rhythm. We have made use of two important notions. The first is the idea that the stress pattern of words, or the rhythmic patterns of whole utterances can be represented as a hierarchical constituent structure by means of a tree diagram, showing the relative patterns of prominence. The second idea is that patterns of prominence and rhythmic alternation can be represented by means of a grid. These notions are distinct though closely related. Some phonologists have argued that only the constituent structures, as formalized in tree diagrams, are needed ('trees only' approach). On this approach we group together feet into larger tree structures and label some of the feet 'weak' and some 'strong'. Others have claimed that we can manage entirely with the grid ('grid-only' approach). On this approach, the notion 'foot' doesn't have any special theoretical status. As far as lexical stress is concerned, the controversy seems to be resolving in favour of a historic compromise in which the mechanics of stress and rhythm are handled essentially by using grids, but with one major concession to constituent structure: the use of the foot.

In many instances, a representation in constituent structure (tree) format will be equivalent to one in grid format and vice versa. However, there are differences in the behaviour of the two types of representation. One important point is that if we represent all stress and rhythmic phenomena using the tree notation exclusively, we will end up with a great deal of tree structure, much of which doesn't really mean anything phonologically or phonetically. As we will see when we consider English rhythm in more detail in the next chapter, the kinds of pattern predicted by the trees approach for English compounds don't necessarily correspond to reality when we take into account the various smoothing out procedures employed, for instance, to avoid lapses. On the other hand, it turns out that some minimal indication of constituent structure is needed to describe certain phenomena in the world's languages. Roughly speaking, we need to be able to represent at least the notion of foot as a hierarchical unit, and arguably we will need the level of phonological word (i.e. a sequence of feet).

The original proponents of the historic compromise were Halle and Vergnaud (1987). They represent stresses as a set of grid marks (using asterisks instead of x's). Stresses are built up in layers of marks. The first layer (Line 0) corresponds just to the stressable syllables. These are grouped together to form foot constituents. This is shown in 7.49 for some of our Maranungku examples in 7.6:

```
7.49        *   *   *   *   *    *        (*   *) (*   *)  (*     *)
         w e l e p e l e m a n t a   →  w e l e p e l e m a n t a
            *       *   *   *             (*       *) (*  *) (*)
         l a ng k a r a t e t i     →  l a ng k a r a t e t i
```

To indicate the final word-level stress we introduce another line of marks, indicating the head of each foot (corresponding, of course, to a stressed syllable). The feet are all either degenerate or trochees, so it is always the left most syllable of the foot that is the head. This process gives us a sequence of new marks at Line 1:

```
7.50        *       *       *      Line 1
         (*   *) (*   *)  (*     *)  Line 0
         w e l e p e l e m a n t a

            *           *    *      Line 1
         (*       *) (*  *) (*)     Line 0
         l a ng k a r a t e t i
```

Finally, we then group together all these into another (this time unbounded) constituent at the word or Line 2 level to indicate where the main stress falls (i.e. the first syllable):

```
7.51        *                    Line 2
        (*     *       *)        Line 1
        (*  *) (*  *) (*     *)  Line 0
     w e l e p e l e m a n t a

            *                    Line 2
        (*         *      *)      Line 1
        (*      *) (*  *) (*)     Line 0
     l a ng k a r a t e t i
```

Needless to say, this is more than just an exercise in alternative notations. The advantages of this approach are connected with Halle and Vergnaud's overall conception of stress theory, which we can't enter into in this modest introduction, but one of the ideas behind this set of notational conventions is to permit us to conflate the grids notation with the trees notation without making use of more 'tree' structure (constituent structure bracketing) than necessary.

FURTHER READING

Introductions to recent models of stress can be found in Durand (1990), Roca (1994). Kenstowicz (1994) provides a more advanced treatment. Very good overviews of the field are provided by Kager (1994) and Halle and Idsardi (1994). A brief summary of the material of section 7.1 is given in Jensen (1993: ch. 4). Hayes' (1981) original treatment, which has been very influential, provides a very clear introduction to the subject for the more advanced student. Although the treatment I have given here is somewhat simplified and doesn't address the issue of parametrization, it should be possible to tackle parts of Halle and Vergnaud's important (1987) monograph (which forms the starting point of most current treatments of stress systems). (See also the further reading for chapter 8.)

EXERCISES

7.1 Stress in Nganasan
Provide an account of the stress system of the Samoyedic language, Nganasan on the basis of the following examples (Tereshchenko 1979). [Secondary stress is also found but we ignore it for the purposes of this exercise.] [Note: [əʉ̯] is a diphthong.]

ŋə́ðusæ	'be visible'	ŋəʤutɨːə	'visible'
dydéː	'dream'	kíta	'cup'
kúʔbasa	'bead'	kuʔbasáː	'of a bead'
mə́ y̜ləməː	'covered in earth'	múli	'ornament'
nitə́ː	'cauldron'	sə́mu	'hat'
sǽtɨmɨmbǽtɨnə	'I finish'	sólətu	'glass'
táːnsa	'lasso'	táːnsanə	'lassos'
xékutɨ	'hot'		

7.2 Stress in Odawa

Provide an account of the stressing of words in the Odawa dialect of the Ojibwa language (Halle and Vergnaud 1987) [we are ignoring the position of main stress]:

bimóséː	'he walks'
bizíw	'lynx'
kitóːtáːwéːwikámikóm	'your store'
nagámó	'he sings'
nibímoséːmín	'we walk'
nigíːnamádáp	'I sat'
nigíːnamádabímín	'we sat'
ninágamómín	'we sing'
ninámadáp	'I sit'
niníbá	'I sleep'
niníbáːmín	'we sleep'
niwíːndigóːwinmín	'we are monsters'
niwíːndigóːw	'I am a monster'
niwíːpimítakkónáːn	'I'll carry it along'

7.3 How are the following compounds stressed? How does the stress pattern relate to the meaning (and hence the constituent structure)? There may be more than one plausible constituent structure for some of these compounds. How do these different structures change (1) the meaning (2) the stress?

government tax inspector
Road Tax inspector
school classroom size
engine fault detection mechanism
music practice room booking form
Road Tax inspector training schedule
linguistics class room changes
linguistics summer school administration problems
mean household income fall rate monitoring programme
executive class business card printing machine design competition

7.4   An argument for feet

The foot can be used to explain the otherwise unexpected patterning of data in the Bedouin Hijazi dialect of Arabic (Al-Mozainy et al. 1985).

Write a rule to determine stress for the words shown in A:

A   maktú:fah   'tied (fem. sg.)'
    ga:bílna   'meet us (masc. sg.)'
    má:lana   'out property'
    ʔistáslam   'he surrendered'
    yáʃrɨbin   'they (fem.) drink'
    ʔínkisar   'he got broken'
    ʔíntiðar   'he waited'
    ʔíftikar   'he remembered'
    ʔíxtibar   'he took an exam.'

This dialect has a vowel deletion process which deletes the second vowel of the last four words. It also triggers a stress shift:

B   ʔinksárat   'she got broken'
    ʔintðáran   'they (fem.) waited'
    ʔiftkáraw   'they (masc.) remembered'
    ʔixtbáraw   'the (masc.) took an exam.'

First, show that the stress in the B words is not in the place you would expect from the words in A. Then use the B words to motivate the notion of 'foot'.

chapter 8

Stress and Rhythm in English

8.1 Lexical Stress in English

8.1.1 Introduction

English, like many languages, has a system of word stress that in part follows phonological rules and in part is idiosyncratic. We might thus say that some words show properties of a fixed stress language, while others exhibit free stress patterning. In general, for a large class of words, it is therefore impossible to predict for certain how a word will be stressed. Moreover, there is psycholinguistic evidence from speech errors that we store the pronunciations of individual words complete with their stress patterns (Fay and Cutler 1977). However, this does not mean that there are no rules or principles underlying lexical stress. On the contrary, there are certain types of stressing which would be rejected as 'un-English' by any native speaker. For example, Liberman and Prince (1977) point out that a nonsense word such as *podectal* would only be pronounced *podéctal* by an English native speaker, and never, say, **pódectal*. Likewise, Hayes 1981 mentions that a Russian word like *Ninochka* (a diminutive of the girl's name, *Nina*), when incorporated into English speech, becomes *Ninóchka*, even though in

Russian the stress falls on the first syllable. This evidence suggests there might be rules or principles of some sort governing lexical stress, as opposed to simple rote memorization of individual lexical items.

A characteristic of English is that stress patterns are frequently affected by grammatical category or morphological structure. The most drastic illustration of this is shown by noun – verb pairs such as *cóntrast – contrást, tránsport – transpórt*, in which the syntactic category of the word determines where the stress falls. More subtly, we find a contrast between a proper name (which we can assume has no internal morphological structure) such as *Dóminic* and the suffixed form *demónic*. The *-ic* suffix causes the stress to fall on the previous syllable in the latter, but since the *-ic* sequence in *Dominic* isn't an affix, the word is given the stress pattern characteristic of this type of word (cf. *ánimal*). For this reason, phonologists frequently divide up English words into morphologically simple (monomorphemic) and morphologically complex. Since there are relatively few ordinary morphemes in English which are polysyllabic, this tends to mean that discussion centres around proper names such as *Winnepesaukee* or *Ticonderoga*.

In principle, stress can fall on any syllable, witness 8.1:

8.1   disyllabic: móral, morále
        trisyllabic: Waterlóo, Torónto, Líverpool
        quadrisyllabic: Kalamazóo, Piccadílly, América, Hígginbotham

On occasions there is vacillation in the stressing of a word. Thus, we hear pronunciations such as *contróversy* and *cóntroversy*, *býzantine* and *byzántine*. These are rather few and far between, however. Dialect differences can be heard too, e.g. British *labóratory* vs. US *láboratory*, British *débris*, vs. US *debrís*. On the whole, American English tends to retain, or at least to attempt to reproduce, foreign aspects of the pronunciation of loan words (even where this is spurious), while British English is quicker to assimilate loans to the native patterns.

Words of two or more syllables may also have one or more secondary stresses. We often refer to the stressed syllable in a word as the **tonic** syllable. Syllables preceding the tonic are therefore **pretonic** and those following are **post-tonic**. Secondary stresses may be either post-tonic, as in 8.2a, or pre-tonic, as in 8.2b:[1]

8.2   a. gýmnàst, déscànt, quásàr
        b. còntradíct, èpiphenómenal, còmpartmèntalizátion

Note particularly the contrast between the examples with post-tonic secondary stress in 8.2a, and similar examples without any secondary stress in 8.3:

8.3   bréakfast, prégnant, rázor

Occurrence of secondary stresses depends in part on the length of the word, in part on its segmental structure and in part on lexical idiosyncrasy (cf 8.2a vs. 8.3). On the whole, US English tends to have a greater number of secondary stresses in post-tonic position than British English. Thus, while British English has *Bírmingham* with no secondary stress, US English may have *Bírminghàm*. Within Britain there is considerable dialect variation. Thus, many accents would have [dɪˈfrɔst] for RP [ˌdiːˈfrɔst] *de-frost*. Finally, secondary stressing frequently depends on speech style and rate.

One of the main signals of secondary stress is lack of vowel reduction, which was introduced in chapter 6. Recall that completely unstressed vowels, especially the short vowels /ɛ ɔ æ ʌ/, are regularly reduced to /ɪ ə/. The original quality of the vowel can often be detected by looking at alternative forms of the word in which the vowel comes under some degree of stress. For instance, in *photograph* ([ˈfoutəˌgræf] or [ˈfoutəˌgrɑːf]) we know that the second vowel has been reduced from /ɔ/ because this is how it is pronounced in *photography* [fəˈtɔgrəˌfɪ]. If we compare the examples in 8.2a with those in 8.3 we see that vowel reduction is the most obvious factor differentiating the syllables with secondary stresses from those without. Compare [ˈʤɪmˌnæst ˈdɛsˌkænt ˈkweɪˌzɑː] with [ˈbrɛkfəst ˈprɛgnənt ˈreɪzə].

8.1.2 Primary stress

In this subsection we will be mainly concerned with developing principles for assigning the main stress to a word. We can begin our discussion with the descriptive generalizations reported in SPE's influential description. The basic point to notice is that nouns and verbs behave differently with respect to stress and that adjectives behave like verbs when unsuffixed, and like nouns when they are suffixed.

Let's begin with the verbs, a sample of which are shown in 8.4 (based largely on Chomsky and Halle 1968: 69):

8.4	I	II	III
	astónish	maintáin	collápse
	édit	eróde	tormént
	consíder	applý	exháust
	imágine	appéar	eléct
	intérpret	obéy	convínce
	prómise	surmíse	adápt
	embárrass	eráse	obsérve

In addition, we can consider the following set of adjectives (selected from Chomsky and Halle 1968: 80):

8.5   I   II   III
       cómmon   remóte   succínct
       hándsome   discréet   imménse
       stúrdy   éxtreme   robúst
       frántic   sincére   corrúpt
       shállow   secúre   occúlt
       wánton   obscúre   diréct
       vúlgar   compléte   augúst

From these examples it is obvious that the words in columns II, III have ultimate (final) stress, while those in column I have penultimate stress. What do the words in II, III have in common which distinguishes them from those in I? The answer is that those stressed on the penult end in a short vowel plus at most one consonant, while those stressed on the final syllable or 'ult' end either in a long vowel/diphthong, or in two consonants.

How can we incorporate this patterning into our description of the stress facts? The basic analysis we will adopt is that proposed by Hayes (1981), working within the framework of Metrical Phonology developed by Liberman and Prince (1977). In chapter 7 we saw that stress systems can be analysed in terms of the type of stress feet permitted in a language. In different languages different types of stress foot are erected at different points in the word (e.g. starting at the left or the right edge). We also discovered that in some cases (e.g. Latin) the way in which the stress feet are positioned over syllables in a word may depend on the phonological structure of the syllable, and in particular, its weight (i.e. whether its rhyme is complex or simple).

We begin with verbs and unsuffixed adjectives. Hayes showed that we can regard this group of words as subject to something very much like the Latin stress rule we saw in chapter 7, provided if we make certain additional assumptions. The key idea is to invoke the notion of extrametricality introduced in the previous chapter: we ignore the final consonant of the word, if it has one, a property known as **Consonant Extrametricality**. This allows us to treat all the words of column I as ending in a vowel. We thus obtain representations such as 8.6:

8.6   I   II   III
       a.   astoni<sh>   maintai<n>   collap<se>
            edi<t>   ero<de>   tormen<t>
            conside<r>[2]   apply   exhaus<t>
       b.   common   remo<te>   succinc<t>
            handso<me>   discree<t>   immen<se>
            sturdy   extre<me>   robus<t>

The final syllable rhymes are shown in 8.7:

8.7   a.   ɪ   eɪ   æp
            ɪ   ou   ɛn
            ə   aɪ   ɔːs
      b.   n   ou   ɪnk
            ə   iː   ɛn
            ɪ   iː   ʌs

Note that in *common* the /n/ is syllabic, and hence part of the rhyme. It therefore is not eligible for Consonant Extrametricality. On the other hand, in the case of *handsome*, I have chosen to represent this as ending in -*əm*. The result is the same whether we regard the final nasal as syllabic, hence not really a consonant, or whether it is the coda, in which case it will be extrametrical. The case of *shallow* seems to contradict what has been said, since the rhyme appears to be heavy (/ou/). However, it turns out that final /ou/ /juː/ regularly behaves as though it were a short vowel (along with \juː: as in *rescue, argue*).

Given Consonant Extrametricality it is easy to formulate the principle governing stress placement for these forms: the final syllable (the ult) gets stressed precisely when it has a heavy or branching rhyme, otherwise, the penult (i.e. the penultimate syllable) is stressed. Now, this is precisely the Latin stress rule. However, since we are discussing English, we will refer to it as the English Stress Rule, ESR.

Armed with the metrical formalism for representing stress we can now analyse these examples by saying that we build a left-headed foot starting from the right edge of the word. Here we are making an important assumption about English, namely, that its feet are trochees. However, if the final syllable (excluding its invisible consonant) is heavy then the foot is erected over that syllable, just as in Latin. These assumptions give us the representations in 8.8:

8.8   a.

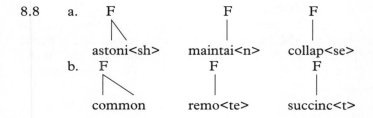

      b.

It is important to appreciate that once we have taken the decision to operate in terms of a particular foot type, such as trochees, we must stick to it – we can't assume that feet are, say, trochaic in some words and iambic in others, for then we would not be able to impose adequate restrictions on the inventory of stress patterns possible in the language. In effect, we would come close to saying that there is no real regularity in the system, an unwelcome conclusion in linguistics.

How well does this work for nouns? Consider the list in 8.9 (cf. Chomsky and Halle 1968: 71):

8.9   I   II   III
        América   aróma   veránda
        cínema   balaláika   agénda
        aspáragus   hiátus   consénsus
        metrópolis   horízon   synópsis
        jávelin   thrombósis   amálgam
        vénison   coróna   uténsil
        ásterisk   aréna   asbéstos

The nouns in 8.9 are similar to the verbs except that they all have a short vowel in the final syllable. They work in exactly the same way as the verbs providing we make one simple assumption: this time we treat the whole of the final syllable as extrametrical, a device known as **Noun Extrametricality**. This gives us representations such as 8.10:

8.10   Ameri<ca>   aro<ma>   veran<da>
        metropo<lis>   hori<zon>   synop<sis>
        aste<risk>   are<na>   asbes<tos>

These have the final rhymes shown in 8.11:

8.11   ɪ   ou   æn
        ə   aɪ   ɔp
        ə   iː   ɛs

We now assume that the ESR applies as normal to those portions visible to stress rules, outside the angled brackets.

Now we must decide what happens to the extrametrical final syllables. To keep the exposition simple, I shall assume that they are attached by means of Stray Syllable Adjunction to the foot level. We will leave the fate of the pretonic unattached syllables till later in the chapter. The stress patterns after ESR and SSA are shown in 8.12:

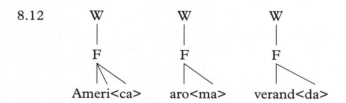

8.12

Now let's consider a different set of adjectives, those in 8.13:

8.13   I   II   III
        munícipal   anecdótal   paréntal
        herétical   adjectíval   dialéctal
        oríginal   mediéval   fratérnal
        magnánimous   desírous   treméndous
        signíficant   defíant   relúctant
        ínnocent   complácent   depéndent
        prímitive   condúcive   expénsive

There are two points to make about these cases. First, we often see a stress
shift, in that the stress pattern on the base word (e.g. *párent*) is often
different from that of the derived adjective (*paréntal*). What seems to be
happening is that the adjectival suffix has attracted the stress to the syllable
before it (columns II, III), or the one before that (column I). Such suffixes
are often called **weak retractors** (or *weak suffixes*). In the case of column
I and some column II, III adjectives this causes problems for the ESR. We
saw above that adjectives pattern like verbs, and hence, show consonant
extrametricality. But this should mean we get the stress patterns of 8.14 for
words such as *heretical*, *primitive* and *reluctant*:

8.14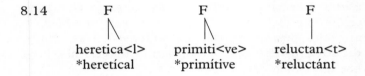

On the other hand, if we treat these words as though they were nouns, and
hence make the whole of the final syllable extrametrical, then we would
obtain the correct stress:

8.15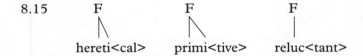

Treating some adjectives as verbs and some as nouns seems rather ad hoc,
however. What unites the aberrant class of adjectives is that they all end in
a recognized adjectival suffix. If we ignore this suffix for the purpose of
stress assignment then our adjectives behave just like the unsuffixed adjectives. In other words, we take 8.16 as our starting representations, and then
treat these as ordinary adjectives:

8.16   a.   heretic <al>
         b.   primit <ive>
         c.   reluct <ant>

This is often referred to as **Adjective Extrametricality**. Taking the rhyme projections and imposing consonant extrametricality on them as usual we obtain representations 8.17:

8.17   F   F   F

          hereti<c><al>   primi<t><ive>   reluc<t><ant>

Not only can we now treat all adjectives as essentially the same, we can also account for additional cases such as 8.18:

8.18   I   II   III
         végetative   commútative   consúltative
         tránsitory   prepáratory[3]   perfúnctory

Here the suffix has two syllables, and both must be disregarded in order to account for the stress.

This straightforward rule, ESR, in tandem with the two sorts of extra-metricality, covers all the major cases. The rule is not without its exceptions. For instance, adjectives such as *módest* fail to fit the pattern, as do a large number of prefixed verbs such as *permít, repél, abét, forgíve*. (The latter will be discussed later). Where there is no more specific rule or principle to account for the form (as appears to be the case with *módest*) we simply have to assume that the stress pattern is stored as part of the lexical representation itself, just like any other lexical idiosyncrasy.

We have seen that adjectival suffixes and the final syllables of nouns are systematically ignored by the ESR. However, not all suffixes or final syllable types behave in the same way. One interesting set of exceptions is a group of nouns (or sometimes adjectives) which end in a long vowelled syllable. In some cases what happens is that the final vowel gets stressed. This is particularly likely to be the case if the noun ends in certain suffixes e.g. *-áire, -éer, -ée, -é/ét* (US only except for *bouquét* which is also British; note also stressed *-étte*), *-ése*. For instance, *questionnáire, enginéer, referée, café* (US), *ballét* (US). In addition, certain syllables behave as though they were suffixes (and are hence sometimes referred to as 'pseudo-suffixes'), e.g. especially *-éen/-íne, -óon, -íque, -éur/-éuse*. Examples are: *turéen, machíne, platóon, antíque, chaufféur, chantéuse*. Other types of example include *políce, bazáar, cheróot, canóe, regíme, stockáde*, and (in British English) *cavalcáde*.

However, there exist a good number of polysyllabic nouns ending in a long vowelled syllable in which the stress falls on the 'wrong' syllable, as in 8.19 (cf. SPE: 78):

8.19   húrricàne, ánecdòte, pédigrèe, níghtingàle, mártingàle, mátadòr,
         formáldehỳde, báritòne, guíllotìne, Árkansàs, ántelòpe, stévedòre,
         hypótenùse, cándidàte , cántalòupe, cávalcàde (US).

The simplest way of thinking of these cases is to assume that the stress appears first on the final syllable, as expected, and that it is then retracted to the previous syllable but one (i.e. the antepenult). This type of stress retraction plays an important role in some accounts of the stress system of English and other languages. Notice that these words retain a vestige of their 'original' stress in that the final syllable retains secondary stress. Also, we find dialect differences or doublets within a single dialect in which the stress genuinely alternates, e.g. *gásolìne ~ gàsolíne, súbmarìne ~ sùbmaríne.*

The verbal suffix *-ate* tends to behave in a rather similar way. Thus, we have examples like 8.20, which we can analyse in more or less the same manner as the examples in 8.19:

8.20   désignàte, cóncentràte, exácerbàte, cónfiscàte, sálivàte

The interesting thing about this type of retraction is that it invariably puts the stress back two syllables from the ending, irrespective of the weight of the intervening syllables. This is in contradistinction to the suffixes such as *-al* or *-ic*. Recall that those suffixes ('weak retractors') throw back the stress in words of the form $\sigma_1 \sigma_2$ *-ic/al* to σ_2 if it is heavy and to σ1 only if σ2 is light. The type of retraction seen in 8.19, 20 is often referred to as **Strong Retraction** (SR) and the affixes which trigger it are called s**trong retractors** (the idea being that these affixes are untroubled by the weight of σ_2).[4]

To formulate this rule, all we need do is to take our trisyllabic words and apply the ESR, giving them final stress. Then we place a trochaic foot over the first two syllables, making that foot the main one in the word. This has the effect of retracting the stress to the first syllable, leaving the final syllable with secondary stress. This is illustrated in 8.21 for *désignàte*:

8.21

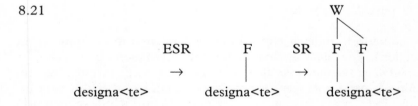

Strong Retraction will also account for words such as *difficult*:

8.22

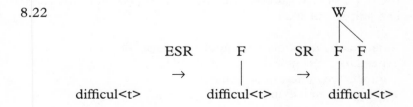

A final quirk in the behaviour of suffixes is shown by the endings *-ic* (*-ics*, *-ism*), *-ity*/*-ety*, *-ify* and a number of others. Consider the examples in 8.23:

8.23   a.   académic (acádemy)
        b.   cataclýsmic (cátaclysm)
        c.   heteromórphic (héteromorph)
        d.   periódic (périod)
        e.   económics (ecónomy)
        f.   electrícity (eléctric)
        g.   notoríety (notórious)
        h.   persónify (pérson)

These endings have in common the property of attracting stress towards the previous syllable, whatever its weight. Other suffixes are similar in that they only seem to attach to words or stems which have final stress (so that again the suffix is immediately to the right of a stress). A number of examples are listed in Kreidler (1989: 311) (who calls these post-tonic suffixes; the tonic syllable is the one bearing the main stress). A variety of ways have been proposed for handling these cases. Perhaps the most convenient and intuitively straightforward way of viewing them is to say that the lexical representation of the suffix includes a chunk of metrical structure which then fits over the stem, as pictured in 8.24:

8.24   a.   F

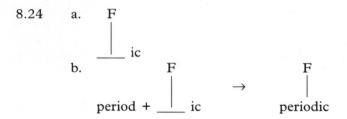

Finally, we come to a somewhat vexed question (related to the topic of the next subsection): how do we account for the alternations in stressing in *párent* ~ *paréntal*, *órigin* ~ *oríginal*, that is, 'weak retraction'? In one sense the answer is already apparent: these are the consequence of the ESR together with Adjective Extrametricality. However, matters become a little more murky when we note that in certain cases adding an affix has no effect at all on stress (contrary to what we have been assuming hitherto). Moreover, this tends to be true of particularly productive affixes. Thus, consider the examples of adjective suffixes in 8.25:

8.25   a.   ámateurish, níghtmarish, coquéttish, tígerish
        b.   repéatable, récognizable, cátapultable
        c.   cómplicated, ínterested, delúded
        d.   ínteresting, hórrifying, intríguing

The reason for this behaviour is that the suffixes concerned systematically have no effect on stress, i.e. they are **stress neutral**. This means that the stress of the derived adjective is exactly that of the base (*ámateur, níghtmare, cátapult* and so on), at least in British English. One popular way of treating the difference between stress neutral and stress affecting affixes is to assume that the word formation component of the grammar is sensitive to this difference. In Siegel's (1974) theory the two types of affix are attached by morphological rules which operate in distinct blocks, or at distinct levels. First, we have affixation of the stress sensitive ('Class I') affixes, then we apply various phonological rules (including stress), then we attach the stress neutral ('Class II') affixes. We assume that it is impossible to 'loop' back into the phonology, so this means that the stress neutral affixes are unable to influence stress by virtue of the way the grammar is organized.

Siegel's theory ('Level Ordering') has been very influential in that it forms an important component of Kiparsky's (1982, 1985) theory of Lexical Phonology. It is beyond the scope of this introduction to discuss this theory (see further reading at the end of chapter 5). The Level Ordering theory has proved problematical and it is not accepted by all of those phonologists who work within an otherwise standard model of Lexical Phonology. However, the observations which gave rise to the theory remain valid. We must be cognizant of the fact that certain affixes are systematically ignored by the stress rules. Perhaps the most obvious case is that of inflectional suffixes. If we consider an ordinary verb such as *edit* we don't want the 3 sg. -*s* suffix to interact with stress assignment at all. This is because we would have to treat the -*s* as the most peripheral element, in which case the final consonant of the verb stem could not be extrametrical (it would not be peripheral). Thus, we would end up with a representation *edit<s>*. This would end in a heavy rhyme, -*it*, which should therefore get stressed (much as in the case of *collapse*). Clearly, since no inflections ever change stress we need to be able to say that the stress pattern of a word is computed independently of its inflectional properties, or in other words that we inflect already stressed words (in English, at least – in other languages stress may actually be part of the inflectional system). For the present, we will simply note that certain types of affix generally fail to affect the phonological structure, including the metrical structure, of the stems they attach to.[5]

Given that suffixes such as -*ic* have idiosyncratic properties, the question arises as to how to handle the cases in 8.25 vis-à-vis the cases such as *paréntal, original* etc. The problem is that the weak retracting suffixes such as -*al* appear to change the stress of the base to which they attach. We accounted for this by assuming that -*al* is extrametrical, and that the ESR applies to the base, but without the application of Noun Extrametricality. But this means that we can't simply say that a stress neutral affixes such as -*ing* is extrametrical, for otherwise we would predict stresses such as **interésting*.

There are two popular solutions to this kind of problem. It is beyond the scope of an introduction like this to delve into the pros and cons of each. The first solution is to say that both types of affix are attached to bases which already have their stress assigned, but that the stress affecting affixes trigger a process which removes all metrical structure on the base (what Liberman and Prince 1977 call 'deforestation', because in their formalism it involves the removal of tree structures). The derivation for *parental* will then be as in 8.26:

8.26   a.   cycle 1

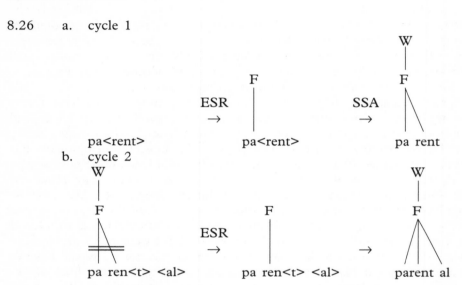

In this derivation affixation is perceived as a cyclic phenomenon under which a battery of rules (specifically the stress rules) first applies to *parent*, and then to *parental*. We can call this the 'cyclic analysis'.

An alternative approach is to say that the stress rules, and indeed other phonological rules, fail to apply at all to bases which have received the special category of affix which we have identified as stress affecting (cf., e.g. Inkelas 1990). Thus, the derivation will be much simpler, in that we treat *parental* as (effectively) like a simple monomorphemic word, with the exception of Adjective Extrametricality, which renders the adjectival suffix invisible, and Consonant Extrametricality. Thus, we obtain the derivation in 8.27:

8.27

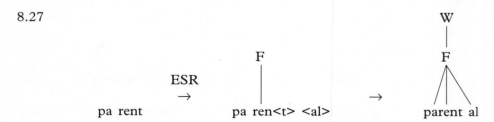

This second derivation seems much tidier than 8.26 because we are not obliged to build up structure only to destroy it again. I shall refer to it as the 'direct analysis'.

There are theoretical reasons which can be advanced in favour of deforestation (the cyclic analysis) (a number are given by Halle and Vergnaud 1987 for instance), though these arguments are by no means universally accepted. One empirical reason for it which is often cited is the claim that the effects of cycle 1 stressing sometimes has to be retained (in other words deforestation isn't always complete). A notorious example is that of *còndensátion* vs. *còmpensátion*. It is claimed that in *còndensátion* there is secondary stress on the second syllable, which is lacking in *còmpensátion*. This is said to be explicable in terms of the stress pattern of the base. In *condénse* the second syllable gets primary stress, while in *cómpensàte* there is no stress there. The primary stress in *condénse* therefore remains as a weak stress (actually a form of ternary stress) in *còndênsátion*. Unfortunately, not all speakers agree with such judgements, and there are other ways of explaining the judgements of those that make a distinction. One plausible possibility is that speakers sometimes add the tertiary stress by analogy with the stress on the base form (the operation of analogy would help explain why speakers' reactions are rather unreliable with these forms). The cyclic analysis has very few other empirical consequences for the description of English stress, or, indeed, for the description of stress systems in most other languages, which is further evidence to support the direct analysis.

The discussion of cyclic and direct analyses of stress assignment leads us on to another question which we have not properly dealt with, that of secondary stress. This is a rather complex matter, and I will just outline some of the basic facts and one influential type of solution to the problem. The first problem concerns the phonetic nature of secondary stresses. Earlier accounts (both structuralist and generative) tend to assume that there are several different degrees of secondary stress. SPE, for instance, assumes five degrees of stress (including total lack of stress). However, it turns out to be very difficult in general to detect more than a three-way opposition between primary stress, secondary stress and no stress. For this reason, we will simplify matters and only assume one degree of secondary stress.

If we consider the purely phonological questions surrounding secondary stress, the first point to make is that we already have an account for some types of secondary stress. The rules we have discussed so far will provide us with a secondary stress on the final syllable of *húrricàne*, for instance. Moreover, whenever we add a stressed affix to a word we tend to retain the stress of the original base, though reduced to a secondary stress. For example, in *mòuntainéer*, we find a secondary stress on the first syllable corresponding to the primary stress on the base of the word, *móuntain*. The effect is rather similar to that of forming a phonological phrase out of two words. Thus, if the word here is given main phrasal accent in the phrase *there's a mountain here* then the sub-phrase *mountain* here will have very similar stress patterning to the word *mountaineer*. Other examples of this would be *órganize ~ òrganizátion, insínuate ~ insìnuátion*. However, the original stress is retracted where the base has stress on its final syllable: *confrónt ~ cònfrontátion*.

In polysyllabic words of sufficient length there will be a string of secondary stresses preceding the main stress. This can be seen if we look at a set of monomorphemic polysyllabic words such as those in 8.28 (where we have words with affixes attached matters become more complex – we can see the stress rules operating unfettered in monomorphemic words):

8.28   Àpalàchicóla, Pòpocàtepétl, hàmamèlidánthemum

The stress on these words can be generated by assuming simply the ESR and Strong Retraction, SR:

8.29   F   SR   F   F   F

          ⟋\   →   ⟋\ ⟋\ ⟋\

        hamamelidanthe\<mum\>   hamamelidanthe\<mum\>

The problem cases are those shown in 8.30, where we have a dactyl, that is a ternary foot of the form *s w w*, at the beginning of the word:[6]

8.30   àbracadábra, Kàlamazóo, Nèbuchadnézzar

The difficulty is that so far our rules only permit dactyls to be formed in one way, by making the final syllable extrametrical and then erecting a trochee over the antepenult and the penult, as in *(hàmamèli) dánthemum*. Since it is only peripheral elements that can be extrametrical, it is impossible to generate the dactyls in *àbracadábra* this way.

Hayes 1982 offers a very plausible way of thinking of these cases. He argues that the SR will produce the following stress patterns with the words in 8.30:

8.31   F   F   F   F

          ESR   ⟋\   SR | ⟋\   ⟋\
          →   →

        abracadabra   abracadabra   a b r a c a d a b r a

This gives the incorrect stress pattern *àbràcadábra*, in which the second syllable is incorrectly stressed (the first syllable is stressed because the SR is permitted to form a degenerate foot in such cases). However, the correct form will result if we assume a rule which destresses an open stressed syllable immediately after a degenerate foot. We can formulate the rule as in 8.32:

8.32
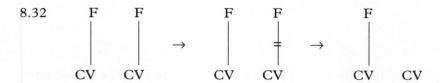

We now end up with a two unfooted syllables in the middle of the word. These are adjoined to the first foot by Stray Syllable Adjunction as in 8.33:

8.33
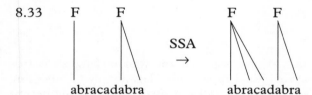

This has the effect of turning *àbràcadábra* into *àbracadábra*[7].

We have seen already how certain types of post-tonic secondary stress develop, namely as a consequence of Stress Retraction. However, there are other types of case in which secondary stresses arise after the main stress. A well known type is shown in 8.34, illustrating the distinction between *gymnast* with secondary stress and *breakfast* without:

8.34   a.   W   b.   W
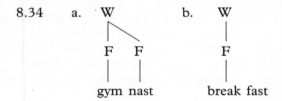

It seems to be largely a matter of idiosyncrasy which words have the secondary stress and which don't.

According to some phonologists, certain types of pre-tonic stresses can be indicated in a similar way. Thus, consider the minimal pair 8.35:

8.35   a. re-fur   [ˌriː'fəː]   b. refer   [rɪ'fəː]

In 8.35a the first syllable has secondary stress (as is clear from the unreduced vowel) while in 8.35b the first syllable lacks any stress. Given our representations for *gymnast* and *breakfast*, it is natural to say that *re-fur* consists of two degenerate feet, the second of which is strong (hence, bearing primary stress) as shown in 8.36:

8.36

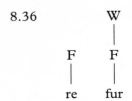

Refer on the other will consist of just one foot. The obvious way of representing this is as an iamb, as shown in 8.37:

8.37   Iambic representation of foot structure for *refer*

However, this contradicts our assumption that the foot in English is trochaic. This assumption has provided a reasonably elegant way of analysing
large tracts of the English stress system, and if we were to suddenly permit
iambic feet we would no longer have any explanation for most of the facts
discussed so far.

Fortunately, there is another way to justify a representation such as 8.37,
without assuming iambic feet, namely, by appealing to Stray Syllable
Adjunction. In the present case, we might assume that the stress rules would
be so formulated as to fail to assign any stress to *re-* in *refer* and that the
stray syllable is adjoined to the foot erected over *-fer* to give 8.37 without
the need to assume that English stress rules assign iambic feet as such.

A third way to represent *refer* would be to assume that the initial stressless
syllable in such cases is tacked on to the whole word, without being incorporated into a foot structure. In other words, we reformulate Stray Syllable
Adjunction so as to attach the stray element to the highest level of prosodic
structure available. This would give us a representation along the lines of
8.38:

8.38

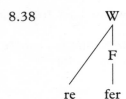

Any of these possibilities would provide a plausible analysis of the two
pronunciations of a word like *maintain*. In many accents (mine included),
this can be pronounced either as 8.39a or as 8.39b:

8.39   a. [ˌmeɪnˈteɪn]   b. [mənˈteɪn]

That is, it can be pronounced either with (8.39a) or without (8.39b) secondary pre-tonic stress. It is intuitively plausible to derive the 8.39b variant
from the 8.39a by some kind of 'destressing' process operating on the first
syllable. If 8.39a is represented as 8.40, then this process can be thought
of as a process in which the first syllable is severed from its foot node
('defooting'), as shown in 8.41:

8.40

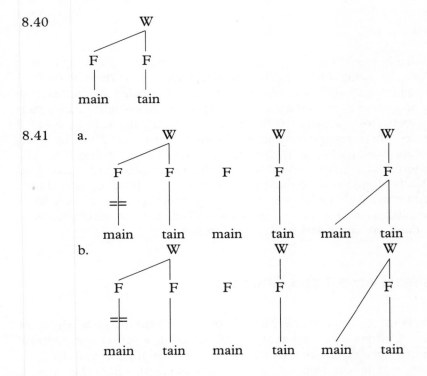

8.41   a.

       b.

This analysis of *maintain*, however, suggests yet another way of treating the
problem of *refer*. Suppose we said that the stress rules apply to both *refer* and
re-fur to stress both syllables. For instance, this would be the case if we
assume that Strong Retraction can apply in both cases (there is nothing in
what we have said so far to rule this out, so it is the most natural assumption). We might then notice that there are a good many words like *refer*
consisting of Latinate prefixes followed by a Latinate root in which the
prefix is unstressed (compare, *despise, incite, provide, perceive, transpire* and
many others). Given this it could well be that there is a special rule which
destresses the first syllable in such cases (in which case the unstressed
syllable could be adjoined to the foot or the word by Stray Syllable Adjunction
8.41a, b).

    There is not much to choose between these analyses. However, there
remains one further intriguing solution for *refer*, which is simply to say that

the first syllable doesn't receive any analysis on its own as part of a foot or any other prosodic unit, as in:

8.42

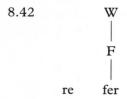

The *re-* syllable would have to be accommodated at some point, of course, for example, by being added to the preceding syllable (if there is one).

These (and other) solutions are currently being debated in the research literature and there is no consensus even amongst phonologists who otherwise share very close views about the nature of English stress. In section 8.3 we'll see how the representation in 8.42 can be put to good use in trying to understand how phrase level rhythmic effects work in English. This discussion should have given some flavour of the complexity of the questions, and the kinds of approach to them that are possible. One thing that should be borne in mind is that whatever proposal we adopt for such cases is likely to have repercussions for the way we view a whole host of other problems. Some of these are discussed in the next section.

8.2 Phrasal Accent and Rhythm

When we come to look at the phonological and especially the rhythmic properties of phrases we find that we are entering a rather controversial area. The main problem is characterizing the nature of rhythm and rhythmic alternations and in determining how rhythm interacts with other aspects of phonology and with syntactic structure. In particular, we will find that decisions have to made as to how much reference needs to be made to syntactic structure in order to understand rhythmic structure.

The main question is whether we need to refer to purely prosodic categories such as those discussed in chapter 5, or whether we can get by with direct reference to syntactic structure. That would mean we wouldn't need any prosodic domains at all, which would be the most parsimonious way of viewing things. There are problems with this assumption, the main one being that we sometimes find a whole host of processes making reference to the same prosodic domain. However, these prosodic domains seldom correspond exactly to a syntactic constituent. Thus, it would be necessary to state all the different types of syntactic triggering context, which would be just a cumbersome way of smuggling in the prosodic domains by the back door. Nonetheless, cases have been proposed in which phonological rules must make direct reference to syntax, so it might well be that we cannot accept the strongest stance, which would be that phonology can refer solely to prosodic domains.

As a result of this we will find that there are several rather different, and, it would seem, mutually incompatible, approaches to this problem and the reader should be prepared to find a variety of views in the literature. This is as it should be, of course: if there were no controversial issues, no one would be bothering to conduct research in the area. An unfortunate side effect, as usual, is that the same terms are frequently used with different meanings by different authors, while distinct terms may sometimes be used to refer to objectively one and the same phenomenon.

Traditionally, those who have examined the accentual properties of phrases (and poetic metre) in English, have made use of the concept of the foot. However, this concept is not (necessarily) identical to the one we have adopted in our study of word stress. Consider the following example (from Halliday 1970: 2, discussing the notion of 'foot'):

8.43   Peter spends his weekends at the sports club.

Halliday points out that there are various ways of pronouncing such a sentence, depending on emphasis, degree of formality, speed of delivery and so on. Two possibilities are shown in 8.44, 45, with respectively faster (allegro) and slower (lento) speech styles:

8.44   Peter spends his / weekends at the / sports club

8.45   Peter / spends his / weekends / at the / sports / club

In 8.44 we have three major accents for the phrase as a whole, on the syllables *Pe-*, *week* and *sports*. In 8.45 we have six accents. Thus, there are twice as many accentual feet in 8.45 as in 8.44. Halliday explicitly likens the foot to a bar (or measure) in music. Terminology is not fully established in this area, but it will be useful to distinguish this type of foot from the notion of foot we have used to describe lexical stress patterns. I'll therefore refer to the latter as the stress foot and refer to Halliday's conception of foot as the *accentual foot* (or sometimes the *rhythmic foot* or *Hallidayan foot*).

The foot here is again seen as trochaic: the accented syllable is always the first in the foot. However, Halliday's descriptive schema permits us to include the correlate to an upbeat (or anacrusis) in music, that is, a bar or measure which starts on a weak, unaccented beat. Another way of thinking of this is to say that the accent of the foot is phonetically missing, though present phonologically. This is referred to as a **silent beat** or **silent ictus**. This is often found at the beginning of a phrase, and is marked with the symbol ‸, as in 8.46:

8.46   ‸In a / moment we'll / come to / Red / Square.

While it is possible to pronounce an example such as this with a slight accent on the first word, it is also possible to begin it with no accent at all until the word *moment*, as shown in 8.46.

Where there is a significant pause in a phrase, say, to mark off intonationally separated phrases, we also find a silent ictus in non-initial position, as in 8.47 corresponding to 8.48, the appositive relative clause discussed in chapter 5, section 5.4.5 (I have simplified the examples slightly):

8.47   //ˌPho/ nolo/ gists// ˌwho / know/ dozens of / langua/ ges// ˌare/ widely ad/ mired//

8.48   Phonologists, who know dozens of languages, are widely admired.

This pronunciation can be distinguished from that of 8.49, corresponding to 8.50, in which the relative clause *who know dozens of languages* is interpreted restrictively rather than appositively:

8.49   //ˌPho/ nolo/ gists who/ know/ dozens of / langua/ ges are/ widely ad/ mired//

8.50   Phonologists who know dozens of languages are widely admired.

I have notated the intonational phrases of these examples by placing them between double slashes, //.

In chapter 5 we saw that there are languages in which short unaccentable words join with full, accented words to form a separate phonological domain, the phonological word. The unaccented words are clitics. In cases such as the Finnish =ko/kö clitic we found that the clitic was suffixed to the word to its left to form not only a single domain for word stress but also that the clitic joined the vowel harmony domain of its host. However, this is a relatively straightforward case, in which it is clear which word is the host and what the effects of cliticization are.

In a language like English we often find that there are small (usually monosyllabic) words which lack accent of their own and which seem to attach rhythmically to other, accented, words. This is seen in our example 8.44. In that pronunciation there are two accentually defined units ('feet') ending in unaccented words, *Peter spends his* and *weekends at the*. Now, the function words, *his* and *the*, are seldom accented (except when they receive some sort of contrastive emphasis). These words, then, tend to behave as clitics, at least as far as accentuation is concerned. In the analysis offered by Halliday, they are treated as enclitics, attaching to a preceding accent. Notice that the verb and preposition *spends* and *at* are also unaccented in this example (though not in the more careful pronunciation shown in 8.45).

Related to this is the problem posed by an example such as 8.51:

8.51   Peter contracted Amanda's affliction.

In this example, using Halliday's footing principles, we would obtain 8.52 as the rhythmic structure:

8.52   //Peter con/tracted A/manda's af/fliction//

In this example the final three words all begin with unstressed syllables, which are grouped with the previous accented word. Thus, the foot boundaries cross the word boundaries. Such a case can be compared with 8.53, in which the foot boundaries and word boundaries coincide:

8.53   Peterson travestied Anderson's fiction.

8.54   //Peterson /travestied /Anderson's/fiction//

Clearly, the overall rhythmic structure of 8.51 and 8.53 are the same, despite the fact that the foot boundaries split words in one case but not in the other. Finally, both are comparable to 8.55 in which the unaccented syllables are all clitics:

8.55   What is the name of the man in a hat?

8.56   //what is the /name of the /man in a /hat //

The problem of English rhythm now revolves around the question of how we treat the unaccented pretonic (prestress) syllables and the unaccented words (clitics) in examples such as these, and how the rhythmic units to which we appeal to analyse such phenomena relate to the units we have already distinguished in examining word stress. At the same time we will need to consider the relationship between the representation of rhythm and rhythmic alternations such as Iambic Reversal (chapter 7). The principal questions are these:

8.57   a. Is there a single unified notion of rhythmic (accentual) foot (or do we get foot-like structures from a variety of different representations)?
          b. Are further levels of rhythmic structure needed (for instance, do we need prosodic domains over and above the stress foot, phonological word or phonological phrase)?
          c. Do the principles of rhythmic construction respect the Strict Layer Hypothesis?

These questions are related, as we will see. To some extent question 8.57a is crucial. Native speakers are apt to perceive stretches of stressed and

unstressed syllables as rhythmically similar, no matter what type of morphological or syntactic structure underlies them. Thus, if we answer 8.57a
negatively, some way must be found to account for this rhythmic similarity.

There are essentially four types of approach to this set of problems. They
differ in the types of assumptions they make about the organization of the
rhythmic units. The fourth of them makes use of the notion of the metrical
grid, which we will look at in greater detail in the next section. The first
three appeal to the notion of hierarchical prosodic structure, represented as
a set of tree diagrams. Before we review the first these, it will be useful to
look at the rhythmic structure of our examples in more detail from the
perspective of metrical phonology.

Let's start with example 8.53, the relatively straightforward one. In 8.54
I analysed this as consisting of four Hallidayan feet. How do these feet relate
to the notion of 'foot' used to describe lexical stress phenomena in the last
chapter (and in §8.1 of this chapter)? Let's suppose for the present that the
two notions are equivalent. This would mean that we can incorporate the
Hallidayan foot into the prosodic hierarchy in the way which we have assumed
since chapter 5. Example 8.54 then consists of four feet, the most prominent of these feet is the last, which contains the word which bears the main
phrasal accent for this sentence. (Many would say that the second foot bears
a secondary prominence, but we'll ignore this.) We can analyse this as in
8.58:

8.58

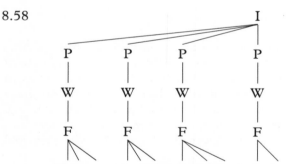

Peterson travestied Anderson's fiction.

In a trisyllabic word such as *Peterson* or *travestied* the final syllable is
extrametrical. We have been assuming that such syllables are tacked onto
the foot level by Stray Syllable Adjunction (to give effectively dactylic feet).
In 8.58 we have a single intonational phrase consisting of four phonological
phrases. Each of these consists of just a single phonological word.

Now let's consider how we might analyse examples 8.51 and 8.55. Here,
we have an interesting problem: the Hallidayan foot defines units such as
Peter con- in which an unstressed syllable of one word has attached itself to
the previous word. This sort of behaviour isn't expected of the stress foot

defined in chapter 7, which is defined over words and cannot therefore straddle word boundaries. For some phonologists this means that the notion 'foot' doesn't play a role in the phrasal phonology and doesn't, therefore, enter into the prosodic hierarchy (Halle and Vergnaud 1987 adopt this position). However, there are various ways of approaching this problem.

The difficulty is posed by (1) unstressed pretonic word initial syllables such as the *con-* of *contracted*, and (2) unstressed functions words. Let's adopt the analysis of the *contracted* cases suggested in the previous section, under which the lexical stress rules simply fail to incorporate such unstressed syllables into the word tree at the lexical level.[8] First, let's assign those syllables which can unambiguously be associated with a foot, namely those that belong to an accented word. We'll remain agnostic as to where to incorporate the pretonic unstressed syllables. This gives us 8.59, 60 (ignoring the intonational phrase from now on):

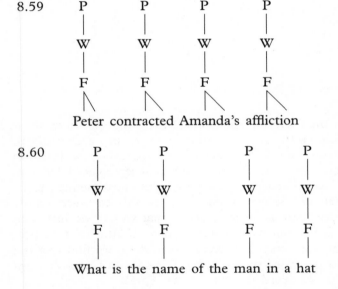

8.59

Peter contracted Amanda's affliction

8.60

What is the name of the man in a hat

The problem now reduces to the question of what to do with the syllables which are left unattached in 8.59, 60.

The errant syllables have to be attached to some unit of prosodic structure in order to be prosodically licensed and thus escape elimination by Stray Erasure. These means we must attach them to higher order units such as the foot, the phonological word, or the phonological phrase. The first problem is that we don't know which direction to attach the stray syllables in. Suppose we say that in 8.59 a stray syllable adjoins to the same W as the other syllables in that morphological word, much as we analysed cases like *parental* earlier in the chapter. This would give us representations 8.61:

8.61

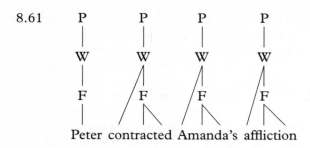

Peter contracted Amanda's affliction

The simplest way to deal with 8.60 would then be to adjoin the clitics in the same direction to give 8.62:

8.62

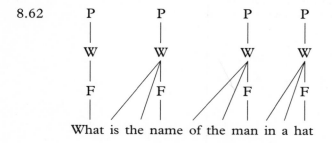

What is the name of the man in a hat

Now, 8.62 goes against the traditional account of these things. Normally, it is assumed that clitics cliticize to the left in English (i.e. they are enclitics). One reason for this assumption is the fate of (certain of) these function words when they become genuine clitics, as when *is* is replaced by *'s* in *What's in the box?* If *is* were a proclitic, attaching to the next element to its right, we'd expect *What 'sin the box?* Judgements in this case are a little subtle, but in other cases there is clear evidence that we are dealing with encliticization. Thus, *will* or *shall* when contracted to *'ll* attaches to a preceding word. When that word ends in a vowel, as in 8.63, we find that the *'ll* clitic has attached to the word on the left (cf. 8.64), and doesn't form a phonological unit with the word to its right (cf. 8.65):

8.63   a.   Joe'll only complain.
        b.   Sue'll only complain.

8.64   a.   [dʒouəɫ ounlɪ]   b.   [suːəɫ ounlɪ]

8.65   a.   *[dʒou lounlɪ]   b.   *[suː lounlɪ]

If we make this assumption then we will obtain representation 8.66 for 8.51 and 8.67 for 8.55:

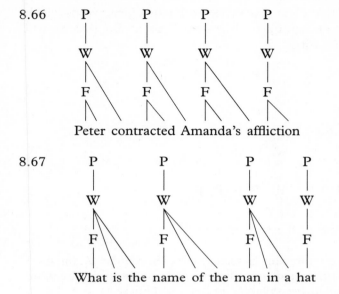

8.66

Peter contracted Amanda's affliction

8.67

What is the name of the man in a hat

In these representations, we effectively mimic the formation of dactylic feet, producing an analysis which is very close to that of Halliday. However, there is an important difference, in that, strictly speaking, these units are not feet but rather prosodic words consisting of a foot and stray adjoined syllables. Therefore, this kind of analysis fails to capture the idea that there is a unified notion of rhythmic foot. As can be seen from 8.66, 67, there is a representational difference between the 'foot' *Peter con-* and *what is the*. In addition, if we assume that extrametrical syllables in words such as *Peterson* (or *America*) are adjoined to the foot, rather than the word level, then there will be a difference between the representations of *Peterson* in 8.53 and *Peter con-* in 8.51 (draw the trees and check this for yourself). However, in the Hallidayan tradition, these have identical rhythmic properties. Another interesting feature of this analysis is that it permits cliticized words to be adjoined directly to prosodic words. This means that we are skipping a level of prosodic organization in the case of those syllables, by not incorporating them into feet. In other words, we have a violation of the Strict Layer Hypothesis.

For some phonologists (e.g. Giegerich 1992) these are important disadvantages, and they would reject such an approach. Before we consider their alternative, let's ask how else we might accommodate clitics in a fashion which respects the Strict Layer Hypothesis. In their original discussion of prosodic domains, Nespor and Vogel 1986 distinguished a special level of Clitic Group (C). A clitic group is said to come between the phonological word (W) and the phonological phrase (P). Clitics are morphologically and syntactically separate words, which, however, have to adjoin to some other phonological unit at some level. Let's assume that the level is that of the clitic group (C) and that clitics are therefore phonological words which cannot form a separate clitic group of their own. This means that we will obtain representation 8.68 for 8.55:

8.68

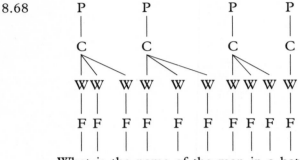

What is the name of the man in a hat

We are assuming that the pretonic unstressed syllables in *contracted, Amanda's* and *affliction* are not incorporated into any prosodic structure at the word level, so that we can treat these syllables rather like clitics, as in 8.69:

8.69

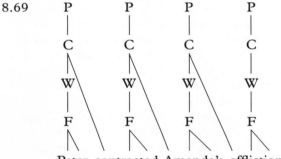

Peter contracted Amanda's affliction

With these representations we are able to maintain the claim that all material is grouped into hierarchically arranged prosodic structure. However, this still doesn't allow us to say that a unified notion of foot governs the rhythmic structure of both types of example, so we still have a negative answer to question 8.57a. This is because in 8.68 we have clitic groups mimicking the Hallidayan accentual foot, while in 8.69 we still have adjacent stressless syllables assigned to different prosodic constituents.

Let us now return to the question of how we might try to capture Halliday's interpretation of the unified accentual/rhythmic foot. In the discussion of troublesome words such as *refer* we saw that one solution to the problem of the unaccented pretonic syllable was to assign the unlicensed syllable *re-* to the nearest prosodic category one level up in the hierarchy, i.e. the foot on *fer*. If we continue to assume that these unstressed word initial pretonics are unlicensed at the lexical level then we could assume that they get attached to the foot level of the previous word. This would mean treating the function words in 8.68 as enclitics and treating the unstressed syllables in 8.69 as a type of 'honorary' enclitic, to give 8.70, 71(ignoring irrelevant levels of prosodic structure):[9]

8.70

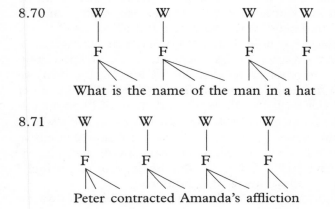

What is the name of the man in a hat

8.71

Peter contracted Amanda's affliction

This means that we also adhere to the Strict Layer Hypothesis. Notice that this doesn't entail that the phrasal rhythmic structure contradicts the lexical structure as such, because lexical rules don't assign any prosodic structure to the relevant unstressed syllables.

One drawback of this analysis is that it makes all stray syllable adjunction leftward. What, then, do we do about unstressed syllables at the very beginning of a domain (e.g. the beginning of the utterance itself)? There are two possibilities. One is simply to assume that in such cases adjunction has to work rightwards. The other, more interesting, proposal is to make use of the notion of a silent ictus mentioned at the beginning of this section. Thus, we might say that in certain circumstances a foot could have an empty head. A representation for an example like 8.46 might therefore be 8.72:

8.72

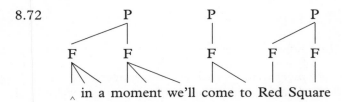

 ˄ in a moment we'll come to Red Square

The idea of using 'empty' rhythmic positions for accounting for such phenomena has been explored in some detail by Giegerich (1985).

An advantage of this approach is that we don't need to appeal to a Clitic Group. This is a rather controversial construct. The main difficulty is finding uncontroversial evidence that there is a separate domain between that of Prosodic (Phonological) Word (PWd) and Phonological Phrase (Φ). In many cases clitics simply attach phonologically to an adjacent morphological word and their phonology (including sometimes their stress) is then incorporated into the phonology of that word. This can generally be adequately described by saying that the language has a category of PWd which is larger than the morphological word. A simple example of this would be the Finnish clitic system introduced briefly in chapter two. A clitic such as -ko/kö 'question marker' undergoes vowel harmony. But all we need to say is that the domain of vowel harmony is the PWd and that clitics form a single PWd with their hosts. We don't need a separate level of Clitic Group for this. To provide absolute proof of the need for a Clitic Group, then, we would need to show: (1) that there was a domain of Prosodic Word distinct from the morphological word, (2) that there was a domain of Phonological Phrase, (3) that there are phonological rules sensitive to either the PWd or Φ, (4) that there are sequences of host + clitic which are not coextensive with either the PWd or Φ and which undergo at least one distinct phonological process not proper to the PWd or the Φ domain. Not surprisingly, it is rather difficult to meet these stringent conditions.

We conclude this section by raising a further intriguing problem of rhythm. There are many phrases consisting of content words and cliticized function words which are homophonous with other content words. Some examples are given in 8.73, 74:

8.73   a.   Tell the Roman off!
        b.   Tell the Romanov![10]

8.74   a.   market a failure
        b.   marketer failure
        c.   mark it a failure

However, not all apparently homophonous phrases are of this type. A frequently discussed case concerns the subtleties of timing and duration which distinguish 8.75 from 8.76:

8.75   Take Grey to London.

8.76   Take Greater London.

In 8.75 *Grey* is noticeably longer than *to*, and it is also longer that the *grea*-syllable of *Greater* in 8.76. The greater duration of *Grey* is generally held to be due to a rule which introduces a slight lengthening of a word final stressed syllable. This clearly fails to happen with *Greater* because the relevant syllable is not word final. Phonological theory now has to provide for some kind of representation difference in the cases to which the lengthening process can be made sensitive. Let's examine the implications this phenomenon has for the various approaches we've seen to rhythmic structure.

The most seriously damaged is the Hallidayan foot approach. This is because these phrases ought to have exactly the same rhythm, as in 8.77:

8.77   a.   /Take /Grey to /London/
          b.   /Take /Greater /London

The Clitic Group approach might try to ascribe the durational difference to the fact that *Grey to* forms a constituent at a rather higher prosodic level than does the word *Greater*:

8.78   a.   b.

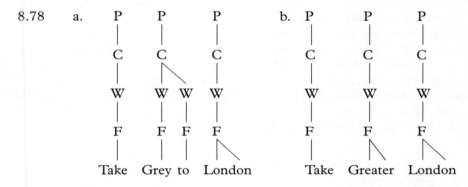

If we eschew the Clitic Group, we might assume a representation such as 8.79:

8.79   a.   b.

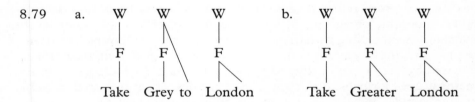

If we allow some of the syntactic structure to remain in the representation (reflected in the prosodic constituency in 8.78 or 8.79) then we can appeal to this structure in the formulation of the lengthening rule. This is easiest where we make use of Clitic Groups, for we simply say that the lengthening occurs after a prosodic word (W). In the case of 8.79 we would have to say that it occurs after the final foot of a prosodic word (so that the rule has to ignore any syllables adjoined to the prosodic word but not properly part of the foot).

Finally, another possibility is to abandon the assumption that phonological clitics are all treated identically. We might, for example, say that *to* is attached prosodically to the expression with which it forms a syntactic constituent, i.e. *London* in the Prepositional Phrase *to London*. We would then distinguish prosodically between /take /Grey / to London/ and /take

/Greater / London. The lengthening of *Grey* would then be a simple consequence of isochrony – *Grey* and *Greater* would both constitute a single
accentual foot and hence should be of roughly the same length. But this
means that *Grey* has to be longer than the first syllable of *Greater*, as observed. This type of solution involves allowing the phonology to have access
to syntactic information (since the syntactic structure is preserved at the
expense of a prosodic structure which is formulated in purely phonological
terms). On the whole phonologists have been loathe to introduce non-
phonological information unless it proves absolutely necessary. However,
everyone seems to be agreed that in principle such cases may exist, so such
a solution cannot be ruled out.

Lengthening rules of this type are currently the focus of a good deal of
research effort from phonologists and phoneticians and the precise nature
of the problem is still not fully clear. We can't review these issues here in
their full complexity (but see further reading to this chapter). Instead, we
must turn to a rather different way that phonologists have developed for
looking at rhythm, one which makes considerable use of the notion of a
grid, which was introduced in chapter 7.

8.3 Eurhythmy

English, as we've seen, tends towards stress-timing, that is, it strives to
distribute stresses, rather than syllables, evenly across time intervals. Another important organizing factor in English speech is the tendency to
maintain an alternating pattern of strong and weak beats. Impressionistically,
the ideal rhythmic pattern is of sequences consisting of a stressed syllable
followed by one or two unstressed syllables. In chapter 7 I also said that the
metrical trees formalism which was used for describing the stress patterns
of compounds, and which, in a rather different form was used in section
one to describe word stress, doesn't lend itself very well to the description
of changes in rhythm.

This is what motivated the metrical grid. It is a relatively straightforward
matter to represent rhythmic alternations over the grid. In this section we'll
build on our discussion of Iambic Reversal in chapter 7 to see how grid
theorists have approached a number of problems in the rhythmic structure
of English using these analytical tools.

8.3.1 Clash resolution by stress shift

We know that English word stress falls on a variety of positions within the
word. Moreover, English abounds in monosyllabic words. Therefore, there

are in principle ample opportunities for long sequences of stressed or unstressed syllables to occur, in violation of the tendency towards alternating
rhythms. English has several ways of accommodating such clashes. As we
saw in chapter 7, one strategy it can adopt is to move the position of some
accents so as to minimize or remove stress clashes. This was seen when we
discussed Iambic Reversal, as when the final stress in *Dundee*, or *Tennessee*
is retracted to the first syllable in *Dundee marmalade*, or *Tennessee Williams*,
as was shown in 7.47, 48 repeated here as 8.80, 81:

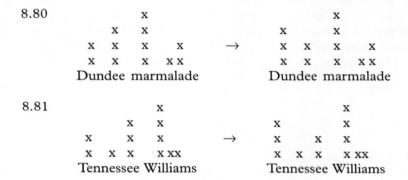

```
8.80              x                             x
            x     x                       x     x
        x   x   x    x        →       x   x   x     x
        x   x   x   x x                x   x   x    x x
          Dundee marmalade              Dundee marmalade


8.81                x                             x
             x      x                     x        x
        x    x      x         →       x     x      x
        x  x  x    x xx                x   x   x   x xx
          Tennessee Williams           Tennessee Williams
```

The situation is a little more involved than this, however, and some phonologists have argued that Iambic Reversal represents part of a broader picture. Let's consider further examples:

8.82   a.   Mìssissippi législature
        b.   Èuropean hístory
        c.   ànalytic fúnction
        d.   prèhistoric mán

In 8.82a it would appear that the conditions for reversal are not met. This
can be seen from grid 8.83:

```
8.83                x
              x     x
        x     x     x    x
        x  x  x  x  x x  x x
          Mississippi legislature
```

Here we see that the stress clash which Iambic Reversal has alleviated
seems to be separated already by the unstressed final syllable of *Mississippi*.
However, the crucial point is that this separation doesn't take place on
the same level on which the clash occurs. To see this, consider 8.84, in
which I've boxed off the portion of the grid at the level at which clashing
is defined:

8.84

```
                    x
            x       x
    x       x   x   x
```

```
    x   x  x x  x x x x
    Mississippi  legislature
```

Intuitively, we might say that the *-pi* syllable of *Mississippi* is too weak and 'low-level' to intervene sufficiently to prevent the stress clash. The result is that the boxed portion of the grid is identical in crucial respects to that for *Dundee marmalade*. There is a stress clash between *-si* and *le-* and this has to be alleviated by moving a stress mark leftwards to give 8.85:

8.85   x
            x   x
            x   x   x   x
            x x x x   x x x x
            Mississippi legislature

We will define a stress clash as in 8.86:

8.86   A stress clash occurs when there is a sequence of two adjacent grid
        marks, not separated by a mark on the next lowest level.

The rider about the next lowest level rules out intervention by syllables such as *-pi* in 8.84, that are 'too weak' and will guarantee that we obtain a regular alternating pattern.

  This account of Iambic Reversal is essentially that proposed by Liberman and Prince (1977) in a pioneering paper on metrical structures. However, Hayes (1984) has argued that we should look at these alternations from a different perspective, which places the emphasis not so much on the shifting of word stresses as on the maintenance of a strictly alternating rhythm across the whole utterance. Hayes assumes that the 'ideal' rhythmic organization for any utterance is a sequence of strong-weak pairs, grouped together to form a larger span of strong weak pairs. The tendency to achieve such rhythmic perfection is what Hayes calls eurhythmy. This ideal grid is reminiscent of a bar of 4/4 time in music, and in the abstract it would look something like 8.87:

8.87   x   x
        x   x   x
        x   x   x   x   x   x
        x x x x x x x x x x x x

Hayes argues that this reflects a number of constraints on rhythmic organization, independently of the alleviation of stress clashes. The first of these is a
tendency to prefer a grid in which there is a row somewhere with a spacing
of four syllables between marks. Such a row is called the **level of scansion**,
and the tendency is enshrined in the **Quadrisyllabic Rule**, 8.88:

8.88   A grid is eurythmic when it contains a row whose marks are spaced
         close to four syllables apart. (Hayes, 1984: 46)

Hayes' principle is illustrated by 8.89:

8.89   x   x
                 x   x   x <<<   x
             x   x   x   →   x   x   x
             x x x x   x x   x x x x   x x
             Mississippi Mabel   Mississippi Mabel

In other words, Hayes attributes the application of Iambic Reversal not so
much to the alleviation of a stress clash, as to the aspiration to achieve a
quadrisyllabic gap between *Mi-* and *Ma-* at the level of scansion. On the
other hand, there are cases in which a clash occurs as defined in 8.91 where
one might expect Iambic Reversal to apply, but where it fails to do so.
Hayes' example is 8.90:

8.90   a.   x   b.   x
                   x - - - - - x   x - - - - - - - x
               x   x   x   ↛   x   x   x
               x xx x x   x   x   xx xx   x
                 Minneapolis Mike   Minneapolis Mike

By 8.86 there is a stress clash in 8.90a. However, there is actually little
pressure to apply Iambic Reversal. Thus, the expression would most naturally be pronounced *Minneàpolis Míke* and not **Mìnneapolis Míke*. Hayes
claims that this is because the distance between grid marks at an appropriate level of scansion is three syllables in 8.90a and five in 8.90b. This
means that both are slightly (and perhaps equally) dysrhythmic, so nothing
is gained by applying the rule, and thereby obscuring the accentual pattern
of the underlying lexical form.

Returning to the 'ideal' grid in 8.87, we see that the second highest level
is the level of scansion for the Quadrisyllabic Rule.

8.91   x   x
         x - - - - - x - - - - x
         x   x   x   x   x   x
         x x x x x x x x x x x x

However, at the next lower level the grid still has an alternating pattern, this time with a period of two syllables. Hayes therefore formulates a **Disyllabic Rule**:

8.92   The domains delimited on the level of scansion should be divided evenly by a mark on the next lower grid level. (1984: 48)

The Disyllabic Rule refers to a tendency for even spacing within larger eurhythmic grids. This is illustrated by the phrase *almost hard-boiled egg*. The initial grid, before rhythmic adjustments, is shown in 8.93 (Hayes 1984: 60):

8.93
```
                              x

                    (x)   x

    x               x   x
    x   x   x       x   x
    x   x   x       x   x
    almost hard boiled egg
```

The representation in 8.93 has a clash between *boiled* and *egg*. This can be partially resolved by moving the circled x in 8.94 to the first syllable of *almost*:

8.94
```
                              x

         < < < < < <(x)   x

    x                   x   x
    x   x   x           x   x
    x   x   x           x   x
    almost hard boiled egg
```

This leaves a further clash between *hard* and *boiled*, which can now be resolved by moving the circled x in 8.95 to *hard*:

8.95
```
                              x
         x                    x

         x        < < <(x)   x
    x   x   x           x   x
    x   x   x           x   x
    almost hard boiled egg
```

The result is a more eurhythmic grid. (This is not exactly how Hages analyses this case but it will do for our purposes.)

8.3.2   Lapse resolution

It is not just clashes which give rise to dysrhythmy. The alternating rhythm tendency will be breached by a long string of unstressed syllables, too. Such a violation is called a lapse. The usual way in which such things are dealt with is for grid marks to be added in between peaks, so as to create smaller alternating peaks. A simple illustration of this idea is given in 8.96 (borrowed from Nespor and Vogel 1989). In 8.96 we see a phrase with a string of un-accented syllables between the accents (ignoring all but the first four levels):

```
8.96                x                    x
                    x                    x
                    x                    x
                    x   x x   x x   x   x
          it wasn't happening if it was raining
```

Now, we could make this pronounceable by simply speeding up the speech rate, so that the distance between the two accents was not too great. How-ever, at a slower pace we would probably add a stress to *if*, thereby breaking up the long stretch of stressless syllables, producing 8.92:

```
8.97                x                    x
                    x                    x
                    x        x           x
                    x   x x   x x   x   x
          it wasn't happening if it was raining
```

At a slower pace still we might find the even more eurhythmic grid of 8.98:

```
8.98                x                    x
                    x                    x
                    x     x     x        x
                    x   x x   x x   x   x
          it wasn't happening if it was raining
```

8.3.3   Clash resolution by stress deletion or insertion

There are occasions when a clash occurs which can't be relieved by shifting an accent leftwards. An obvious case in point is when the clash occurs at the very beginning of a phrase, as in 8.99:

```
8.99              x                x
            x     x                x
            x     x                x
            x     x    x    x    x x x
          three books were on the table
```

One way of relieving such a clash is to reduce the accent on *three*. This requires a process deleting a grid mark from that word. This will have to be the topmost mark in order to result in a well formed grid, giving 8.100:

8.100
```
              x                    x
              x                    x
      x       x                    x
      x       x    x    x    x x x
      three books were on the table
```

However, a similar process is evident from an example such as 8.101:

8.101
```
                         x
      x           x    x  x
      x    x    x    x  x
      x  x x   x x   x  x
      crocodiles often eat fish
```

It would be somewhat unnatural to pronounce 8.101 with equal stress on *often* and *eat*. Although *eat* is the main verb of the sentence, it would usually suffer deaccenting to give something like 8.102:

8.102
```
                         x
      x           x       x
      x    x    x    x    x
      x  x x   x x   x    x
      crocodiles often eat fish
```

On the other hand, we could retain the relative prominence patterns in an example such as 8.101 and relieve the clash a third way, by the introduction of a 'silent beat'. This is a short pause or lengthening which behaves, phonologically, like an extra unstressed syllable. In stress-timed languages it is quite common for the prosody to be 'stretched' in this fashion. In many syllable-timed languages such as Italian, this would not be so acceptable (cf. Nespor and Vogel 1989). Example 8.103 shows 8.100 with a extra silent beat, shown as an asterisk:

8.103
```
               x                   x
      x        x                   x
      x        x                   x
      x   *    x     x   x   x   x x
      three  books were on the table
```

There is much discussion as to the best way of handling such effects, whether clash alleviation is solely the result of bending to the power of eurhythmy or is the result of language particular rules. If there are language particular rules, the question then arises as to how best to formulate them. When I introduced the idea of stress clashes, I notated the change wrought by Iambic Reversal as a movement of a grid mark. However, given that we independently need to appeal to adjustment processes of Beat Addition and Beat Deletion, we could just as easily regard Iambic Reversal as a composite of deletion and addition (where necessary).

The use of the metrical grid to capture these rhythmic relationships means that we don't need to analyze them in terms of the behaviour of feet. This means that we don't have to worry about the discrepancy between the notion of foot used in describing lexical stress systems and the 'Hallidayan' foot.

FURTHER READING

Fudge (1984) provides a very good, essentially theory neutral introduction to the description of the English lexical stress system. Another useful survey is that provided by Kreidler (1989). There is one theoretically oriented textbook introduction to English stress and rhythm, Hogg and McCully (1987), though some of the discussion is rather advanced. Jensen (1993) provides a brief overview of English stress. Giegerich (1992) gives more extensive discussion of stress and rhythm (from a tree-theoretic perspective). A useful survey of wider issues concerning stress and rhythm is provided by Couper-Kuhlen (1986).

EXERCISES

8.1 Use Hayes' model to account for the stress patterns on the following words [if you're not sure of the stress use a standard pronouncing dictionary]:

Nouns
breakfast, computer, marigold, radio, Alexander, Anastasia

Verbs
amaze, deliver, allow, elevate, paralyse

8.2 The stress patterns of the following verbs do not follow straightforwardly the principles given by Hayes. What is special about them? What implications might this have for stress rules?

Verbs
to breakfast, to word-process, to asterisk

8.3 The following words have more than one acceptable stress pattern. Which pattern (if any) would be predicted given Hayes' rules? Could both patterns be predicted, given slightly different assumptions about the basic form?

A   'contro,versy ~ con'troversy
B   'kilo,meter ~ ki'lometer
C   'byzan,tine ~ by'zantine
D   'tele,vision ~ ,tele'vision

8.4   Using the representational techniques described in this chapter (or, if necessary, an extension of those techniques), explain how you would capture the following stress patterns. [Ignore changes in vowel quality. If you are not a native speaker of English, check the stress patterns in a pronouncing dictionary.]:

auction ~ auctioneer	complicate ~ complication
ellipsoid ~ ellipsoidal	erudite ~ erudition
horrify ~ horrific	insular ~ insularity
Japan ~ Japanese	notorious ~ notoriety
organize ~ organization	permeable ~ permeability
person ~ personify	prohibit ~ prohibition
Roman ~ Romanesque	Slovene ~ Slovenian
Venice ~ Venetian	viscose ~ viscosity

8.5   Provide a complete explanation for the following rhythmic and vocalic alternations:

A   a.   Don't divulge secrets
           [dount ,daɪ'vʌldʒ siːkrəts]
     b.   Don't divulge secrets
           [dount ,dɪ'vʌldʒ siːkrəts]
     c.   Don't divulge secrets
           [dount 'daɪ,vʌldʒ siːkrəts]
     d.   *Don't divulge secrets
           [dount 'dɪ,vʌldʒ siːkrəts]

B   a.   They'll re-fund our project . . .
           [. . . ,riː'fʌnd aʊə prɔdʒɛkt]
     b.   They'll re-fund OUR project.
           ['riː,fʌnd "aʊə prɔdʒɛkt . . .]
     c.   They'll refund OUR deposit (but not yours . . .)
           [rɪ'fʌnd "aʊə dɪpɔzɪt . . .]
     d.   *They'll refund OUR deposit . . .
           ['rɪ,fʌnd "aʊə dɪpɔzɪt . . .]

where " indicates emphatic accent.

8.6   Formulate Iambic Reversal as a combination of Beat Addition and Beat Deletion for all the cases mentioned in this chapter.

Notes

CHAPTER 1   PRELIMINARIES TO PHONOLOGY

1   In such circumstances we would not speak of coarticulation but of assimilation (see chapter 2, section 2.4.3).
2   This way of stating things will be substantially emended presently, so do not take it too seriously for the moment.
3   Try to resist the temptation to ask what happens to, say, the 't' sounds of *cat, Carter, Patrick* and so on. This is all dealt with in much more detail in chapter 6.
4   Using simple set theoretic terminology, we would say that the B positions constitute the complement set of the A positions and vice versa.
5   The 'a' vowel in 1.5–7 stands for the vowel I shall represent later in this chapter as [æ].
6   In some cases uvulars behave as though they were more related to pharyngeals and glottals and would thus be classed as gutturals. It is currently unclear how best to regard uvular sounds.

CHAPTER 2   PHONOLOGICAL PROCESSES

1   It is worth stressing that the second column of examples represents the more normal pronunciation, and that the first column represents a special speech style

which would not normally be used by native speakers, except over noisy telephone lines or when teaching foreigners English pronunciation. It is necessary to make this point because you will often be told that the pronunciations represented in the second column are 'sloppy', 'lazy', 'uneducated', and that they testify to a loss of cultural standards, a decline in moral standards amongst the young, and are generally indicative of an attack on the family, motherhood and the Great British (or American) Way of Life. Such judgements are, of course, like most folk judgements about language and accent, based entirely on ignorance of the facts and on deep-seated prejudice.

2   We're oversimplifying here, somewhat, since the phonetics of these alternations is rather more complex than I've made out.

3   Or in some RP accents, [ɪz]. We'll ignore this difference from now on.

CHAPTER 3   SYLLABLES AND SYLLABIFICATION

1   My dictionary includes one counterexample, a dialectal word *gowk* /gaʊk/.

2   In other words, the scale helps to define sets of *natural classes* – see chapter 4.

3   Recall that a consonant with a tilde ~ through it is pharyngealized; [ħ ʕ] are pharyngeal fricatives.

4   There is one systematic exception to the ban against two obstruents in a coda, and that is that /sp, st, sk/ clusters are permitted, as in *asp, cast, risk*. Notice that here, again, it is /s/ that is behaving out of line.

CHAPTER 4   DISTINCTIVE FEATURES

1   It is usual to abbreviate the names of features. These should be self-explanatory. However, commonly used abbreviations for the features are found in appendix 4.3.

2   What exactly it means to say that a feature characterization is undefined will become clearer as we proceed.

3   We will ignore the guttural sounds for the present.

4   Some care is needed here because there are languages in which precisely this sort of thing happens. That is, in some languages there are sounds which are, for instance, both labial and velar (see p. 19). Such a sound is usually transcribed in IPA as [k͡p] or [g͡b], and can be found in a number of African languages, such as Yoruba, Igbo or Kpelle (these last two have such sounds in their names). Other such doubly articulated sounds are also possible. The point about these sounds is that they are comparatively rare in the world's languages, (i.e. they are *marked* sound types) and special provision needs to be made for them in linguistic theory. What we should avoid is a theory which predicts that such sounds will be as commonplace as /p t k/.

5   The fact that it is impossible to specify a sound as [+high, +low] leads many linguists to question the validity of this particular choice of features. There are good reasons for replacing these binary features with a different set or with a

set of unary features, much as we have done for place of articulation. Consideration of these possibilities would take us too far afield at this stage, but you can find a discussion of unary vowel features in the appendix 4.2.

6 However, recall from note 5 that many phonologists are understandably unhappy about the existence of such implicit redundancy relations, and view this as a failing in the specific distinctive feature system which gives rise to them.

7 It is often said that removing redundancies lessens the load on memory. The idea, presumably, is that the linguistically defined feature matrices are stored directly in the brain in more or less that form, and removing redundancies would therefore 'free up' memory space. Unfortunately, however, very little is known about the psycholinguistic mechanisms of storage that would subserve lexical entries of this kind. Moreover, removing redundant information and filling it in by rule requires processing capacity. One thing that brains seem very good at is storing vast quantities of information, and it is frequently found that the brain stores information redundantly in order to reduce processing costs rather than reducing redundancy. An analogy might be helpful: I have several types of address book, kept in different places (at home, in the office, on a computer and so on) and many of the addresses are repeated. This is wasteful of storage space, but very convenient, because I don't have to carry one address book around with me all the time. Also, if I lose one of the address books I can probably reconstitute most of the addresses from the other books. In general, it is very difficult to argue about the nature of linguistic representations from psycholinguistics (especially in areas of psycholinguistics where we are largely ignorant). To do so is to run the risk of confusing the two Chomskyan notions of 'competence' and 'performance'.

8 Interestingly, the original sound historically is the /e/, not the /o/. Thus, the name p^jotr 'Peter' had /e/, (deriving from the Greek petros 'rock'), just as other languages (including most other Slavic ones), but this type of /e/ got 'labialized' before a hard consonant. Now, however, it makes more descriptive sense to regard the /o/ as the underlying sound and say that the alternation is a case of palatalization between two palatalized consonants. This situation, when a derived sound (here /o/) is reinterpreted in a grammar as the underlying sound, and the original underlier becomes the derived sound is known as **rule inversion**.

9 Presumably, in a complete grammar of Russian, such a rule would be couched in terms of an assimilation process spreading the frontness of the palatalized consonants from both directions onto the vowel. Processes of this sort are not well understood and Russian has not been analysed in these terms, so it is difficult to know exactly how the process should be formalized. However, this doesn't matter in the least for this illustration. All that is important is the final results of the alternation, i.e. the fact that it is /o/ alternating with /e/.

10 In this illustration, we haven't had to appeal to any redundant features. However, this does not mean that redundant features can never be accessed by lexical, structure preserving rules. Under those circumstances we simply have to assume that the redundancy rules have begun to operate and have filled in the relevant feature specifications. A general principle then tells us that those specifications have to be provided before the first rule applies which makes appeal to them.

11 I shall question this assumption in chapter 6.

12 Elements can also be used to describe consonants, of course. Discussion of this can be found in Lass (1984), Durand (1990) and Harris (1990, 1994) with somewhat different theoretical bases in each case.

CHAPTER 5 RULES AND DOMAINS

1 You may wonder what the use of such a rule could be. This will be seen later when we discuss ordering relations between rules.
2 Although the specification COR is redundant for sounds already marked [−anterior] (only coronal sounds can be marked for [anterior], whatever the specification) when stating a process such as this it is necessary to 'fill in' the connection between the [anterior] feature and the COR node which it depends on, otherwise the diagrams would not make much sense.
3 'Adjacent' can't always be taken literally. It is very common for consonants and vowels to behave as though they were transparent to each others features, so that many assimilation processes affecting vowels do indeed skip over intervening consonants. To a lesser extent, we also find assimilation processes affecting consonants which ignore intervening vowels. However, there are good grounds, both phonetic and phonological, for considering consonants and vowels to exist in separate planes or tiers for many purposes. This means that processes which only apply to vowels or to consonants can also be said to respect the principle of locality. For instance, a vowel v_3 in a sequence $v_1, \ldots v_2 \ldots v_3$, can't affect v_1 if v_2 is the kind of vowel that can also affect v_1.
4 These representations abstract away from other rules devoicing final obstruents and reducing unstressed vowels. Recall that the symbols p^j l^j etc. represent palatalized consonants.
5 It is beyond the scope of an introductory text to delve into the intricacies of theories of lexical phonology, since it entails a reasonably sophisticated understanding of morphological theory. However, the further reading offers introductions to the theory.
6 Presumably the /n/ in *entró* undergoes this rule, too, though Harris does not mark it as having done so.
7 Nespor and Vogel are at pains to reanalyse reference to the rhyme as reference to the syllable. I retain Harris' original formulations here to illustrate the possibility of reference to a rhyme constituent.
8 If you are unfamiliar with syntactic tree diagrams, or if you are used to radically different types of syntactic tree, concentrate on the labelled brackets rather than the trees. The tree diagrams are not essential to understanding the points raised here.
9 Looking through recent articles in phonology for more modern examples of these abbreviatory conventions turned up no clear examples of their use, except occasionally as a kind of informal shorthand. Rubach's (1993) analysis of Slovak phonology, for instance, contains sixty rules, none of which use the abbreviatory conventions I shall list below.
10 Readers who know Polish may object that the form here should be *ʧɛʨi*. This is true, but Rubach accounts for this by means of another rule which turns /s/ into /ʨ/ before /i/.

CHAPTER 6   POSTLEXICAL PROCESSES IN ENGLISH

1   In reasonably fast speech this representation would be further simplified by degemination of the long sibilant. See Section 6.3.1.1 below.
2   A related difficulty is that handbooks describe the facts in different ways. This is partly because the authors are describing slightly different dialect patterns and partly because they are concentrating on different aspects of the problem for pedagogic purposes and therefore simplifying the facts in certain places. (My presentation of the data largely follows Kreidler, 1989: 106, 116, who tends to make more distinctions than most.)
3   Inalterability, and the related property of Inseparability, are discussed in more detail in Kenstowicz (1994: 410ff).
4   Giegerich (1992: 221) accounts for such instances by appeal to ambisyllabicity. However, his explanation crucially hinges on the assumption that preglottalling is possible in *mattress* but not in *hopeless* or *equal*. My judgements coincide with those of Wells and not with Giegerich's for these cases, but it must be admitted that the facts are not entirely clear.
5   By convention, this notation is taken to mean that there can be no other foot within these boundaries.
6   It remains unclear exactly how to deal with words such as *petrol*, which are subject to a good deal of variation. The formulation as given will apply to *petrol* if the /t/ is ambisyllabic. Informant responses even within a single dialect tend to differ, so I shan't go further into the matter.

CHAPTER 7   STRESS AND RHYTHM

1   Since we are only interested in the stress I have given more of a transliteration than a transcription, using the following conventions: č = [ʧ],y = [i̯],C′ = palatalized consonant, though I haven't been consistent in transcribing palatalization.
2   In point of fact, the English stress system should probably be analysed exclusively in terms of trochaic feet, and we will see in chapter 8 that 7.4b, c may have to be given a more sophisticated representation. However, these examples suffice for the basic purposes of illustration.
3   Recall from chapter 3 that the mathematical term 'algorithm' means a mechanical procedure or set of instructions, which when followed generates a desired output.
4   This language is often referred to as Eastern Cheremis in the Western literature. Mari is the official name for the two literary dialects (Meadow-Mari and Hill-Mari).
5   This is not to say that the rule works for everything we would like to call a compound. For some discussion of the problems see Spencer (1991: ch. 8).
6   Because an iambic rhythm, $w + s$, is reversed to give a trochee, $s + w$.

CHAPTER 8   STRESS AND RHYTHM IN ENGLISH

1   Remember that we are marking primary stress with ′ and secondary stress with ` when marking orthographic forms. When stress is marked in transcriptions the usual IPA conventions (see chapter 2) apply.

2   This, of course, will only constitute an extrametrical consonant in a rhotic dialect.

3   The unexpected short /æ/ in this word is due to a general process under which a long vowel shortens when followed by a disyllabic suffix. The same thing is found with well-known alternations such as *divine ~ divinity, serene ~ serenity, sane ~ sanity, profound ~ profundity, verbose ~ verbosity.* Many phonologists still follow SPE in assuming that this is the result of a phonological rule, known as Trisyllabic Shortening (TSS).

4   The origin of the terms 'strong/weak retractor' is that when we consider alternations such as *órigin ~ oríginal* it looks as though the 'basic' stress (on *órigin*) has been shifted under the influence of the affix (though Hayes' analysis of the ESR doesn't actually treat the alternation in such terms).

5   The matter is complicated by the fact that some of these suffixes exist in two forms, one of which does affect stem phonology and one of which doesn't. This can sometimes lead to minimal pairs such as *compárable* 'capable of being compared' and *cómparable* 'similar', or more drastically, *uncompárable* 'not capable of being compared' and *incómparable* 'extremely good'.

6   Note that this and some other words discussed here are exceptions to Noun Extrametricality.

7   This is not the only way to account for such cases, of course (Halle and Vergnaud 1987: 232ff give a detailed alternative within a somewhat different theory of stress, heavily influence by Hayes' work). In addition there are pretonic secondary stress types that I have not accounted for here.

8   We could always adopt one of the other analyses in which the unstressed syllables are licensed lexically by attachment to the next foot or word level, but then we'd simply have to reattach those syllables elsewhere. Adopting the assumption that these syllables are completely unlicensed prosodically at the lexical level thus saves a little time and space in the exposition.

9   Giegerich (1992: 264ff) offers essentially this solution, though within a slightly different descriptive framework, which makes use of (yet another) slightly different notion of foot.

10   Speakers of Russian must be careful to give this name its anglicized pronunciation with stress on the first syllable (not the second, as in Russian).

References

Abercrombie, D. 1967. *Elements of General Phonetics*. Edinburgh: Edinburgh University Press.

Al-Mozainy, H. Q., Bley-Vrohman, R. and McCarthy, J. J. 1985. Stress shift and metrical structure. *Linguistic Inquiry*, 16: 135–44.

Archangeli, D. 1988. Aspects of underspecification theory. *Phonology*, 5: 183–208.

Avanesov, R. I. 1972. *Russkoe Literaturnoe Proiznošenie* (*The Pronunciation of Literary Russian*. In Russian). Moscow: Prosveščenie.

Batalova, R. M. and Krivoshchekova-Gantman, A. S. 1985. *Komi-Permjatsko – Russkij slovar'* (*Komi-Permjak – Russian Dictionary*). Moscow: Russkij Jazyk.

Baur, A. 1969. *Schwyzertüütsch*. Winterthur: Gemsberg Verlag.

Berko, J. 1958. The child's learning of English morphology. *Word*, 14: 150–77.

Bolinger, D. (ed.) 1972. *Intonation*. Harmondsworth: Penguin Books.

Bolinger, D. 1986. *Intonation and Its Parts: Melody in Spoken English*. Stanford, CA: Stanford University Press.

Borden, G. and Harris, K. 1984. *Speech Science Primer*. Baltimore: Williams and Wilkins (second edition).

Broe, M. 1992. An approach to feature geometry. In G. Docherty and R. Ladd (eds), *Papers in Laboratory Phonology II: Gesture, Segment, Prosody*, Cambridge: Cambridge University Press.

Broselow, E. and McCarthy, J. J. 1983. A theory of internal reduplication. *The Linguistic Review*, 3: 25–88.

Browman, C. and Goldstein, L. 1986. Articulatory gestures as phonological units. *Phonology*, 6: 201–51.

Brown, G. 1977. *Listening to Spoken English*. Harlow: Longman.

Brown, G. 1990. *Listening to Spoken English*. Harlow: Longman (second edition).

Carr, P. 1993. *Phonology*. Basingstoke: Macmillan.

Catford, J. 1988. *A Practical Introduction to Phonetics*. Oxford: Clarendon Press.

Chomsky, N. and Halle, M. 1968. *The Sound Pattern of English*. New York: Harper & Row (SPE).

Churchward, C. M. 1953. *Tongan Grammar*. Oxford: Oxford University Press.

Clark, J. and Yallop, C. 1990. *An Introduction to Phonetics and Phonology*. Oxford: Blackwell.

Clements, G. N. 1985. The geometry of phonological features. *Phonology Yearbook*, 2: 225–52.

Clements, G. N. 1990. The role of the sonority cycle in core syllabification. In J. Kingston, and M. Beckman (eds), *Papers in Laboratory Phonology I: between the Grammar and Physics of Speech*, Cambridge: Cambridge University Press.

Clements, G. N. and Hume, E. 1994. The internal organization of speech sounds. In J. Goldsmith (ed.), *Handbook of Phonology*, Oxford: Blackwell.

Clements, G. N. and Keyser, S. J. 1983. *CV Phonology*. Cambridge, MA: MIT Press.

Clements, G. N. and Sezer, E. 1982. Vowel and consonant disharmony in Turkish. In H. van der Hulst and N. Smith (eds), *The Structure of Phonological Representations* (Part II), Dordrecht: Foris.

Condoravdi, C. 1990. Sandhi Rules of Greek and prosodic theory. In S. Inkelas and D. Zec (eds), *The Phonology–Syntax Connection*, Chicago: University of Chicago Press.

Couper-Kuhlen, E. 1986. *An Introduction to English Prosody*. London: Arnold.

Cruttenden, A. 1986. *Intonation*. Cambridge: Cambridge University Press.

Crystal, D. 1969. *Prosodic Systems and Intonation in English*. Cambridge: Cambridge University Press.

Dixon, R. 1980. *The Languages of Australia*. Cambridge: Cambridge University Press.

Durand, J. 1990. *Generative and Non-Linear Phonology*. Harlow: Longman.

Elbert, S. and Pukui, M. K. 1979. *Hawaiian Grammar*. Honolulu: University Press of Hawaii.

Fay, D. and Cutler, A. 1977. Malapropisms and the structure of the mental lexicon. *Linguistic Inquiry*, 8: 505–20.

Fromkin, V. and Rodman, R. 1993. *Introduction to Language*. New York: Holt, Rinehart & Winston.

Fudge, E. 1969. Syllables. *Journal of Linguistics*, 5: 253–86.

Fudge, E. 1984. *English Word Stress*. London: Allen & Unwin.

Fudge, E. 1987. Branching structures within the syllable. *Journal of Linguistics*, 23: 359–77.

Gibbon, D. 1976. *Perspectives of Intonation Analysis*. Frankfurt: Peter Lang.

Giegerich, H. 1985. *Metrical Phonology and Phonological Structure: German and English*. Cambridge: Cambridge University Press.

Giegerich, H. 1992. *English Phonology*. Cambridge: Cambridge University Press.

Gimson, A. C. 1980. *An Introduction to the Pronunciation of English*. London: Edward Arnold (third edition).

Gimson, A. C. 1993. *An Introduction to the Pronunciation of English*. London: Routledge (fifth edition, edited by A. Cruttenden).

Goldsmith, J. 1976a. *Autosegmental phonology*. MIT PhD dissertation (published 1979). New York: Garland.

Goldsmith, J. 1976b. An overview of autosegmental phonology. *Linguistic Analysis*, 2: 23–68.

Goldsmith, J. 1990. *Autosegmental and Metrical Phonology*. Oxford: Blackwell.

Goldsmith, J. (ed.) 1994. *Handbook of Phonology*. Oxford: Blackwell.

Goodwin, W. W. 1894. *A Greek Grammar*. Basingstoke: Macmillan.

Guerssel, M. 1986. Glides in Berber and syllabicity. *Linguistic Inquiry*, 17: 1–12.

Gussmann, E. 1980. *Studies in Abstract Phonology*. Cambridge, MA: MIT Press.

Hale, K. 1973. Deep-surface canonical disparities in relation to analysis and change: an Australian example. *Current Trends in Linguistics*, 11: 401–58.

Halle, M. 1973. Prolegomena to a theory of word formation. *Linguistic Inquiry*, 4: 3–16.

Halle, M. 1992. Phonological features. *International Encyclopedia of Linguistics*, 8: 149–76.

Halle, M. and Clements, G. 1983. *Problem Book in Phonology*. Cambridge, MA: MIT Press.

Halle, M. and Idsardi, W. 1994. General properties of stress and metrical structural. In J. Goldsmith (ed.), *Handbook of Phonology*, Oxford: Blackwell.

Halle, M. and Mohanan, K. P. 1985. The segmental phonology of Modern English. *Linguistic Inquiry*, 16: 57–116.

Halle, M. and Stevens, K. 1971. A note on laryngeal features. *Quarterly Progress Report*, 101: 198–22. Cambridge, MA: Research Laboratory of Electronics, MIT.

Halle, M. and Vergnaud, J.-R. 1987. *An Essay on Stress*. Cambridge, MA: MIT Press.

Halliday, M. A. K. 1970. *A Course in Spoken English: Intonation*. Oxford: Oxford University Press.

Halliday, M. A. K. 1980. *A Course in Spoken English: Intonation*. Oxford: Oxford University Press (second edition).

Hamilton, W. S. 1980. *Introduction to Russian Phonology and Word Structure*. Columbus: Slavica Publishers.

Harris, James. 1983. *Syllable Structure and Stress in Spanish*. Cambridge, MA: MIT Press.

Harris, John. 1990. Segmental complexity and phonological government. *Phonology*, 7: 255–300.

Harris, John. 1994. *English Sound Structure*. Oxford: Blackwell.

Harris, John, and Kaye, J. 1990. A tale of two cities: London glottalling and New York City tapping. *The Linguistic Review*, 7: 251–74.

Hawkins, P. 1992. *Introducing Phonology*. London: Routledge.

Hayes, B. 1981. *A Metrical Theory of Stress Rules*. MIT PhD dissertation, distributed by Indiana University Linguistics Club (published 1985). New York: Garland.

Hayes, B. 1982. Extrametricality and English stress. *Linguistic Inquiry*, 13: 227–76.

Hayes, B. 1984. The phonology of rhythm in English. *Linguistic Inquiry*, 15: 33–74.

Hayes, B. 1986a. Inalterability in CV phonology. *Language*, 62: 321–51.

Hayes, B. 1986b. Assimilation as spreading in Toba Batak. *Linguistic Inquiry*, 17: 467–99.

Hayes, B. 1989. Compensatory lengthening in moraic phonology. *Linguistic Inquiry*, 20: 253–306.

Hayes, B. 1990. Diphthongization and coindexing. *Phonology*, 7: 31–72.

Hogg, R. and McCully, C. 1987. *Introduction to Metrical Phonology*. Cambridge: Cambridge University Press.

van der Hulst, H. 1989. Atoms of segmental structure: components, gestures, and dependency. *Phonology*, 6: 253–84.

Hyman, L. 1975. *Phonology: Theory and Analysis*. New York: Holt, Rinehart & Winston.

Ingria, R. 1980. Compensatory lengthening as a metrical phenomenon. *Linguistic Inquiry*, 11: 465–95.

Inkelas, S. 1990. *Prosodic Constituency in the Lexicon*. New York: Garland.

Inkelas, S. and Zec, D. (eds) 1990. *The Phonology–Syntax Connection*. Chicago: University of Chicago Press.

Itô, J. 1989. A prosodic theory of epenthesis. *Natural Language and Linguistic Theory*, 7: 217–59.

Itô, J. and Mester, R.-A. 1986. The phonology of voicing in Japanese: theoretical consequences for morphological accessibility. *Linguistic Inquiry*, 17: 49–74.

Jakobson, R. 1939. Observations sur le classement phonologique des consonnes (Observations on the phonological classification of consonants. In French). Proceedings of the 3rd International Congress of Phonetic Sciences, 34–41. (Reprinted in *Roman Jakobson, Selected Writings I*, The Hague: Mouton, 1962).

Jensen, J. 1993. *English Phonology*. Amsterdam: J. Benjamins.

Jones, D. 1967. *Everyman's Pronouncing Dictionary, Containing over 58,000 Words in International Phonetic Transcription* (thirteenth edition, edited by A. C. Gimson). London: Dent.

Joseph, B. and Philippaki-Warburton, I. 1987. *Modern Greek*. Beckenham: Croom Helm.

Kager, R. 1994. The metrical theory of word stress. In J. Goldsmith (ed.), *Handbook of Phonology*, Oxford: Blackwell.

Kahn, D. 1976. *Syllable-based Generalizations in English Phonology*. MIT PhD dissertation, distributed by Indiana University Linguistics Club, (published 1980). New York: Garland.

Kaisse, E. and Shaw, P. 1985. On the theory of Lexical Phonology. *Phonology*, 2: 1–30.

Kanerva, J. 1990. Focusing on phonological phrases in Chichewa. In S. Inkelas and D. Zec (eds), *The Phonology–Syntax Connection*, Chicago: University of Chicago Press.

Katamba, F. 1989. *Introduction to Phonology*. London: Longman.

Katamba, F. 1993. *Morphology*. Basingstoke: Macmillan.

Kaye, J. 1990. 'Coda' licensing. *Phonology*, 7: 301–30.

Kaye, J. Lowenstamm, J. and Vergnaud, J.-R. 1985. The internal structure of phonological elements: a theory of charm and government. *Phonology Yearbook*, 2: 303–26.

Kenstowicz, M. 1994. *Phonology in Generative Grammar*. Oxford: Blackwell.

Kenstowicz, M. and Kisseberth, C. 1977. *Topics in Phonological Theory*. New York: Academic Press.

Kenstowicz, M. and Kisseberth, C. 1979. *Generative Phonology: Description and Theory*. New York: Academic Press.

Kenyon, J. and Knott, T. 1953. *A Pronouncing Dictionary of American English*. Springfield, MA: Merriam.

Kibrik, A. E., Kodzasov, S. V., Olovjanikova, I. P. and Samedov, D. S. 1977. *Opyt strukturnogo opisanija arčinskogo jazyka*. Vol 1. (*Towards a Structural Description of Archi*. In Russian). Moscow: Izdatel'stvo Moskovskogo Universiteta.

Kiparsky, P. 1973. 'Elsewhere' in phonology. In S. Anderson and P. Kiparsky (eds), *A Festschrift for Morris Halle*, New York: Holt, Rinehart & Winston.

Kiparsky, P. 1979. Metrical structure assignment is cyclic. *Linguistic Inquiry*, 10: 421–42.

Kiparsky, P. 1982. From Cyclic Phonology to Lexical Phonology. In H. van der Hulst and N. Smith (eds), *The structure of phonological representations (Part I)*, Dordrecht: Foris.

Kiparsky, P. 1985. Some consequences of Lexical Phonology. *Phonology Yearbook*, 2: 83–136.

Kisseberth, C. 1970. On the functional unity of phonological rules. *Linguistic Inquiry*, 1: 291–306.

Koutsoudas, A., Sanders, G. and Noll, C. 1974. On the application of phonological rules. *Language*, 50, 1–28.

Kreidler, C. 1989. *The Pronunciation of English*. Oxford: Blackwell.

Ladd, R. 1980. *The Structure of Intonational Meaning*. Bloomington: Indiana University Linguistics Club.

Ladd, R. 1986. Intonational phrasing: the case for recursive prosodic structure. *Phonology Yearbook*, 3: 311–40.

Ladd, R. 1992. An introduction to intonational phonology. In G. Docherty and R. Ladd (eds), *Papers in Laboratory Phonology II*, Cambridge: Cambridge University Press.

Ladefoged, P. 1993. *A Course in Phonetics*. Harcourt, Brace Jovanovich (third edition).

Ladefoged, P. and Halle, M. 1988. Some major features of the International Phonetic Alphabet. *Language*, 64: 577–82.

Lass, R. 1984. *Phonology*. Cambridge: Cambridge University Press.

Lewis, G. 1967. *Turkish Grammar*. Oxford: Clarendon Press.

Liberman, M. and Prince, A. 1977. On stress and linguistic rhythm. *Linguistic Inquiry*, 8: 249–336.

Lieberman, P. and Blumstein, S. 1987. *Speech physiology, speech perception, and acoustic phonetics*. Cambridge: Cambridge University Press.

Lisker, L. and Abramson, A. 1964. A cross-language study of voicing in initial stops: acoustical measurements. *Word*, 20: 384–422.

Mackridge, Peter 1985. *The Modern Greek Language*. Oxford: Oxford University Press.

McCarthy, J. 1988. Feature geometry and dependency: a review. *Phonetica*, 43: 84–108.

McCarthy, J. J. and Prince, A. 1994. Generalized Alignment. In G. Booij and J. van Marle, (eds), *Yearbook of Morphology 1993*, Dordrecht: Kluwer, 79–154.

McCawley, J. 1972. The role of notation in generative phonology. In M. Gross (ed.), *The Formal Analysis Natural Languages*, Mouton: The Hague.

Nespor, M. 1990. On the separation of prosodic and rhythmic phonology. In S. Inkelas and D. Zec (eds), *The Phonology–Syntax Connection*, Chicago: University of Chicago Press.

Nespor, M. and Vogel, I. 1986. *Prosodic Phonology*. Dordrecht: Foris.

Nespor, M. and Vogel, I. 1989. On clashes and lapses. *Phonology*, 6: 69–116.

Novikova, K. A. 1960. *Očerki dialektov Evenskogo jazyka: Ol'skij govor, čast'1 (Sketches of the dialects of the Even Language: the Olsk Dialect, Part 1*. In Russian). Moscow–Leningrad: Izdatel'stvo Akademii Nauk SSSR.

Odden, D. 1994. Tone: African languages. In J. Goldsmith (ed.), *Handbook of Phonology*, Oxford: Blackwell.

Paradis, C. 1988–9. On constraints and repair strategies. *The Linguistic Review*, 6: 71–97.

Pierrehumbert, J. 1988. The phonetics and phonology of English intonation. MIT Ph.D., distributed by Indiana University Linguistics Club, Bloomington, Indiana.

Pike, K. 1948. *Tone Languages*. Ann Arbor: University of Michigan Press.

Poser, W. 1989. The metrical foot in Diyari. *Phonology*, 6: 117–48.

Radford, A. 1988. *Transformational Grammar*. Cambridge: Cambridge University Press.

Roca, I. 1994. *Phonological Theory*. London: Routledge.

Rubach, J. 1984. *Cyclic and Lexical Phonology*. Dordrecht: Foris.

Rubach, J. 1993. *The Lexical Phonology of Slovak*. Oxford: Clarendon Press.

Sagey, E. 1986. *The Representation of Features and Relations in Non-linear Phonology*. MIT Ph.D. dissertation (published 1990). New York: Garland.

Scatton, E. 1976. *Bulgarian Phonology*. Columbus: Slavica Publishers.

Schane, S. 1973. *Generative Phonology*. Englewood Cliffs: Prentice-Hall.

Selkirk, E. 1984a. On the major class features and syllable theory. In M. Aronoff and R. Oehrle (eds), *Language Sound Structure: Studies in Phonology Presented to Morris Halle by his Teacher and Students*, Cambridge, MA: MIT Press.

Selkirk, E. 1984b. *Phonology and Syntax*. Cambridge, MA: MIT Press.

Siegel, D. 1974. *Topics in English Morphology*. MIT Ph.D. dissertation (published 1979). New York: Garland.

Skorik, P. Ja. 1961. *Grammatika čukotskogo jazyka, tom 1* (*A Grammar of Chukchee*, vol. 1. In Russian). Leningrad: Nauka.

Spencer, A. 1991. *Morphological Theory*. Oxford: Blackwell.

Stafford, R. 1967. *The Luo Language*. Nairobi: Longman.

Steriade, D. 1994. Underspecification and markedness. In J. Goldsmith (ed.), *Handbook of Phonology*, Oxford: Blackwell.

Tereshchenko, N. M. 1979. *Nganasanskij jazyk* (*The Nganasan Language*. In Russian). Leningrad: Nauka.

Trubetskoy, N. 1939. *Grundzüge der Phonologie* (English translation, C. Baltaxe 1969). *Principles of Phonology*. Berkeley: University of California Press.

Ultan, R. 1978. A typological view of metathesis. In J. H. Greenberg (ed.), *Universals of Human Language, vol. 2. Phonology*. Stanford: Stanford University Press.

Volodin, A. P. 1976. *Itel'menskij Jazyk* (The Itel'men Language. In Russian). Leningrad: Nauka.

Wells, J. 1982a. *Accents of English: the British Isles*. Cambridge: Cambridge University Press.

Wells, J. 1982b. *Accents of English: beyond the British Isles*. Cambridge: Cambridge University Press.

Wells, J. 1990. *Longman Pronunciation Dictionary*. Harlow: Longman.

Wright, J. and Wright, E. M. 1928. *An Elementary Middle English Grammar*. Oxford: Clarendon Press.

Yip, M. 1994. Tone in East Asian languages. In J. Goldsmith (ed.), *Handbook of Phonology*, Oxford: Blackwell.

Zhukova, A. N. 1972. *Grammatika Korjakskogo Jazyka* (*A Grammar of Koryak*. In Russian). Leningrad: Nauka.

Language
Index

References to English are to specific rules or principles cross-referenced in the subject index.

Subject Index

Page numbers in boldface indicate the place where a term is first explained, characterized or defined. For reference to individual distinctive features see under the entry *distinctive feature* (and also Appendix 4.3, pp. 141–4).